Race to the Swift

Thoughts on Twenty-First Century Warfare

RICHARD SIMPKIN was for thirty years an officer of the Royal Tank Regiment, his active service in the Middle East (during which he was awarded the MC and taken prisoner) being followed by peace-time service in most parts of the world. Graduating from Staff College in 1951, he went straight on to the Royal Military College of Science, graduating from the Technical Staff Course with a specialization in vehicles in 1953. An instructional tour in 1957–9 was divided between the directing staffs of the Staff College and the Royal Military College of Science (combat vehicle technology). From 1960 to 1963 he headed the equipment branch of the Royal Armoured Corps Directorate, being responsible for user trials of the Chieftain tank and for development of the Operational Requirements of the Scorpion reconnaissance vehicle family and the Swingfire anti-tank guided weapon system.

In 1963 he was awarded the OBE and took command of the 1st Royal Tank Regiment. After a short second tour at the Royal Military College of Science as Military Director of Studies (Weapons and Vehicles), he was promoted Brigadier in 1968 and appointed Director of Operational Requirements 3 (Army) in the Ministry of Defence, covering equipment policy for the direct fire battle and all aspects of mobility. He decided to retire early in order to embark on a second career, and in 1971 set up a language consultancy which he expanded into a private company in 1973.

Richard Simpkin died on 3 November 1986. In his obituary *The Times* called him 'one of the foremost military thinkers and writers of recent times', and *The Daily Telegraph* said that his 'writings have had a notable effect on western military minds'.

Race to the Swift

Thoughts on Twenty-First Century Warfare

RICHARD E. SIMPKIN

Foreword by
General Donn A. Starry, US Army (Retired)

BRASSEY'S

LONDON

First English Edition 1985
Reprinted 1986, 1988
Paper Edition 1994
Paper Edition reprinted 2000

UK editorial offices: Brassey's, 9 Blenheim Court, Brewery Road, London N7 9NT
UK orders: Littlehampton Books, 10 – 14 Eldon Way, Lineside Estate, Littlehampton BN17 7HE

North American orders: Books International, PO Box 960, Herndon, VA 20172, USA

A member of the Chrysalis Group plc

Richard E Simpkin has asserted his moral right to be identified as the author of this work.

Library of Congress Cataloging in Publication Data
available

British Library Cataloguing in Publication Data
A catalogue record for this book is available from the British Library

ISBN 1 85753 135 3 Flexicover

Printed in Great Britain by
Creative Print & Design (Wales), Ebbw Vale

To
my beloved wife Barbara
a peaceable person,
in the probably vain hope
that a better understanding of war
may help prevent or limit it

Foreword

THIS book is about the future—the future of armed force and military forces as instruments of national policy in a world in which the shadow of nuclear weapons, growing conventional and nuclear military capabilities of the Soviet Union and its surrogates, and militarization of conflict in the Third World are root problems daily grown and growing more contentious.

It is difficult indeed to postulate the future of military matters. For military establishments and strategists alike demonstrate a marvelous propensity for summing up at the close of each armed confrontation and forthwith setting about getting ready to fight over again, better, the conflict from which they just emerged. This is a charge that cannot be leveled at Dick Simpkin and this book. Whether one agrees with the Simpkin solution or no, the basic ingredients essential to a look ahead are here, and provide a solid basis for the dialogue which must ensue as concerned and responsible officials set about seeking consensus over what must be done and how.

It is also interesting and quite relevant to observe on both sides of the North Atlantic, important similarities in thinking about these essential matters. About those similarities a foreword seemed relevant to the challenging hypotheses the author presents.

Since the early 1950s, the United States and its principal allies in many theaters have elected to invoke technology—in the form of nuclear weapons, to offset a superiority in numbers enjoyed by potential antagonists.

Nowhere is this circumstance more dramatically demonstrated than in NATO Europe. The hard facts, then and now, were and are that the countries of NATO cannot or will not support the large numbers of traditional divisions and air wings thought to be required for conventional defense of NATO's Central Region. As Supreme Allied Commander in Europe, General Dwight Eisenhower proposed 96 divisions and 9000 aircraft for the conventional defense of NATO's Central Region. This proposed requirement was forthrightly rejected by the NATO ministers in 1951 as politically infeasible and economically unaffordable.

Later, President Eisenhower embraced the notion that NATO would rely on 26 divisions (12 to be provided by the West Germans), 1400 tactical aircraft, and 15 000 tactical nuclear weapons. While nearly all of these nuclear weapons were built—nuclear artillery shells, nuclear warheads for surface-to-surface and surface-to-air missiles, nuclear bombs for tactical aircraft delivery, deployments to Europe were limited by President Kennedy's Secretary of Defense, Robert S. McNamara, to about 7000 weapons. Nonetheless, presence of these weapons allowed enormous reductions in the originally proposed conventional force levels, and the threat of their use against massed conventional force attack effectively denied the Soviets a meaningful conventional offensive capability for more than two decades.

Now Soviet advances in nuclear weaponry—strategic, operational and tactical, have overtaken the Eisenhower solution. It is no longer credible for Allied forces in Europe, or elsewhere for that matter, to threaten early use of nuclear weapons in response to a conventional attack. We now need another solution to the problem of how to cope with a Soviet-style mass tank/infantry attack, whether delivered by Soviet, Soviet surrogate, or other forces. It is equally essential that means be found to decouple operational level warfare from an automatic knee-jerk sort of strategic nuclear response, for while that chip may have weighed in heavily at a table seating Kruschev and Kennedy, today's power balance clearly identifies it as a nonrelevant piece in any contemporary bargaining.

Operational and tactical level realities in every likely theater of war— Europe, Korea, the Middle East—are however that joint and combined commands will ever be confronted by at least an initial, if not a continuing enemy force superiority. Forces employing Soviet-style operational con- cepts will be echeloned in depth so as to build up momentum—the product of mass and velocity—in order to maintain a continuing and relentless attack designed to overwhelm and defeat friendly forces with conventional, or possibly with a combination of conventional, chemical and theater nuclear weapons. Given the modern conventional weapons systems in the hands of the Soviets, Soviet surrogates, and other forces around the world, nuclear retaliation could be seen as the only alternative to conventional defeat. It is the growing conviction of many that this is an unacceptable alternative; that war fighting Allied or Joint Force commanders must have the conventional force and weapons systems capabilities to counter initial overwhelming superiority in the air and on the ground without breaching the nuclear threshold—beyond which no one can know the consequences.

Related to this dilemma is the progressive militarization of conflict in the Third World—militarization with modern weapons systems. Today, smaller nations with perhaps smaller, but quite modern, conventional forces and smaller nuclear stockpiles, could quite likely adopt the notion that their quantitative disadvantage can be offset by technology—nuclear weapons, for the same reasons that the NATO Alliance adopted that stance many years ago. This just increases the risk of nuclear war, and at the same time, risks the spread of nuclear conflict, from wherever it may have begun. We are on, if indeed not already across the threshold, of a time when irresponsible governments or leaders could use nuclear devices in a variety of modes, for a variety of reasons, all of which, to us, may seem totally irrational and irresponsible. The pervasive trauma over nuclear modernization with which some on both sides of the North Atlantic are seized today, must not be allowed to obscure the increasing difficulty of coping with the possibility that nuclear weapons could well be used in circumstances and for reasons that quite upset the conventional wisdom and protocols that have grown up over the years of the nuclear era. It is therefore imperative that we seek and find a nuclear formula more relevant to the realities of today's nuclear circumstances for the cloudier the nuclear equation becomes, the more we require strong, yet relevant conventional force capabilities simply so that matters may be resolved without risking nuclear disaster. The imminent danger is that the nuclear debate tends to obscure the importance of conventional force capabilities. This encourages further neglect of conventional force needs to the point that conventional defenses in NATO and conventional force capabilities elsewhere tend towards a point of no return.

These considerations dictate that, in Europe for example, NATO strategy must, from the outset, be designed to cope with the Soviet integrated battlefield threat. This includes conventional, nuclear and chemical combined arms capabilities. The growing threat of nuclear capabilities elsewhere suggests such strategy need be appropriate in other theaters as well.

Soviet-style operational concepts embrace two fundamental concepts:

• In the first, mass, momentum, and continuous combat are the operative tactics. Breakthrough is sought as the initiator of collapse in the defender's defense system. All arms and all weapons systems—conventional, nuclear, chemical—are to be planned for integrated employment.

• In the alternative, surprise is substituted for mass. In NATO, this could involve a number of divisions formed into Operational Maneuver Groups (OMG) conducting independent attacks. Without warning, they would seek to deny to defending forces the opportunity to get set forward.

Both concepts are essentially maneuver-based schemes, with a single purpose, to disrupt the operational tactics of the defender, albeit by different methods.

It is with these fundamental problems that any attempt to set forth operational concepts relevant to the realities of today and the future, must inevitably cope.

As the reader shall see shortly, by similar and quite parallel trains of thought, notions in both the U.S. and the U.K. about the need to refashion military operational concepts for future warfare, have arrived at somewhat the same conclusions. Principal among these are:

• Nuclear weapons, especially at operational and tactical levels of warfare, have become nonrelevant means of seeking the political goals likely to be considered appropriate, especially by First and Second World governments.

• Attrition warfare—the wearing down of an enemy by continuing application of massive forces and fires (including and especially nuclear fires) is no longer an appropriate operational concept for military forces of the Free World powers. We in the West will continue to be outnumbered; surely by the Soviets, and possibly quite likely by the growing military capabilities of Third World powers in many regions of the world.

What then is to be done?

The basic question to be asked and answered is whether or not it is possible to fight and win outnumbered without having to invoke the use of theater nuclear weapons. Here the history of warfare is instructive. For at the operational and tactical levels of war the history of battle teaches that time and again the outcome of battle more often than not defies what one might have expected given the force ratios extant at battle's onset. In other words, within reasonable limits it matters not whether one outnumbers or is outnumbered by the enemy; the outcome of battle turns on factors other than numbers. This is not to suggest that numbers are not at all relevant; they are indeed important. It does however suggest that within reasonable limits—say one attacking six to six attacking one, success is most often achieved by means other than just outnumbering the other fellow. For the side which believes itself foredoomed by the realities of national policy to be ever on the low side of the numbers equation, this is indeed encouraging.

What does win?

By far the majority of winners in battles in which the beginning force ratios were generally within the "reasonable" limits suggested above, were those who somehow seized the initiative from the enemy, and held it to battle's end. Most often the initiative was successfully seized and held by maneuver. This seems to be true whether defending or attacking, outnumbered or outnumbering.

Armed with that foreknowledge, how might we regard the use of military force and armed forces as the instrument of national policy in the difficult and changing world suggested above?

In peacetime, the purpose of military forces, especially in the context of operations in areas considered critical to national interests, is to reduce to a minimum the enemy leadership's incentive to seek military solutions to political problems. But when political authorities do commit military forces in pursuit of political aims, military forces must win something, else there will be no basis from which political authorities can bargain to win politically. Therefore, the purpose of military operations cannot be simply to avert defeat—rather, it must be to win. This means then that especially in NATO, the Middle East or Korea, any defensive strategy must extend beyond simply denying victory to the other side. It must, instead, postulate a definable, recognizable (although perhaps limited) victory for the defender.

Defensive strategies in key areas of the world must be designed to preserve, for the defender, the territory, resources, and facilities of the defended area. In virtually none of the critical areas of the world to which U.S. forces (for example) are likely to be committed, is there sufficient maneuver room to accommodate a classic defense-in-depth strategy based on a battle of attrition. The defense must, therefore, begin well forward and proceed aggressively from there to destroy enemy assault echelons and at the same time to slow, disrupt, break up, disperse, or destroy follow-on echelons in order to seize the initiative quickly at tactical and operational levels.

The operative tactics to implement this concept must provide for quick resolution of the battle under circumstances that will allow political authorities to negotiate with their adversaries from a position of strength. Clearly, then, one goal of the Operational Battle must be to lessen the probability of prolonged military operations. Further, the operative tactics should seek simultaneously to:

• Deny the enemy access to objectives he seeks.

• Prevent enemy forces from loading up the assault force fight with reinforcing echelons and thus achieving by continuous combat what might be denied by a stiff forward defense against "reasonable" odds.

• Find the opportunity, seize the initiative—by maneuver to attack and destroy the integrity of the enemy operational scheme, forcing him to break off the attack or risk resounding defeat.

To achieve these goals the battlefield and the battle must be extended in three ways:

First, the battlefield is extended in depth. Enemy units not yet in contact are to be engaged to disrupt their momentum (break up mass, slow down velocity), and complicate command control.

Second, the battle is extended forward in time to the point that current actions, attack of follow-on echelons, logistical preparation and maneuver plans are interrelated to maximize the likelihood of winning the close-in battle as time goes on.

Lastly, the range of assets brought to bear on the battle is extended toward increased emphasis on higher levels of command employing joint service acquisition means and attack resources.

What emerges is a concept of battle—an Airland Battle, in which the goal of collapsing the enemy's ability to fight drives us to unified employment of a wide range of systems and organizations on a battlefield which, for corps and air wings, is much deeper than that foreseen by previous doctrinal concepts.

Is this battle/battlefield extension possible?

We believe that it is; further we believe that technology now in hand and that likely to soon become operationally useful—principally electronics technology, sensor technology, microprocessor technology, rotorcraft and related avionics technology, combine in unique ways to make the Airland Battle possible. Having acknowledged the nonrelevance of the previous technology solution and the realities of Soviet style operational concepts of mass-momentum continuous land combat, we believe it possible to once again marshal technology's offerings to support an operational concept designed to make possible maneuver warfare in the face of superior numbers. Maneuver warfare designed to wrest and retain the initiative and to win the Airland Battle at the operational and tactical levels of warfare.

Whether or not the notions embraced by Dick Simpkin's closing chapters, those dealing with the relevance of organized forces, defense of the NATO centre and small force maneuver theory, are solutions or even relevant concepts for solution to the problem of operative tactics to meet challenges about which we both generally agree, remains for the reader to judge. However, the need for change cannot be denied. Nor can it be denied that Dick Simpkin has cast some first bold strokes, and that in *Race to the Swift* one finds core ideas which must be brought to bear in any attempt to peer into an always murky future.

GROSSE POINTE,   DONN A. STARRY
February 1985

Acknowledgements

Once again my thanks go first to my wife for the enormous support she has given me in editing, and to Jeannette Ritchie for all her excellent work on the word-processor and her help with numerous chores.

Professor John Erickson of the University of Edinburgh again rallied round unstintingly with material, advice and moral support. While I was researching and writing this book, I had the privilege of discussion with many old friends and new. Among the old, I want to acknowledge my deep indebtedness to General Sir John Hackett and General Dr Ferdinand von Senger and Etterlin—likewise to the latter's wife Ebba, whose little book of *belles lettres* has given me many moments of pleasure and some valuable clues (Chapter 15). It was also both pleasurable and useful to have a talk with Brigade General a.D. Edel Lingenthal, an old colleague on the MBT80/KPz.3 working group, and Frau Gisela Lingenthal, *née* Manstein, when they dropped in for tea last summer during a tour of Scotland.

Among the new, the discussions I was able to have at the United States Army War College with Generals Graf Kielmansegg and von Mellenthin were of immense value, as were the brilliant briefings of Carlisle's military Sovietologist, Dave Glantz. Just as valuable were my contacts with Major General Rick Brown at Fort Knox, Brigadier General Ed Burba at Fort Benning, and their respective teams, also with Lieutenant Colonel Jack English and his colleagues during an earlier visit to a symposium at Combat Training Centre, Gagetown, Canada. Major General Tony Trythall, now Managing Director of Brassey's, chipped in with valuable expert advice on the education of officers and junior leaders. It would be folly to tackle a book of this kind without some opportunity for discussion, but I was exceptionally fortunate in being able to listen to, question and argue with so many men of such distinction and wisdom—and patience!

I am deeply grateful for the help and moral support of Al Garland, Editor of *INFANTRY*, and Major Chuck Steiner, Editor of *ARMOR Magazine*, the latter throughout his tour of 4 years in that chair. My contacts with Wolfgang Flume (*Wehrtechnik, Military Technology*) have also been useful.

Above all, it is high time I acknowledged the debt I owe to Brigadier Bryan Watkins, now Editor of *British Army Review*. He is a friend of some

40 years' standing; and a close and staunch one in the 35 years since, as heretical kindred spirits, we shared a hut on Fan Ling Racecourse, reorganising the world with the help of many a limerick (my speciality) and rude recitation (his), and of not a little rum. Without his unstinting help and support over the past few years, I doubt whether this book or its predecessor would ever have got themselves written.

Like its predecessor, this book could not have been written in Elgin without the excellent services which the British Library Lending Division, Boston Spa, provide for their Registered Users (which, being a company, we are). Various members of their staff have gone to great lengths to sort out problems for me. Now that she has moved to another department, I can perhaps mention by name Ann Norris, formerly with Serial Accessions. By the same token the Moray District Library Department and the Elgin Public Library have helped me a great deal—particularly Lesley Reid in bibliographical research, Alastair Campbell ·in calling in books from rockiest mountain and rushiest glen, and the staff of Elgin's Reference Library—an exceptional one of which far larger cities might be proud.

Credits

Rights

The extensive quotations from Sun Tzu's *The Art of War* (trans. Griffith) are made by kind permission of the Oxford University Press, under a reciprocal agreement with the Pergamon Press Group.

I am grateful to Schild-Verlag, Munich, for their kind permission to quote from Guderian's *Panzer-Marsch!* (see Bibliography).

My thanks are also due to the Editor of *Europaische Wehrkunde* and Dr Dieter Ose for their kind permission to use, in translation, quotations taken from Dr Ose's article "Der Auftrag" (see Bibliography).

Although for one reason or another questions of copyright as such do not arise, I should like to acknowledge to Lady Liddell Hart and Adrian Liddell Hart my indebtedness to Sir Basil's writings.

Graphics

Graphics by Pergamon Press Drawing Office.

Some of the graphics started life as foils or slides prepared for me by USAARMS Fort Knox, USAIS Fort Benning, US Army War College Carlisle, or CTC Gagetown. Others have appeared in slightly different form in *ARMOR Magazine*, *British Army Review*, *INFANTRY* or *Military Technology*. The Editor of *British Army Review* kindly provided bromides of some figures. I should like to thank the authorities/editors concerned for their kind of agreement to the use of this material, and their graphics teams, together with (yet again) the Pergamon graphics team, for the talent and patience they have shown in giving shape to my thoughts.

Contents

Introduction

> "It will be better to offer certain considerations for reflection, rather than to make sweeping dogmatic assertions." MAHAN

"The few books which treat of war as an art are but small in esteem", wrote Marshal Saxe. This still holds good today—cold comfort for anyone embarking on such a project. I have found that writers on the generalities of war come in three kinds. First, and perhaps most valuable to the aspiring great captain, there are the quasi-mystical works with some intrinsic literary merit. Saxe's *Rêveries* is an example of this genre, albeit a strange one. De Guibert's *Essai Général de Tactique*, which Napoleon is purported to have taken into the field with him, is in part another such, and the more general parts of Triandafillov's *Kharakter operatsii sovremennykh armii*, with their elegant Cartesian dialectic, have something of the same effect. Perhaps this mainly French tradition reaches its climax in the writings of the poet-mystic-pilot Antoine de Saint-Exupéry, lost on a secret flying mission in 1944. But works in this genre communicate mainly on the aesthetic level; they are not amenable to analysis or extrapolation.

Then there are the analytical historians of war, from Thucydides and Tacitus to Liddell Hart, Alan Taylor and Michael Howard. Their technique of first examining examples in depth, then drawing general conclusions from them, is a particularly valuable one for the non-historian. It both provides him with the facts and exposes the writer's thinking to him. The limitation of these authors is inherent in their approach; they are apt to stop one stage short of expounding practical principles. The exception is Mahan. I vividly recalled a hasty dip into his chapters on the Russo-Japanese War from my Staff College course almost 35 years ago; and it was with enormous pleasure of every kind that I reread *Naval Strategy* in full. I cannot imagine why the United States Army's "Reformists" (the protagonists of manoeuvre theory) spend their time agonisingly re-enshrining Clausewitz when they have a far sounder authority close at hand in the shape of Mahan—and a far greater one, Sun Tzu, brought to them by the scholarship of an American general.

This leads me to the third group—the didacts, the names one usually associates with theory of war—and to a splendid exception which proves both prongs of the pitchfork I am about to drive home. Sun Tzu lived well over 2000 years ago, but might have been writing not so much yesterday, as tomorrow. And his translator, General Samuel B. Griffith, not only offers a translation of high intrinsic literary quality, but takes us into his author's mind with his background information and notes.

Being a professional translator, I have a profound mistrust of translations, so I went back to the original wherever I could. As I shall show in Part 1, this paid off, especially in the case of Clausewitz. But the didacts' morass of pseudo-philosophy, axioms and minutiae reminded me of nothing so much as John Bunyan's Slough of Despond. As I wallowed in it, I became at once increasingly discouraged from attempting to write about the theory of war, and more and more determined to find a different approach, emulating the scope of Sun Tzu and the clinicalness of Mahan, but developing my arguments from disciplines other than history and warfare. While I agree that military history provides valuable depth of perspective and a common background, I do not share the historian's view that it is the only proper path to military wisdom. I have thus sought to steer a middle course between the analytical historians and the didacts, diverging from the latter in four major respects.

They were writing in an age when war was an accepted instrument of policy, with the aim of instructing princes or general staff officers in the conduct of war. Recourse to armed force was still regarded as acceptable in the times of Fuller and de Gaulle; as Michael Howard puts it, Caucasian culture was still "bellicist". Today, while war between organised forces remains a favourite third world sport, the mass centre of public opinion in the first and second worlds seems no longer to regard deliberate resort to conflict between organised forces as an acceptable instrument of policy. This is not to say that public opinion rules out armed defence against military threats, or entirely disapproves of the ever more frequent and effective acts of the kind generally known as "revolutionary warfare". On the contrary, under the name of "government sponsored terrorism" these acts are establishing themselves as a recognised form of application of armed force. Then again, my aim is not to instruct but to enlarge understanding of the mechanisms of modern warfare among soldiers and politicians, and in other informed circles. My hope is that this understanding, by diminishing the passion and the mystery of war, will encourage the solution of disputes by non-violent means, or at least by pre-emptive and dislocating operations rather than blood baths.

The didacts' way has been to build a framework of purportedly enduring axioms and to clad this with a plaster of ephemeral and often rococo detail. Even in the case of the Russians, Triandafillov and that undogmatic genius Tukhachevskii, technology has invalidated most of the detail they set out in the twenties. As some of Clausewitz's asides show, the notion of developing an intellectual discipline by building a vast edifice of meticulously classified detail is a reflection of the descriptive phase in the evolution of the hard sciences. It remained a highly respected approach, matched incidentally by trends in literature and the arts, through most of the last century and well into this one. My view of what a theory should be is just the opposite of this—a general explanation of the principles underlying a phenomenon. As one's understanding advances, analysis progressively strips away surplus material until the heart of the matter is laid bare. In this way one arrives at propositions, the equivalent of scientific "laws", which represent the simplest and most general statements attainable with present understanding—and thus the ones most likely to endure.

Partly for the above reasons, the didacts make no attempt to relate war to any other discipline or phenomenon. Where they emerge from purely narcissistic thinking, these authorities bombard the reader with terms and assumptions unintelligible to the layman, or with unexplained historical examples meaningless to the non-historian. What is more, this liking for contemplation of their navels makes both their terminology and their arguments suspect. For instance, in the usual interpretation of Clausewitz—though not I now think the correct one—the import of his *Vernichtungsprinzip* (lit. "principle of annihilation") shifts from "destruction" in Book 1 to "dislocation" in Books 7 and 8 (see Chapter 1), permitting the proponents of both major theories of war to stand pat on his authority. I am convinced that it is entirely feasible, indeed absolutely essential, to relate warfare to established disciplines which are widely accepted and understood.

Fourth, most of the didacts have tried to dress their systems up in quasi-philosophical robes—something that most if not all were at least as ill-fitted to attempt as I am. Admittedly this was a fashionable trend—a matter of courtliness, almost of courtesy—in the days when most of them were writing. But they were either obsessed with the glories of war or writing for those so obsessed; such murmurs of a still, small voice as one finds are apt to be blotted out by the sound of the trumpet. Some of the concepts of war are intellectually not of the easiest; but for that very reason they need to be set out and discussed in the simplest possible terms.

There is one thing, though, on which I go all the way with the didacts. Again and again, after a long section devoted to the most Euclidean of reasoning, they observe: "But of course it is the worst of mistakes to see armed conflict only as a matter of geometry" (or mathematics, or whatever). This is the problem in trying to discuss war within the two-dimensional grid of the printed page. Like three-dimensional chess or the three-dimensional noughts and crosses beloved of the wardroom, war has to be viewed on three levels at once. By the same token, it has to be explained in terms not of one other discipline, but of three. And the nub of the matter lies in the interaction of these three levels, each subject to its own set of laws, in the mind of the commander.

The first level is that of classical physics. This discipline provides a model for the physical aspect of war—on the one hand for the synergetic and dynamic effects which characterise manoeuvre, and on the other for the constraints imposed by terrain and available technology. Being probabilistic, modern physics might well offer a link between this level and the next; unfortunately it would also put the analogy beyond the reach of this writer and, I suspect, of most readers. I am not suggesting that all officers should be trained in physics or that physicists would make great captains. I happen to find this the easiest way to approach the problem. Even for those who do not, this analogy with an established discipline helps to confirm the validity of the argument and to identify where and why it breaks down (as in Chapter 8). To keep the book in balance and, I hope, readable, I have omitted mention of the various blind alleys I followed before arriving at the concepts I put forward.

The second level (going up) rests on risk, chance and surprise—in sum, on statistics. Clausewitz's greatest contribution to military thought may have been to bring out the role of chance in war, and in his day it was difficult to go much further. Now that technology has reshaped the role of chance and mathematics has given us some understanding of it, it should be possible to analyse this whole aspect in objective terms, even in part to quantify it. This I have attempted to do in Part 3. I may have gone adrift here by taking too narrow a view of "risk", but at least my analysis narrows down the grey zone and offers some lines of thought which look profitable.

At the third and most important level, the imposition of the commander's will and the clash of wills, one turns naturally to psychology. In the anglophone world of the thirties and forties, "psychology" meant by and large "Freudian psychology", so at least one had some idea what "turning to psychology" implied. Freud may have worn a figurative grey macintosh, but at worst he provided a coat rack shared by professionals and laymen in many countries. Now we have about five major schools, all of them differing widely—often to the point of contradiction—in terms and concepts, and none of them much known to, or respected by, the layman—or, I suspect, within the profession. One is thus deprived both of a conceptual base and of the terminology to go with it, and this makes objective discussion of the psychological aspect of war extremely difficult. I have therefore contented myself with bracketing in rather crudely on the "clash of wills", and explored in depth the rather simpler but equally important problem of troop control. For, important as it is to know your enemy, I cannot help feeling that inhibiting the opposing commander's response by swift and purposeful action is more likely to achieve a psychological victory than agonising over what he is likely to do.

As I remarked earlier, I can see no way of making a general synthesis of the three levels within the bounds of a written presentation. In fact I consider it would be dangerously simplistic to attempt this—the more so since all three act on both doctrine and command decisions in quite different ways. This is one reason why I shall probably join my distinguished predecessors in Marshal Saxe's celestial wastepaper basket. So in the last part of the book I have tried to draw the elements of my thesis together by looking at the interaction of the three levels in certain aspects of the future of armed conflict which I believe to be relevant to today's worldwide sociopolitical situation.

At the risk of indulging in the wishful thinking of one in his dotage, I see the West European peace and environmentalist movement in general and the Federal Republic's Green Party in particular as the heralds of an advance in civilisation comparable in magnitude to that which occurred between the Middle Ages and the start of the Industrial Revolution. Certainly—and I make no apology for repeating this—West European bodies politic, though not as yet their politicians, are coming to see socially approved intraspecific mass slaughter (the ethological definition of war) as a less than ideal way of going about one's business. Clearly this is not going to result in the instant elimination of war or the threat of it from the advanced world. But it is going to modify traditional military principles and aims, such as the necessity of "going over to the offensive", or the mission of defeating the enemy as opposed to containing him.

By the same token, this viewpoint adds force to questions already being asked, notably in the Soviet Union, about the "usability" of organised forces. Again, this is not going to lead to the immediate disbandment of standing armies. But it may well mean that organised forces take over from nuclear weapons as the "unusable" deterrent, while such armed conflicts as to occur are conducted by small specialised forces employing manoeuvre theory, as well as by clandestine elements of every kind. The "usable" complement to such forces would be a mass militia capable only of local defensive action.

General Donn Starry in his Foreword, and I myself through most of this book, have dwelt on the similarities of the military problems faced on both sides of the Atlantic, and of the approach to solving them. But one must likewise, I think, identify the way in which underlying socio-political trends differentiate Europe on the one hand from *both* superpowers on the other. The Soviet Union and the United States today, like Europe's imperial rivals of yesterday, are constrained by their very status to adopt a fundamentally offensive posture—ideologically, economically, through surrogate conflicts, by military confrontation, by revolutionary warfare and, in the last resort, by some level of direct conflict between their organised forces.

The shift of the foci of power to Moscow, to Washington DC and, more gradually, to Riyadh, leaves Europe on the defensive—struggling to maintain its values and its very existence. That the Warsaw Pact and COMECON are held together by fear needs no stressing. Less evident perhaps, especially from across the Atlantic, is the fragility of NATO and the EEC. The cohesion of both these groupings—at least in anything resembling their present form—depends on the present right-wing governments of Britain and the Federal Republic. The next German federal election could well put a SPD/Green coalition into power; and this would hang an enormous question mark over the form, if not the fact, of continued German participation in NATO. Britain's current policies on NATO and the EEC hang on a minority government (42 per cent when elected, some 37 per cent at the time of going to press). And polls on both these policies have consistently shown over 60 per cent of the British electorate to be opposed to them.

Thus, however prudently and judiciously an SPD/Green coalition or a British Labour government might act, the next two or three years could see a dangerous destabilisation of NATO in general and the NATO centre in particular. Like a physical power vacuum, a policy vacuum in Western Europe would benefit only the Atlantic Alliance's enemies. On the military side, the time for radical thinking was the day before yesterday. Proponents of the EEC have a little longer.

Finally, therefore, I have moved back in time to glance at some more immediate problems. The broad long-term political trend is towards the left just as certainly as the broad long-term sartorial trend is towards informality. But I subscribe to the substantial school of thought which sees the possibility of a direct Soviet attack on Western Europe largely as a figment of the imagination of ideologues on both sides of the Atlantic and the North Sea. Western politicians are preoccupied with maintaining the last peace just as surely as any soldier ever set about preparing for the last war. Nevertheless, opinion is on the move. When I visited the United States in March 1984 I was told at a formal briefing that, although the Warsaw Pact threat to the NATO centre was still the ultimate threat, *it was no longer seen as the most likely threat.* Oddly enough, what first brought this home to me was a weekend visit to Malaysia 15 years ago, when I heard the formerly peacable, light-hearted and charming Malays giving vent to the chesty grunts of Islamic nationalism. And this impression was reinforced over and over again by experience with my industrial clients exporting to French-speaking Islamic markets.

Western Europe, and *mutatis mutandis* the Soviet Union and her satellites as well, face a serious threat from Islam militant, on a front stretching unbroken from Algeria to Afghanistan, with outposts further east. This threat was an economic one in the seventies; it has become one of revolutionary warfare in the eighties. Two, probably three, Islamic nation states have nuclear weapons already; so there is no reason whatever to suppose that, by the turn of the century, the threat will not become one of organised forces with nuclear back-up. The trouble is that the Koran provides these cultures with standards of humaneness on a par with those of the most brutal periods of the Middle Ages, coupled with a total readiness to embark on, and die in a *jihad.* These people are more than ready to use the weaponry both halves of the rich north so obligingly provide them with. I close, then, with a glance at both the similarities between manoeuvre theory and the doctrine of revolutionary warfare, and the use of manoeuvre theory to counter this threat.

Despite the Islamic nuclear threat, I have deliberately excluded discussion of nuclear and chemical warfare. This omission is based on a set of assumptions which are coming to be more and more widely held. The use of nuclear weapons against each other by NATO and the Warsaw Pact is no longer credible. With the deployment of designated "theatre weapons", any use of battlefield nuclear weapons would instantly escalate at least to a "theatre exchange" in Europe. Every theory of war I have encountered is based on a situation that changes at a rate slow enough for its further course to be influenced by response. A nuclear exchange on the scale now predictable is thus different in kind from non-nuclear warfare. I would go further. Nuclear weapons indisputably represent an extreme of physical violence. But readers who stay with me as far as Chapter 17 ("Acceptable aims") may join me in questioning whether a nuclear exchange is a purposeful act of war, or mere ideological "MAD-ness".

Much the same arguments apply to the use of chemical warfare, lethal or incapacitating, against centres of government and population—something which is entirely feasible. By contrast, from the physical point of view, selective tactical employment of chemical weapons differs only in degree from that of other ammunition. The case put forward by Haldane, Liddell Hart and many others in the twenties—that the use of chemical agents against troops was more humane than the use of steel and high explosive— has been ignored rather than refuted. In fact, the characteristics of modern chemical agents add much force to it. My own view, first put forward in an essay published in 1960 and now shared by many who specialise in the psychology of war and human factors, is that, whatever their direct military effect, modern high-grade agents might well bring hostilities to a halt by putting conditions on the battlefield beyond the bounds of the human organism's psychosomatic tolerance. In any event it is remarkable how, within a bellicist culture, governments of every shade and ideology join hands in ruling out chemical warfare.

I hope what I have said above will establish a link between me and readers rash enough to join me on this difficult exploit. But because the route is a severe one, I should like to belay the rope which links us by touching on my habit of thought. For I have come to wonder whether causal or "linear" reasoning is really much help in innovative thinking, let alone in making its products palatable. *Homo anglo-americanus* may possibly be *sapiens*; but no way is he *rationalis*. Even the French and Germans, one increasingly finds, are apt to hide a light of intuition under a bushel of ratiocination, while for the Russians the billowing clouds of Marxist-Leninist verbiage seem little more than a smokescreen behind which they can emote in decent privacy.

Born, bred and schooled a dyed-in-the-wool rationalist, I like to argue my way through, step by agonising step, to a conclusion, a process that endears me as little to the Anglo-Saxon reader as my use of the first person does to a German one. And just as facts have to be learnt and digested before they can decently be discarded, this reasoning process has to be gone through. Yet I have come to see two drawbacks to doing it in public—apart from the fact that some readers may not stay with me.

The first is that a linear logical process cannot produce a balanced solution to a complex problem. In *Antitank* I took technology as the determinant and finished up with an impossibly large and expensive division. I have since found, incidentally, that using force structure or concept of operations as a leitmotiv leads to much the same result. Thus, as many have been kind enough to say, *Antitank* was a doubly valuable exercise. But it was not, and was not intended to be, a blueprint for an army of the future.

The second limitation of rigorousness is that it shuts out important perspectives which lie off the main line of argument. One cannot turn and gaze up every little glen as one drives along the valley; yet the reader probably knows the valley road and wants to be shown the track up the glen. For instance—and I am basing this discussion on my own experience because this is how I came to it—if one is writing or talking about the design of armoured vehicles from a technological viewpoint, one can certainly introduce and give due weight to specific human factors. But one cannot present the ergonomic aspect as a coherent whole. That calls for a different book, and the key synthesis at the man/machine interface has to be left to the reader. This is the "two-dimensional" limitation I referred to earlier; I have tried to overcome it in this book by coming at the problem two different ways.

What is more, I am convinced that, "OK" or otherwise, the spoken word now rules again. To communicate effectively, the written word, so long the arbiter of style, should now follow the patterns of the spoken. I recall an outstanding teacher of languages—of Russian origin, I think, but no matter—once saying to me—"Grammar and syntax are like a pair of crutches. Once you are fully fit, you throw them away." Similarly, I have come to think both a predominantly factual and a rigorously argued approach, like the use of a computer, are in effect mere rungs on the ladder of credibility. Having surmounted them, one can step off the ladder onto a platform which allows more freedom of movement.

Nevertheless, I have attempted a fairly formal structure without wasting my publisher's money and my readers' time by trying to go the whole hog. Never, even to please my German friends, would I forgo the first person or adopt a more formal style. What I write is, I hope, firmly founded on research and analysis. But it is one man's thoughts, nothing more; it would be less than honest to give my ideas a gloss of objectivity by corseting them in formal dress. By the same token, in response to feedback from some academic readers and most others, I have dispensed with footnotes and detailed references. Most of the key sources are well enough known to be familiar to any reader likely to want to refer to them.

I opened with four aspects on which I diverged from the didacts of military theory. Let me close with a fifth. However ephemeral some of their detail, they set out to produce a definitive "system of war", a master plan. In this immensely complex and terrible business of modern armed conflict, I shall be more than happy if I have managed to carry the reader a few steps down the path towards "knowing that he knows not".

Elgin
July 1984

List of Illustrations

List of Tables

Key to Symbols

I have used NATO symbols (STANAG 2019) with certain simplifications familiar to those who know the system. This is a brief guide to the system for those not conversant with it.

Formation/unit symbols are based on a "golden square" reactangle whose size is not significant (1). They are completed by a type symbol (2) (or occasionally by a combination of these); a level (size) symbol (3), and sometimes a descriptive abbreviation (4) (e.g. MED = medium, MOR = mortar, 122 = calibre of field gun) to the left of, or if needs be below the symbol. Abbreviated formation/unit names are placed to the right of the symbol, and sub-unit letters/numbers to the left.

—x x— **Boundaries** are single full lines, with the level symbol at intervals.

○ **Full lines** indicate existing organisations, occupied positions, etc.

◌ **Broken lines** indicate future (dis)positions.

Locations are indicated by —

a line from the centre of the base for a complete formation/unit

an initially vertical line from the bottom left corner for HQs, etc.

Type symbols

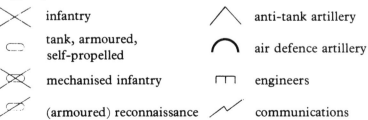

╳	infantry	◠ anti-tank artillery	
⊂⊃	tank, armoured, self-propelled	⌒ air defence artillery	
⊠	mechanised infantry	⊓ engineers	
⊘	(armoured) reconnaissance	∿ communications	

⛨	parachute troops	┼	medical
∞	rotary-wing aviation	**PRO**	military police, traffic control
•	artillery (tube or mixed)	⟩—⟨	maintenance, repair
⬚	rocket artillery	⊘	service, supply (general)

Weapon system symbols

◇	reconnaissance patrol, vehicle	⊐	(medium) anti-tank guided missile system
⊟	main battle tank		heavy ATGMS on tracks

Level/size symbols

.	section	xx	division
...	platoon	xxx	corps
I	company	xxxx	army
II	battalion	xxxxx	front (army group)
III	regiment	⌐⌐	(over level symbol) group
x	brigade	(+), (−)	considerably reinforced/reduced

PART 1

The State of the Art

"War is a trade for the ignorant, a science for men of genius."　　　SAXE

"Military education hitherto has not been designed to teach a scientific approach to problems, but rather to develop executive skill and foster the spirit of loyalty."
　　　LIDDELL HART

". . . consequently, when a great captain does arise, irrespective of the circumstances which surround his successes, his system, even if he has no system, is turned into an infallible doctrine, a dogma which becomes a millstone"　　　FULLER

1

The 50-year Cycle

"The student will observe that changes in tactics have not only taken place *after* changes in weapons, which reasonably is the case, but that the interval between such changes has been unduly long."   A. T. MAHAN

Introduction

The earliest major work on the theory of war was almost certainly Sun Tzu's *Art of War*, probably written in the fourth century B.C. Of all the works I have studied, it vies with Mahan's *Naval Strategy* as the most relevant for the present and future. Its literary quality survives translation; many passages use communication at the aesthetic level to convey the art of command; and the detailed precepts are stated with such simplicity that they are easy to transpose into a modern idiom. The classical and post-classical eras produced a valuable crop of analytical historians, from Thucydides, who slightly preceded Sun Tzu in time, via Tacitus, to Procopius, who wrote in the sixth century A.D. Those times likewise gave rise to poets of war who rank among the "all-time greats" of world literature, like Homer (if he had a personal existence) and Virgil. Then again there were the descriptive historians whose accounts of war are so clear as to provide models ripe for analysis, among them Julius Caesar, one of the few in history to wield the pen as effectively as he did the sword.

There followed the long-drawn-out rise and fall of the knight in armour, punctuated, for instance, by the phenomenon of Genghis Khan and the theorising of Machiavelli. Interestingly, the aloof absolutism which characterises *The Prince* soon vanishes in Machiavelli's *Art of War*, where he obscures the broader issues by leaping into the cockpit of controversy—thus setting the example for most of his successors. The eighteenth century up to the French Revolution produced more than its share of great captains by land and sea, together with a sprinkling of significant military writers. One might mention, for example, de Bourcet and de Guibert, who provided, respectively, the structural and training basis for Napoleon's army and the diet which nurtured his military genius; or in less serious vein Heinrich von Bülow, whose purely geometrical theory of war, published at the end of the century but a product of age of elegance, was a baroque disaster in every

3

sense of that phrase. But it was Napoleon's army, the child of the French Revolution, which set the spring of modern theorising about war a-bubbling—simply because Napoleon's conduct of war gave soldiers, historians and dilettantes alike something to think, talk and write about.

There were two far more solid grounds than this, however. Before and during the eighteenth century, the functions of head of state, political direction of the war, and command of the army in the field were often combined in one and the same person. This was particularly the case among the Continental powers. There too, when the head of state did not conduct the war himself, he tended to delegate this task to his heir or to a near relation trained in the same tradition, a principle epitomised in Machiavelli's *The Prince*. By the same token, up to and during the epoch of the "wars of kings", armies were small enough to be effectively commanded by one man. "By God! I don't think it would have done if I had not been there", the Duke of Wellington said of Waterloo.

On the one hand, the fabric of advanced nation states became more complex, resulting in the appointment of a "secretary for war" or such. On the other, military men being great imitators of success, the size and character of Napoleon's forces sparked a trend towards mass armies, which soon combined with the railway to produce the "nation in arms" concept. Thus the conduct of war came to involve not just one key man, who could get on with doing what he thought best, but at least four—the head of state, the secretary for war (and/or the chief of staff), the commander-in-chief in the field, and one or more higher formation commanders. What is more, just as a cabinet of ministers came to surround the head of state, a staff grew round the commander in the field.

All this complexity brought in its wake three needs. One was to define the functions, powers and responsibilities of all these people. The second, far more important, was to provide them with a jargon in which they could communicate with a good chance of being understood. Third, and no less important, came standard procedures and a common doctrine. This situation bred the first wave of modern theorists, from which the names to survive were Clausewitz and Jomini—both of whom first published in the 1830s, and who were, needless to say, arch enemies. But before addressing the Clausewitz enigma or looking beyond I should like to open up the main theme of this chapter.

The 50-year cycle

Henry Stanhope pointed out in *The Soldiers* that, for some good reasons and many more bad ones, an army is at root a social organisation rather than a functional one. Even a small army is a very large organisation by any standards. Regular officers recruited in peacetime are seldom the most dynamic of revolutionaries, and those that are tend not to attain positions of real power. Thus an army by its very nature possesses an organisational inertia several times greater even than its size would suggest.

On BBC television recently, a leading feminist—not Germaine Greer, but some British native product—observed that "you'd never change men"; male chauvinism, she bemoaned, would only die after boys had grown up among feminist attitudes. This contention is strikingly borne out by the pattern of military innovation. Time and again, where a radical change in equipment, doctrine or force structure is concerned, one finds a gestation period of between 30 and 50 years or more between the technique becoming feasible, or the need for change apparent, and full-scale adoption of the innovation. This delay varies somewhat with time and place only because of variations in the factor that governs it—the career span of an officer rising to the highest rank. When the pressures of war distort this pattern, the ensuing peace almost always brings a restoring backlash. One could fill a book with historical examples, but I shall mention just two, the first a dual one.

The American War of Independence (say 1780) saw the expansion of musket-armed light infantry beyond company level on the British side, and the fielding of organised units of riflemen on the American. But it was well over 30 years before the British Army introduced the Baker rifle into general service. Likewise, contact in that war with von Wurmb's *Jäger* sowed the seed of skirmishing in the British mind. This bore notable fruit in Sir John Moore's Experimental Corps of Riflemen and the Light Division he built round it. But the "line infantry" remained just that until, almost a century and many thousands of wasted lives later, the Boer commandos imposed a discipline of fire and movement. Then again, acceptance of the "Fuller plan" (for the use of tanks in deep penetration) as the "basis of tactics" for 1919 shows that, after $3\frac{1}{2}$ years and, this time, millions of wasted lives, the Allied high command had finally started to think in terms of manoeuvre. And thanks to Foch's change of heart these ideas did carry some influence in the postwar French Army. But in Britain they were not so much discarded as buried in quicklime; and in the United States Army the tank arm was disbanded and responsibility for the tank given to the infantry. Admittedly "armoured" thought was reinstated in both armies after 25 years rather than 50. But the timing and extent of this swing was dictated partly by the circumstances of the North African Campaign, mainly by the German armoured threat as a whole.

From earliest times, technology has influenced the form of war in some way or other. But it was not really until the years leading into the (first) Industrial Revolution, again the turn of the eighteenth and nineteenth centuries, that technology began its tumultuous burgeoning, and machine power really came to be employed first in static, then in mobile applications. The pace of the electronic revolution leaves us breathless, as the mechanical one may well have done our forebears, but it is too early to see how far this will influence the rate of progress in military equipment. So far, accelerating technological advance has failed to produce a commensurate speeding up of innovation; and even on the purely technological side, spurts fostered by the threat or actuality of war have been offset by a backlash once this pressure was removed. In every field, the peacetime first-line service life of a given generation of major equipment tends to be ten times that of its wartime life—say 20 years as opposed to 2.

There is also a good deal of evidence that the first-line life of a particular *form* of a given category of equipment spans about two peacetime generations, so that its total life runs to 50 to 60 years. By a change of "form" I mean here a change substantial enough to influence doctrine and/or force structure. Since this is rather surprising—or at least it was to me—I have demonstrated it in Fig. 1. I hope these examples will serve both to bring out the principle and to show that "50" is a very flexible figure. There have been flashes in the pan like the ultra-heavy artillery gun, stayers like the machine gun, and "old faithfuls" like the cargo truck, which has confounded the predictions of the twenties and by and large warded off all challenges from tracked and aerial vehicles.

There are, in fact, at least five good reasons for this rule-of-thumb figure of 50 years—enough to make me suspect that it will at least fight a sporting rearguard action against the electronic cavalry charge. The first, also to be seen in commerce and industry, is the career-span factor. For instance, full acceptance and integration of computers will have to wait until the computer-literate schoolchildren of today become the power generation of the day after tomorrow. A second and related reason is the difficulty of training people on sophisticated equipment. The Federal Republic must surely rank with France and Sweden among the world's most advanced countries in both technology and education, and 5 years ago she was proclaiming that advanced equipment was *per se* easier to use and thus posed no training problem. Now, for her third generation of postwar equipment (the 1984 Leopard 3 tank project, for instance), ease of training and operation take precedence over all aspects of performance. And where the limits of the human organism's physical performance as well as complexity are involved, as with fighter pilots, the overall success rate in training (from initial selection to full operational qualification) has fallen to under 5 per cent.

Similarly promoted is finance. Even relatively simple weapon systems like the battle tank or the attack helicopter are coming up with unit production costs of between two and eight million dollars; and their "real unit cost slice" (including development, infrastructure and logistic backing) is several times greater. Only the largest and healthiest economies can sustain these kind of costs at all; and even they have to amortise the outlay over a period which overstretches the design's development potential and carries it well into technological obsolescence.

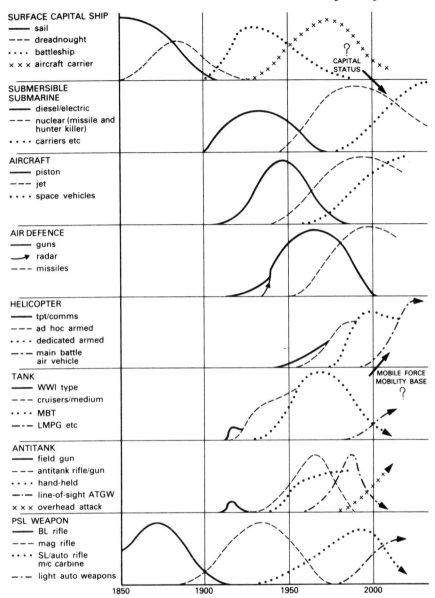

FIG. 1. *Schematic to illustrate principle of fifty-year cycle.*

Then there are three time factors in the proper sense of that term—first, research and development time. Automation has enormously speeded up the design and development of systems involving only one discipline, most notably of course that of electronic systems. But it has not, so far at least, managed to straddle the interdisciplinary interfaces of a complex weapon system. There is a great deal of evidence from both the first and second worlds, and recently from third world countries like Korea which have now moved into the development as well as the production of relatively complex equipment, that the R & D cycle is lengthening. Where in the seventies one talked of 10 years from project definition to introduction, one now is now less than sanguine about 12 years as a planning basis. Admittedly war sees years cut to months. But in both the Second World War and the Vietnam conflict this led to a small number of total failures and a much larger one of end products, like the early German jets and the original Sten gun, which were considerably more dangerous to their users than to the enemy. "Crash projects" and telescoped development have been attempted in peacetime too. But I know of none, in any military field and in either NATO or the Warsaw Pact, which has not resulted either in abandonment or in the later-than-normal introduction into service of an unsatisfactory model. Quite apart from funding problems and hiccups in research programmes, it is extremely difficult to draw up a sensible requirement for a successor until an equipment is at least in the user trial stage—and this means 7 or 8 years from the word go.

Then come the problems of introduction itself. Even where user trials and prototype acceptance go smoothly, there is a delay of at least a year before preproduction models can be delivered for troop trials and training evaluation, and a rather longer one before production models start flowing and cadre training can start. So one is looking at a period of 4 or 5 years between acceptance and the first field force unit going operational. Finally, there is the pipeline time as such, dictated by funding and production, training and logistic resources, sometimes—as with the extension of runways—by infrastructure too. From all this I conclude that the 10 years of a half-generation, the 20 years of a generation, and the 50-year lifespan of a given form of equipment are all likely to be with us for some time.

I first hit on this notion of a 50-year cycle from the pattern of development of theories of war, something I now see as an effect rather than a cause of it. I am personally convinced that the "career span" factor is the determinant. But if one takes the sorting out of military ideas after the Napoleonic era as a starting point, and singles out from the technological area step advances in means of locomotion (Fig. 2), one perceives an interestingly consistent pattern. To explore this further, I shall examine each peak of theorising in turn.

The Clausewitz enigma

If the wits are right in dubbing Proust "the world's most quoted and least read novelist", Clausewitz must be his non-fiction counterpart. The first modern wave of theorising stemmed from the ferment thrown up by Napoleon—both the nature of his army and the conduct of his campaigns—

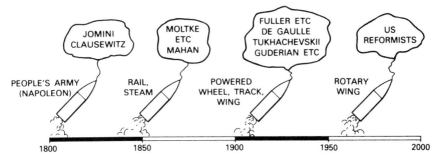

FIG. 2. *Innovations in mobility and peaks in theorising.*

and from the trend towards mass armies set in motion by the early promise of the railway. Jomini, the other name to survive from this wave, is certainly the more lucid and to my mind the sounder, just because he accepts the limitations of the type of theory he proposes. But it is Carl von Clausewitz who symbolises the theory of war in the public mind. Some see him as a kind of latter-day Mars breathing death and destruction, others as the thinking man's antidote to militarism. The addicts of attrition and the masters of manoeuvre both stand pat not just on the same thesis but on the very same term in it—the *Vernichtungsprinzip*. Even the analytical historians hold opposing views on him. Realising from the start that I could not ignore Clausewitz and remain credible, I decided to try and get to the bottom of all this.

Much in Clausewitz remains obscure, partly because he evidently intended it to be so, partly because he had philosophical pretensions which he was incapable of sustaining. Book 2 (*Theory of the Art of War*) shows him repeatedly forced to fluff the upper limit of his thesis (the borderline between theory and "genius") in his efforts to synthesise a comprehensive theory. I am ill qualified to comment on his philosophical approach. But having found one leading authority attributing his thinking to Kant, another to Hegel, and a third maintaining a deafening silence on this aspect, I felt reasonably justified in using the word "pretensions". In fact I was reminded of nothing so much as the quatrain of Richard Porson, an eighteenth-century satirist, on his "Visit to the Continent":

> "I went to Frankfort and got drunk
> With that most learn'd professor, Brunck;
> I went to Wortz and got more drunken
> With that more learn'd professor, Ruhnken."

Despite this and my lack of the equipment or the inclination for scholarly exegesis, the way the solution to the main problems fell like chestnuts in my lap astonished me. I used the Bonn 1952 edition of *Vom Kriege*, partly because many Germans seem to regard it as the best modern edition, partly because of the excellent preface by Werner Hahlweg. In between Marie von Clausewitz's Foreword and her husband's Introduction comes a progress report (the *Nachricht*) found among his papers. This is in fact in two parts, the second a note probably written on the last occasion he handled his papers before leaving to join Gneisenau as chief of staff in Poland, from where he was to return with a fatal infection of cholera. In the main "progress report" (page 78) he uses entirely unambiguous language to state the position. Book 7 (The Offensive), he writes, is only a first draft ("sketches"), developed as a "mirror image" of Book 6 (The Defence). More important, Book 8 (The War Plan), while ultimately to be the culmination of the work as a whole, is likewise a first draft, written with the aim of clearing his mind and of providing a reference base for revision of the first six books.

In the second note he re-emphasises the point like this:

> "In its present state, the manuscript on the conduct of major war which will be found after my death can be regarded as nothing more than a collection of working papers from which a theory of major war should be developed. I am still unhappy with most of it, and Book 6 is really no more than a shot in the dark. . . . The first chapter of Book 1 is the only thing I regard as being in final form; it will at least serve to give the whole the general direction I intended."

When one looks at Book 1, Chapter 1, and Book 8 in the light of these statements, they seem to offer clear-cut solutions to the two main problems about Clausewitz. Sections 24 to 27 of this chapter leave no doubt whatever that Clausewitz viewed war as "a true political instrument, a continuation of political intercourse, an execution of it by other means". He goes on to consider and dismiss the argument that certain types of war are ends in themselves. He then points out that war, although subordinate to politics, has a nature of its own, and that politics must not demand of war things which are contrary to that nature, describing the proper recognition of this relationship as "the first, most sweeping and most decisive act of the judgement exercised by the statesman and the commander in the field".

It is widely—and, I had hitherto assumed, correctly—supposed that Clausewitz began by using the term *Vernichtungsprinzip* (lit. "principle of annihilation") to mean physical destruction or disruption of the enemy force in battle, and progressively widened its meaning to cover dislocation and psychological disruption too. Taking the opening of Book 1, Chapter 2, and Book 8 together, one must, I think, discount this view. At the beginning of Chapter 2, he lists the three "general (military) objectives" as "the enemy's forces, territory and will", and goes on to make this categorical statement, its first sentence in the German equivalent of italics for emphasis:

"The (enemy) *force must be destroyed, i.e. brought to a condition in which it can no longer continue the conflict.* We hereby declare that from here on we shall use the expression 'annihilation of the enemy force' to mean this and nothing more."

The impression I have formed is that shortly after this, when he turned his mind to the battle, his thinking became increasingly fuddled with Wagnerian harmonies featuring the trumpet in the top line, and that it was not until much later, in time and in his progress with his writing, that he had worked this martial music out of his system.

This brings out one of the reasons why Clausewitz is so widely misunderstood. His papers are drafts written mainly over a period of 15 years during which he aged from the mid-30s to just on 50, some of them first put on paper earlier still. He himself claims to have finally revised only the first chapter of all, though internal evidence suggests that he had done some work on the rest of the first book at least. To anybody who writes, the original bears all the marks of a draft. There are the blurrings and lapses of syntax, the *non sequiturs*, the occasional incorrect or inconsistent use of a word. What is more, there are all the signs of the emotional top-hamper one has to "write out" of one's head to clear the way for reason, and subsequently to discard or completely rewrite. Another familiar sign is the way the quality and clarity of his language trails off as he tackles a difficult idea. Some passages where these factors compound each other could mean anything—or nothing; they can only be interpreted from their context. Over and above this problem, my own experience of translating pseudo-philosophical German in a number of other fields—including, oddly enough, jazz—tells me that this is an extremely difficult task, sometimes even a fruitless one. The translator suffers from exactly the same problems as the author did, the ones I outlined above, and produces a text which is partly unintelligible and wholly unreadable. One reason for this is the way German modes of thought are so closely bound up with the structure of the German language, an effect compounded if one is working on a draft. In striving to offer an acceptable translation, one is forced so far away from the form of the original that the import of the translation may tend to diverge progressively from that of the original rather than to fluctuate about it.

This may, I suggest, be one reason why Clausewitz has been so massively and tragically misunderstood by those who read him in translation. A second reason is one put forward by Liddell Hart and other authorities, and confirmed by the impressions I myself have formed. Neither the down-to-earth Anglo-Saxon nor the Frenchman with wits sharpened on Cartesian dialectic has much time for the pseudophilosophical meanderings of the German mind. The non-German reader grabs the headings, or a catch-phrase from the early part of a long sentence, and leaves it at that. It's just too bad if, as rather often happens in Clausewitz, the latter part of the sentence happens to reverse the meaning of the first—or something in Book 8 happens to contradict Book 1. But the third and probably the strongest reason for this gross misunderstanding—and here again I lay no claim to originality—is the liking of the military mind for imitating success regardless of the circumstances, and for preparing for the last war. It was Moltke's successes in the wars of 1864, 1866 and 1870/71 that put Clausewitz into the international charts.

The only problem was that the Prussians themselves, inspired by the military successes of Frederick the Great and Napoleon, and by the possibilities of the railway, by no means accepted Clausewitz's theses. In fact the only evidence I can find of the German officer's approval of Clausewitz is the use Beck made of him to counter Ludendorff's doctrine of war for its own sake (page 27). Reading Jomini and Clausewitz together in the original, one is struck by the readiness of the "philosophical" Prussian to come down from his eyrie and dig his talons into his more down-to-earth Swiss opponent. The latter part of Book 2 and external evidence adduced by Werner Hahlweg are alike in suggesting that both Clausewitz's teaching when Commandant of the Prussian Staff College and his writings were strongly opposed, attracting disdain rather than acceptance. One wonders why he did not wish to publish before his death, even if he had lived long enough to do so. In fact, putting two and two together and making five, I have gained the impression that Clausewitz's preoccupation with the "bloody battle" during the earlier years he was writing, the years following the Congress of Vienna, may well have been a reaction, which he later sought to correct, against a school of thought favouring the indirect approach or even heading towards pacifism. I leave this thought as a nice problem for some historical research student.

Some authorities believe that the elder Moltke was, in the formal sense, a student under Clausewitz, presumably at the Staff College. Since Moltke was born in 1800, and did not transfer from the Danish to the Prussian Army until 1822, I cannot see quite how the dates might fit. But it is more than probable that Moltke was somehow exposed to Clausewitz's ideas during the formative years of his career. Moltke's thinking, while irreproachable in detail, seems to have been torn between the scope for *mass* manoeuvre offered by the railway, a single overwhelming sweep from the start of mobilisation to final victory, and the need to retain suppleness by the development of directive control (*Auftragstaktik*). More important, Clausewitz's subordination of military aims and actions to the political aim became less and less acceptable as the Prussian eagle spread its wings and grew to adulthood. However much this bird was itself concerned with agility, what the British, French and Russian saw, as watchers or as rivals, was its size and the striking power of its talons. Putting this together with Clausewitz's early emphasis on the battle and the "destruction" (taken literally) of the enemy force, and on his distortion of the Napoleonic concept of "absolute war" (again in Book 8), they arrived at the doctrine now known as attrition theory, one as easy on the generals' minds and instincts as it was hard on their soldiers' bodies. However unacceptable one may find this theory in human terms, and however disastrous it may have proved in colonial wars, the failure of the two German operational offensives of the First World War forces one to concede that, in major war, positional warfare may have been the correct response to the technological setting of the time. Where Foch went adrift was rather in applying to this setting and to the scope of the Schlieffen Plan the dimensions of the Napoleonic battlefield.

I do not for one moment suppose that what I have said will do more than stir the fires of the controversy over the interpretation of Clausewitz. But I hope it may show why, where it stems from Clausewitz at all, the thinking I shall put forward derives from the *final* shape of his theory—from the supremacy of the political aim over all matters military; from battle as only one means among many of achieving the military aim; *but* also from the futility of threats of any kind which are not backed by physical and moral readiness to fight if needs be. One thing that boils to the surface again and again in Clausewitz's text is his mental struggle to synthesise the various aspects of his thesis into a coherent, all-embracing theory which takes account of the realities of chance and generalship. As I explained in the Introduction, I have stopped short of attempting a general integration. And in support of this decision I should like to quote from the second short note of the *Nachricht*, probably written the last time Clausewitz looked at his papers.

> "In their actions most just follow a 'feel', based on subjective judgement, which fills the bill more or less well depending on the degree of genius they possess.

> "All the great captains have acted in this way, and part of their greatness and genius has lain in their knack of hitting the nail on the head. This will always be the way things get done; and 'feel' is more than adequate in this respect. But when it comes not to acting, but to convincing others in discussion, what counts is clear thinking and getting the nub of the matter across. Up till now development of this skill has come so little way that most discussions take the form of ill-founded toing and froing. Either nobody budges an inch; or mutual respect leads a mere compromise drawn down the middle, a solution of no intrinsic merit whatsoever."

The role of the theorist is not to provide off-the-shelf systems of warfare but to provide a vehicle for discussion of war, and material for training minds to make war more skilfully—or to avoid it.

The operational level and total war

The Dolomite-like appearance of the first peak of modern theorising on war is probably due to the coincidence that Clausewitz's papers and Jomini's major work closely coincided in time. By contrast, the second has all the convexity of the Cairngorm, a magnificent training ground but, for me at least, lacking in aesthetic appeal. It runs perhaps from the end of Franco-Prussian War to the retirement of Schlieffen in 1905. Its scope was mainly confined to Germany and Russia; as explained above, the Anglo-French addicts of attrition were busy digging in on their misinterpretation of Clausewitz. The United States Army seems to have relegated to the history books the brilliance of the commanders in the War of Independence and the Civil War, and consolidated a similar position. Only at the United States Navy War College did the teaching and writing of Mahan provide one of the brightest lights ever to shine over these glowering seas.

Moltke (the elder) and Schlieffen, both doers and pragmatists rather than thinkers, are the great names of this period. But the views which were developing in the German General Staff over these years, and which seem to owe far more to Jomini than to Clausewitz, were chronicled and discussed by a number of military authors like von Verny du Verdois, von Blume, von Scherff and von der Goltz. The size of and complexity of armies created a grey zone between strategy and tactics (as then defined) and imposed the need for the definition of a third level, spanning from theatre/army group or army, to corps and sometimes, in Moltke's eyes at least, reaching down to division. The term the French adopted and the British followed was *la grande tactique* (grand tactics). On the German side the word chosen was *operativ*, quickly borrowed by the Russians as *operativnyi* and now rendered in English as "operational".

This latter group of terms quickly began to gather round them their modern connotations of dynamism, synergetic effect, responsiveness and self-containment, of which much more later. It also gave rise to a fundamental divergence of views. Moltke maintained that the operational plan should seek to ensure that the first contact between main bodies occurred under the most favourable circumstances possible, and that "no plan survived contact". After this it was a matter of responsiveness and opportunism. He therefore laid extreme emphasis on every aspect of directive control, in particular on the right of the commander on the spot to react to the situation as he found it without going back for further orders.

Schlieffen, coming into a position of influence when the French and German armies had attained something like the complexity and the mobilised strength with which they would open the First World War, took the opposite view. He felt that uncertainty over the location, nature and outcome of the first main force contact stemmed in general from lack of a scenario (as we should now say), and in particular from the age-old need to seek out the enemy. His eyes were firmly fixed on war with France; he could see little option for the French Army but to close forward to the frontier over its whole length at the same time as the Germans did; and the millions disgorged from the railheads on both sides could scarcely fail to find each other.

Given these constraints and the means of transportation of the time, Schlieffen preferred to predetermine when, where and how first contact would occur, and to make an operational plan carrying from mobilisation right through to strategic decision. No-one can say how this concept would have fared if the Schlieffen Plan had been implemented in its original form as opposed to being toned down by the younger Moltke, or, perhaps more important, whether it would "have done if Schlieffen had been there"; nor whether it would have got an earlier and more severe come-uppance if Foch had held the main French reserves in front of Paris rather than forward in the Napoleonic lozenge. In the event, the Allies were able to block the right hook because it was too slow, and because its trajectory lay on an exterior line with respect to the bulk of the Allied forces. We shall see the elder Moltke's approach reincarnated in the Wehrmacht's practice, the Soviet Army's preaching, and American "Reformist" thought. We may note, in passing, how Schlieffen's ideas bear on the Israeli situation; and we may wonder whether Soviet *practice* does not in fact lie nearer to Schlieffen than to Moltke.

There was another way, more fundamental still, in which nineteenth-century Prussian opinion diverged from Clausewitz's insistence on the dominance of the political aim. Stemming probably from the glories of Frederick the Great, from sharing Clausewitz's initial distorted interpretation of Napoleon's concept of absolute war, and from the growth of mass armies with the implication of a "nation in arms", the concept of war as an end in itself steadily gained ground. This trend seems to have started to run out of control with the accession of Kaiser William II in 1888 and the resignation of Bismarck 2 years later. I have found no record of Hindenburg's view on this. For present purposes it is probably enough to note Ludendorff's explicit and total denunciation of Clausewitz's modifying principles in favour of "total war". One cannot help wondering whether this was at the root of Churchill's concept of total war, leading to the Western Allies' insistence on unconditional surrender.

"Tanks only" in the twenties

I shall explore developments in Germany and the Soviet Union in depth a little later. Here I want to look at the upsurge of new thinking mainly associated with the names of Fuller, Liddell Hart and de Gaulle. These names are usually linked to mechanisation and the tank, but in Britain at least they were firmly tied to the considerably greater one of Haldane, the protagonist of chemical warfare. In fact chemical warfare, mainly in association with the bomber, rather than mechanisation, is the real leitmotiv both of Fuller's work and of Liddell Hart's earlier (1925-ish) writings. A quick glance at de Gaulle's book *Le Fil de l'Epée* makes one wonder whether he was ever motivated by anything except *la gloire*. But the British writers, Fuller and his fellow soldiers just as much as Liddell Hart, were moved above all by revulsion against the futile mass slaughter of the First World War. My own impression is that, just like the murk of many passages in Clausewitz, the layers of cloud which enfold Fuller's propositions have their origin in a conflict between his militaristic and extreme right-wing attitudes on the one hand and his basic humanity on the other. Excellent writer that Liddell Hart is, his contributions of the mid-twenties to this theme were, as he himself later admits, too overstated and emotionally charged to carry conviction. Similarly I suspect that Fuller was driven to the extremes of his "tanks only" views by the pigheadedness of the opposition.

In all these writings there was a clear doctrinal link between chemical warfare, aviation, mechanisation including off-road logistic vehicles, and the emphasis on *mechanised* airborne troops. In one combination or another, these ways of war offered a means of obtaining a quick decision without a battle. The bombing of centres of government and population with incapacitating chemical agents would produce a decision with a minimum of death and lasting disablement by dislocating the national ability to take decisions and/or breaking the will of the body politic. The few casualties would be civilian ones, including women and children; but in an epoch when wartime forces were composed mainly of conscripts and reservists, this distinction was largely a sentimental one.

At operational level, the enemy's main force would be turned and dislocated. If there was an open flank or an interrupted front, the mechanised force would go round it or through the gaps. If not, mechanised airborne forces would jump over the enemy, and/or the mechanised force would break out through a gap created by chemical warfare. Mass infantry, preferably lorry-borne, would be needed only to mop up, deal with prisoners, and secure and administer territory gained. Applying the "fleet in being" theory (of which more later), the existence of "gasproof" air and mechanised forces with a chemical capability, even if inferior in conventional fighting strength, would very often pre-empt military action by the enemy and severely hamper any operations he did attempt. This is, I think, a fair statement of the essence of the Fuller–Liddell Hart thesis.

But when one explores both this doctrine and de Gaulle's more down-to-earth proposals in depth, one finds that both are flawed. In terms of military soundness and Gallic chauvinism alike, de Gaulle had a great deal going for him. His first bite at the cherry, *La Discorde chez l'Ennemi* (1924), suggests that his thinking stemmed from a remark of Ludendorff's—"Employment of tanks in mass is our greatest enemy." And it is in this book that he admits to a complete lack of technological knowledge or even awareness. His key work, *Vers l'Armée de Métier* ("Towards an all-regular army"), published in 1934, shows that he had studied Fuller and Liddell Hart but did not at that stage accept the "tanks only" argument. The armoured division he proposes is overgrown, tank-heavy and short on artillery even by thirties standards. But it is an all-arms force with good information-gathering resources; and it contains 500 tanks—something of a "magic number", as we shall see. In a memorandum to the commander-in-chief and chief of staff of the French Army, written in November 1939 but unpublished until 1980, he lays great stress on fully mobile radio command facilities, one of the keys to responsiveness, but seems to be leaning, doubtless through frustration, towards the "tanks only" viewpoint. While he might well have been unable to stem the tide of conservative military opinion, he in fact seems to have struck two rocks. The first, which carried away his credibility, was a proposed jump to 50- or 60-ton tanks from the then "heavy tank" going weight of some 18 tons. The second, which sunk him, was the strength of feeling in the French body politic of the day against a sizeable force of standing combat units as opposed to specialist units and cadres.

By far the best critique I have found of Fuller's views on land warfare is Tukhachevskii's preface to the Russian translation of Fuller's *Reformation of War*, republished in the Russian marshal's *Selected Works*. The value of mechanised airborne forces is a hobby-horse which the two men shared and which the Soviet Army later fostered. This apart, Tukhachevskii may do rather less than justice to the influence of certain specific ideas of Fuller's on the evolution of Soviet thinking. But this brilliant advocate of the all-arms battle flattens the "tanks only" heresy with a smart left-and-right. He stresses the need for both infantry and artillery to help get tanks forward, and points out that the turning action of a mobile force can only be developed if there is a main force to provide a fulcrum and to hold the enemy forward. We shall discuss later how far and how favourably or otherwise Fuller's and Liddell Hart's thinking influenced the Germans. But after a migration whose path I have not traced, the "tanks only" heresy finally came home to roost on the east bank of the Suez Canal in October 1973.

Ferment in the eighties

If we take the thirties, when Tukhachevskii's and Guderian's mechanisation programmes were in full swing, as the effective apogee of a 50-year cycle, we might now expect to be at the zenith of the next one. And we find several of the advanced world's major armed forces in a greater or lesser state of flux. Technologically, overhead attack of armoured vehicles is taking over from line-of-sight systems. This will both deprive the tank of its antitank role and call for a change of form in the principal classes of armoured vehicle. In conjunction with this trend, the helicopter is tending at once to supplant the armoured vehicle and to encourage a shift to faster, lighter armoured vehicles. The rotary-wing principle, now evolving into the day of the tilt rotor, will also allow navies to respond to the dictates of advanced means of detection and attack and go below the surface. The Soviets, for instance, appear to be building a series of nuclear-powered, aircraft-carrier sized submarines; these could (and almost certainly will) replace both helicopter carriers and assault ships, surfacing only to fly or float off their payloads. In conjunction with the hunter-killer and missile submarines already long in service, this points the way to underwater naval task forces. More broadly still, the question marks which hang over electromagnetic guns, directed energy weapons and robotics may, over the next 50 years, turn into exclamation marks of guardsman-like stature.

However, thanks to scale and bureaucracy, the mills of Marx grind almost as slowly as the mills of God—though far less surely. In the West, the British Army continues to hang on by its toenails to what it has got as it approaches its thirtieth consecutive year of financial squeeze. With the last of the Wehrmacht-trained officers gone, the Federal German Army, condemned by its government to a doctrine of positional defence, seems to have lost the Prussian spark of creativity and to be wallowing in a slough of administrative problems. It is to the "Reformist" movement in the United States Army that one must look for innovation. *Field Manual 100-5 Operations*, promulgating a switch from attrition theory to manoeuvre theory, is a very good start.

To round off this scene-setting operation, I would draw the reader's attention to the Swedish Army and the Swiss Militia, and indeed to the whole broad concept on which those countries base their defence policy. For they are the only advanced countries I can think of whose defence policies have been completely successful since inception. History suggests that there will always be a "top nation" and a challenger. Even if it can be restrained short of war, superpower rivalry is bound to continue. But the emergence of the European peace movement as a solid political force opens new perspectives. Given time, the erstwhile "imperial powers" of Europe, now deprived of all of their empires and most of their power, may eschew their bellicist hankerings and exchange the semblance of power for the reality of influence by making themselves, like Switzerland and Sweden, at once models worthy of imitation and very hard nuts to crack.

2

Blitzkrieg

[From the section "Principles for employment of tanks"]
". . . (The tank) is therefore the weapon of potentially decisive attack. Mobility and firepower will only be exploited to the full if the attack achieves deep penetration and the armoured force, having broken out, can go over to the pursuit. . . . The higher the concentration of tanks, the faster, greater and more sweeping will be the success—and the smaller our own losses. . . . Tanks must attack with surprise, and as far as possible where the enemy is known or presumed to be weak. . . . The tank needs supporting arms which complement it and can go everywhere with it. . . . Even in defence, the tank must be employed offensively. Concentration is even more important here, so that the enemy's superiority can be offset at least in one spot."

HEINZ GUDERIAN, *Panzer-Marsch!*

Introduction—attrition theory and manoeuvre theory

A year or two after the war, I was browsing in the cellar of Camilla Speth's bookshop on the Kurfürstendamm when I lit on one of the more agreeable surprises of my life—a German book of nonsense verse on a par with Lear or Lewis Carroll—the *Galgenlieder* ("Gallows songs") of Christian Morgenstern, one of Germany's leading twentieth-century lyric poets. One sonnet, *The Knee* ("A knee goes lonely through the world, . . ."), says as much about the fruitless butchery of the First World War as the better-known line of Siegfried Sassoon—"But he did for them both with his plan of attack." Before we examine the German military reaction to that defeat, it may be as well to define the two main theories of war and the relationship between them.

As a serving officer striving to reconcile British and German views on armoured doctrine and thence on the philosophy of tank design, I went along, partly from experience of similar discussions with the United States, partly from sheer desperation, with the thesis put forward by Field Marshal the Lord Carver in *The Apostles of Mobility*. He sees the views of the various leading armies as points on a spectrum running from emphasis on direct protection (armour) to emphasis on mobility. From my studies of the last few years, I would respectfully but diametrically differ from this view, at the same time offering an explanation for it. My immediate purpose here is just to summarise my view, leaving amplification and justification of it until later in the book.

19

We saw in the previous chapter how American, British and French dedication to attrition theory stemmed partly from misunderstanding of Clausewitz, partly from blind imitation of the successful Prussians (who had in fact understood Clausewitz but largely rejected him). Some authorities suggest that these Armies' liking for attrition theory arose from their experience of colonial warfare, as contrasted with the Continental European wars between nation states or alliances of roughly equal sophistication and power. But the lessons of the Boer War, some extremely bloody clashes with fanatical Muslims, and even the near-miss of the Germans' 1914 offensive did nothing to shake the addicts of attrition. On the American side, belief in material progress seems to have been translated into the blind faith in the power of materiel which was the hallmark of their doctrine in both World Wars, which cost them defeat in Vietnam, and which they are only now beginning to slough off. The British and French attitude, which still prevails on one side of the Channel and persisted until quite recently on the other, probably results from the way soldiers' blood and courage have proved more readily available in those two countries than generals' brains, and on what it is hard to resist calling the Anglo-French disease—the enduring if quaint conviction that blood-letting is good for the nation's health.

For attrition theory (also known as "position theory") is about fighting and primarily about casualties, though at sea and in the air, and more recently on land, it takes account of material losses too. An adherent of this theory of war simply seeks to achieve a shift of relative strengths in his favour by imposing on the enemy a higher casualty rate, or more broadly "attrition rate", than he himself suffers. In physical terms, this is a two-dimensional model, the relative rates of change of mass with time (Fig. 3a). True, this represents change—as by most definitions does any form of warfare. But it is essentially a static concept, which takes no account of dynamic effects. The curves on the graph stand for nothing more nor less than smoothed histograms compiled from, say, weekly strength returns. Troop movements are simply a means of getting to a position in time to await or give battle; subject to this, their speed is only of secondary importance.

To achieve the shift of relative strengths, the addict of attrition seizes and holds a piece of ground—or in the case of naval warfare a forward base, a stretch of narrow waters or the like—which lies between the enemy and the attainment of his strategic aim. This ground must also confer on the side which holds it a tactical advantage, such as height *per se* or the domination of an obstacle or defile. The enemy then pounds himself to pieces on the rock (the fundamental British tenet), or sets himself up as a target for the "fire base" established on it (the American view). Once the relative strengths have shifted in the defender's favour, he "goes over to the offensive". If the enemy still does not repent of his political sins and sues for peace, or if his

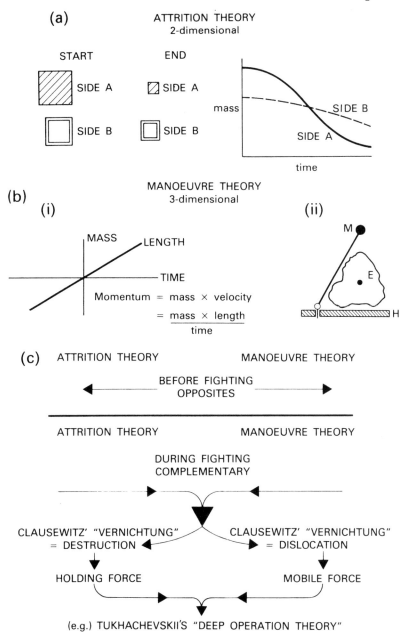

FIG. 3. *Attrition and manoeuvre theory. a. Attrition theory depends on change in relative strengths. b. (i) Manoeuvre theory is 3-dimensional, with momentum as key quantity. (ii) Basic manoeuvre theory model—H = holding force, M = mobile force, E = enemy. Note "hinge" between holding and mobile forces. c. Attrition theory and manoeuvre theory are* opposites *before outbreak of hostilities,* complementary *in war.*

own government has by then lost sight of its political aim in favour of military revenge, the addict of attrition advances cautiously and tidily on a broad front to seize another piece of ground which directly threatens some vital interest of the erstwhile aggressor. The process is repeated until one side has gained overwhelming strength (Second World War) or becomes exhausted (First World War). The Second World War, not least the protracted uncertainty over which way the Russian bear would jump, also demonstrates a principle of Clausewitz—fighting apart, the addict of attrition's only way to change relative strengths is by knocking out secondary members of the opposition or acquiring allies.

Manoeuvre theory, by contrast, regards fighting as only one way of applying military force to the attainment of a politico-economic aim—and a rather inelegant last resort at that. True success lies in pre-emption, or in decision by initial surprise. Missions and objectives down through the levels are logically related to the strategic aim, and are concerned with enemy forces and resources. Ground seldom features as an objective except when it stands for a geographically fixed enemy resource—like a centre of government, naval base, airfield or bridge—or when a particular topographical feature provides access to, or control of, a key resource.

Manoeuvre theory draws its power mainly from opportunism—the calculated risk, and the exploitation both of chance circumstances and (to borrow a tennis term) of "forced and unforced errors" by the opposition; still more on winning the battle of wills by surprise or, failing this, by speed and aptness of response. But on the physical level manoeuvre theory is a dynamic, three-dimensional system. One is now concerned not just with mass and time but with the interaction of mass, time and space—or, in the terms of dimensional analysis, of mass, time and length (Fig. 3b(i)). This threefold relationship is best and most commonly represented by the quantity known as momentum. To oversimplify grossly, one now sometimes has to understand strength or combat worth not just as mass, but as momentum—mass times velocity. One can in fact hang this physical aspect on three concepts—mass (inevitably), leverage and tempo, a complex parameter broadly standing for rate of progress towards accomplishment of the mission.

A lever requires a fulcrum to develop its effect, and this implies the existence of at least two distinct masses on the side employing manoeuvre theory. Since these two elements interact dynamically with the enemy, whose force, however distributed, will have a mass centre somewhere, one arrives at the fundamental schematic of manoeuvre theory as a three-element system (Fig. 3b(ii)). The operation of the system turns on the relative positions of the three elements, and on the absolute and relative rates at which those positions change.

Yet, however manoeuvre theory may seek to forestall combat, history leaves no doubt that the exercise of this theory frequently leads to extremely bitter fighting at critical points. By the same token, the role of the static or slower-moving element is to slow down the enemy; and once hostilities have broken out, this will have to be done by engaging him. One thus sees a duality of relationship between attrition theory and manoeuvre theory (Fig. 3c).

Before hostilities start, they are opposites. Attrition theory relies for pre-emption on the status quo, a difference in strength so large as to make fighting seem pointless even to the addict of attrition. Manoeuvre theory calls for *active* measures to achieve pre-emption if possible, decisive surprise if not. Failing these, fighting will take place; and once fighting begins, attrition theory comes into play. In fact the static or slower-moving element is really about fighting. The mobile element is about moving, dependent for its potency on momentum; but it will have little effect unless its mass continues to pose a real threat by its potential firepower and potential mobility. Thus once fighting starts, the two theories become complementary. Manoeuvre theory represents an added dimension superimposed on attrition theory. Or conversely, attrition theory provides manoeuvre theory with the sheet anchor it needs to stabilise it in the storms of war.

Turning to blitzkrieg, with this in mind, we shall see that the German doctrine had several theoretical weaknesses, quite apart from its practical ones. It underplayed the importance of the slower-moving element; and partly for this reason it underestimated the importance of attrition.

The term "operational"

Under attrition theory the same basic techniques are repeated on a larger and larger scale up through the levels. There is no definable cut-off point within a theatre of operations, short of strategic level that is. The Anglo-French term "grand tactics", and the way it slipped almost unnoticed from Anglo-American usage, imply that the difference through the levels is only one of degree. But manoeuvre theory postulates the interaction of two separate elements on the same side (Fig. 3b(i)). There is a need to distinguish between what goes on within each of these elements and the way the two interact. Thus there is a need to define three levels, the third interposed between tactics and strategy but concerned with actions within a theatre. So I feel duty bound to join various offical agencies of the British and United States armies in taking yet another stab—my fifth in 2 years, I think—at defining the word "operational" (*operativ, operativnyi*). Trying to define the noun "operation" does not in fact help much; but once one can pin down the adjective, the meaning of the noun spins off.

I am now reasonably satisfied, for reasons which will come out later, that the word "operational" has acquired not two military meanings but three. First there is the familiar one, also used by the Germans and the Russians, of "having directly to do with warlike operations", contrasted with "administrative" or "logistic", and with the attributives "training" and "exercise" (as in "training expedient", "exercise restriction"). Second comes the organisational one of level—from theatre down to division, or thereabouts, serving in fact to indicate a level at which the two elements called for by manoeuvre theory interact. This was fine as long as a given level of formation represented a roughly constant capability. But technological advance, mainly in mobility, and the constant search for new tactical techniques have invalidated this match. More and more, small special force detachments like the one that, despite lack of official admission, undoubtedly did take out the Super Etandards on the Argentine mainland in the Falklands War, or the Shi'ite fanatic who blew up the United States Marines' base in Beirut, are achieving successes of "operational" and even strategic importance.

Thus, both in general military understanding and in its association with manoeuvre theory, "operational" has taken on a third meaning divorced from organisational level. As I at least now see it, for a concept, plan or warlike act to be considered as "operational", it must meet five criteria. It must:

> have a *mission* lying at one remove, and one remove only, from an aim which can be stated in politico-economic terms (in other words from a strategic aim);
>
> by a *dynamic, closed-loop system*, characterised by speed and appropriateness of response;
>
> consist of *at least three components*, one of which reflects the opponent's will;
>
> be *synergetic*—that is, its whole must have an effect greater than that of the sum of its parts;
>
> be *self-contained* within the scope of its mission.

As we shall see, the blitzkrieg concept stemmed from thinking of this kind.

The postwar ferment

As one who prefers to view history through the wrong end of a telescope—preferably with the lens cap on—until forced to turn the instrument the right way round, I cannot see the provisions of the Treaty of Versailles as other than reasonable. But to the Germans—and seemingly to many historians from among their erstwhile enemies—they were dragon's teeth. Militarily, they deprived Germany of all weapons capable of offensive use; more important still, they slashed armed forces of millions to a total of 100 000. The compound ferment of the "stab in the back"—a necessary if questionable belief—and of defeat itself was matched by a very real need to find "a better way of fighting", though not in the humanitarian sense in which Liddell Hart was to coin this phrase. Unfortunately, trying to get at the bits of the inside story of the Reichswehr that matter, and of its growth into the Wehrmacht is like panning for gold. There is much that glisters; there is pretty authoritative cover of organisation, training policy and tactics; there are regimental and formation histories with a considerably higher professional content than their British counterparts; there are acres of discussion of blitzkrieg by German and foreign authors, seemingly based for the most part on reminiscence.

But my fairly thorough and protracted search, guided by a number of American and German authorities, has failed to come up with anything approaching a definitive statement of the operational concept of blitzkrieg. Somewhere deep in the Library of Congress, where most captured material was sent, valid documentation of this kind may exist. But it does appear to be historical fact that the Germans succeeded in burning the classified files of the Oberkommando der Wehrmacht and the Oberkommando des Heeres. And those who were in key positions before 1935 are mostly long since dead. (Were Guderian still alive, he would have been 97 by the time this book is published.) I have therefore relied mainly on discussions over the years with German officers of Wehrmacht vintage, including two particularly brilliant and distinguished men. First, though, I want to lay a brace of red herrings.

The first, which will wave its tail again briefly in the next chapter, concerns the German–Soviet experimental and training centres of the twenties. When I wrote *Red Armour*, I still shared the widely held view that blitzkrieg and Tukhachevskii's deep operation theory were two sides of the same coin. Then, by a happy coincidence, I finally got my hands on a copy of Tukhachevskii's *Selected Works*, and on some key German articles written 20 years or more ago, just before I attended a Symposium in the United States, where I had the opportunity of talking further with my German friends. I now incline to the view that the main thing the German and Soviet concepts have in common is a tendency to produce maps covered in fat arrows as opposed to anglophone goose eggs.

For good reasons, which I shall bring out in a moment, German documentation on the experimental centres is heavily biased towards the aviation centre at Lipetsk. I have found nothing that comes near John Erickson's lucid and scholarly treatment of this question in *The Soviet High Command*—apart from some unpublished source material which he kindly provided me with and which entirely bears out his analysis of the facts. Briefly, the Germans established a mission headquarters in Moscow with access to the Soviet Chief of General Staff, and three joint centres—one at Lipetsk for aviation (including air observation of artillery fire), one at Volsk (codename TOMKA) for chemical warfare, and one for tanks and mechanisation at Kazan. The whole arrangement was terminated in 1932. Lipetsk was a going concern by 1925 and put in almost 7 years' of useful work. The Germans were able to put a lot of pilots through advanced courses; and the Soviets profited enormously in both training and technology. The chemical warfare centre at Volsk was probably established by 1926, but further negotiations in the following year cut its activities back. In 1928 theoretical co-operation at the centre itself was reported to be going well; but technical problems, increasing Soviet chariness about field trials and, doubtless, political sensitivity made this project a very stop–go one. There is no record of any positive results; but Volsk may well have produced some kind of negative evidence which led the two countries to abstain from chemical warfare in the Second World War.

Despite an imposing organisation with training, development trial, user trial, logistic and administrative wings, and an ambitious programme of courses, Kazan never really got off the ground. The setting up of the centre does not seem to have been finally agreed until early in 1927, and the first tanks, shipped in sections, were not due until spring 1929. An interesting sidelight is that some of the sixty British tanks ordered by the Soviet Union in March 1930 were passed on to Germany through Kazan. But the Red Army had received no Soviet tanks in quantity by the time the centre closed in 1932. While tactical training for tank officers was planned, most of the courses that actually took place seem to have been at trade training level, for crewmen and fitters. There is a record of a conference at Kazan on 30 August 1929 which may have covered operational and tactical doctrine. But there is no evidence at all of Kazan having had a decisive influence on German thinking.

More interestingly, neither Tukhachevskii nor any of the big names in German armour seem to have played much direct part in this co-operation. During the period in question, Tukhachevskii was first Chief of Army Staff, then Commander, Leningrad Military District. But the dominant Russian figure was Voroshilov; Tukhachevskii's relations with the Germans appear to have been very reserved, and in 1931/2 he was excluded from the German–Soviet staff talks—or at least ceased to take part in them. All this is surprising, the more so in view of his visits to the German and French war ministries and staff colleges, and of the "German connection" on which his trial was based. One explanation is that his political reliability was already suspect, but in my view, as I shall bring out in the next chapter, he may well have been busy rethinking his ideas at this time. All in all, there is little to suggest that either Soviet thinking in general or the fruits of all this co-operation had any great effect on the development of German doctrine.

My second and similar red herring is the influence of British thinking on blitzkrieg. True, the key men in the Reichswehr read Fuller's and Liddell Hart's publications. True, Guderian and his colleagues met both these men on a number of occasions. Certainly they, like the Russians, picked these

British brains. And I am still convinced (as I wrote in *Tank Warfare*) that Liddell Hart's thirties' thinking and writing provided Guderian at once with a skeleton of principles for his doctrine and a yardstick by which to measure it. But there are three reasons why I by and large accept the German contention that British influence in the formative stages was minimal. First, the seminal thinking took place *before* much of Fuller's work was published, and before the Salisbury Plain experiments. Second, the tank emerged as a conclusion from the German studies; it was not their starting point; and the German tactical concept was fundamentally an all-arms one. Third, the German thinking may seem revolutionary in British terms; but in the context of German military thought over the previous 50 years or more it was *evolutionary*.

The main problems which faced von Seeckt as head of the Truppenamt (Chief of Army Staff), and then of the Reichswehr, concerned force structure, training and procurement. One suspects that it was mainly to ease the last two of these that he fostered the German–Soviet co-operation. Clearly the only way to make the Reichswehr the nucleus of a substantial fighting force was to structure it, albeit clandestinely, as a cadre; there seems good reason to accept the German contention that this cadre of 100 000 was the finest organised body of men ever assembled in peacetime. On the other hand, the time available for expansion might prove to be very limited; so the need for "a better way of fighting" was evident to all.

As early as 1922 Guderian, then a staff captain in the transport directorate of the Ministry, had set about exploring in depth the military implications of the internal combustion engine on land, in the air and at sea. He demonstrated from history how the great captains of all times had been constantly on the lookout for new means of achieving a quick decision by a mobile form of warfare and how, to this end, they had increased the numbers of their fast-moving troops. Guderian was an infantry officer, and his key idea at this stage was to restore the mobility and offensive capability of the infantry by having them ride not just forward but *into battle* on vehicles. At this stage he saw tanks as a means of sustaining this mobility.

But the many excellent cavalry minds in the Reichswehr were just as active, if not more so. Some, including Beck himself, felt that they were rejecting Ludendorff's views and going back to the correct interpretation of Clausewitz, though Werner Hahlweg records von Kleist's comment that "Clausewitz rated low back in my days at Staff College". Be this as it may, their thinking seems to owe more to Sun Tzu. Their basic approach was that if you were never going to be strong enough to fight and win a battle, you had to achieve operational aims without fighting one. This meant above all moving faster than the enemy could respond—"getting inside his decision loop" as the Americans put it today. The first move was to turn the enemy tactically, by a surprise penetration down a boundary or other weak spot (often referred to as a "slashing attack"), or better still through a gap. They were firm advocates of the indirect approach, and of the principle, stated by Jomini and re-emphasised by Mahan and Liddell Hart, that the hazards of difficult terrain are always preferable to the hazards of combat. Anything more than a passing encounter battle, a light skirmish, had to be avoided. Otherwise your breakout force would be at best slowed down, and at worst destroyed. Once a fast-moving force had got into the enemy depth and dislocated him at tactical level, it had to continue gaining depth fast enough to keep one jump ahead. As depth increased, the opposition would weaken; and even if it did not, the leverage exerted by the force would increase.

There were thus two schools of thought, the "enlightened infantry" view and the cavalry one. Needless to say there was a third powerful view, initially held I think by von Seeckt himself, favouring infantry on their feet supported by artillery as the decisive arm. Looking at this triangular situation, one is inclined to think that Guderian's design for the *Panzertruppe* was a compromise. So it is interesting that Germans brought up in the cavalry tradition saw it as an "extreme" solution. One can perhaps resolve this apparent paradox by looking on the one hand at the structure of the *Panzertruppe* as a whole, and on the other at the initial organisations of the three types of division it contained. In terms of speed and cross-country capability alike, the physical mobility of the force fell short of what the cavalry would have liked. This was partly due to the emphasis placed by Guderian on fighting power, partly to the technological limitations of the time, compounded by the effect of the Versailles Treaty restrictions.

By contrast the tank–infantry ratios within divisions were extreme. The *Panzer* division proper came in two kinds, tank heavy by 2 to 1 and 4 to 3 respectively. The *Panzergrenadier* divisions formed by conversion of infantry divisions started with a 6 to 1 preponderance of infantry, but this was later reduced to 4 to 1. The "light" divisions, found mainly by mechanisation of the cavalry, were initially 4 to 1 infantry–heavy (although this "infantry" was bred in the cavalry tradition). However, it became more and more usual to reinforce them with an independent tank brigade of three battalions, a practice which led to their progressive conversion to balanced *Panzer* divisions.

Viewing all this with foreign hindsight, one tends to think that the build-up was set rolling as at the touch of a button by Hitler's rise to power. Not so. During the 9 years following Guderian's initial studies, practical activities were confined to experiments by the seven-battalion strong Motor Transport Corps, using commercial vehicles with or without mock-up tank bodies. Theoretical studies continued in Berlin; probably the value to the Germans of the Soviet–German project lay more in the thinking it inspired in Berlin than in what was achieved on the ground at Kazan. It was not until 1931, when Guderian became chief of staff of the Transport Inspectorate, that things really began to move. Shortly after Hitler came to power, the work was transferred to a new Motorised Troops Directorate (lit.

"Headquarters of the motor *combat* troops"—my italics), with Guderian, now a Colonel (General Staff), as its chief of staff. Not until 1935 did the first field trials of a tentative armoured divisional organisation take place. These went well, resulting in the formation of three armoured divisions, with Guderian himself taking over *2. Panzer-Division* as a test-bed. Shortly afterward three "light" and four motorised (*Panzergrenadier*) divisions were formed, and these ten divisions were grouped into three corps (later to be known as *Panzerkorps*), as army group troops.

Although the Germans themselves rate Guderian less highly than does foreign opinion—perhaps because of his failure in front of Moscow—it is primarily to him that the credit for the structure, tactics and equipment of the *Panzertruppe* must go. Looking at what happened in other armies, one has to regard the creation of armoured divisions and corps as a milestone in itself. But it is noteworthy, even if coincidental, that 1935, the year of the first trials at divisional level, was also the year in which Beck was appointed Chief of General Staff. Although he resigned less than 3 years later and in fact became the leading military figure in the anti-Nazi resistance movement, Beck's is the name which keeps on coming up in discussion when one seeks to pinpoint responsibility for the operational doctrine which came to be known as blitzkrieg.

Operational doctrine

I use the word "doctrine" advisedly, in preference to "concept" or "theory". Certainly the impact of blitzkrieg on those on the receiving end of it was so dramatic as to make it seem revolutionary. But the more closely one looks at the German technique, the more one sees it, on the one hand, as a pragmatic managerial response to an extremely difficult situation, on the other as an evolutionary development, exploiting new means, of the operational thinking of the elder Moltke and Schlieffen. The situation was a difficult one, for the *Sturm and Drang* of Hitler's ambitions considerably outpaced the attainable tempo of technological development, equipment procurement and build-up and training of forces. I for one would not entirely go along with van Crefeld in singling out the German General Staff's powers of organisation as the key feature in the Wehrmacht's superiority (see Chapters 15 and 16); their command and control technique was more important still. But the selection and training of the Reichswehr did produce an exceptional concentration of managerial talent, both top management (General Staff) and middle management (warrant officers and sergeants). At the same time, a military tradition at both levels, conserved in face of defeat by Ludendorff's claim of a "stab in the back", ensured that these men viewed war with the professional detachment necessary for clear thinking.

As to theorising, my impression is that von Seeckt, Beck, von Brauchitsch and their colleagues reacted to Fuller, and later to de Gaulle and Tukhachevskii, in much the same way as the elder Moltke did to Clausewitz—a way which accords with my own view that the value of theories of war lies not in laying down a blueprint but in promoting understanding of this phenomenon. Like mental sauna-bathers, they allowed the Briton's vapourings, the Frenchman's hot breath and the Russian's cold wind of reason to flow over them, and came out all the fitter to get on with the job.

The two German operational offensives of the First World War (in 1914 and 1918) had only just failed to achieve a decision. And they had evidently failed because their overall tempo was too slow. The punches were telegraphed in preparation and laboured in execution; as a result, the defender, despite his own sluggishness, was able to block them. The leaders of the Reichswehr did indeed form a crack parachute division under Student, and their successors used Student and his men to good effect in Crete. But unlike the British School and Tukhachevskii, they seem to have seen airborne forces very much as an optional extra—a judgement subsequently confirmed by history. For them the role of the powered wing was to help the powered wheel and track roll faster by supporting them with information and with fire. Their central thought was to develop a small force of high quality with mobility an order of magnitude higher than the rest of the army. They accepted that, to start with, this force might represent only 5 per cent or so of available mobilised strength. No matter. Its combat worth would lie in surprise and speed of execution—the cavalry approach.

Employing either strategic or operational surprise, this force would penetrate to great depth, beyond the enemy reserves, while avoiding battle. This would dislocate the enemy force physically and shatter its commanders psychologically. Any response they could make would certainly be overtaken by events and probably be irrelevant to the German operational aim. With luck the armoured spearheads would go far and fast enough to cut the enemy's main communication arteries, perhaps even to seize an undefended centre of regional or national government and thus act directly on the enemy's political and popular will.

A much more open question is how the originators of the doctrine saw this mobile force being handled once it had broken free. In the Polish campaign the underlying thought seems to have been the seizing of topographical objectives in great depth, a river line with its crossings or a communications node, and reliance on this act to dislocate the enemy psychologically. Because the Polish Army for the most part defended forward, German infantry formations were still fairly close behind the armour and in a position to deal with these dislocated forces. In the French campaign, the pace of which perhaps astonished the German commanders even more than it surprised the opposition, one sees a tendency to prefer operational objectives which would separate elements of the Allied forces from one another and/or cut the line of their retreat. And this mixed approach was by and large reflected in Yugoslavia and Greece. In North Africa, by contrast, perhaps because of the terrain and the shape of the usable area of operations, one sees a shift towards turning (which the Americans call "enveloping") and the fuller envelopment implicit in the European understanding of that term. This tendency became more and more marked as the Russian campaign developed and a succession of massive Soviet forces were cut off, encircled and (in the Clausewitzian sense) "destroyed". Certainly when the Germans were forced onto the strategic defensive, controlled manoeuvres of a rather classical kind became the order of the day for their armour at both operational and tactical levels.

All this has led Matthew Cooper and others to suggest that envelopment was the leitmotiv of the Germans' armoured operations in depth. Even in Manstein's defensive operations in the Ukraine, which have recently become the object of intensive study in the West, physical disruption or dislocation, as opposed to envelopment, was often both the stated aim and the actual outcome. I am inclined to think that they saw envelopment as a matter of opportunity, a response to a situation, rather than a fundamental element of planning.

Let me pose a quasi-paradox which we will explore further in Part 2. The Germans were undoubtedly aware that, in manoeuvre theory as in basic physics, a lever requires a fulcrum. This is clear from the way in which their counter-offensive operations were aimed at "lifting the Soviet mobile forces off their hinges" (*die sowjetischen Stossgruppen aus den Angeln zu heben*) as a prelude to disrupting or enveloping them. But they were faced with a disparity of tempo between their armour and their main force which was bound to separate the two widely in depth as an offensive operation progressed. As long as it keeps rolling and also retains *potential* energy and *potential* momentum (firepower and mobility, that is) a mobile force itself acts as the fulcrum for a psychological lever arm which it projects along its thrust line in front of itself. The Germans have long had a unique understanding of the importance of the commander's will, and I view this psychological leverage, which we shall see taking physical shape later in Part 2, as the guiding principle of blitzkrieg.

The influence of Hitler

Both his ex-enemies and his surviving generals have a common vested interest in heaping blame on Hitler, and this is of little help to anyone trying to draw military lessons from the Second World War. Before attempting to evaluate blitzkrieg, I should therefore like to toss in a balancing, if not entirely a balanced, view. To do this properly would take a book to itself— one which I have little desire to write—so my intention is to provoke second

thoughts rather than to offer conclusions. Although he exploited nationalism, racism, the spirit of revenge and dreams of national aggrandisement,
the real propulsive force behind Hitler's rise to power was economic. He had
studied Clausewitz and understood him far better than most. But, like the
Marxism it in many ways resembled, his thinking saw political and strategic
issues as having economic roots. His impatience evidently stemmed not
only from personal ambition and the need to sustain the dynamism of his
movement, but from feelings of economic insecurity in an unloving world.
By the same token, perhaps because he doubted the Western Allies' will and
ability to open a second front and overestimated the strength of the "West
Wall", he seems to have seen the main danger to Germany as economic
exhaustion rather than military defeat.

From 1936 onwards Hitler was undoubtedly moving a great deal faster,
both in actions and in planning, than his generals would have liked. This
precipitateness, as well as the moral aspects of Nazi war plans, may well have
underlain Beck's resignation in 1938. Hitler began to press for the launching
of the French campaign while the operations in Poland were still in
progress. The data originally set was November 1939, and arguments over
postponement turned into a kind of running fight. Hitler's original plan
appears to have been to overrun France and make peace with Britain in time
to face eastwards again by summer 1940. Once the French Campaign was
under way, the pace of events took even the senior commanders by surprise,
and it was Hitler who urged them to press on however high the risk. From
the Rhineland up to Operation Barbarossa all his horses came in—even the
ones his generals saw as rank outsiders. Early triumphs on the Eastern
Front, coupled with Rommel's militarily minute but strategically important success in Africa, seem to have focused Hitler's attention on gaining
control of Suez and the economic resources of the Ukraine, then opening up
a land route to India, and so putting the entire Middle East in pincers. His
decision to divert forces southwards into the Ukraine probably played a
large part in the failure to complete the advance on Moscow and to occupy
Leningrad. And it is Moscow, not Stalingrad, that German officers in key
positions at the time see as the turning point of the war.

From 1943 onwards, Hitler insisted on holding as far forward as possible
so as to retain control over the economic resources of the Donets Basin. This
undoubtedly deprived Manstein of the depth of manoeuvre and speed of
response which might have resulted in a German operational victory
decisive enough to turn the tide eastwards again. But with hindsight it is a
nice question whether there would have been any stopping the Red Army if
it had broken clear west of the Dnieper before the 1943 spring thaw. In the
event, the compromise arrived at between Hitler and Manstein gained the
Germans some 7 months; and the critical delay was a military one—the
postponement of Operation Citadel (the Kursk counter-offensive) from
April to August.

It may even be fair to say that Hitler's interventions in the conduct of the war were reasonable attempts to conserve politico-economic aims in face of a resurgence of the "war for war's sake" tradition which had germinated in Schlieffen's time, sprouted vigorously in the younger Moltke, and achieved full growth in Ludendorff.

Finally under this head, let me throw in a point for the reader to make what he likes of in terms of the relationship between Hitler and his generals. Taking Manstein as an example of an outstanding and highly respected commander (though in his case not a particularly lovable one), I asked the senior intelligence officer of his headquarters (Army Group Don/South) what would have happened if Manstein had openly disobeyed Hitler and been removed, perhaps disgraced or executed. His answer was, in effect— "Absolutely nothing, except that we'd have had a new commander-in-chief." Seemingly the troops' loyalty was exclusively focused on Hitler. Goebbels' internal propaganda, built on Hitler's early military successes, must have been a good deal more purposeful and effective than the tirades he directed at Germany's foes. One of his greatest achievements, this officer remarked, was to create a "Hitler legend", and to isolate this image from the increasingly questionable and widely rumoured policies and practices of the Führer's entourage.

Critique

The odds stacked against the Third Reich as the War went on may have been overwhelming. The critical failure in front of Moscow may have been partly due to Hitler's decision to turn south as well. The defensive successes achieved against the Red Army in 1943 and 1944 may have been notable ones. But there is no getting away from the fact that Germany embarked on the war with blitzkrieg and the *Panzertruppe* as her decisive instrument by land; and the war ended in unconditional surrender after Germany had been completely overrun from east and west. This fact should give the proponents of manoeuvre theory, especially of manoeuvre theory in the defence, considerable food for thought. The addict of attrition can argue, with a good deal of force, that manoeuvre theory comes apart when the going gets rough. The question is whether blitzkrieg diverged from manoeuvre theory in crucial respects, or failed to take account of the complementarity of manoeuvre theory and attrition theory following main force contact. With hindsight the German doctrine appears open to criticism on both these counts.

Hitler got involved in a major war long before his war machine was militarily or economically ready for one. As a result, the Wehrmacht achieved the brilliance of a first-rate team but never the "strength in depth" of a great one. Both the Army and the Air Force started the war with too few men trained in key skills, and with too few training resources to keep up with attrition even when things were going well. Development was rushed. To quote but a few examples, the Me-110 fell between two stools in its characteristics and had dangerous vices. The Panther (Pzkw.V) tanks for which Operation Citadel was delayed had severe carburation problems; when they did not catch fire of their own accord, they were apt to be set on fire even by hits which did not penetrate the armour. And the Me-262 jet fighters were too unreliable and too dangerous to handle for their outstanding performance to be of much value.

Production of top priority materiel like combat aircraft and tanks was just about adequate though permanently crisis-ridden. But the flow of important equipment on slightly lower priority was never more than an intermittent and ill coordinated dribble. When the French campaign was launched in May 1940, only two out of the eighty *Panzergrenadier* battalions then in existence had the Sdkfz.251 armoured half-track. The rest had to make do with the larger unarmoured version or with rather indifferent wheeled softskins. Even when the availability of armoured personnel carriers peaked, at the time in fact of Operation Citadel, only twenty-six out of 226 *Panzergrenadier* units (under 12 per cent) were armoured. With unspectacular but essential equipment like trucks, the situation varied from the chaotic to the laughable. Then again on a particular day early in 1943, the Northern and Central Army Groups on the Eastern Front numbered just three fit tanks between them! Even in Manstein's Army Group Don/South, granted priority for reinforcement, armoured divisions (*sic*) were lucky to have two figures' worth of fit tanks to their name. Contingency items like winter clothing either did not exist or could not be moved; and this was a major factor, perhaps the decisive one, in the failure to take Moscow.

The distinguishing feature of the blitzkrieg offensive is avoidance of battle. And it is here, I think, that Guderian's organisational solution diverged from the cavalry operational concept applied to it. This brings up the whole question of mobility ratios which we shall be examining in Part 2. The "light divisions" were capable of swift and silent movement over unlikely terrain. But they lacked the punch even to pose a credible threat, let alone to implement it. Both the tank-heavy and the balanced types of *Panzer* divisions achieved a high enough tempo to keep one jump ahead as long as the (literal) going was good and the logistics worked. But once slowed down and weakened by Russian conditions and logistic overstretch, they began to lack both the agility to avoid battle and the punch to give it.

Even more important, the rest of the German Army was still muscle-powered, tied to the speed of the boot and the hoof. The failure to provide a sound fleet of logistic vehicles (see above) combined with the wanton destruction of Russian-gauge rolling stock to rupture the chain of resupply. As armoured offensives gained depth, and even in defensive operations, the *Panzertruppe* and "the rest" usually found themselves fighting two different battles, if not two different wars. Although, as mentioned above, the armoured forces themselves created psychological leverage in front of them, separation between them and the main force became so great as to make nonsense of any physical leverage developed between the two. At higher tactical level, the tank-heavy *Panzer* divisions (which were in the majority) tended to run out of infantry when they encountered serious opposition, difficult terrain, or both these in combination. This is to my mind the most credible of the many explanations offered for the hold in front of Dunkirk which, by allowing much of the British Army to escape, became the first turning-point of the war. Unless there was a railway in the right place, secure and operating, there was just no means of rapid reinforcement. Even in 1943, "the rest" remained entirely dependent on the railway for rapid troop movement, and the *Panzertruppe* too depended on it for resupply and reinforcement.

This chronic condition of logistic overstretch and lack of punch at the sharp end had an extremely serious consequence. Magnificently as they manoeuvred and fought, and valuable as their operational successes were, the *Panzertruppe* seldom won *decisive* operational or strategic success in battle. They were halted and forced back in front of Moscow, held outside Leningrad, thrown back at Alem Halfa, prevented from breaking into or out of the Stalingrad ring, defeated at Kursk, halted at Bastogne. The German Army's greatest success in battle as opposed to manoeuvre was probably in Italy, and this was a positional defence conducted by infantry and based on ground of immense tactical strength. With this exception, once the Soviets and the Western Allies had agonisingly hauled themselves up by their bootstraps into the first division, the Germans were soon shown up as lacking "strength in depth".

Though I have not seen it spelt out elsewhere, Soviet-inspired hindsight also suggests to me that the *Panzertruppe* ran extremely high and largely avoidable operational and tactical risks by failing to mount intelligence operations commensurate with the scope and tempo of their manoeuvre. Their aerial reconnaissance was excellent as long as the air situation allowed it to be. Their armoured reconnaissance was skilful, at once discreet and bold, though perhaps lacking in depth. And their signals intelligence (intercept), on which they relied very heavily, was outstanding. But a recent opportunity I have had to study operations in the Ukraine shows the General Staff's approach to intelligence—though far ahead of British and wartime American practice—was essentially derived from the requirements of positional warfare. There is no sign of the carefully directed gathering and updating of information on the enemy depth which the Red Army practised in war and the Soviet Army has developed into a key aspect of its operational concept. German "operational reconnaissance" was equivalent to the British concept of "medium reconnaissance", not the Soviet one. As we shall see, manoeuvre theory calls for a clear-cut concept of "operational intelligence" (as compared with tactical or strategic intelligence) and the resources to implement it. I raise this issue now because I shall explore the relationship between information and risk fully in Part 3.

The Wehrmacht was undoubtedly caught in the web of a mismatch between the scope and urgency of politico-economic aims on the one hand, and limitations in human and material resources on the other. What is more, the racist and generally oppressive policies inherent in Nazism proved to be a severe military handicap. Without these, resistance movements in the West would have been hard to sustain; the Baltic States would have provided more numerous, better and more reliable troops than they in fact did; and Georgia and the Ukraine would have been a source of high-grade recruitment rather than vicious partisan opposition. This is a key lesson for the masters of manoeuvre. But in comparing the little one knows of the development of blitzkrieg with even the embryonic form of Tukhachevskii's deep operation theory, one cannot help wondering whether Soviet success, in particular the rapidity with which they were able to improve their tactical and operational techniques, did not owe much to a theoretical foundation which was at once sound, adaptable, clearly stated and widely disseminated.

3

Deep Operation Theory

"... artillery, tanks, aviation and infantry, cooperating amongst themselves,
simultaneously inflict a defeat on the enemy's combat order throughout its whole
depth."   TUKHACHEVSKII, as quoted by LOSIK

Tukhachevskii and Triandafillov

At the same time as von Seeckt and his colleagues were beginning to
brood over blitzkrieg, Tukhachevskii was standing back mentally from the
traumas of the Red Army's formation and the tumult of the Civil War, and
starting to shape lessons for the future from his experiences. He was also
able to draw on a tradition of manoeuvre in general and the turning
movement in particular, continuing unbroken from the eighteenth-century
writings of General Ukuniev (quoted by Jomini), an earlier advocate of co-
operation between arms. This tradition was probably derived, as Duffy and
Bellamy have postulated, from Genghis Khan's way of war and, following
this path back through time, from Sun Tzu. It is not without significance
that at least four Russian translations of Sun Tzu have been made. Among
the many levels of interpretation to which the Chinese master's "ordinary
force" (*cheng*) and "extraordinary force" (*ch'i*) lend themselves is the
physical one which equates "ordinary force" (with which one engages the
enemy) to the "holding force", and "extraordinary force" (with which one
wins the battle) to the "mobile force". Again Sun Tzu's analogy of a torrent
of water ("Now the shape of an army resembles water") perfectly expresses
the dynamism of manoeuvre theory and, incidentally, the untranslatable
German concept of *Schwerpunktbildung*, of which "development of a centre
of effort" is a totally inadequate rendering.

As the epigraph of this chapter suggests, the focal points of
Tukhachevskii's thinking were the all-arms battle and the principle of
simultaneity—one which is by no means easy to grasp. He interpreted
simultaneity as bringing the largest possible number of troops into contact
at the same time, and thus as requiring a concept which offered the
"maximum contact area". In his twenties' writings he argued that this
called for a mass army operating over a *broad* front. The contact was frontal

37

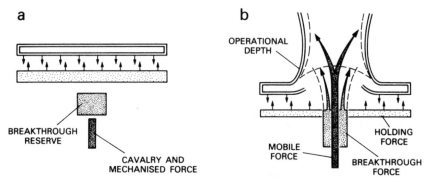

FIG. 4. *Tukhachevskii's "maximum contact area" concept. a. broad front. b. deep battle.*

(Fig. 4a). To succeed, you had to have a sufficient density of troops over the whole front not only to pin the enemy down but to achieve a favourable ratio of attrition rates, *plus* enough reserves to achieve decisive superiority at the critical time and place. All this was the task of infantry, artillery and tanks acting in concert. Then, with the enemy pinned down everywhere and broken at the chosen point, you could launch your cavalry, with air and mechanised support, through the gap. Although this concept allowed for operational manoeuvre to achieve a decision, it owed a great deal to attrition theory.

Against this background, the impact of Triandafillov's work *The Character of the Operations of Modern Armies* becomes clear, as do the respective contributions of these two brilliant Tsarist-trained officers to the evolution of the Soviet concept of land warfare. Triandafillov focuses on the importance of the "shock army", a powerful, versatile force composed of all arms including aviation (and, incidentally, having a substantial offensive chemical capability). He envisages the development of modern armies in two stages, the first of which is still infantry-centred and corresponds reasonably closely to Tukhachevskii's broad front concept.

In Triandavillov's second stage, the "shock army" remains responsible for the break-in but is completely reshaped to contain what we should now call the "mobile force" as well. "Manoeuvre tanks" (contrasted with "powerful tanks" and "tankettes"), in conjunction with special motorised forces, referred to as "mechanised cavalry", operate in depth as "strategic cavalry". In a further stage of development, these tank and mechanised forces become organic to corps, armies, and even divisions, and are complemented by motorised machine gun battalions and self-propelled artillery. Triandafillov also introduces, albeit tentatively, the other key concept peculiar to the Soviet approach, the *interchangeability* of combat troops and fire.

Figuratively speaking, this second stage concept, coupled with the notion of interchangeability, revolutionised Tukhachevskii's approach to simultaneity. More literally, it turned his thoughts neatly through 90 degrees (Fig. 4b), from the "broad front" to the "deep battle", while conserving the principle of maximum contact area. The first (incomplete) edition of Triandafillov's book was published in 1930, and Tukhachevskii's "deep battle" concept, the first stage of his "deep operation theory", and took firm shape about 1932—whence my remark in the previous chapter that Tukhachevskii's absence from the German–Soviet staff talks may have been due to his preoccupation with this fundamental rethink. The new approach launched the formation of the Red Army's mechanised corps and culminated in "PU-36", the 1936 Field Service Regulations which Tukhachevskii certainly masterminded and probably wrote.

In the following year Stalin, using as excuses the lessons of the Spanish Civil War and Tukhachevskii's alleged involvement with the *Abwehr* (the German intelligence service), but almost certainly seeing a potential rival, had the great man and five of his six most able colleagues shot. The mechanised corps were disbanded or penny-packeted, tank formations were limited to brigade level with a high proportion of independent tank battalions; the infantry regained their dominance, and deep operation theory gave way to attrition theory. This purge and reversal of policy largely accounts for the course taken by the Russo-Finnish War, and was a major factor in Hitler's decision to launch Operation Barbarossa.

The Second World War ("The Great Patriotic War")

To the retreating Russians, often completely surrounded and more often still threatened with envelopment, the early German successes must have looked like deep operation theory in action. This factor, the evident need for drastic changes, and almost certainly pressure from officers who had been up-and-coming disciples of Tukhachevskii's resulted in the Supreme Headquarters (*Stavka*) Directive of 10 January 1942. This Directive, together with two implementing orders promulgated later that year, effectively reinstated deep operation theory and set in train the reorganisation it called for. The four tank armies formed by the time of Stalingrad had a tank strength of 400 to 450 on paper. During 1943 this figure rose to about 500, a figure we shall see to be a key one in manoeuvre by armoured forces.

The two sides' operations in the Ukraine between Stalingrad and Kursk, say in the first 9 months of 1943, illustrate the whole essence of modern manoeuvre theory. In the first phase of the post-Stalingrad offensive, 5 Tank Army was used for the break-in, with independent tank corps and brigades—representing the old organisation and the first stage of the metamorphosis—in the follow-up force. This evolved fairly rapidly into a three-phase, or three-echelon, pattern. In a front (army group) offensive the independent tank brigades and battalions were assigned to infantry formations for the break-in; tank and mechanised corps were employed to complete the penetration, screen off its flanks, and perhaps seize short-range operational objectives such as rail junctions or bridges. Tank armies, sometimes stiffened with an additional tank corps or so, formed the front's mobile group, then still known as the "shock group". This group was held back until it could be launched cleanly beyond "operational depth", the depth, that is, at which a manoeuvre would force the enemy to react at operational level.

At this point development of the concept came up against two conflicting calls on the limited armoured and mechanised resources available. On the one hand, as the mobile group demonstrated its potential, there was a tendency to enhance its power and scope by giving it more tanks, by expanding it in fact into a two- or even three-echelon force. This bigger and more complex force naturally required a larger mechanised infantry (motor rifle) component too. As a result, the second (breakthrough) echelon of the main force, made up of independent tank and mechanised corps, was weakened, its role being restricted to completing and securing the penetration.

On the other hand, even the three-echelon pattern (break-in, break-through, break-out) often failed to ensure a clean launch for the mobile group. The initial response to this was simply to make the mobile group complete the penetration and fight its way clear. As a result it was slowed down, weakened, disorganised and logistically overstretched to the point where it became easy meat for a German counter-offensive, usually executed at *Panzerkorps* level. As a result, the Red Army effectively added a fourth phase to its offensive concept. The third echelon's task became not just to complete the penetration of the defence, but to secure a deployment area, a kind of bridgehead, for the mobile group to shake itself out in.

These problems were fairly quickly and very effectively solved because they were basically amenable to an increase in mass, and the Soviet war effort was by that time geared to achieving this. Shortcomings in command and control, and in artillery and air support, proved to be less tractable. When the new rules were promulgated in October 1942, only a sprinkling of officers in the tank arm, and any survivors of Tukhachevskii's mechanised force who happened to be around, had much feel or liking for them. The readiness of the gunners and the infantry to pick holes in the new concept was fostered by the rules as they stood being far from workable. The gross underestimation of the breakthrough problem discussed above was compounded by limitations in movement techniques, and by lack of the standing operating procedures (SOPs) needed for deployment from the move, for passing successive echelons though one another, and for carrying out rolling reliefs.

Just as embryonic were the kind of communications needed to control mobile operations. The communications complexes with which the Red Army ended the war, employing up to six major nets in an army headquarters, were the outcome of lessons learnt the hard way. This lack of the physical means of troop control compounded the two-pronged psychological problem that plagued the Red Army then as it does the Soviet Army today—the run-of-the-mill Russian officer's tendency to do nothing until not just told to but actively prodded; and his understandable fear of reporting an adverse situation lest he be held to blame for it. As the wastage rate among divisional and higher formation commanders shows, the only way of achieving any flexibility at all was forward command of the most extreme kind.

Death in battle at the head of one's troops was undoubtedly preferable to the price of failure—public execution, or the miseries of a penal battalion culminating in dismemberment on a minefield. But this rather snide comment does not serve to explain the contrast between the excellence of the top-flight Soviet officers and the mediocrity of the rest—something just as conspicuous and just as enigmatic today as it was then.

More serious still, and more recalcitrant than the problems of tactics, even than those of command and control, were the inability of the Soviet artillery of the day to support mobile operations, and the total absence of the kind of control and liaison arrangements needed for effective close air support. Lacking anything resembling an armoured personnel carrier, the Red Army was forced to mount its mechanised infantry in softskins of limited performance, or to have them ride on tanks. In either event, the German artillery was usually able to separate the Soviet infantry from their tanks at a very early stage in the battle. This vulnerability of the mobile force to artillery fire doubled the difficulty of advancing beyond artillery range. The mobile force lacked both the direct support it needed to maintain momentum, and the counter-battery capability which might at least have postponed the separation of tanks and infantry. I find it interesting that the Soviets were prepared to divert large numbers of tank hulls for assault guns (SU guns) but none, as far as I know, for "self-propelled" artillery mountings in the accepted sense of that term, or for armoured personnel carriers.

Be this as it may, from late 1943 onwards the artillery component of tank and mechanised corps was stiffened by the addition of a regiment's worth of assault guns. These were used almost entirely in the direct fire role for which they were best suited, leaving the counter-battery problem unsolved. As far as I know, the only truly mobile indirect fire weapon system the Red Army fielded during the war was the truck-mounted multi-barrelled rocket launcher (the "Stalin organ", now beloved of "phase three" revolutionary forces). Even had the technology and production resources been available, the conservatism of the Russian artillery arm, redoubled by the evident inadequacy of its procedures for mobile operations, might well have failed to achieve the proper support. It is significant that the Soviet Army, with an artillery arm as preeminent in history as that of the French, was by many years the last advanced army to acquire proper self-propelled artillery.

Both artillery and air support were—and still are—severely hampered by the absence of requests initiated at low levels and passed upwards. In most advanced armies, even major fire plans are built up in this way. But in Soviet eyes a request like this would be seen either as cowardice, or as an infringement of the higher commander's authority—two particularly well-trodden short cuts to the nearest penal battalion. In any event, despite the success of the joint aviation centre at Lipetsk, the Red Army never developed the kind of techniques for close air support which were pioneered by the Wehrmacht and effectively picked up and developed by the Western Allies. Despite the lavish scale of tactical air and the presence of an air army within each front (army group), close air support operations were mounted and co-ordinated at front level, with army-level flank liaison between the air army and the tank or all-arms army to be supported. The postwar Soviet Army did introduce a forward air control organisation capable of putting tentacles (as we should call them) forward to division. But only very recently has this shown any signs of functioning in the way familiar to Western soldiers and airmen; and the latest information suggests a reversal of that trend.

From the end of 1943 onwards, there were few changes in concept, organisation or tempo. As always in Soviet practice, the formations of the mobile force tended to grow in size, a 1945 tank army having a tank strength of rather over 500. By the same token, the scope of operations—in particular their depth—progressively increased; but this was due mainly to deterioration in the quality and strength of the opposition. The tank army, reinforced as appropriate, became the normal mobile group of a front, and tank army operations between late 1943 and 1945 show a remarkable consistency of tempo. Their overall duration was about 30 days, split more or less evenly between mounting and execution. The best time to launch the mobile group was considered to be D + 4 or D + 5, at an "operational depth" varying between 35 and 60 kilometres beyond the initial lines of contact. The tank army tended to gather momentum through the 10 days or so of its operation, achieving an average rate of advance of some 50 kilometres per day. The break-in and break-through battle likewise accelerated from a typical 5 kilometres on the first 2 days to perhaps 25 kilometres per day on the fifth.

Ground forces in the postwar period

In the 40 years since the end of the Second World War basic deep operation theory has shown little change from the original pattern—a holding force, also responsible for the break-in battle, and a mobile force whose conduct is based on turning the largest possible enemy mass. The principle of "slow in, fast out"—deliberate action/tight rein in the break-in, and dash/loose rein in the break-out—is unchanged. But in practice the Soviets' extremely advanced C^3I systems have almost certainly deprived the mobile force commander of his previous freedom of action and resulted in a kind of "forward command from the rear". In effect, an army commander can now directly control a company group without moving from his headquarters; and it would be very un-Russian of him to resist doing just that thing.

The tank corps became a tank division, with some 340 tanks and 230 infantry fighting vehicles (IFVs)—a strength in main tactical tracks significantly higher than that of the wartime tank army. The corps level disappeared from the main force structure, the terms "corps" and "brigade" being reserved for specialised formations; and the tank army grew to a strength of about 2400 main tactical tracks. The all-arms army, of four mechanised divisions and one tank division, shows a very similar figure for main tactical tracks, but is about half as strong again in artillery and men. By and large both tank and mechanised formations have the same major equipments and thus the same physical mobility. But the planned overall tempo of the tank force is roughly twice that of the all-arms force—and four times that of the wartime tank army.

The heavy break-in/fast break-out pattern remained virtually unchanged until about 1960. Then the first phase of the "revolution in military affairs" ushered in the heyday of the battlefield nuclear weapon, and of the employment of tanks in mass. The vast tank formations rolled forward over a nuclear and chemical carpet, with little need to fight or manoeuvre, the all-arms force being relegated to a secondary role of providing diversions and mopping up. For evident reasons, it was at this stage too that the concept of interchangeability of combat troops and fire came into its own. For the nuclear weapon did more than just neutralise its target; it achieved a large measure of destruction, and incapacitated the remnants for long enough for fast-moving tanks to close up to them.

In the Soviet Union, the end of this phase was marked by a non-nuclear scenario for the river crossing in Exercise Dnieper, the showpiece manoeuvres held to celebrate the fiftieth anniversary of the Revolution. The intervening years have seen a succession of three major changes, with a fourth, the employment of helicopters at operational level, very well on the way.

The swing away from reliance on battlefield nuclear weapons coincided with the introduction of the BMP1 infantry fighting vehicle—a world first in its class. The Soviets had long maintained that the "heavy break-in battle" was not a fundamental part of their concept but an expedient forced on them by "limitations in training and equipment". The evident potential of the BMP sparked a lively and enduring controversy, extending to proposals for the use of light armoured forces at operational level. What did emerge was the resurgence of the "slashing attack", so strongly favoured by the Reichswehr's cavalry officers (page 27), as an alternative to the heavy break-in. This slashing attack goes in through a gap or down an enemy boundary, and turns in diagonally, say along the rear boundary of a defending division or corps. This tactical turning movement, coupled with flank screening, opens a corridor for the mobile force proper. Alternatively the "slashing" force may itself push straight on to an operational objective, with an all-arms force as immediate follow-up to secure the corridor, then the mobile force as a third echelon.

The Soviet Army more than most is riddled with internecine strife; as in the British and United States Armies, the motor rifle arm saw itself as the rightful heir to the infantry's traditional dominance. The success of tank-based mobile groups in the war had led to the enshrinement of the tank and domination by the tank arm; and the nuclear heyday reinforced this trend. The turn away from nuclear weapons and the coincident appearance of the BMP gave the motor rifle arm a chance to reassert itself. In the twenties, before he turned to mechanisation, Tukhachevskii's main theme had been the evolution of the all-arms battle; and the motor riflemen picked this theme up where he had left it. This switch of emphasis, still occupying the key position in every issue of *Voennyi vestnik*, will have taken nearer 20 than 15 years to promulgate—an indication, as mentioned earlier, of the scale of the Soviet armed forces and of the diversity of their manpower.

The third development is the emergence of the operational manoeuvre group (OMG). Historical perspective is not my strong suit, but I am puzzled at the sensationalist way in which most military Sovietologists presented the OMG—in fact a Polish term, not a Russian one—as an innovation ("A new challenge to NATO!"), and have maintained that its original form represented a development of the "raid" tactic (of which more below). To anyone with a feel for the linear imperative of troop movement, the OMG is essentially evolutionary in nature. Let me drive this point home with a simple statement of fact. Suppose that a 1980-ish Soviet tank army is moving westwards on a single route at normal Soviet speeds and densities, and that its tail is just clearing Berlin. With organic vehicles only, its head would be somewhere near Aachen; with the normal slice of front troops and specialist units thrown in, its head would be somewhere on the Jabbeke motorway, between Brussels and Ostend. And this is based on approximate road distances, not measured as the crow flies.

This vast body of troops is just about five times the strength of the 1945 tank army in main tactical tracks. Conceptually at least, it was a splendid complement to the battlefield nuclear weapon, because all it had to do was to roll forward over the nuclear carpet until it reached the area of its objective, spreading out and using its tracks to surmount or bypass damage to routes. In terms of genuine manoeuvre, it is virtually unmanageable. There is a good deal of German and Soviet evidence that the "magic figure" of 500 main tactical tracks represents about the largest mechanised force that can be manoeuvred as a single entity. Thus the bringing into play of an OMG based on a tank division—of just about this size—is simply a return to postnuclear realism.

However, this form of OMG had two drawbacks. The tank divisional commander, still short of infantry even after the balancing exercises of the seventies, was expected to peel off infantry-heavy battalion groups as raid forces. The Soviet General Staff evidently understood, as many Western commentators did not, that he was unlikely to see these troops again within the time-frame of the operation. More important still, he was going to have to keep looking over his shoulder—something very unwelcome to any armoured commander and totally out of place in the context of a Soviet mobile force. In the Second World War the Soviets had regarded separation (in depth) between the head of the mobile force and the line of the holding force as something to be actively striven for—as indeed it is. But with the tempos hoped for in the eighties, separation between the tactical *tail* of the mobile force and the holding force was likely to be such as to prevent the development of leverage.

These two problems were solved by introducing into the OMG a second echelon in the shape of a mechanised division. This division can lead if the terrain calls for it to do so. But its normal role is to mount all raids, screening operations and other distractions, to support the tank division forward tactically and by control of movement, and to maintain the lever arm between the mobile force and its hinge. Hiving off a headquarters to command this group would leave a standard front short of one operational level headquarters, so a purpose-designed corps level OMG headquarters has been introduced. Once again, one senses an emergent conflict between flexibility on the one hand, and size and complexity on the other. As we shall see, this conflict in turn suggests the need for new approaches to the implementation of manoeuvre theory.

The fourth firm trend, stemming, in part at least, from the postnuclear rethink, is the introduction of the airborne assault brigade, an operational helicopter formation, into front and tank army troops. The principle underlying this will form one of the main themes of this book. But before turning to the whole business of *desanty*, I should like to mention yet another trend, now moving from the stage of reasonable prediction to that of stated intention, in the ground force proper. It is the product of the Soviet operational art and technological advance acting in concert. The mechanised division has the same physical mobility as the tank division; but it is a more massive organisation with a tank–infantry ratio of 7 to 10 (in fact almost 8 to 10) as against 10 to 6, and is usually handled more deliberately. With the growing emphasis, likewise soundly based on technology, on the all-arms battle as opposed to the tank's dominance, it would make very good sense to have just one type of division geared to the main battle tank. There are now firm indications of a plan to replace the existing tank and all-arms divisions by a single type of "shock division", and to pair this with an "airborne division". The latter would double in the airborne and light mobile force roles, and provide a mobility step between the heavy track and the rotor.

Desanty

The Russian word *desant* (plural *desanty*) has the basic meaning of "descent"; but its military connotations are so wide-ranging and so important that I shall borrow it. As a noun or an attribute, the Russians use it to describe the arrival in enemy-held or unsecured territory of any force, individual or warlike object, in any direction other than the shortest straight line drawn from his or its point of departure, and/or by any means other than his or its own steam. Thus the word was formerly used of infantry riding forward on tanks or crossing a river in assault boats. Nowadays it is used tactically, for instance, of a mechanised infantry company which swims a river in its vehicles and moves along the far bank to bounce a bridge. Operationally and strategically, it extends on the one hand to major airborne and amphibious operations, on the other to the insertion of agents or special forces detachments. This concept of desanty is fundamental to contemporary deep operation theory, indeed to modern manoeuvre theory as a whole.

One of the notions which Tukhachevskii drew from either Fuller (who specifically proposes it) or from Triandafillov (who implies the need for it) and made very much his own is the idea not just of airborne forces, but of *mechanised* airborne forces. He evidently saw from the start the basic weakness of a force whose mobility plummets from that of the transport aircraft to that of the boot—three orders of magnitude nowadays—as its men jump or touch down. This lack of tactical mobility at once telegraphs paratroops' objective and makes them unable to organise themselves before a vehicle-based enemy can respond.

It took the Soviet Army almost 35 years to bring this concept to fruition with the introduction of the BMD multipurpose airportable armoured vehicle, and even then their direct firepower was limited to the ASU 85 airborne assault gun, an outstanding vehicle when first introduced in 1962, but no match for the main battle tank. The feasibility of the "light mobile protected gun", in effect a light tank with full tank firepower, has been proven in the West; and the Soviets have the technology in the shape of the BMP vehicle family and a choice of several candidate guns. Given the BMD, now almost certainly in second generation form with most of its problems ironed out, this "light tank" is the key to a single force which combines the concept of mechanised airborne troops with that of a light mobile force, and for that matter of an amphibious seaborne assault force.

This vehicle has been long expected, and the firm indications of organisational change touched on above suggest that it is well on the way. An "airborne/light" division of the kind depicted would at once provide a mechanised airborne, airportable and economically seaportable force of high combat worth, and bridge the awkward mobility gap between rotor and heavy track on the one hand, and rotary and fixed wings on the other.

For although the United States Army rushed into the air cavalry business with cries of "vertical envelopment", it was the Soviets, with manoeuvre theory in their bones, who grasped the true significance of the helicopter, built up a massive body of rotary-wing technology, and stuck with the concept through all its teething troubles. At tactical level, the employment of heliborne troops was thrashed out in the context of river crossing. Mainly for organisational and training reasons, the most usual scale of these tactical lifts was two battalions; but it varied from a reinforced battalion to a weak regiment. The next step was logistic—the use of heavy-lift helicopters to replenish the tanks of the mobile force.

The latest published information suggests that the integration of helicopters at tactical level has now spawned an "air-ground assault group" in place of the normal raid force. This appears to consist of an air element of a dozen or so assault helicopters, and a ground element which includes a few armed helicopters for fire support and a small tactical lift (perhaps one battalion on minimum scales). My own impression is that this is yet another kite flown in the satellite specialised press to titillate Western commentators into sending a *frisson* through the NATO top brass. There seems no reason to suppose that tactical integration of helicopters has progressed as far as it has in the United States Army. Meanwhile, Soviet rotary-wing technology is falling back, especially in the fields of avionics and optronics.

Once the assault helicopter, in the shape of the Model D and later versions of Mi-24 (Hind), had been proven in service, and the tactical concept of its employment had been evaluated at regimental level, the Soviet Army was ready to move on to the operational use of helicopters. The introduction of the (rotary-wing) airborne assault brigade in 1979 or 1980 was a triple step forward. It provides a permanent formation, considered by the Soviets to be the equivalent in combat worth of a tank division, with physical mobility an order of magnitude higher than the mechanised mobile force, thus adding a new layer to the deep battle. Its dismountable element consists of specialised helitroops, the entire brigade being found by the Airborne Forces, now a separate service and still five places above the army in the pecking order for manpower selection. Third and most important, it provides operational commanders with a powerful force free of the linearity which governs the controlled movement of troops in ground vehicles and— less obviously but almost as strictly—in fixed-wing aircraft.

This ability to concentrate and disperse independently of prepared surfaces is what the rotary-wing revolution is really about, and we shall be exploring its significance in Part 2. At present, though, there is one great drawback. In *ad hoc* heliborne actions, where a medium helicopter transport battalion flies in, lifts the men of a designated mechanised regiment, deposits them, and flies away, these men's operational and tactical mobility is reduced to that of the boot once they dismount. In the airborne assault brigade, with organic helicopters, the dismountable element retains operational mobility. But there remains an awkward gap in tactical mobility once men are on out on their feet. Briefly for the moment, there are two ways of overcoming this. One, represented by the von Senger "main battle air vehicle" concept of air-mechanisation, is to treat attack and assault helicopters like tanks and infantry fighting vehicles. The other is to mechanise operational rotary-wing formations by equipping them with light armoured vehicles carried under heavy-lift helicopters for operational moves. It will be fascinating to see which way the Soviets go. They have the scale and the technology to do both, backing the airborne division with heavy-lift helicopters, and providing the rotary-wing airborne assault formations with machines suitable for intimate and sustained participation in the tactical battle.

No less interesting is the impact of the helicopter on strategic mobility. The strongest indication that the Soviets have appreciated this lies in their initial build of four or five nuclear-powered submarine catamarans, the size of the largest United States aircraft carriers. This information has been confirmed from several sources, but a news item published in July 1984 cast some doubt on it. If it is correct, the first of these catamarans will be long down the slip, perhaps even commissioned, and the second well into construction by the time this book is published. One of the more likely roles for these vast submarines could well be that of helicopter carrier. The potency of the threat posed by one or more airborne assault brigades brought to the enemy's rear or to a distant theatre in this way needs little emphasis.

To drive home the significance of *desanty*, I can perhaps use the "fifth column" analogy which was coined in the Spanish Civil War and has become a household word. For the four types of organised force we have been discussing—heavy mechanised forces, light mechanised forces, helicopter forces and airborne forces—represent "the four columns marching on Madrid". The Soviet "fifth column" stands for the whole span of activities from information-gathering by patrols of divisional deep reconnaissance companies to sabotage and state-sponsored terrorism at strategic level. Although the Soviets draw a formal distinction between strategy and the "operational art", the concept of the turning movement, the indirect approach, permeates their thinking from battalion to Politburo level. As that scholarly and lucid translator from the Chinese, General Samuel B. Griffith, points out, a remark made by Shaposhnikov when Chief of Staff of the Red Army echoes to the point of paraphrase Sun Tzu's teachings on this aspect of war:

"(The prerequisite to victory) is to make perfect preparations in the enemy's camp so that the result is decided beforehand. Thus the victorious army attacks a demoralised and defeated enemy."

Primary responsibility for military special forces (which exist alongside those of the KGB) is vested in the Airborne Forces (VDV). The main distinction between the "professionals" of Spetsnaz, long-service soldiers ranking from sergeant upwards, and others with special force training is that the "professionals" are trained for insertion by free-fall parachute. The Airborne Forces have been expanding their special force element for some time. There are indications that their aim is to train all their personnel "to special force standards", but it is not entirely clear what this might mean— possibly the same standard as short-service members of Spetsnaz proper, and the men of divisional long-range reconnaissance companies. This could mean that close on 100 000 men—or 20 000 detachments of five—would be trained in the more elementary types of semi-clandestine and clandestine operation. The mind boggles.

Today's worldwide spectrum of activities by irregular forces suggests that the strategic scope for special forces with capabilities ranging from clandestine hit squads through *coup de main* to powerful raids is limited only by the sponsor's imagination. Strategic and operational missions alike represent additional layers in deep operation theory; above all they are a means of implementing the principle of simultaneity. If successful, they would paralyse the opposition at all levels from cabinet to the higher operational commands as soon as the leading troops were committed, or more probably before this. The paralysing of government might suffice to destroy the political will to resist.

This picture is formidable enough, but superimposed on it is the politically orientated KGB network of agents and special forces, who will have been working at one remove again from the military special forces to undermine the unity of alliances and of states within them. And over and above the KGB's "organic" personnel are indigenous agents—estimated, for instance, at about 20 000 in the Federal Republic alone. By way of summary I can only reiterate what I wrote in *Red Armour*—"While massive enough, the frontal threat on which [the West] focuses its attention is only the tip of the iceberg—a good analogy since, it is said, a third to a quarter of an iceberg shows, and this is roughly the proportion of the Soviets' total offensive power that their organised land force represents."

Critique

I have not attempted to analyse deep operation theory in detail at this stage. The Soviet model is the only one in existence at the moment, and at theoretical level it is better developed and documented than any other version of manoeuvre theory in history. I shall therefore take it as the basis of Part 2, in which I shall examine the physical level of manoeuvre theory. How far it matches the theses I shall develop in the later parts of this book, I leave it to the reader to judge. For whether or not I am right in suggesting that the Wehrmacht's practical potential outmatched its theoretical back-up, the Soviets themselves leave one in no doubt of their reservations about their ability to implement deep operation theory to the full. There are two main reasons for these questionings. One is transient. The other is the Soviet armed forces' Achilles heel, which might even prove as enduring and ultimately fatal as that legendary failure of immersion.

First, if Chapter 1 is right, we are now at one of the peaks of theoretical speculation which presage radical change. The main instruments of the late twentieth-century change are evidently electronics and the rotary wing. In particular the dominance of indirect fire achieved by surveillance and fire control on the one hand, and by terminal guidance on the other is bringing the Soviet principle of interchangeability home to roost. Whether they are in armoured vehicles, on their feet, or dug in, troops deployed at high density will certainly be pulverised into incapacity and probably "destroyed" in a markedly more literal sense than Clausewitz intended. Against troops in the field, the levels of effect once associated with battlefield nuclear weapons can now be achieved by non-nuclear means. All this fits into Soviet operational teaching, but literally turns their tactical concepts—and everybody else's—inside out. As I have tried to suggest in Fig. 5, the "anvil of troops" ringed by fire has to become an "anvil of fire", better perhaps a "cauldron of fire", ringed by enough troops to seal the edges, observe indirect fire, and thicken it up with direct fire when targets present themselves.

Yet, for the Soviets more than most, the abandonment of high troop densities is a leap in the dark. They can field the technology; but their ability to train commanders or troops in this new way of war is another thing again. As a result, they are piling new layers of capability, like the operational employment of helicopters, on old. The resulting "club sandwich" is getting difficult enough to dish up; the chances of its reaching the table and getting eaten without collapsing sideways are increasingly remote. At the same time, technology is making the filling of each layer more and more complicated, too sophisticated perhaps for some of those who will have to prepare it. At some point the Soviets are going to have to cast aside much of their massed forces and "baroque" equipment, and shift the focal point of deep operation theory from the old layers to the new. Russian history suggests that they will do this later rather than sooner.

The second and more lasting weakness stems from the Russian character and is compounded by the paranoia that seems to permeate the Marxist-Leninist system from top to bottom. The amount of noise the Soviet Army makes in public about flexibility, initiative and tempo shows how well aware its higher echelons are of weaknesses in these respects. Let me quote

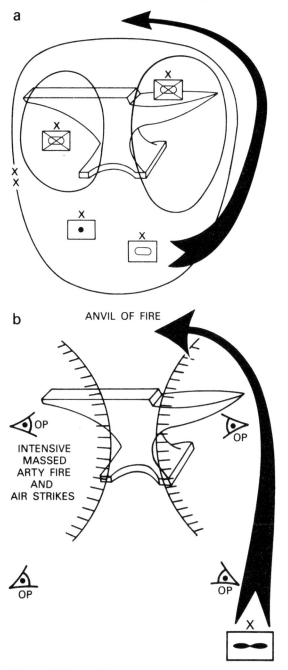

FIG. 5. *a. The anvil "of troops"—a conventional hammer and anvil defence by a mechanised division with a tank-heavy brigade. b. The anvil of fire, a killing area shaped by defending troops but not occupied by them.*

just one example—the "hasty battalion attack". Nowadays this term would make even the addicts of attrition think in terms of a period of 2–3 hours between receipt of orders and accomplishment of the mission. So my attitude has been as rigorous as that of the religious and scientific establishments towards parapsychology. When *Red Armour* went to press, I had written simply that the tempo of the "hasty" attack was an enigma. Since then I have added to my collection three more unequivocal accounts from *Voennyi vestnik*, and had all the evidence independently checked. The tempo of the hasty battalion attack is *not* 2–3 hours from receipt of orders to accomplishment of mission, but *18 to 22 hours from receipt of orders to launch* (H hour).

Again, one sees the *Voennyi vestnik* series on the all-arms battle, which has been running since January 1981 and virtually amounts to a complete tactical manual, trying to drive home the same lessons on co-operation between arms that Tukhachevskii was trying to instil in the twenties—or, *mutatis mutandis*, that General Ukuniev was banging on about 200 years ago. When I was young and strove for a sophisticated image, I used to spend hours looking for hidden charms in the jokes in the *New Yorker*, only to discover that the intended joke was the one I had first thought of. Dangerous as it is to underrate a potential enemy, the Soviet Army's achieved performance sometimes seems so indifferent as to defy credence.

The run-of-the-mill Soviet officer—and that means most officers serving with troops up to and including battalion commanders—apparently has only one response to a situation. This is to play it by the book as far as he can, and then to sit back and await new orders. Indeed, since promotion beyond battalion commander (roughly the equivalent of company commander in most Western armies bar the German) is unlikely even in war for those who do not qualify at a special-to-arm academy, and since an active mistake might point the way to the nearest penal battalion, he has little reason to do otherwise. By the same token, such men tend not to report adverse situations promptly and fully, lest they be blamed for them. Thus, even with modern communications and means of surveillance, any system which relies on requesting or awaiting new orders will seldom offer the speed and aptness of response to the actual situation which manoeuvre theory calls for. Quite apart from its effect on morale, "forward command from the rear" cannot work.

Apart (presumably) from the new breed of warrant officer, the "officer's right-hand man" introduced as a link between officers and senior NCOs (*sic*), the professional and personal quality of NCOs in field force units appears to be at best mediocre. In the Soviet Army as in those of the Federal Republic and the United States, the quality of senior NCO is an acknowledged weakness; and my impression is that the Soviet training organisation in its various forms sucks up the best, bleeding field force units more heavily than they can stand.

What is more, relations through the ranks are so appalling as to be hard for a Western professional soldier to envisage. At a symposium I attended in Canada, Peter Vigor, then head of the Sandhurst Soviet Research and Study Centre, was asked how a Soviet NCO might tell one of his men to do some simple thing. His sample order contained, I think, seven words, five of them variants on the soldierly expletive which the Russians, in a true spirit of democracy, use freely through the ranks. This is a record I have only once heard equalled. Working on a muddy side-slope, one of my Centurion crews had just got a thrown track back on and tightened, when the track-adjusting mechanism came away. Falling back into the mud with the 3-foot spanner and its contents on top of him, the driver uttered the immortal phrase— "The ****ing ****er's ****ed, **** it!" Perhaps Peter Vigor too was indulging in a touch of poetic licence. But if there is one assertion in this book that my whole experience, research and reason tell me is beyond dispute, it is that manoeuvre theory can only be exploited to the full by the practice of directive control (*Auftragstaktik*) in the full German meaning of that word.

PART 2

The Physics of War

"Principles and rules in the art of war are guides which warn when it is going to go wrong."   A. T. MAHAN

"To dogmatise upon that which you have not practised is the prerogative of ignorance; it is like thinking that you can solve, by an equation of the second degree, a problem of transcendental geometry which would have daunted Legrange or Laplace."   NAPOLEON (trans. MAHAN)

4

Ground

"When one man defends a narrow mountain defile which is like sheep's intestines or the door of a dog-house, he can withstand one thousand. This is the situation in respect to terrain."   SUN TZU

Introduction

As a proponent of manoeuvre theory in war—if war there must be—and in argument too, I care even less than the reader probably will for the way I am taking shelter behind a glacis of other people's caveats and a moat of my own. I do so to leave the reader in no doubt that I seek on the one hand to challenge his cast of mind rather than to inform him; and on the other to protect both his perspective and my own against being distorted by the apparent mass centre of this book. My treatment of the physical aspect of manoeuvre theory constitutes the longest and probably the strongest part of the book. This does not mean that it is the most important! Not only does morale enhance the real worth of a military force many times over; as we shall see, exploitation of the dynamics of manoeuvre theory calls for rare excellence in training and the exercise of command.

I very much like Mahan's remark about principles and rules being "guides which warn when it is going to go wrong". I would go further and equate them to the "constraints" which a commander employing directive control (Part 4) imposes on his subordinates. If you don't understand and respect the physics of the thing, your plan is not going to work, and it may bring other related plans down with it. *But* compliance with these ground rules offers no positive assurance that your plan will succeed, or even that it is truly relevant to your mission. Success depends on skill in the art, leadership, and above all creative thinking—all of them fields in which the rules are, to say the least, a shade skimpier and more pliable.

Ground is man's natural element, and an infinitely complex one. War on land differs in three fundamental respects from war at sea, in the air or in space. War in the fluid media is ultimately concerned with the possession or control of ground, even if all or part of this ground be seabed; the only exception to this is the economic need for access to marine life. On land man can choose his degree of dependence on machines; in the fluid media, he cannot live or move without them. The fluid media are either uniform, or have an unchanging gradation of properties, except where they adjoin land—narrow and shallow waters, for instance, or low-lying fog. Ships and aircraft are no longer susceptible to weather conditions unless in the vicinity of land. Land, by contrast, varies in a most complex manner with space, and to a lesser but significant extent with time. Only the relatively minute areas covered by man-made surfaces offer constant and predictable characteristics.

Ground is in fact so complex, and the ramifications of its interactions with man's sensory perceptions, man's body and man's machines are so manifold, that detailed analysis even of limited aspects and areas is only just beginning to come within the reach of the most powerful data processing systems and the most sophisticated electronic presentation techniques. By and large, the "eye" or "feel" for ground which pervades the animal and vegetable kingdoms alike remains a far better and more versatile tool than any foreseeable artefact. Nevertheless, I have found a very crude "steam" analysis helpful in many ways, not least in providing a framework into which the physical aspects of the military value of terrain can be fitted. This grossly simplified model takes no account of the economic or political value of ground, of the influence of plant growth and building on visibility, or of the above-surface effects of weather on man's ability to use ground. I think it more useful to keep the model simple and cover these aspects separately.

A basic terrain model

The principal parameter, which I shall call *wavelength*, represents the average distance between two similar peaks—as it might be between successive tactical bounds. We can describe a wavelength for each of a number of successive orders of magnitude. If we start with an ant's-eye view, which is about as far down the scale as I at least can envisage, a strip of a worm-cast, perhaps 1 millimetre in diameter, is a significant obstacle to be surmounted. About the lowest wavelength man, or at least the soldier, is interested in is 100 millimetres, about a hand's width with fingers and thumb closed together. As Table 1 shows, successively higher orders of magnitude have quite distinct and specific military significance.

One point needs to be made here, both as a word of warning and as an indication of why detailed terrain analysis is so appallingly difficult. When a wavelength or frequency pattern of this kind is put to him, the musician, the physicist, and many an engineer will envisage a vibration system which can be broken down into a tidy set of sine waves representing the fundamental and a series of harmonics. This does *not* hold for terrain, because each element of wavelength is attributable to a different cause. To "go to the ant" again for a moment, the orders of magnitude he is interested in will be determined by the position of an individual soil particle within the

TABLE 1   *Military significance of terrain wavelengths*

$\text{m} \times 10^n$	"Waveband" common-sense unit	Significance
10^{-1}	100 millimetres to 1 metre ⎫	ride
10^0	unit metres ⎭	
10^1	tens of metres	infantry fieldcraft
10^2	hundreds of metres ⎰	tank fieldcraft
	⎱	platoon tactics
10^3	unit kilometres	company/battalion tactics
10^4	tens of kilometres	brigade/divisional tactics
10^5	hundreds of kilometres	operational level

distribution of particle size, the composition and moisture content of the soil, and so on. At the orders of wavelength which give the vehicle designer to think about ride, such factors as stones and short-term erosion patterns dominate. As we go further up the scale, geological history and make-up become the dominant factor.

The second parameter is **roughness**, perhaps better called steepness or brokenness in the longer wavebands, but let us stick to the one term. We can think of this as the amplitude, or height, of the terrain profile with respect to each waveband (Fig. 6). We can if we need to express roughness as a

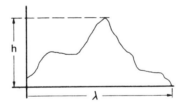

FIG. 6. *Schematic of terrain profile = wavelengths λ (Table 1), h = maximum height, h/λ—"roughness".*

percentage of the highest wavelength in the band—like the Continental expression of gradients, but with a somewhat different meaning. Evidently a given stretch of terrain may have quite different "roughnesses" at different wavebands. And once again these roughnesses, being variously caused, need have no mathematical relationship to one another. Looking back at Table 1, we see that the military worth of each waveband within a given piece of terrain depends largely on the degree of roughness in that waveband. But this evaluation turns on the military situation too. Good ground for the defender is difficult ground for the attacker; smooth ground for the tank man is dangerously open for the infantryman. The relative importance of the different wavebands may vary with the military situation, but their military significance will not—or at least will do so only at the upper and lower extremes of roughness. By contrast, the relationship between roughness and military worth is governed entirely by the military situation.

The third parameter I will call **strength**. Civil engineers will know it as "soil-bearing pressure" (or maximum shear stress), vehicle designers as the factor that limits nominal ground pressure and, under certain conditions occurring mainly in alluvial soils, battle mass or gross vehicle mass. Water obstacles and crevasses can be seen as pieces of terrain with zero strength. Unless he can jump them or swim them, man can surmount them only by using some kind of artefact. With the exception of cavalry and pack animals, and perhaps of infantrymen attempting fire and movement across peat bogs, strength only comes into play from the 10 metre waveband upwards. We shall touch on climatic extremes later, but it is worth noting here that in latitudes beyond the temperate zone, indeed well within it where large continental masses are concerned, the strength of the terrain changes radically with the seasons. Both freshwater ice and sea ice offer good routes across major obstacles; snow makes wide stretches of otherwise easy terrain passable only to specially trained men and specialised vehicles; over vast areas, the mud produced by the autumn rains and the spring thaw makes movement off prepared surfaces next to impossible.

I hope some readers at least may find this simplistic and rather dry attempt at analysis as helpful as I do. One can get a quick insight into the "orders of magnitude" approach by thinking of the different impression one gets of the same piece of country from walking it, from driving a jeep along its tracks, from driving a car along its normal roads, from traversing it on a motorway, and from flying low over it in an aircraft. I have included the model for two reasons. First, it provides some kind of theoretical, or at least generalised, basis for most of the factors the soldier has to consider when assessing terrain. It covers the broad concepts of mounted and dismounted fieldcraft, including helicopter fieldcraft (nap-of-the-earth flying); the quality of "going" and hence the speed of movement; the tactical value of ground; and the operational suitability of large areas for particular types of troops or shapes of manoeuvre.

Second, the more Soviet tactical sketches and maps with Soviet overprints I study, the more convinced I become that this is the way a Soviet officer looks at a map. This opinion stems partly from a general subjective impression, partly from struggling to look through the eyes of someone trained to think in terms of manoeuvre theory and equilibrium. I can only speak for myself, but I hope what I say may ring a bell with others. When I look at, say, one of the Ordnance Survey 1/25 000 Series maps, I conjure up not a bird's-eye view but a vertical display which changes as I change my imagined position. This is broadly equivalent to the actual view I get as I walk along a track or drive along a road. I see the country "unrolling" in front of me. This technique holds, with less detail of course, for good maps down to about 1/250 000 in scale (like the NATO series of Europe); beyond this lack of information reduces one to a bird's-eye interpretation. By contrast and for evident reasons, one looks at nautical charts with a bird's-eye view, and has to make a conscious effort to visualise a marked channel or a shore feature as it will appear—whence the immense value to me at least of those little sketches inset into Admiralty charts.

I would ask the reader to examine the way he reads a map. For if I am right, if the Soviet officer and his attrition-minded counterpart do in fact envisage map data differently, this relates to a fundamental difference in approach between them. The manoeuvre-minded envisage land the same way as a sailor envisages sea—as something to be moved across, a means of getting from A to B, or at least of getting *at* B, where B is an operational objective. What I have termed roughness and General Sir John Hackett has much more elegantly called "the movement of ground" is a hindrance. For the man brought up on attrition theory, even if he later extends his outlook to encompass manoeuvre theory too, roughness is first and foremost a tactical asset—a resource to be exploited. This difference in outlook also explains why Wehrmacht-vintage Germans accuse the Americans and British of "always thinking tactically, never above corps level", and why they can contemplate ultra-high mobility vehicles indulging in a kind of naval warfare on land which is anathema to us. I cannot help finding it ironic that we, as an ex-top maritime power with many generals coming from the same families as admirals, should be obsessed with hillocks, while the Germans and the Russians seem happy to regard undulations as waves.

Choke points

In the model just discussed, one was looking at ground along the direction of movement; the wavebands were, so to speak, longitudinal ones. One could develop a similar model, normal to the line of movement and based on *lateral* wavelengths. But this is not particularly profitable, because one is interested in only two effects. One is physical width limitation. This is of the order of unit metres and is generally concerned with man-made features—roads, bridges, agricultural tracks, forest rides and the like. As a rule, if the width limitation is above the general surface level and of limited length, a gap between buildings for instance, it is easily cleared (Fig. 7a). If it is long (like a wood, Fig. 7b), or is constituted by the surface on which vehicles run (Fig. 7c), surmounting it will certainly be a major task and may be impossible.

I make this rather obvious point to highlight the concept of **traffic-ability**, a term equally applicable to terrain and to the vehicles which cross it, and one which was fundamental to blitzkrieg with its emphasis on avoidance of battle, but has until recently featured hardly at all in the thinking of mechanised addicts of attrition. Back in the fifties Detroit Arsenal coined a term "mobiquity" (the ability to go anywhere), but this somehow came to

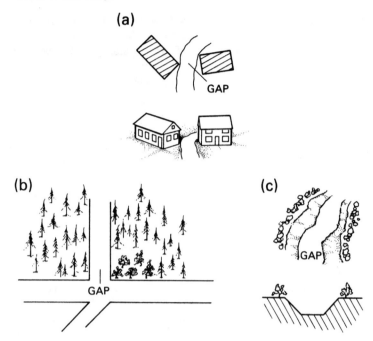

Fig. 7. *Some typical man-made choke points with widths of unit metres. a. gap between buildings. b. forest ride. c. sunken lane.*

be associated mainly with the ability to cross soft ground. This results in disproportionately wide vehicles, which have correspondingly poor traffic-ability in other respects. In developed countries, most of all perhaps in developing ones, there is a tremendous military advantage in keeping within the width of the largest commercial and agricultural vehicles. Gross vehicle mass, roughly speaking the counterpart of the "military load classification" (MLC) of routes, is also important here, both directly and because, especially in tracked vehicles, width marches with it. The curves in Fig. 8, showing total support effort and trafficability as functions of vehicle mass, are schematic but well founded. They bring out almost dramatically the penalty of going above the commercial limit, currently 38 tonnes (just over MLC 40). The commercial width limit is settling down at 2 metres (plus 10 per cent tolerance), a very difficult one to meet with tracked vehicles, or with the various types of ground effect machine that now seem to be creeping back into fashion in some quarters.

The second lateral effect is the tactile defile, lying mainly in the "hundreds of metres" waveband but sometimes extending to unit kilometres. Here again one must draw a distinction between long defiles like mountain passes, and venturi-shaped (double funnel) defiles often associated with an obstacle and thus with a physical choke point. These

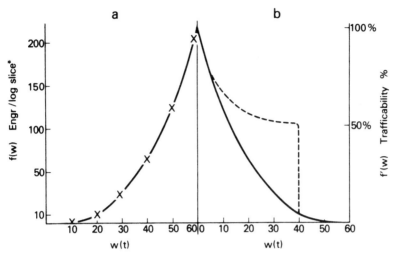

(arbitrary units × 10³)

Fig. 8. *The implications of vehicle mass a.* Engineer/logistic effort. *Formerly logistic slice was taken to vary as the square of weight and engineer effort as something over the cube. Nowadays it seems reasonable to use the cube (*shown*) as a rough estimate for both. b.* Trafficability. *Common sense and evidence from German studies suggest that the basic trafficability/weight curve is around the mirror image of the engineer/logistic effort v weight curve (*full line*). Development of the communications system for a specific purpose will distort this curve in something like the way shown (*broken line, in this case with 40 t as a risk load for MLC40 routes*).*

venturi-shaped defiles may lie within a long and rather broader defile, a constriction in an upland valley for instance, or in generally open terrain like the North German Plain. In a period which features speed and scope of manoeuvre in conjunction with the dominance of massed indirect fire, the choke point and defile are probably the most important topographical features from the military point of view.

The only real way of overcoming the hazards of the long defile is to turn it by getting off the ground—one aspect of the revolutionary effect of the helicopter. The venturi-shaped defile with one or more physical choke points has at first sight a more pronounced influence still on manoeuvre; but in most instances both the problems it poses can be resolved. Once again helitroops can play a major part, in this instance by seizing the defile before the enemy's defence is prepared and the bridges are blown. A more conventional approach is to exploit the capabilities of light amphibious vehicles. By using minor approaches to close up to the obstacle on a wide front and then swimming it at a number of places, a manoeuvre force can avoid funnelling in and retain the balance needed to reinforce success. This is a good if somewhat down-to-earth example of Napoleon's dictum that "a plan, like a tree, must have many branches if it is to bear fruit".

This may be a convenient point at which to discuss the problem of submerged crossing or snorkelling by tanks and other vehicles too dense to swim even with a screen. For a long time after the Soviet Army demonstrated this capability, one tended to think of it as having primarily tactical value. One envisaged "monsters of the not too deep" rolling up the bank to charge down the defender. The Federal German Army, lumbered with an infantry fighting vehicle that neither sinks nor swims, insists that snorkelling is a realistic tactical expedient for the defender who knows and controls the ground he is manoeuvring over. This just may be true, although I would hate to think that the security of the NATO centre depended on it. But the tactical use of snorkelling by the attacker has to be regarded as a bonus, and the Soviet Army increasingly treats it that way. They hold a modicum of tracked self-propelled bridge/ferries (the GSP, which resembles NATO's Gillois and M2, or its successor) well forward, and use these to get tanks and armoured medium artillery (the M1973, mounting a 152 mm gun on the GANEF hull) across. With all their infantry fighting vehicles and armoured personnel carriers, as well as their 12 mm armoured artillery, amphibious, they have a high potential for quick opposed crossings, even without resort to a tactical helicopter force.

After some years of trying to clear my mind on snorkelling, the view I have formed (which I believe matches current Soviet thinking) is that the value of this capability increases as one moves back from the line of contact. If one looks at it as a means of maintaining operational tempo and reducing vulnerability to air attack and long-range artillery fire, in other words of avoiding both bunching and queueing, one gets a completely different picture. To take the NATO centre as an example, the Warsaw Pact can prepare, and almost certainly has prepared, multiple submerged crossing sites astride their main routes over the Elbe, the Oder and the Vistula—perhaps as far back as the Dnieper. They can prepare such sites secretly and at leisure, maintain them by periodical inspection and repair, and make reasonably sure that they are secure against enemy action.

Obstacle crossing

Nevertheless, with the almost certain appearance in most major armies of the nineties of the amphibious light armoured force based on the "light mobile protected gun" and the infantry fighting vehicle, the preparation of submerged crossing sites is a matter of limited and passing interest. Far more important is the tactical crossing of both wet and dry gaps by both light and heavy armoured forces. I do not want to deal with the tactical aspect here; the Soviet model is a good one and has been widely described and discussed. What those concerned with evaluating obstacles in attack or defence, and with choosing crossing sectors, seldom seem to appreciate is that the gap itself, whether filled with water or with air, is generally the easiest part of the problem. There are three distinct elements to an obstacle—the approach (and exit), the banks, and the gap itself (Fig. 9). Thus one of the trickiest natural obstacles to get across quickly is the narrow, deep, steep-sided dry (or virtually dry) gap, such as the *balkas* of the Ukraine or the beds of flood rivers in alluvial plains just below mountain ranges.

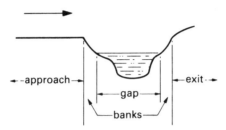

FIG. 9. *Schematic to show the three elements of a water obstacle.*

On ground of marginal strength, like much of the North German Plain, seemingly adequate approaches and exits, even established tracks and unmetalled roads, deteriorate very rapidly. One has seen a shower falling when a crossing is well under way bog it down completely. The most vulnerable stretches, because they probably have the lower shear strength and are subjected to the severest stress, are those just short of and beyond the banks. The near side gets battered by engineer vehicles and crossing traffic manoeuvring; the far side, almost by definition an up-gradient, suffers from crossing traffic struggling out. In many parts of the world, the New Territories of Hong Kong being one such where I learnt this lesson the hard way, causeways, embankments and sharp-edged banks in alluvial soil are subject to sudden collapse under the weight of a heavy vehicle of an area two or three times that of the vehicle's track plan. I have experienced this in North Germany too, for instance along the banks of the little River Innerste, virtually a dry gap for part of the year, and in the low-lying parts of Schleswig-Holstein.

With dry gaps and fords, the near bank may need dozing in, or even shelving off by a ramp vehicle of the type the Soviets use; but the exit bank evidently poses the greater problem. In deep wet gaps with a significant current, amphibious vehicles have a particular characteristic which few planners or users seem aware of until they have learnt by experience, and which is doubly important with the present swing away from hydrojets and back to water propulsion by wheels or tracks. When a swimming vehicle is entering or leaving the water across a sharp edge, there is a point at which one end is supported by the ground while the rest is afloat and subject to the current. This has the effect of swinging the vehicle parallel to the bank. It may then be capsized by the inshore track or set of wheels riding up the bank; at best it will be very difficult for the crew to get it to swim clear of the near bank or face up square to the far one. To overcome this, preparation of the banks may well have to extend far enough beyond the edge of the water to float off and ground vehicles progressively. Where this is impossible, some form of swinging cable (as for a cable ferry) may be needed.

I have gone into some detail here to underscore the point that, given amphibious vehicles, self-propelled bridge/ferries, ribbon bridges, and "tactical" earth-moving plant, the difficulty of achieving a crossing turns far more on the nature of the banks than on the characteristics of the gap between them. Thus a narrow canal with little or no current may prove to be a more severe obstacle than a wide, shallow-banked, fast-flowing river or a tidal estuary. Canals in alluvial soil with a high water-table (and here I am again thinking of the North German Plain) may present a really tough problem. There may be a towpath, even one of vehicle width, along the bank. But there are unlikely to be many metalled approach roads; canals are still very much a world of their own. Unmetalled approaches and exits, dozed and otherwise, may well collapse or turn to deep liquid mud almost as soon as they are prepared. Bridge/ferries and other amphibious vehicles may find it hard to get into the water, let alone out of it. And a vertical bank of light alluvial soil which has no metalled towpath and is lightly revetted if at all offers a less than ideal bedding even for a shortish MLC 80 bridge.

It is useful to think of the severity of obstacles in terms of the total delay they cause, including the loss for other purposes of road space taken up by crossing equipment. The opposed crossing of double obstacles, such as a river and a canal running parallel to each other with a narrow strip of ground, perhaps an embankment, between them, almost always imposes far greater delay than would two similar obstacles well separated. Double crossings also involve disproportionately high tactical risk.

As a parting thought on waterways, in whichever direction with respect to the line of operations they may run, one is wrong to look on them simply as obstacles. In the Soviet mind at least, they may be another way of achieving *desanty* (page 46). For instance, with the addition of an amphibious light mobile protected gun to the existing Soviet family of armoured vehicles, it would be entirely feasible to insert a small balanced force—say the battalion group which typifies their raid forces—by motoring it along a waterway, or even by floating it silently down a reasonably fast-flowing river. I suspect most soldiers envisage this as much too slow. But a force moving at part throttle, say 3 knots, down a river with a 3-knot current would cover over 250 kilometres in 24 hours.

Cover and intervisibility

Technology is changing the military value of many terrain elements, not least that of cover. On the one hand, just as near infrared devices and image intensifiers largely put paid to the cover of darkness, airborne and surface-to-surface thermal imaging systems, using the far infrared band, are changing traditional ideas about cover from view and camouflage. While some still question the tactical value of these systems because of limited discrimination in steady ambient temperatures and of poor image quality, the next generation of surveillance, vision and sighting systems, in which the signals from various types of sensor will be combined and optimised by an image processor, will eliminate most of these problems. Moving and stationary military objects will then be as easy to "see" round the clock in what we are used to thinking of as "cover from view" as they now are in broad daylight in the open. In fact only dense forests of tall trees and built-up areas with tall buildings and narrow streets—environments in which it is difficult to move and impossible to carry out organised offensive action—will offer any certainty of concealment. Undoubtedly both passive countermeasures (clothing and paints) and active ones such as swamping heat sources will be developed. But it is hard to see these clawing back the lead which thermal sensors have established.

Men on their feet in the open, or even in open trenches, have long been vulnerable to indirect fire. Armoured vehicles were until very recently immune to indirect fire from all but the heaviest artillery, so that "cover from fire"—direct fire, that is—provided them with the same kind of protection as the infantryman of old enjoyed behind his fortifications or his parapet, or even just an earth bank. Now compact and relatively cheap terminal guidance systems, using a variety of target signatures, have made it possible to engage pinpoint hard targets effectively with indirect fire. And after standing still for decades, the technology of chemical-energy explosives has suddenly started to roll again. A number of "smart" armour-defeating bombs for heavy mortars are already in service, and a similar projectile for the medium (81 millimetre) mortar will probably have completed the final "engineering" stage of development by the time this book appears. So it is time for a rethink not just above "cover from view" but about "cover from fire" as well.

To complete the picture—an apt expression here—advances in fire control systems for direct fire weapons, complemented in some instances by full-trajectory guidance, have pushed the effective range of direct fire engagement of pinpoint targets out to and beyond the limits of inter-visibility imposed by terrain. And the mounting of cruise-profile guided weapons on helicopters which can pop up from behind cover has in effect extended these limits. Both for this reason and because intervisibility ranges are a subject prone to misunderstandings—and thence regrettably to distortions by technologists with an axe to grind—a word about them may be helpful. A glance at the last three cases depicted in Fig. 10 shows that, unless rigorously defined, "intervisibility" can mean whatever the person using the word wants it to. Thus the figures for direct fire engagement

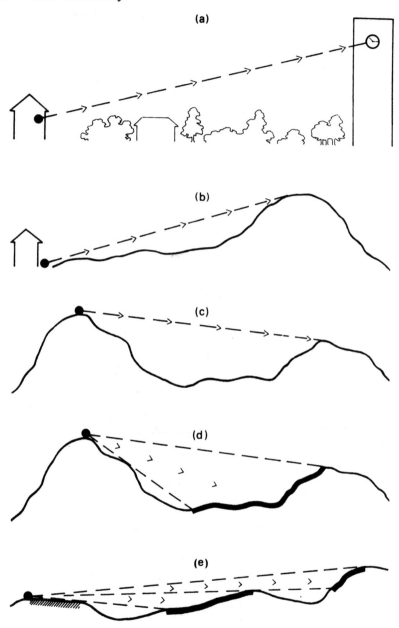

FIG. 10. *Types of intervisibility. a. Point-to-point. b. Point-to-crest. c. Crest-to crest. d. Crest-to-area. e. Area-to-area.*

ranges which various countries have produced at various times are largely meaningless unless supported by a tactical scenario and an indication of the type of weapon system.

The curves at Fig. 11 are therefore generalised ones, aimed at showing the pattern rather than indicating the figures. The first point is that openness or closeness of terrain makes far less difference than one would expect. I think this is a dual effect readily explained in terms of our basic model. Our ideas of "openness" and "closeness" relate mainly to the 100-metre and higher wavebands. On the one hand desert, and probably many other types of *naturally* flat terrain, have enough roughness in the 10 to 100 metres band to provide cover for objects 2 to 3 metres high. On the other, the rougher parts of broken terrain, which would offer the best concealment, tend to be the least suitable for manoeuvre by tracked vehicles.

The curves of Fig. 11 could be converted as they stand to cost-effectiveness or "diminishing returns" curves by simply writing "cost" along the bottom and "percentage of targets" up the side. But the second

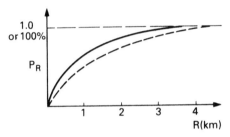

FIG. 11. *Generalised curves to show ranges of acquisition/engagement for rolling European terrain (eg Flanders, full line) and featured desert (eg Libya, broken line). P_R is the probability that an event will occur at or below range R. Lack of definition of conditions has always made figures on this the subject of violent controversy. For some reason, both battle analysis and trials consistently come out with lower figures than subjective experience would suggest.*

area of controversy demonstrates the difference between basic cost-effectiveness analysis and cost-benefit analysis; it likewise highlights the danger of applying the law of diminishing returns without being sure exactly what the parameters signify. A cut-off at, say, the 80 per cent point does, it is true, affect only 20 per cent of possible targets. But the hidden assumption is that similar targets have the same *tactical* value wherever they are in the direct fire zone. This is patently untrue. One knows from experience that targets at the two extremities of the zone are far more important than those in the middle of it. For the defender, engagement of targets at the far end of the zone will make the enemy react prematurely; with luck they may make him over-react and misjudge the layout. For the attacker, the ability of supporting weapon systems to take out targets from overwatching positions may save, or at least postpone, the 50 per cent drop in tempo that would result from his leading sub-units having to deploy and resort to fire and movement. And very short-range targets are evidently critical for both because they offer an immediate, extreme, and perhaps critical threat.

Both these factors tend to shorten the pattern of range distribution, a tendency often reinforced by the soldier's demand for simplicity and the politician's for cheapness. There is however another factor which acts in the opposite sense. In all the studies of this kind I have participated in and most of those I have examined, it is not always clear whether one is talking about sightings or engagements or, if the latter, whether the target was in fact exposed long enough for the attacking weapon system to engage it. The exposure time of a given vehicle following a given path over a given piece of ground will vary with the relative heights of observer and observed, and with the distance between them (Fig. 12). The ability to see into "dead" ground depends on the angle of sight; and for a given height difference the angle of sight depends on range. This bears out the commonsense expectation that exposure times will tend to be shorter at the longer ranges.

In sum, "Naught shelters thee." Today's military machine is as all-seeing as the Hound of Heaven—though significantly less benevolent in intent.

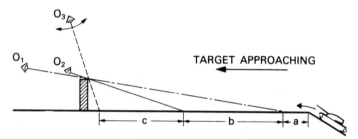

Fig. 12. *Schematic to indicate how movement exposure time varies with relative height of observer and observed, and/or with the distance between them. O_1 will catch only a brief glimpse (the time the target takes to traverse distance a); O_2 will get a longer look over $(a+b)$, and O_3 will have the target in view over $(a+b+c)$.*

Urban terrain

I prefer to use the American term because it brings out that built-up areas, just as much as wild or rural ones, represent a terrain type with military characteristics of its own. In Europe, and to a lesser extent in the rest of the first and second worlds, urban terrain covers a large and increasing proportion of the land surface. Admittedly urban terrain is only one type of man-made or man-dominated terrain. But most other types have their parallels in nature. Even the most featureless of agricultural land reclaimed from the sea is not too different from the Russian steppes or the flat lands of other continental masses. Urban terrain is, I suppose, very broadly comparable with forest, woodlands and scrubland. But it differs fundamentally in that most of the traversable surface is prepared to a uniform standard of minimal roughness and of great strength.

I used the analogies of forest, woodland and scrubland advisedly, for I believe there are three broad categories of urban terrain which have significantly different characteristics from the soldier's point of view. The first of these is represented by almost all old towns and sizeable villages, and by most modern city centres, business quarters, industrial zones and housing estates. Here the roughness in the 1 to 10 metre waveband may even approach 1000 per cent (a 100 metre tower block on a 10 metre square base, that would be); it remains very significant even in the 100 metre to 1 kilometre band. The result is that ground-level intervisibility is generally limited to the width of streets and squares, the length of straight stretches of street, and the run of the occasional larger open space. Even looking down from a dominating rooftop allows one to see very little of what is going on at ground level. Those in the streets are completely exposed to the most elementary forms of attack, such as dropping grenades, from those in or on buildings. And even if the victims can see the attacker, they often cannot get at him or fire back effectively without clearing through the building.

We thus arrive at the conventional tactics of street fighting. This is fine for a country village of one street and a few small houses; but in even the smaller towns it soaks up troops like a sponge—a battalion to a block or even to a building—and is grossly extravagant in time and casualties. All this is anathema to the master of manoeuvre; as Sun Tzu puts it—"The worst policy is to attack cities." The only reason likely to lead an attacker into a "man-made forest" of this kind is the dislocation of a centre of government or, I suppose, the capture of some major resource like a broadcasting facility or a national computer centre. For the defender, especially one fighting on his home ground, military and humanitarian considerations will combine to keep him out of these areas, unless he is able, with a minimal use of his manoeuvre forces, to block a major thrust line by channelling the attacker into a city and forcing him to clear through it. This is one of the situations where home defence forces, regular and otherwise, come into their own.

The second category of built-up area, which I have compared with woodland, is that of some modern towns and small cities planned on a low population density (by urban standards) and mainly residential in character. It also covers "garden suburbs" and other modern residential suburbs. Layout is characterised by multi-lane double carriageways on the approaches, round the edge and, as boulevards, through the centre. Buildings are relatively low, limiting the roughness to, say, 100 per cent in the 1 to 10 metre waveband—an order of magnitude lower than the "downtown" category; and they are well spaced, so that there are tactically useful arcs of ground-level intervisibility, even if distances are limited to 100 or 200 metres.

Apart from a few major complexes, such as civic and shopping centres and light industrial zones, this terrain is suitable for minor tactical manoeuvre by mechanised and airmechanised forces. It is roughly comparable in openness to *bocage* country, but much easier to move through because it is traversed by wide roads whose verges may well offer cover from view for a section or a single vehicle. These areas, then, are broadly comparable in military terms to types of natural terrain generally regarded as usable. Whether the attacker goes through them or round them will depend on the lie of the trunk roads he wants as axes, and on the character of the surrounding countryside. The defender will presumably try to keep clear of them on humanitarian grounds. But he may well be forced to block in them or concentrate artillery fire on them to create for himself an "anvil" or pivot of manoeuvre.

The third category of urban terrain, fairly so-called I think because it forms part of a conurbation and is man-dominated if not entirely man-made, is the kind of commuter area that is growing up, for instance in the north of the Federal Republic, in Scandinavia and in parts of the United States. Houses tend to be low and rambling, at a density perhaps of rather under ten to a hectare (four to an acre), with gardens, orchards and hedges. Feeder roads are metalled, but narrow and perhaps bedded for light traffic only. These areas may develop in any moderate type of natural terrain, but in close or broken country the natural features tend to dominate over the man-made ones. On open, flat or gently undulating terrain, such as the area north and northwest of Hanover, the effect of this development is to make the country markedly closer without radically changing its military character. The pattern is, so to speak, one degree closer than agricultural areas where smallholdings predominate.

I mention this category because planning forecasts, descriptions made for civil purposes, and even maps can be misleading. For example, in the sixties the German planners were predicting a conurbation centred on Hanover and extending to Brunswick, Celle, Bad Nenndorf and Hildesheim. This is a rough circle with an average radius of 50 kilometres or so, and an area of almost 8000 square kilometres, lying astride one of the main Warsaw Pact thrust lines. The implication was that the whole area would become unfavourable for an armoured offensive, and that this would change the character of the defensive battle. On a rough analysis by eye on a medium scale map, this area breaks down by the three "urban" categories into something like 20 per cent "downtown", 30 per cent "suburban", and 50 per cent "commuter". So it is by no means the kind of obstacle the planning forecast at first sight implied. The "suburban" and "commuter" categories of urban terrain might in fact, like the Ardennes, offer a sound axis for a surprise thrust.

Extreme terrains and climates

"That you may march a thousand *li* without wearying yourself is because you travel where there is no enemy", Sun Tzu tells us. And Liddell Hart stresses that "natural hazards are less dangerous than fighting hazards". The value of being able to use extreme terrain is solidly borne out by history from Ancient China through classical times to the Second World War, and now in Afghanistan. Naval history has likewise demonstrated the strategic advantages to be had from seaworthiness and seamanship. Given modern aids, the same goes for the ability to survive and operate in extreme climates. We tend to think of land mobility entirely in terms of the wheel and the track, and thus to focus our minds on prepared surfaces and on types of natural terrain where vehicles can operate. The "firepower—mobility—protection" triangle has far wider application than the design of tanks. If we extend our understanding of "mobility" to cover versatility as well as speed, and of "protection" to cover elusiveness as well as armour (as Field Marshal the Lord Carver does with his definitions of "indirect" and "direct" protection), we can set about comparing the combat worth of a well-equipped platoon of Gurkhas with that of a troop of main battle tanks. Similarly a troop of well heated, soft-skinned oversnow vehicles which can move on loose snow and negotiate glaciers may be worth a regiment of non-arcticised armoured vehicles confined to packed snow.

The ability and will to go where the enemy cannot, still more where he thinks you cannot, is an immeasurable asset. But one of the advantages of "natural hazards" over "fighting hazards" is predictability. This divides extreme terrains and climates, or rather combinations of extreme terrain and climate, into two classes. More narrowly, it highlights the point I made earlier about "mobiquity" (in the Detroit Arsenal sense) and trafficability. If you are going to stake success on this type of indirect approach, you have to be virtually certain that it is in fact within your capability.

This is perhaps most easily seen in the context of vehicles. Experienced tank commanders will take their tanks through narrow gaps because they can find out whether or not the gap is wide enough before much harm is done; because many gaps can very easily be widened; and because if one vehicle gets through, the rest will. They will *not* willingly use side slopes or (as was borne out yet again in the Falklands War) soft going, because the only way to prove the route is to put a vehicle over it; and even if the first vehicle gets through, there is no guarantee that the rest will. The combination of jungle, mountain and monsoon, and Arctic or Antarctic ice in spring and autumn, are other instances of low predictability.

Another factor which unduly limits thinking about the use of extreme terrain is the insidious doctrine that "like fights like"—one to which I shall return in Part 5 but which I should like to harass a little here. This is a view that one might expect to be held by the addicts of attrition with their liking for "fair play" and "a jolly good scrap". Surprisingly, though, this view is pressed even more strongly by the masters of manoeuvre, notably some Wehrmacht vintage Germans; and by defence analysts with a strong humanitarian streak who feel that it is wrong, for instance, to pit men on their feet against machines. If you pit two similar but unequal organisms or machines against each other—a heavy tank against a light tank, a bantamweight boxer against a heavyweight, a female tennis champion against a male one—the probability is that the stronger will win. This is especially so if they are constrained to similar behaviour by their nature or by "the rules of the game". If two essentially dissimilar opponents are matched and their behaviour limited only by their respective physical characteristics—a tank-hunting team against a tank, a helicopter against a submarine, or a guerrilla force against an organised one—you have a completely different kind of contest, one which the seemingly weaker contender is apt to win.

Operational and tactical value of ground

Each major step forward in technology evidently changes the military value of terrain characteristics and particular topographical features. We have noted, for instance, how the severity of a water obstacle increasingly depends on the approaches and banks rather than the stretch of water itself. The evolution of firepower has progressively eroded the strength of high ground and steep slopes. Once indirect fire becomes the dominant element in the engagement of armoured vehicles that it already is against men, the sole remaining physical advantage of high ground will be the fields of view it offers—though I suspect it may long retain its psychological importance! In conflicts where at least one side is mechanised, defiles and inverted defiles (narrow steep-sided ridges, that is) have taken over from hills as key tactical features. If we take the defile, inverted or otherwise, and turn it through 90 degrees, we find not only obstacles based on a wet or dry gap, but bands of what the Americans so aptly call "hindering terrain".

This may be soft going traversable only along strips of firm ground or even causeways. Hitherto marshes and the like have offered about equal difficulties to attacker and defender, because of the difficulty of finding cover from view, let alone from fire, and of emplacing and extricating heavy weapons. But modern surveillance capabilities, linked to the ability to call down long-range indirect fire with instant accuracy, now gives the defender an edge. Of much greater advantage to the defence is close country, urban and natural alike. Where movement and tactical manoeuvre of vehicles are concerned, one can regard close country as a complex of extremely narrow defiles, narrow enough for an immobilised vehicle to block a route. If these bands can be made dangerous enough to the attacker to force him to clear through them with infantry, they have considerable defensive strength

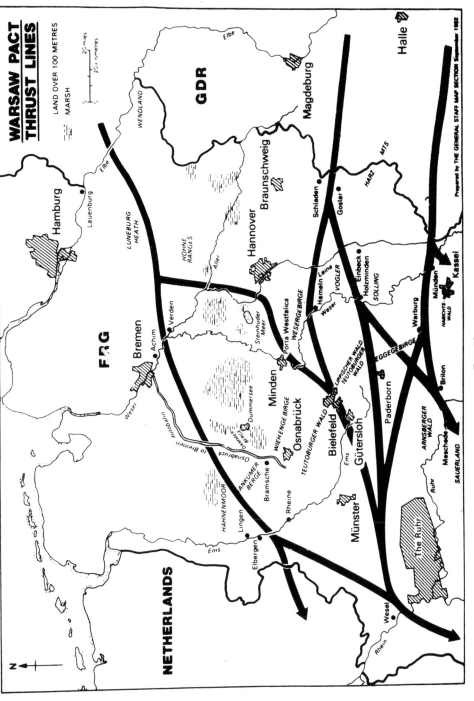

FIG. 13.

against an opponent employing manoeuvre theory. Whatever the basic type of country, few sweeping operational maneouvres can be made without encountering a band of hindering terrain of some kind or other. There is at least one across every likely thrust line of a Warsaw Pact offensive against the NATO centre (Fig. 13); and accounts of operations in the Ukraine in 1942/3 also provide striking examples of its influence on both sides.

The reader may wonder why I have discussed types of terrain in some depth and skated over an assessment of their military value. I have done this because one of the major effects of the helicopter (Chapter 7) is to revolutionise the tactical evaluation of ground. It does this because it *allows you to use ground tactically without depending on it for mobility.* This new capability will in fact reconcile one of the conflicts between the two fundamental theories of war. The master of manoeuvre will be able to join the addict of attrition in looking at accidents of terrain as aids to fighting, if he has to fight, rather than as obstacles to movement.

Politico-economic value of territory

We saw in Chapter 2 how Hitler's decision to divert a substantial force southwards to the Ukraine contributed to the failure, seen by many Germans as critical, of the advance on Moscow. Churchill's disastrous and futile diversion of Wavell's troops from North Africa to Greece was in like vein. The Falklands adventure might well have added yet another verse to the long chapter of accidents of this kind. And the NATO centre provides an extreme and enduring example of the conflict between political, economic and cultural interests on the one hand, and military planning on the other. The Federal Republic is the second or third most powerful and certainly the second most enthusiastic member of NATO. She is also its main frontier state. Without the strength of her Army and the depth provided by her territory there would be no way of holding the NATO centre. Yet it is her Government's entirely understandable insistence on a forward positional defence that puts paid to any realistic chance of success for a non-nuclear defence of the NATO centre by the forces available. As a result, there is an extreme risk of a conflict in Europe going nuclear and/or chemical and bringing about the annihilation of the West German population—a result amounting to the ultimate negation of German policy.

This glaring contradiction bears out very well the balance which Clausewitz actually struck (as opposed to the many different interpretations of his views on this matter). "War", he wrote, "has its own grammar, but not its own logic." While the military aim must remain subordinate to the political aim, governments, having gone to war, must respect the nature of war as a complex phenomenon, and not impose on their generals constraints which conflict with this nature.

As well as extending extreme economic value to large areas of sea, technological advance has had a threefold effect. It has augmented (in fact to the point of absurdity) the capability of direct attack on political and economic centres. It has greatly magnified the short-term vulnerability of advanced societies—socio-economic complexes, if you like—to even the very limited physical interference represented by strikes in key sectors, let alone the effects of warlike action. And by creating levels and densities of population too high to subsist on an agricultural economy, it has made the long-term survival of peoples dependent on the functioning of this very sensitive industrial and commercial complex.

In the eighteenth century, when Europe at least had abandoned the barbarities of the Middle Ages and wars were "kings' wars" fought with small armies, the gap between the minimum of armed force compatible with a major political aim and the maximum damage warring societies could tolerate was a wide one. From the Napoleonic Wars onwards this gap has progressively narrowed. If it still exists at all, it is the eye of a needle through which the camel of mass organised forces can scarcely pass. This is the idea that underlies Soviet thinking on the "unusability" of organised forces, which we shall examine in Chapter 18. One might also see it as the seed of wisdom in the tumultuous Greenery of the European peace movement. If war is indeed to be subject to a rational political aim, the steadily mounting politico-economic value of the territory of advanced societies will impose increasingly rigorous constraints on the scope and way of war.

5

Mass

"Multitudes serve only to perplex and embarrass." SAXE

"Generally, management of many is the same as management of a few. It is a matter of organization." SUN TZU

Introduction—the Lanchester equations

Until very recently it would have been fair to say that no physical force of direct military significance was thinkable without mass. Now directed energy weapons have placed mass (the mass of the projector) at one remove from the effect on the target. But the statement will still serve our purposes here. Surprising, then, that little thought seems to have been given to what actually represents mass in the physics of war.

One would have thought that mass would be easy enough to envisage in terms of the large discrete units which operate in fluid media. But going back for a moment to the days of sail, one finds that ships were counted and classified, but that no single parameter was used to quantify fighting power. Since smaller ships, such as frigates, were seldom able to engage ships of the line without closing them and getting blown out of the water, only ships of the line were taken into account, and these were graded by the number of guns firing broadside—H.M.S. *Cornwallis* (74) for instance. Evidently in a broadside duel the ship with the greater number of guns is statistically the more likely to win. Just as, evidently, the admirals of the day—or at least the relatively few competent ones—had some mental formula for combining numbers of ships and numbers of guns to determine relative strengths. And this brings us to what, I suspect, is the first problem in defining military mass—that one can only do so meaningfully in relative terms. This is because the expression "relative strengths" implies that the two sides face each other in a common situation, and this fixes or shuts out a proportion of the host of hidden variables to which military mass is subject.

Lanchester, working at the Royal Aircraft Establishment, Farnborough, early this century, was the first person I know of to propose a mathematical relationship between numbers and quality (the latter represented in the naval example above by the number of guns). And Lanchester is worth listening to, for he correctly recommended the adoption of eight medium machine guns (as opposed to fewer heavier weapons) for the Hurricane and the Spitfire, and thus might almost be said to have determined the course of the Second World War. The Lanchester equations at once illustrate the scope of the problem and define its limits. For duels and indirect fire he proposed his Linear Law, by which you need twice as many or twice as good for a two to one chance of success. For situations where all units on one side can take on all units on the other, as in the direct fire battle, he proposed his Square Law, which states that you need twice as many *or four times as good* for a two to one chance of success. So in attempting to relate mass to fighting power one starts with an error zone of a power—here a factor of two.

Usable mass

Before pursuing the meaning of quality, let us suppose for a moment, however simplistically, that numbers of ships, aircraft, tanks, or men under arms can be taken to represent combat worth. The next question then becomes what proportion of their available forces the two sides can apply to a given situation.

Most people readily envisage that long sea and/or air lines, of the kinds that affect most possible cases of intervention by the first and second worlds in the third, impose a limitation on the force employed. The overall tempo and touch-and-go character of the Falklands War perfectly demonstrate this point. The United States' hesitancy (at the time of writing) in supporting the moderate Arab Gulf States provides another example. Admittedly there are at least two good geopolitical reasons for this. But in any event the logistic problem of mounting and sustaining any substantial sea or air operation beyond the Straits of Hormuz, let alone action on land, is immense. Strategically the Gulf is the lobster pot it looks like on the map.

By contrast, few appreciate that similar restrictions apply to land lines in developed territory. We saw in Chapter 3 (page 44) that a Soviet tank army with normal attachments, moving on a single route, would occupy the motorway from Berlin almost to the Channel coast. To drive this point home, it is worth glancing at the other side of the coin. The deployment of NATO forces would mainly take place in West German territory—over a road system, that is, which is probably the world's most modern and which was largely developed within the framework of NATO requirements. Yet only one east–west route of Military Load Classification (MLC) 50 or higher—capable, that is of taking tanks and some other key vehicles—is available to each assigned division. (Figure 8, page 63, also relates.) A division strung out on a single route is virtually deprived of operational mobility. By the same token, even in an offensive launched after mobilisation, limitations of road space dictate that the Warsaw Pact would lead with only fifteen to twenty divisions (*plus* perhaps four or five airborne divisions inserted in great depth). Thus if NATO were fully deployed, the initial clash would take place between forces of similar size—about the same size, incidentally, as the force the Soviets might hope to get away with assembling for an attack with strategic surprise.

Thus both sides on the NATO centre have about the same immediately usable mass, and this roughly corresponds to the size of force that saturates the surface communications system. At this point the difference between attrition theory and manoeuvre theory leaps into the foreground. Under attrition theory, the difference in attrition rates between two forces of roughly equal quality would not be all that great, so that the Warsaw Pact, with its vast follow-up forces already poised in locations from Poland's western frontier to the Dnieper and beyond, could be expected to win. Under manoeuvre theory, where a smallish force may disrupt or dislocate an extremely large one, the issue would be much more open. The problem, to which we shall return in part 5, is that NATO is not currently geared to the employment of manoeuvre theory, nor are its forces quite large enough to do so over its central front.

Physical fighting power

I have reserved the term "combat worth" for the total military value of a force, and I shall develop this concept in Chapter 8. Here I am concerned with mass, and thus with the much narrower, essentially tactical concept of **fighting** (here *contrasted* with moving). Whatever form it may take, fighting is essentially an exchange of energy. Firepower is the ability to transfer energy to the enemy, survivability the ability to avoid or absorb this energy. Movement within narrow confines is not completely excluded. It provides a means of bringing firepower to bear; and it contributes to survivability. But except in the rare cases of aircraft, ships or tanks ramming one another, movement plays no *direct* part in the energy exchange. To approach a concept of quality one needs first a concept of physical fighting power (physical because it excludes generalship and morale), and then a concept which relates this to mass. Suppose, then, one postulates a quantity **"physical fighting power per unit mass"**, and then sets out to define or model its parameters.

I first met the marketing triangle (Fig. 14) in a commercial context. But for the idea underlying the extension of it on which I am about to embark I am indebted to Professor Ronnie Shephard, whom I have known for many years and regard as outstanding among British operational researchers. One of the great strengths of the marketing triangle is that it allows one to study three complex parameters in linear terms, even to quantify them relative to one another, by means of a simple plane figure. One can therefore extend the model in four steps—area, depth, volume and solid shape—without

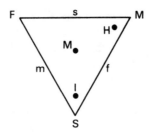

FIG. 14. *Marketing triangle of firepower (F,f), mobility (M,m) and survivability (S,s). H = helicopter force, I = infantry dug-in, M = balanced (heavy) mechanised force.*

overstepping the bounds of Euclidean geometry and thus of my own and many others' understanding.

If the three sides of the triangle stand for three interacting parameters which together describe physical fighting power, then it is entirely logical to consider its area as representing physical fighting power. And to make this concept a useful measure of quality, we need, as we just saw, to relate it to mass as "physical fighting power per unit mass". Having done this we can introduce mass as the third dimension (depth), the "z axis" of Cartesian coordinates, if you like (Fig. 15a).

This is in fact the key step in trying to reach an understanding of military mass, but it is worthwhile following the argument through. If one now integrates along the z axis for a given mass, one obtains a solid, a bar of

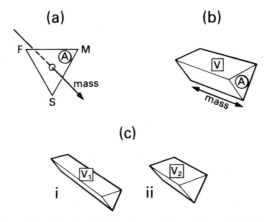

FIG. 15. *Extensions of marketing triangle model—a. Area A of triangle FMS (Fig. 14) represents physical fighting power; this can be integrated along an axis representing mass. b. Volume V of solid generated from A represents total fighting power of available (or usable) mass; for reasons explained in the text, this is not a useful concept in absolute terms. c. For constant volume ($V_1 = V_2$), shape represents quality. A long thin bar is a backward conscript army, a short squat one an advanced professional army.*

triangular section (Fig. 15b), which I most easily envisage as the carton of a Toblerone chocolate bar. This solid offers one or two useful notions.

Its volume corresponds to the total fighting power of the available or the usable mass. This is in fact of little value because, for reasons which I shall explore in a moment, one cannot quantify physical fighting power in absolute terms. The cross-sectional area represents quality and is thus related to quality of human resources and degree of technological advance; the length represents mass. So the **shape** describes the quality of a force (Fig. 15c). A long thin bar corresponds to a conscript force formed by a backward nation; a squat block of equal volume depicts a small professional force found by an advanced one.

Unfortunately all one can do with the last three steps of the above exercise is to tuck them into the back of one's mind for future reference as a guide to thought. Much as I should like to extend this three-dimensional model to overall combat worth, I cannot do so for two reasons. First, as already stressed, I can see no useful way of quantifying physical fighting power in absolute terms. Second, while it is nice to be Napoleonic and talk of the moral being to the physical as three to one, I would have some hesitation in applying this factor to a purportedly mathematical model—and I would be even more loath to suggest any other figure.

Practical units of military mass

As I pointed out at the start of this chapter, there has always been a certain amount of subjectivity in defining and quantifying the mass of naval and air forces. And the Lanchester equations tell us that, in the absence of a single unit of mass that takes account of quality too, this subjectivity is largely justified. But for the soldier the answer has always been a simple one. The unit of mass is the man. And however much man may vary from individual to individual and society to society in intellectual, moral and cultural attributes, he remains pretty constant in terms of physical strength.

Both distinguished Germans of Wehrmacht vintage and, as far as I can estimate, the Soviets stay firmly with this concept despite the influence of technology on the land battle. But I do not really think it will do as it stands, for it contains a battery of hidden assumptions, some of them patently false. What is more, a touch of *reductio ad absurdum* shows it to be contrary to common sense. This said, it is admirably simple and serves reasonably well in comparing two land forces of roughly equal sophistication in a setting where the same fairly light restrictions on usable mass apply to both sides. Thus it works for the NATO centre in terms of the simultaneously usable masses discussed above.

Taking the man as a unit of mass in the modern land battle assumes that every type of combat and combat support soldier—every soldier, that is, who contributes directly to physical fighting power—has the same chance of survival. More fully stated, the combination of the physical threat with which he is directly faced and the direct and indirect protection with which he is provided gives every soldier, from the paratrooper to the infantryman to the tank man to the heavy rocketeer, the same expectation of life in contact with the enemy.

The signpost to a better understanding of mass is the Soviet principle of interchangeability (of shell and bayonet), and the path a careful study of the Soviet norms for artillery ammunition, in particular of the equivalences. These I know to have been developed from battle experience, sophisticated modelling, and extensive trials. They bring one smartly back to the old familiar notions of intensity (the equivalent of tempo in manoeuvre) and weight of shell.

This, coupled with the basic mental association of mass and weight, was one factor that led me to examine weight as a parameter of military mass. The other was a study I was asked to do on the United States "high technology light division", one of two structural projects for light divisions in the pilot stage as I write. In applying a very wide range of options to the problem, I discovered that both physical fighting power and combat worth as a whole were linked not to the number of men but to airlift weight. Just as Soviet thinking would lead one to expect, the equivalence of a balanced mechanised battalion group to a (more or less) standard infantry brigade was there. But the best basis of comparison was airlift weight.

This led me to re-examine at staff check level the equivalences based on numbers of men which I had found in *Red Armour*. My new figures showed a consistent trend, though a more conservative one than those based on manpower—one in fact that might well be nearer to reality. But I also discovered that for large complex formations weight was a much more tedious parameter to work with than numbers of men! What did emerge was a concept of **organic weight per man** (organic as in vehicle, not cultivation). In the Soviet formations I looked at, this seemed to vary from rather under 1 tonne/man (including helicopters) for the airborne assault brigade, through something over 1 tonne/man (excluding transport aircraft) in the airborne division (the version with about one-third of its "infantry" in BMDs) and well over 2 tonnes/man for the mechanised division, to almost 4 tonnes/man for the tank division. I have deliberately kept these figures vague to pre-empt nit-picking; but I think readers will agree that they make good sense.

This allows us to go on using the soldier as the basic unit of military mass, one that is extremely convenient as well as being widely understood and accepted. To this we can apply "organic weight per man" as a multiplier where fighting is concerned, that is for the holding force and in estimating the threat posed by the mobile force. As we shall see, tempo becomes the principal multiplier where manoeuvre is concerned. In some instances, which I shall deal with in Chapter 8, both apply.

Going back to our model of the extended marketing triangle (Figs. 14 and 15), we can now say that the area of the triangle represents organic weight per man, and that the volume of the solid generated by the product of this and the number of men (mass) represents physical fighting power. Here, though, one must note the erroneous hidden assumption that all soldiers have the same moral fighting power!

Fighting multipliers

The American term "combat multiplier" means a factor by which you can multiply mass to arrive at combat worth and applies across the board—to fighting and manoeuvre alike, or to any mixture of these. One needs, I think, to break this concept down in two ways. First, there are **fighting multipliers,** related to physical fighting power and to situations involving attrition, and **manoeuvre** multipliers. This is not an absolute distinction because it is blurred by the complex interactions demonstrated in the "firepower–mobility–survivability" triangle (Fig. 14); but it is a useful one, and a safe one provided that these interactions and the psychological overlay are kept in mind. The second breakdown, again to some extent blurred by interactions, is between **intrinsic multipliers** arising from the constituent nature of the force, and **extrinsic multipliers** derived from environment or circumstance.

Important as the intellectual and moral factor is, it cannot be quantified. Napoleon put it at three, Tennyson at ten. Many historical examples show that it can be higher still; and compounded with surprise it can attain almost any level you care to think of. The physics of the thing will do no more than get you into the right parish—or stop you going to the wrong one. It is your will, skill and judgement that gets you to the church on time.

Having established organic weight per man as an intrinsic fighting multiplier, I took a second look at the Lanchester equations. I found that, for a conflict between two large, sophisticated mechanised forces, one did not go far wrong with a "1.5 power law"—a half-way house between Lanchester's two cases. By contrast, if one tries to compare forces of grossly disparate nature and/or quality, as in the case of an advanced army taking on a guerrilla force, one goes wildly adrift. What is more, as the Americans learnt in Vietnam and the Soviets are learning in Afghanistan, weight per man can turn from a multiplier into a demultiplier—a spoiling factor.

This "half-way house" Lanchester equation, like so many of its kind, in fact constitutes a particularly luscious primrose path leading to an absolute concept of military mass. I have to admit I followed this for a while; it took a wet walk with my dog on an anything-but-primrose cliff path to make me retrace my footsteps. But two general points do emerge. One is that the higher the level for which the equation is struck, the higher both the organic weight per man and the proportion of indirect fire weapons will be; in other words increasing the proportion of indirect fire weapons has a dual effect on physical fighting power. Second and much more important these days, increasing the proportion of indirect fire weapons enhances the degree to which quality can offset numerical inferiority.

As the simplicity of attrition theory suggests, fighting multipliers are few in number and do not compound one another to anything like the same extent as manoeuvre multipliers do. The principal extrinsic fighting multiplier is **ground**, classically assessed as giving the defender a three to one advantage. The deliberate *preparation* of defensive positions is probably best seen as an *improvement in* the tactical strength of ground, though it also provides troops with direct protection. In the past deliberate preparation was undoubtedly a fighting multiplier; but in face of today's surveillance resources and the accuracy and intensity of modern fire, it has probably become an invitation to destruction.

We took a hardish look at ground in the preceding chapter. The point perhaps worth re-emphasising here is the essential duality of ground from the military point of view. It is both a fighting multiplier and a manoeuvre multiplier. Most often ground which is a fighting multiplier for one side is a manoeuvre demultiplier for the other, and *vice versa*. But if a defender chooses to employ operational manoeuvre, he may well, as we shall see, need to move faster than the attacker; and he may need to do this across the grain of the ground. Thus open terrain, firm and fairly smooth but not featureless—"good tank country" in fact—may favour a defence based on operational manoeuvre rather than an attacker using similar techniques.

This leads one to enquire whether **tactical manoeuvre** can fairly be regarded as an extrinsic fighting multiplier. Certainly limited manoeuvre at the lower levels has almost always played a part in positional warfare; and certainly the ability to carry out such manoeuvres enhances fighting capability. On the other hand, if one accepts that the term "operational" has a meaning associated with manoeuvre theory but independent of level (page 24), and that attrition and manoeuvre theory are complementary once hostilities have started, then surely one must also accept that manoeuvre theory can be applied at any level, even within a concept or situation dominated by attrition theory. There is an interesting grey zone here, though, to which my attention was first drawn by a question from a student at the United States Army War College. Few, I think, would describe a "did for them both" frontal attack as a manoeuvre. In fact Collins and Webster confirm my own feeling that, on both sides of the Atlantic, the word "manoeuvre" has connotations of dexterity and cunning, of the indirect approach. One reason I have ducked translating the Russian word *desant* (page 46) is that I should like to use "manoeuvre", but that word must mainly be reserved to render *manevr*. I am inclined to think that manoeuvre theory comes into play whenever one makes any movement which deviates from the most direct approach physically possible, one of the conditions for *desanty*.

Robotics and unmanned fortifications

Again it is a nice question whether military robotics, which has so far been primarily concerned with motion (of aircraft, ships, and most categories of wholly and partly guided projectile), should be linked to mass or to mobility. I suggest there are two reasons for treating this technology as a fighting multiplier. First and as a matter of principle, automatic devices and systems either extend the scope of the soldier's senses and/or augment his physical strength; in the latter case they increase the soldier's military mass just as the weight of equipment with and behind him does. Or they replace the soldier completely, not (as yet) cloning him but reproducing a particular combination of his capabilities. These devices and systems are therefore fighting multipliers in the most literal sense.

The second reason applies mainly though not entirely to the tactical level of land warfare. Controversial as it may be at the politicostrategic level, the Tomahawk cruise missile demonstrates that an unmanned aircraft can carry out nap-of-the-earth flight, or at least low-level contour flight, at high speed. As far as I know Tomahawk is not designed to receive post-launch commands; an unmanned craft that had this facility would be wide open to the electronic warfare threat, a threat which affects communication with manned craft too. The reason for training fast jet pilots (despite the vast expense and a wastage rate of over 90 per cent) and their equally expensive navigators, is not to fly or navigate the machine, but to put a human head or two in a position to make on-the-spot tactical judgments and to deal with flying emergencies. The same is true of ships. Even in crowded shipping lanes, everything is left to "George", however unsophisticated or unreliable that particular "George" may be. As I have often seen when sailing in the Channel at night, the officer of the watch sleeps in comfort until woken by an audio alarm signal from the radar, and then rushes from his duty cabin onto the bridge wing in his pyjamas—or whatever!

This may not be good practice, but it mostly works because the radar and the alarm signal are extremely reliable. The officer of the watch has trustworthy communication with the sensor and, in this instance by being on the spot though inactive, he can quickly assume control. We are now at a point where routine control of some rail systems is fully automated—like the underground railway which yaks away in charming Dalek tones at Atlanta Georgia's vast airport. Automatic control of traffic on motorways is likewise approaching technological feasibility, however far it may be from economic viability or psychological acceptance. But I at least cannot envisage cross-country driving, or the precision and complexity of manoeuvre called for in

tactical nap-of-the-earth flying by helicopters, being successfully automated. The remote "crew" of a robot tank would need an optical quality
stereoscopic video link and a multi-channel command link, both not just
extremely reliable but secure against all forms of interference including the
spectrum of active electronic warfare threats. This means the "crew" would
have to be within a few hundred metres of the robot, preferably if not
essentially on visual path to it.

For the next step in this argument I am indebted to a seminar I led while
visiting Sweden in 1981. One of the ideas my hosts wanted to examine was a
robot tank troop with a troop command vehicle. They felt, I am sure rightly,
that each robot would require a two-man "crew". This resulted in the layout
sketched at Fig. 16, putatively based on an infantry fighting vehicle hull, for

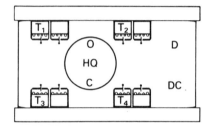

FIG. 16. *Schematic of a platoon command vehicle for a platoon of four robot tanks
(from a doodle I made during a seminar at Bofors Armaments in 1981). The vehicle
is a box-bodied armoured vehicle—an overgrown M113, if you like. At the front are
the driver (D) and deputy commander (DC, ie platoon sergeant) who acts as vehicle
commander. The platoon commander (C) and his operator (O) are on a raised
rotating platform with top vision (not shown). Each robot tank has a command post
(T$_1$ – T$_4$) with two monitors and two sets of controls, operated by its
commander/gunner and driver.*

a troop of four robot tanks. Now this would be a large vehicle, impossible to
armour heavily on all aspects. It would have a conspicuous and distinctive
visual signature. Even when it could remain in cover from direct surface fire,
the enemy would have little difficulty in working out its location once the
robot tanks were in contact. The command vehicle would be vulnerable to
helicopters and to the spectrum of overhead attack now available. One hit
would disable four robot tanks and wound or kill ten highly-trained men.

To my mind this argument rules out robotised ground vehicles and
helicopters as normal equipment for mechanised and air-mechanised
forces. Both the extent of automation practicable in aircraft and ships, and
the successful use of mobile robots in some specialised applications—
notably bomb disposal—are misleading. On the one hand vehicles moving
in fluid media do not have to cope with the complexities of the shorter
wavebands of terrain (page 59). On the other, in bomb disposal for

instance, the human operator and his link with the robot are not under threat. He can observe visually as well as by a video link, and he can be connected with the robot by cable.

This problem of vulnerability of the control centre applies with equal force to any static system of fortifications which requires continuous human control during operation. The enemy is going to discover in advance where the control centre is. If it is near to the system, he is somehow or other going to knock it out. If there are distant duplicated control centres, he is going to sever the communications link at its weakest point. It is naive not to assume total penetration of key areas of secrecy which exist physically in peacetime.

I would go all the way with John Keegan and others in saying that "fortifications" is no longer a dirty word. Admittedly any static system can be turned if the enemy sweeps wide enough; and it loses much of its value when penetrated at any one point. As against this it is a purely defensive system which buys time, aspects I shall return to in Part 5. Meanwhile I would contend, though, that for the reasons set out above, the notion of "push-button" fortifications is a pitfall. One can bypass it to either side. One direction veers towards fairly heavily manned fortifications, employing a variety of sensor and weapon systems remoted over short distances, but stopping short of true automatic control even at the lowest tactical level. This concept ties down, with static direct protection only, a significant, even a large proportion of the available combat soldiers, who could otherwise be given protected mobility and operate as a manoeuvre force.

The alternative is a *fully automated* system of fortifications. This would be completely installed and operate in the monitor state in peacetime. Its primary arming system would rely on a single human action, but this would be backed by a programme for automatic arming in response to certain patterns of sensor inputs. The disarming system could be shielded by several stages of human and electronic coding, and could be further protected by requiring inputs at a number of geographical points, or by decentralisation to sectors. The question is at what point a "man-made obstacle belt", a form of defence known to be of limited operational value, becomes a "system of unmanned fortifications".

The distinction is, I believe, that the one is tactically passive while the other, though operationally passive, is active and responsive at tactical level. Let us start by considering a conventional minefield of anti-tank mines with single-pressure fuses, and anti-personnel mines with tripods and tripwires. This will often be associated with either a natural water obstacle or an anti-tank ditch, sometimes with other forms of obstacle like dragon's teeth (Fig. 17a). Since a belt like this takes a long time to prepare, the enemy will almost certainly know its location and layout. This belt will cost the enemy some casualties and impose some delay on him, but if it is not covered by fire, it presents him with a straight military engineering problem. Anti-lift devices, multi-pressure fuses, and hollow-charge mines with influence fuses

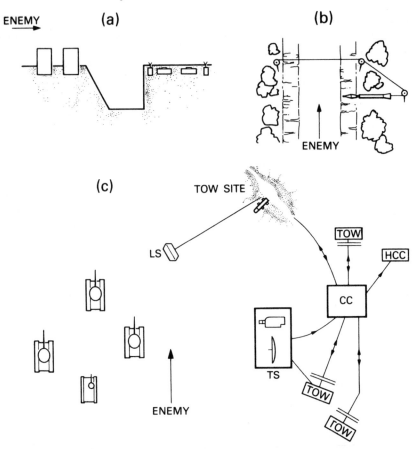

FIG. 17. *Tactically passive and active unmanned elements (all schematic, not to scale). a. Conventional man-made obstacle—dragon's teeth, anti-tank ditch, and minefield with anti-tank and anti-personnel mines. b. Fougasse, rigged from a rocket-launcher and a pull-cord (or pressure-tube). c. Unmanned tactically active anti-tank element based on the TOW guided missile system. Four TOW sites (say) are linked to a control centre (CC), which receives information from tactical sensors (TS) and reports to a higher control centre (HCC) capable both of coordinating several control centres and of bringing down indirect fire. Once alerted and cleared to fire, the TOW receives local target data from a local sensor (LS, say a microphone).*

make his task more difficult, but do not change the essentially passive nature of the obstacle. It will not hurt the enemy unless he enters it.

Next let us look at a fougasse (Fig. 17b), a very simple device made up of a mine like the French MICAH (which projects a steel plate) or a rocket-launcher (such as the Soviet RPG7V), and pull-cord or pressure tube. Since it senses the target and delivers a projectile to it, this fougasse represents a tactically active system, albeit an elementary one operating over only a few metres.

Then let us replace this fougasse with, say, a TOW anti-tank guided missile system, and locate the projector not 2 or 3 metres away in the bank of a lane but 2000 or 3000 metres away in a sunken emplacement (Fig. 17c). We can link this TOW launcher via an automatic control centre to a system of tactical sensors and a command processor. This "platoon headquarters" system orders the TOW system to prepare for firing and authorises it to fire. A pressure, visual or audio sensor in the target area (the "detachment commander") gives the launcher a reference time and position at which to start tracking. A visual or far infrared on-launcher sensor (the "sighting system" and "controller" combined) acquires the target, fires the missile and tracks the target, thus guiding the missile onto it.

This on-launcher sensor detects a hit from the flash and heat. A microprocessor uses hit azimuth and time of flight to locate this hit, and reports back to its command centre. Identifying this as a "hit" report, the "platoon headquarters" passes it back and across to the nearest automated fire control centre ("forward observation officer") which brings down a concentration of artillery of mortar fire if tubes are available and other conditions for engagement are satisfied.

This is *not* fantasy. Everything I have described is based on fairly elementary seventies technology. This microcosm contains the essential elements of a system of unmanned fortifications, and I leave it to the electronically minded reader to develop it further. Since a system of this kind, once in place, would not interfere greatly with normal use of the land, the depth and sophistication of it is limited only by cost. Capital outlay would be high, but maintenance costs trivial compared to those of an equivalent mechanised force. One can envisage systems of this kind as a fortified zone along a frontier (the Inner German Frontier for instance), as blocking positions at the throat of an otherwise open thrust line, as cover for unlikely but dangerous approaches (like the Ardennes in the Second World War), and *mutatis mutandis* for coastal and air defence. I do not want to be too specific here, but it strikes me that they could offer a sound alternative to the permanent strong points in the form of lattice battle proposed by Major General Livsey under the name of "active defence".

Unmanned fortifications are static and purely defensive; they are different in kind from manoeuvre forces. So I do not think one can fairly regard them as a fighting multiplier, a factor applied to the number of soldiers in the way that organic weight per man can be. On the other hand, they can be compared to a well-prepared positional defensive system in terms of the attrition and delay likely to be imposed on the enemy in penetrating them, and of the restrictions on the size and tempo of deployment of his mobile force. One can thus express the strength of unmanned fortifications in terms of infantry brigades or divisions committed to positional defence. Like such manned forces, they will be strengthened if a manoeuvre force can interact with them to contain the attacker's breakout force and/or attack the "hinge" formed at the point where this force emerges from the corridor of penetration. Unmanned fortification systems could well be regarded, then, as **equivalent defensive masses**; in other words a "division's worth" of unmanned system would be credited with the number of men and organic weight per man of an infantry division.

Conclusion

As far as I can discover, the concept of military mass is largely unexplored territory. There was no reason for historians or military authors writing before the 1920s to explore it, since the unit of mass in land warfare was quite obviously the soldier. The British school of the twenties ducked the problem; and the Germans of the twenties and thirties, along with the Soviets then and since, stuck firmly by the soldier. I have demonstrated here, to my own satisfaction at least, that they were and are right. I have deliberately left the issue of the unit of mass in naval and air warfare open, since I can see no evident solution and I lack the necessary feel for warfare in the fluid media. But I think we have made some progress. As we shall see in the following chapters, the distinctions between intrinsic and extrinsic multipliers, and between fighting and manoeuvre multipliers are useful ones. The underlying concept of physical fighting power is likewise an important one. By establishing organic weight per man as an intrinsic fighting multiplier, we have gained ourselves a means of comparing the fighting power of various types and levels of formation. This we shall develop further in considering manoeuvre power, bearing in mind, though, that its validity depends on the setting.

A half-way house between the classical Lanchester models confirms common sense, showing that a shift from direct to indirect fire tends to upgrade the combat worth of quality in relation to that of mass. Finally, I have put down some markers on robotics and static unmanned systems in land warfare, contrasting that technology's limited value for mobile systems with its great promise for static ones. In sum, I hope I have established a common understanding with the reader of the fundamental if uninspiring concept of military mass, from which we can move on together to examine the dynamic aspects of manoeuvre theory.

6

The Bursting Dam

"The nature of water is that it avoids heights and hastens to the lowlands. When a dam is broken, the water cascades with irresistible force. Now the shape of an army resembles water. . . . Avoid (the enemy's strength) and strike his emptiness, and like water, none can oppose you."   CHANG YÜ (in SUN TZU)

"Generally, in battle, use the normal force to engage; use the extraordinary to win."
                                                                        SUN TZU

"Thus, while we have heard of blundering swiftness in war, we have not yet seen a clever operation that was prolonged."   *Ibid.*

"It may be that in the future I may lose a battle, but I shall never lose a minute."
                                            NAPOLEON (trans. LIDDELL HART)

Introduction—dynamic forces

With origins going back to ancient Indian cultures, chess has long held its position as one of the world's great games. It combines different types of piece each subject to its own rules, objective predictions, the use of subjective judgement to synthesise those predictions, and study of the opponent, all in a way that makes it a valuable analogy of war, a hackneyed one in fact. A game of chess is made up of a series of separate moves, each made with extreme deliberation. On television one sees the game speeded up by time-lapse photography; and one can readily envisage this technique being employed to give an impression of continuous movement, just as it is in fact used to demonstrate the growth of plants. One may thus see the increase in the physical mobility of troops from the boot and the hoof to the track and the rotor simply as a time-lapse treatment of war. In fact this is, I am sure, just how the attrition-minded see modern warfare—as a rapid succession of discrete situations.

This is an incomplete view, the two-dimensional view on which attrition theory is based. However rapid, a succession of discrete situations remains just that; it does not become a dynamic system, capable of developing dynamic forces. Being concerned only with mass and time (Fig. 18a), attrition theory has no room for dynamic forces. To take account of these, one has to add the third dimension of length, thus introducing the idea of change with respect to space as well as to time (Fig. 18b).

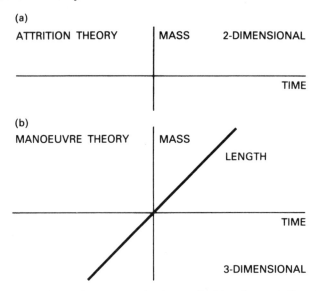

FIG. 18. *Attrition and manoeuvre theories. a. Attrition theory—2-dimensional (mass, time). b. Manoeuvre theory—3-dimensional (mass, time, length).*

But if you do not think that dynamic forces influence warfare you may not believe that they exist at all. Take speech, to start with. Pretend you do not know Portia's "quality of mercy" speech or Viola's "willow cabin" lines, and imagine them delivered at an even pace with the flatness of a voice synthesiser. You might get the message, but I doubt you would be any the better for it. The value of these passages lies in the combination of language (mass) and delivery (dynamics); and the greater of these is dynamics. Or listen to an orchestra rehearsing—or a pop group or a jazz combo for that matter. The conductor asks the first clarinet to sort out a turn; or seeks to improve balance by getting the second violins, violas and cellos to play a passage slowly without the melody line; or gets the ensemble to practice a series of chords one by one. Taken out of the context of a rehearsal, these sounds are totally meaningless. Music communicates wholly at the aesthetic level, and depends entirely on its dynamics to do so. Sun Tzu was much given to bells and gongs; Genghis Khan's taste in music remains a mystery, at least to me. But it never ceases to strike me that the modern world's three most successful practitioners of manoeuvre theory, the Germans, the Russians and the Jews, are also the most musical peoples of our civilisation.

The development of leverage

It may seem strange to lump two main distinguishing features of manoeuvre theory, leverage and tempo, together in a single chapter. To demonstrate that there is a good physical reason for this, one should perhaps put the cart before the horse and enter the discussion via a conclusion. Briefly the relationship of **momentum** to manoeuvre theory is not just a duality but a trinity. Fundamentally, momentum represents the resistance of a moving body to any change in speed or direction (strictly speaking, that is, to any change in velocity). Being the product of mass and velocity, momentum also represents the **physical manoeuvre value** of a force, the counterpart to its physical fighting power (pages 81 and 85). Third, momentum, being mass times velocity or mass times length over time, also stands for **rate of change of leverage**—a quality I at least regard as the clue to understanding the physical aspect of manoeuvre theory.

With all this in mind we can look at how the practitioner of manoeuvre theory develops this leverage. I have adopted the term "leverage" because the Americans have made it stick. But I think a far more indicative way of expressing the concept is "turning moment"; the association between this and the classical military term "turning movement" provides an instant understanding of the military significance of leverage. In the general physical sense first of all (Fig. 19), leverage is produced by the action of a rigid bar of given length (the lever arm) constrained at one end by a fulcrum (or as I shall call it "hinge") and having a force applied or capable of being applied to its other end, as for instance by the action of gravity on a mass. The leverage or (turning) moment is the product of this mass (m) and the length of the lever arm (l).

It is a very small step from this general principle to the basic manoeuvre theory model of holding force (H), mobile force (M) and enemy (E) (Fig. 19b). But "turning" in the military sense implies an actual or potential constraint on the freedom of movement of the body of troops "turned".

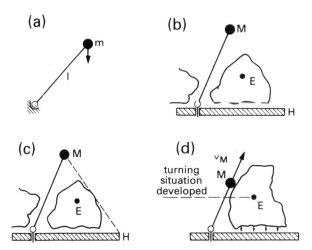

FIG. 19. *The development of leverage (see text).*

This gives rise to a fourth condition, that the body to be "turned", or at least its mass centre, must lie within a triangle formed by the two ends of the lever arm and the other extremity of the holding force (Fig. 19c). Otherwise, like an over-large nut flies out of the nutcrackers and across the room, it will simply be pushed sideways, retaining most of its freedom of action, notably the ability to "counter-turn" the holding force.

Thus useful leverage will depend not only on the value of the mobile force, of which more in a moment, but on *its position relative both to the holding force and to the mass centre of the enemy body in question.* It is at this point that the relative velocities of the three elements (their speeds and directions of movement, that is) come into play. Let us call them just relative "velocities" for now, and let us start by assuming the enemy sits tight with the holding force hard up against him. To establish leverage in this simple situation, the mobile force (M, Fig. 19d) simply has to advance beyond the enemy mass centre (E). Its velocity (v_M) will determine how long it takes to do this, and the rate at which the leverage, once established, is increased by its further advance. I am sorry if the reader is spitting mad at the seeming childishness of all this, but from it springs a string of key points.

Relationship between theories

If some quirk of geography or circumstance allows the relative positions of the three elements (H, M and E) to be established without hostilities breaking out, the attacker's aim may be gained by leverage alone. This is preemption, of which more later. It represents an application of pure manoeuvre theory; attrition theory would have indicated quite a different course of action. Thus the two theories are opposites. If, however, the holding force has to fight, attrition theory—a shift in relative strengths, comes into play as a factor affecting the actions of the two main forces (H and E). On the other hand, the attacker's operational aim is to get the mobile force forward and exercise leverage. Thus, once fighting starts, attrition theory becomes complementary to maneouvre theory, in fact an element in it. Put another way, manoeuvre theory literally and figuratively adds a new dimension to attrition theory.

Holding force roles

This brings us to the roles of the holding force. Its first task is evidently to clear a passage through the tactical depth of the enemy defence so that the mobile force can pass through and break clear. It then becomes a mounting for the hinge the mobile force requires if it is to develop leverage—in fact the fixed half of the hinge as well. But once the mobile force is clear, the holding force's main concern becomes the mass of the enemy force facing it. Evidently it must preoccupy the defender and prevent his tactical reserve counter-attacking sideways onto the hinge. But more important still, it must *hold the defender forward*, if possible even *draw* him forward, so that the mobile force can advance beyond his mass centre (Fig. 19d).

Startling as the physical and psychological implications are, it is a well-known tactical fact that two forces in battle tend to be drawn together. Psychologically, as Sun Tzu points out, a side which turns its back on the enemy (or the modern equivalent) admits defeat; both control and morale will be impaired, and may collapse if the force fails to break clean and elude pursuit. Physically, in the days of hand-to-hand combat and in modern times alike, troops attempting to retire must undergo a period of extreme risk from the moment they begin to break until they are out of reach of the winning combat arm's weapons. Further, they must come into the open when they break, and are thus vulnerable to artillery fire.

This is why, in a withdrawal by a mechanised force, tanks with their protected mobility are normally used to cover the rest out. Tanks or no, the weaker side often has to launch a short sharp counter-attack to get a clean break. Expecting this, the winning side will thicken its forward troops or even launch a counter-counter-thrust. Since this quasi-magnetic effect is widely exemplified in history and is well understood by the attrition-minded, I need not say more. To use one of the pieces of Irish I find so indispensable, the attacker (H) has to push hard to pull the enemy towards him. Evidently this pressure, while holding the enemy forward tactically, will also tend to force his mass centre back in operational terms; we will look at this situation in a moment. As Schlieffen understood better than most, this pinning down or drawing on of the enemy by the holding force is *fundamental* to the functioning of manoeuvre theory.

Interior lines

Before going on to look at the lever arm in more detail, I must digress to bring out a point often overlooked by those concerned with planning counter-moves to manoeuvre-based offensives. The concept of interior lines is familiar to all soldiers in the logistic context but not, I think, to attrition-minded tacticians as a factor in the conduct of their battles. The effect is most easily seen in the case of an offensive launched by a break-in battle on the Soviet model (Fig. 20). Once the attacker starts to develop a bulge beyond operational depth—beyond, that is, the enemy's tactical defended zone, he has the advantage of interior lines. And the mobile force extends this to operational level as it advances to form the lever arm and fans out or swings across tactical boundaries. To contain or defeat the mobile force, the defender cannot afford to be ponderous; as the diagram underlines, he must be more responsive and fleeter of track than the attacker. If the defender has an operational reserve, the possible fourth element in an operational system based on manoeuvre theory, this will have

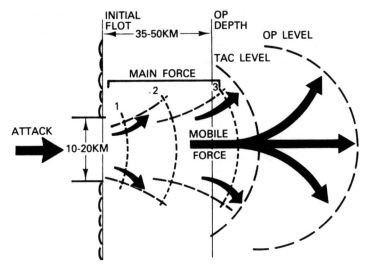

FIG. 20. *Attacker's internal lines (schematic based on Soviet "heavy break-in" battle).*

to move very fast indeed—the thought underlying the von Senger concept of "a new operational dimension" in the shape of a rotary-wing operational reserve. More of this in the next chapter.

Variations in the lever arm

Still keeping the holding force and the enemy stationary, I next want to look in rather more detail at the lever arm. We have so far tacitly regarded it as a single formation (as it might be a Soviet tank division) pushing its mass centre as far and fast as possible up its thrust line to form the lever arm. And since the attacker's aim is to gain as much depth as possible, this thrust line is an axis—a straight line or something very like it. Physicists call this movement from point to point "translational motion" (Fig. 21a). Once it is past turning depth, the mobile force may well be required to swing across the enemy axis in an enveloping move (in the sense in which everybody except the Americans understands that term). If we envisage this as a kind of sweep (Fig. 21b), we can regard it as a mixture of translational and rotational movement. In other words, as common sense would suggest, the mobile force can have any combination of translational and rotational motion.

Thus it can have pure rotational motion—trace out a circular path. Suppose now that the side employing manoeuvre theory (*HM*) is not attacking but defending (Fig. 21c). The holding force is blocking a defile, forming an "anvil" of troops or shaping an anvil of fire. In this case the holding force of troops might even be replaced by an unmanned

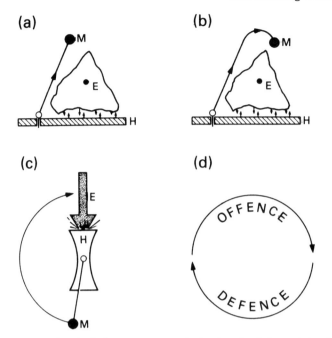

FIG. 21. *Variations in the lever arm. a. translational motion (advance). b. mixed translational and rotational motion (envelopment). c. rotational motion (hammer and anvil defence). d. offense-defence continuum.*

fortifications system (page 90) in the blocking role. Suppose that a mobile force is lying behind this block, and moves in a circular path to strike the enemy's flank and tactical rear once he has impacted on the anvil. This is nothing more nor less than the familiar "hammer and anvil defence".

This gradation of forms of motion brings out one of the fundamental differences between the two theories, one highlighted by Jomini but having even more force today. *Under manoeuvre theory, offence and defence are not the opposites they are under attrition theory but points, or rather arcs, on a continuum* (Fig. 21d). Offensive defense merges into defensive offense and *vice versa*. I take this to be the meaning of the Soviet saying that "defence is the mirror image of offence". In any event it provides the theoretical basis for such NATO concepts as "counterstroke", the "airland battle", and "strike deep".

In fact, as we shall see in Part 5, these concepts call for a triple hammer—a mechanised one at low(ish) tactical level; an airmechanised one at higher tactical level; and an operational hammer of fire and fixed-wing air, perhaps backed up by an airmechanised force.

This notion of multiple hammers serves to switch one's thoughts back to the offence, in particular to a complex mobile force as opposed to a simple one. With a single-element mobile force, the operational commander is faced with a dilemma. On the one hand, the distance in depth between the head of the mobile force and the front edge of the holding force (which the Soviets term "separation") needs to grow as far and as fast as possible in order to establish and increase leverage. On the other, as this mobile element moves forward, it leaves to its flanks more and more attractive secondary objectives, accessible but unattended to. Much more important, if the operational lever arm becomes over-extended, it will—just like a mechanical lever—break. Worse still, once there is a gap, it becomes relatively easy for the defender to "lift the mobile force off its hinges" (*die Stossgruppe aus den Angeln zu heben*), a phrase which occurs again and again in German accounts of Manstein's defensive operations in the Ukraine. In either event, much if not all of the leverage is lost and, if its presence has not reduced the enemy to rabbit-like paralysis, the mobile force becomes something of a hostage to fortune.

These problems are largely solved (though others, notably of movement, are created) by employing a mobile force composed of two elements, like the Soviet "front-level operational manoeuvre group" (page 45). Until the minimum depth for the exercise of leverage is reached, the mobile force moves as one group (Fig. 22a). The leading element concentrates on getting forward, while the second element's task is to support it in every possible way, to ward off any counter-moves, and to hive off small task forces ("raids" as the Soviets call them) to deal with selected objectives to the flanks of the thrust line. Once the minimum depth for leverage is reached, in fact probably at a point coincident with a key topographical feature such as a water obstacle, the follow-up element (M_2, Fig. 22b) goes firm, securing a corridor in depth, and providing an *advanced hinge* for the lead element (M_1). This train of thought is a long-distance express; so let us leave it standing at its first stop and restart it in Chapter 9.

For this notion of a forward hinge gives rise to an even more striking idea, one which lies at the route of the integration of helitroops into airmechanised operations. Perhaps the most familiar analogy is that of an advanced naval base, or perhaps of a strategic airhead. Certainly Mahan illuminates the idea by remarking that "the fleet itself is the key position of

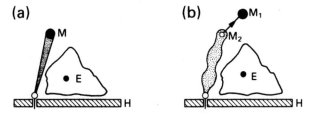

FIG. 22. *Two-element mobile force. a. Mobile force initially moves as one force. b. Follow-up force M_2 forms advanced hinge for M_1.*

the whole", and later explaining that a forward base seized and established by the fleet becomes the pivot for mobile operations by some or all of the fleet. This thinking has two applications to modern land operations. The follow-up element of a mobile force can close forward onto itself, forming a new hinge without having to maintain contact with the original holding force. And helitroops can establish an *operational airhead* as a base for mobile actions, just as airborne troops can establish a strategic one.

Relative velocities

Having examined the ramifications which may arise with the holding and defending forces (H and E) static, we can come to grips with the real essence of manoeuvre theory, the significance of the relative velocities of the three elements. Analysis both of Soviet offensive operations from 1943 to 1945 and of hypothetical examples based on recent Soviet writing suggests that, once the mobile force has broken out, if not before, the holding force, while holding the enemy forward in operational terms, will start to roll him back tactically and thus itself to move forward. This analysis likewise shows that, for healthy growth of the lever arm and timely establishment of a turning situation, the velocity—to keep in these general terms for the moment—of the mobile force must be at least twice that of the holding force (Fig. 23a).

On the other hand, in these early stages, when the mobile force is not properly shaken out and the hinge is vulnerable, there is a tendency to lose

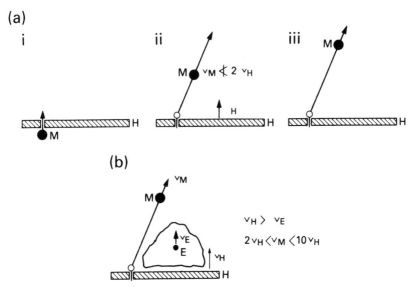

FIG. 23. *Development of the lever arm—conditions for relative velocities of elements after breakout (a) and when operation is fully developed (b).*

cohesion and control if the ratio of these velocities is much higher than three to one. This does not mean that the head of the mobile force should hold back at a time when the whole operation is both literally and figuratively gathering momentum. But it does mean that the initial mobile force must be tracked rather than rotary wing. A ratio of ten to one in the velocities of the two elements, while entirely acceptable once the operation is fully developed (as we shall see), would evidently lead to overstretch of the lever arm, loss of leverage, and rupture of the integrity of the operation. This in no way rules out the *tactical* employment of helitroops to help get and keep the mobile force rolling.

Once the attacker establishes a turning situation, the defender, while taking counter-offensive action at tactical level, will probably be forced to start an operational withdrawal—to shift his mass centre rearwards, that is. Should he sit tight and fail to disrupt the hinge, the turning movement will become an envelopment, perhaps ending in complete encirclement.

With all three elements of the system on the move, the first essential is that the holding force should be able to keep closed up to the defender, that is to maintain a forward velocity higher than his rearward one (Fig. 23b). Similarly, to be sure of maintaining leverage and ideally to increase it, the mobile force must be able to sustain its minimum two to one margin of velocity over the holding force. In fact, as historical examples and theoretical study again show, it is at this stage that the mobile force should and often can accelerate, particularly if part of the initial mobile force has established an advanced hinge or forward base (Fig. 22). And this is the stage at which helitroops, with a velocity an order of magnitude greater than that of the holding force, can be employed at operational level without loss of cohesion.

General characteristics of mobile and holding forces

Before pursuing this line of thought further, one should perhaps open up, for development later, three general points, two concerning the characteristics of the mobile force and the third those of the holding force. Since the quantity governing the combat worth of the mobile force is momentum, mass times velocity, its role could at first sight be filled by a large, slow-moving force. There are two fundamental reasons why this is not so. The first is the set of velocity relationships just discussed, which imposes a minimum velocity. Failure to meet this condition was the underlying cause of the failure of the two German operational offensives of the First World War.

The second is the need for flexibility. Suppose for a moment that a mobile force just meets the minimum velocity requirement but derives most of its momentum from mass. Once the force is launched, this mass cannot easily be varied. Under certain rather specific circumstances a large part of this mass may go firm (Fig. 22). In this event the rest of the force, being restricted in velocity, cannot greatly increase its momentum. And it is militarily impossible to shed chunks of the force like a balloonist throwing sandbags overboard. By contrast a mobile force which derives most of its momentum from velocity can readily attune its momentum to the requirements of the moment.

This thought leads us to a second set of limits on the mass/velocity balance of the mobile force—the need to pose and sustain a threat. Perhaps the most striking evidence of this is the disdain with which the Germans in the Ukraine treated Mobile Group Popov and its counterparts when they ran out of fuel. In the strict physical sense, when the force slows down or halts, its momentum is destroyed. However, since (as long as it has fuel) it carries within itself the capability of regenerating momentum by accelerating or moving off again, we can fairly think of a reversible transformation between *actual and potential momentum* analogous to that between potential and, say, kinetic energy. It is this "potential momentum", the ability to speed up or renew movement, that constitutes the manoeuvre component of the mobile force's threat.

But to make the threat stick the force must also have potential physical fighting power (Chapter 5) in the shape of the firepower it carries. This in turn sets a lower limit to mass. This concept of *potential* fighting power is an important exception, which some Soviet authorities seem to recognise better than others, to the "interchangeability" of firepower and combat troops. When fire is put down, the consequences may be devastating, but they are actual and measurable; it no longer poses a threat. Unless one uses delayed effect munitions, the only way to impose a firepower threat is to place projectors where they can deliver it. This is exactly how the mobile force produces the fighting component of its threat; and this indispensable fighting component of the threat imposes a lower limit on the contribution of mass to the momentum of the mobile force.

In the Second World War one of the factors which, in my view at least, led to the Germans' failure, and which undoubtedly caused the Red Army difficulties surmountable only by overwhelming mass, was an excessive difference in the velocities of the mobile and main forces. In the German offensives, the *Panzertruppe* tended to move five or six times faster than the rest. Either the mobile force pressed on, over-extended the lever arm and had to fight a battle of its own without benefit of leverage. Or, when logistics dictated, the mobile force was held back until the rest caught up, giving the Red Army time to respond to the situation. This collapse of operational integrity is always liable to occur if the difference in velocity between mobile force and holding force is dictated by the physical mobility of the holding force. In the Second World War this was inevitable.

In today's technological environment, and with the main forces of advanced armies fully mechanised, there is no reason why both elements should not have the same physical mobility. This is the case in the Soviet and Federal German Armies, and in the 1986 force structure for the United States Army. The tank and mechanised divisions (in the American case the Type A and B Heavy Divisions) are both equipped with the same type of tank and infantry fighting vehicle. To use the Soviet model once more, a mechanised division is perfectly capable of forming or leading an operational manoeuvre group and would do so in difficult terrain. The difference in velocity rests almost entirely on training and handling. The employment of a holding force and a mobile force with similar physical mobility contributes greatly to flexibility and smoothness in the early stages of an offensive operation. But it does not detract from the value of light armoured and rotary-wing forces as the advance develops.

Special cases

With these points in mind, we can revert to the theme of relative velocities and examine three special cases in which all three elements of the manoeuvre theory system are on the move, and which thus call for an increase in the velocity of the mobile force. The first of these is **envelopment** in the European sense of the term, in which the enemy's axis is cut behind his main force, possibly as a second step towards encirclement (Fig. 24a). Broadly speaking there are two ways of doing this, both of them involving a mobile force of at least two distinct elements. In one (Fig. 24a(i)) the follow-up part of the original mobile force (M_2) goes firm to form an advanced hinge, on

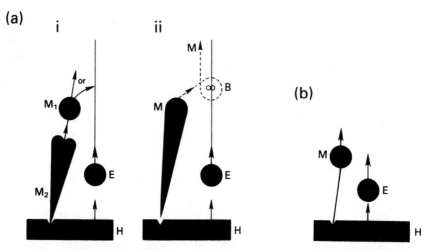

FIG. 24. *Envelopment and pursuit. a. Envelopment—(1) with two-element mobile force (2) by insertion of rotary-wing blocking force. b. Pursuit; this is what the Soviets call "combined pursuit", with the holding force frontal to the enemy and the mobile force parallel to him.*

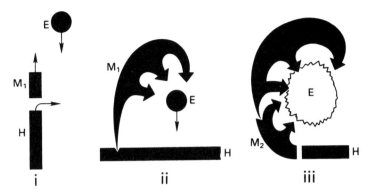

FIG. 25. *Development of the encounter battle.*

which the lead element pivots, swinging inwards to cross the enemy axis and establish a blocking position. This phase of the operation must be completed before the enemy can organise a substantial force of combat troops in depth to protect his axis and/or to attack the advance hinge—and of course before he can pull back out of the trap. The alternative (**Fig. 24a(ii)**) is to insert a block of helitroops and to swing the initial mobile force inwards to join up with it and form a combined blocking position and advanced hinge. This use of helitroops lies right on the tactical/operational borderline. I personally see it as operational, partly because I think the Soviets would use a (rotary-wing) airborne assault brigade; but many readers may well disagree.

In an envelopment operation it is as well to assume that the enemy will have started pulling out, or will start to do so, because the problem is easier if he sits tight. But the remaining two cases highlight the importance of relative velocities because everybody is going flat out. In the **pursuit** (Fig. 24b) both sides are moving in the same direction, so the *relative* velocities are small. If one assumes that the main mechanised forces of the two sides have about the same physical mobility, there is no way a pursuing mobile force found from these main forces is going to get behind the enemy and establish a turning or enveloping situation—unless, that is, some freak political, geographical or military circumstance allows it to be prepositioned forward. With the enemy disorganised, a light armoured force, able to get over the ground, say, half as fast again as the main forces, would have adequate physical fighting power and should be able to turn the retreating enemy. All the indications are that, by the nineties, light armoured forces will be able to do all that heavy ones can except to launch a deliberate attack on an enemy organised in a defensive position with main battle tanks. What is more, the employment of such a force would make the insertion of helitroops to block in depth far safer, because it could link up with them more quickly.

One now sees instantly why the masters of manoeuvre set such store by the encounter battle (Fig. 25). Here the two sides are moving towards each other, so that their relative velocities are at a maximum. The diagram depicts the development of this battle far better than I can describe it verbally. But there are two points to be made. Because it can be achieved rapidly and, with the enemy moving forward, fairly safely, envelopment now becomes a very attractive alternative to a continued advance. Just as pursuit brought out the need for a light armoured force, the encounter battle demonstrates the importance of being able to form a mobile force from any part of the main force. The third stage in the diagram shows a second mobile force, found from the *rear* of the original column, turning forwards and inwards to complete the "lobster claw" of a single envelopment. It would often be more appropriate to set up a double envelopment by finding a second mobile force from the right (originally the *front*) of the holding force.

Tempo

Having looked at these two extremes of relative velocity, we might turn to consider just what "velocity" means in the setting of manoeuvre theory, a setting in which this basic physical term sits none too happily. When I first adopted the Russian term "tempo" outside the Soviet setting, in a lecture at the United States Army War College as it happens, it had a mixed reception. Some felt that I was overcomplicating the whole business of manoeuvre theory, one that was already making many an imagination boggle. However, since two extremely distinguished German officers of Wehrmacht vintage, both of whom have also held senior NATO appointments, not only approved the term but adopted it in their utterances, I felt—and feel— justified in standing my ground. The concept of "tempo" is a nettle that has to be grasped if one is going to understand or employ manoeuvre theory.

I suppose one might loosely describe tempo as "operational rate of advance", by analogy with tactical rate of advance. But tempo is in fact a complex of seven elements, all of them complex in themselves and all of them mutually interacting:

> physical mobility,
> tactical rate of advance,
> quantity and reliability of information,
> C^3 timings,
> times to complete moves,
> pattern of combat support,
> pattern of service (logistic) support.

Each of these elements is subject to the "friction" of war—to my mind Clausewitz's most important single contribution to military thought.

"Action in war is movement in a hindering medium", he writes, ". . . Don't expect precision."

I propose to take no fewer than five bites at this large and rather bitter cherry of tempo. First, below, I shall explore it sufficiently to discuss its relationship with leverage in the dynamics of manoeuvre warfare. In the next chapter I shall look at the movement aspect, contrasting surface and rotary-wing movement. Then in Chapter 11, in the context of surprise, I shall endeavour to bring out the respective importance of relative and absolute tempo. And I shall deal with the intelligence and C^3 sides in Chapters 12 and 16.

One can define the **overall tempo** of an operation as *the distance from the initial line of contact to the back of the final operational objective, divided by the time (in days) from the receipt of orders by the operational commander to accomplishment or abortion of the mission.*

Having once swallowed that bellyful, one can start digesting it by breaking it down into **mounting tempo** (from receipt of orders up to the first crossing of the initial line of contact) and **execution tempo** (from that time on). Mounting tempo is largely determined by movement and C^3 timings, which I shall touch on below, and explore in more depth in Chapters 7 and 16 respectively. Execution tempo again breaks down into tempo up to operational depth, normally determined by the activities of the holding force and thus by mass; and tempo beyond operational depth, governed by the actions of the mobile force and thus by momentum.

Broad features of tempo

At this point I think it will help to put down some markers about tempo, based on the Soviet model as it has developed from the Second World War to the present. Dearly as one would love to make a similar analysis of blitzkrieg, the data does not appear to exist in manageable form—or at least I have been unable to find it.

Soviet operational tempo is characterised by a **dual symmetry**—of space and time. I do not fully understand this, and the best physical analogy I can find to help is the symmetry of a golfer's swing before and after striking the ball. But the consistency of this pattern, and the way it has persisted from the forties to the present despite a fourfold increase in overall tempo, convince me that this symmetry is fundamental to the successful employment of manoeuvre theory. The spatial symmetry I have tried to illustrate in Fig. 26. This schematic was originally a multi-flip foil designed to suggest the way (I think) a Soviet operational commander works from the extremities inwards in planning an offensive operation—the precise opposite of the way an addict of attrition works. Similarly one finds that, with remarkable consistency, the mounting time is roughly the same as the

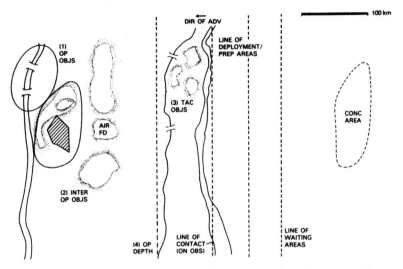

FIG. 26. *Schematic to illustrate Soviet planning sequence, and spatial symmetry. The commander seems to plan* inwards *from the final operational objective, and to make his initial dispositions in such a way as to produce an appearance of equilibrium.*

execution time. We can express this dual symmetry simply by saying that mounting tempo and execution tempo are similar.

This dual symmetry is likewise evident in the mounting of the operation; and likewise it has survived a fourfold increase in tempo. The essence of this is that the C^3 process, troop movement, and essential logistic positioning and movement flow in parallel. As the leading companies reach the assembly area, the company commanders receive their orders (in the Soviet case very simple ones), and the combat and service support elements complete deployment in their initial positions. More of this in Chapter 16.

As one might expect, execution tempo, while averaging out equal to mounting tempo, shows a much wider variation between broadly similar operations—up to 20 per cent, in fact. Here Soviet figures suggest a fourfold increase in the tempo of the advance to operational depth over the past 40 years. In the Second World War, the preferred day for insertion of the mobile force was $D + 4$ or $D + 5$; now they expect to insert single-echelon operational manoeuvre groups (OMGs) on D day, and "front-level" OMGs on $D + 1$ or $D + 2$. There are two reasons for this. One is the influence of modern firepower on the tempo of the "heavy break-in" battle; the other the growing tendency to avoid this battle and open the operation with a slashing attack or, better still, an encounter battle.

Thus the fourfold increase in execution tempo as a whole is achieved partly by earlier insertion of the mobile force and partly by a doubling of the tempo of the manoeuvre phase. Execution tempo shows a pattern of

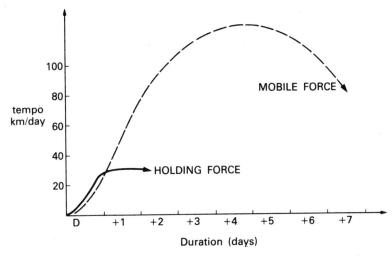

FIG. 27. *Typical Soviet execution tempo for a front-level operation—holding force (full line), mobile force (broken line). Note the smooth transition on breakout, which is important.*

progressive increase (Fig. 27) through the operation. While the average tempo of the mobile force is twice that of the holding force, the two merge at operational depth or thereabouts, as resistance to the holding force decays while the mobile force is still shaking out. Tukhachevskii's writings and historical examples suggest that this smooth progression is another important factor in the successful conduct of manoeuvre warfare.

Factors degrading tempo of execution

Clausewitzian friction, whatever its contributory causes, is at root a physical phenomenon which will come home to roost in the physical aspects of mounting an operation, and in its execution. But just because friction is such a valuable umbrella concept, one is tempted to abuse it by writing off all kinds of degradation against it. Certainly the greater the degrading effect due to specific identifiable causes, the more these causes will compound one another and be compounded by friction. But the determinant of tempo of execution will most often be the tactical rate of advance of the leading troops. Ideally this would be equal to the best practicable running speed of controlled movement, which in turn is governed by physical mobility.

The first identifiable factor is **bad going**, which directly degrades physical mobility. This may be due to terrain. Both Soviet and NATO planning speeds for columns including heavy tracks are reduced by about 40 per cent for difficult routes (through hills for instance). This reduction is less for wheels and light tracks, but here allowance also has to be made for bad surfaces. Darkness has a similar effect; even if night-driving aids make it physically possible to drive at daytime speeds, the "friction loss" is greater at night. A more dramatic effect still, and one easily lost sight of when one's eyes are focused on Europe, results from the absence of roads. Even the good going in parts of the Libyan desert or the Yemeni littoral is what Clausewitz would have called a "hindering medium", while much of the Sinai desert and the Sahara is impassable even to tracks without considerable mobility support. This effect makes itself felt just as forcibly when the military situation calls for off-road movement over developed terrain.

In many types of terrain, the degradation imposed by bad going can be reinforced at rather small effort by **mobility denial**. Deliberately laid minefields may still have a part to play in association with other forms of natural or man-made obstacle and with fortifications; but it is doubtful whether large minefields on their own are any longer worth the effort. The combination of aerial surveillance techniques on the one hand and deep reconnaissance and espionage on the other make advance detection virtually certain. Given this, the time taken to clear mines will be fairly short, and readily calculable by both sides.

By contrast scatterable minelets, whether delivered by air or artillery or dispensed by hand from vehicles, can completely disrupt an advance; what is more, their presence or even the possibility of it is likely to temper dash with caution. The Soviets prove this point by listing means of delivering minelets as one of the very few targets their medium reconnaissance patrols should disclose their presence by attacking. In close country, ambush and "tank hunting" tactics can be even more devastating. The multiplier here is that a knocked-out vehicle, more particularly a pair of knocked-out vehicles one behind the other, and more still an obstruction like this covered by observed fire, can block a narrow enclosed route for quite a while. If the risk of blockage can be made high enough, the advancing side will be forced to bring up infantry in force, dismount it and clear through. Quite apart from disruptive effects further back, this will reduce the rate of advance not just from track to boot but from track to probing boot.

Then there are the essential procedures the attacker must carry out to develop his operation. However strong his predilection for moving in column, he is sooner or later going to have to deploy at some levels. Since this basic physical factor does not seem to be widely appreciated in Western armies, it is worth examining in detail. Suppose that a Soviet advance guard is emerging from a one-route corridor or topographical choke point. At best planning speed and normal density (interval between vehicles) the pass time of the vanguard battalion group (the time the column takes to pass a point, that is) is about 35 minutes (Fig. 28a). When it shakes out to tactical intervals, something it will have to do at least in part before its tail clears the mouth of the choke point, the pass time becomes 1 hour and 35 minutes (Fig. 28b). Now suppose that, for one or more of many tactical reasons, the

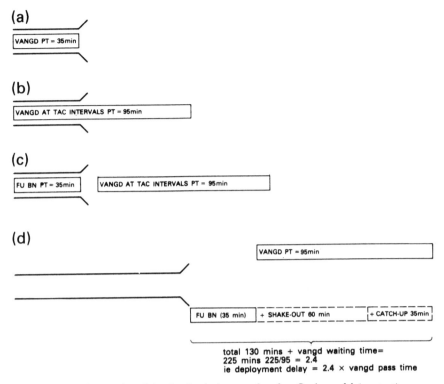

(a)

| VANGD PT = 35min |

(b)

| VANGD AT TAC INTERVALS PT = 95min |

(c)

| FU BN PT = 35min | | VANGD AT TAC INTERVALS PT = 95min |

(d)

| VANGD PT = 95min |

| FU BN (35 min) | + SHAKE-OUT 60 min | + CATCH-UP 35min |

total 130 mins + vangd waiting time=
225 mins 225/95 = 2.4
ie deployment delay = 2.4 × vangd pass time

FIG. 28. *Illustration of time lost by deployment, based on Soviet model (see text).*

advance guard is to fan out to two up. The second battalion group cannot start deploying until the vanguard is clear of the choke point. Admittedly this second group need not shake out until it is clear of the axis. But it will have to do so then (Fig. 28c). During this time the vanguard will have moved on and the second group will have to come up parallel with it before the required deployment is complete (Fig. 28d). As a useful rule of thumb, one can say that *the time lost by deployment will be from one and a half to two and a half times the normal pass time of the leading tactical group.*

The next major degradation of tempo occurs when the leading troops are forced to resort to **fire and movement**. As is well known, *each level of fire and movement practised halves the tactical rate of advance.* In fact it reduces tempo further still, and this is a good point at which to extend Clausewitz's analogy of friction. Engineers distinguish between "rolling or sliding friction", the friction between two surfaces in relative movement, and "static friction", graphically abbreviated to "stiction", the resistance to bringing two surfaces into relative movement. Not surprisingly, stiction is always the greater. One has only to look at mechanised or dismounted troops practising fire and movement to see that, however well trained they are, there is a delay each time one sub-unit comes to rest and the other moves off. Similarly, anybody who has ever moved in convoy knows that the same effect resonates through a column every time it halts and moves off again.

Paucity or innaccuracy of information impacts mainly on the tempo of command and control; this we shall explore in Part 4. But it also has a twofold effect on tempo of execution. No matter whether a tactical commander is in doubt about where the enemy is, or his leading sub-unit has simply lost the way (as very often happens in the best circles!), uncertainty has a kind of treacly effect—just as it does if you are driving along looking for a turn-off, or a particular street or building. Over and above this, the concept of tempo implies purposefulness—movement *towards* an objective or result. We all know the way a prose passage or a piece of music, developing smoothly towards its climax, suddenly seems to lose direction and start weaving about. The deeper-seated effect of uncertainty on tempo is closely analogous to this.

All these factors and the indefinable residue of friction compound one another, so that the operation tends either to sprint for the tape or, literally and figuratively, to grind to a halt. This is something one finds in the operation of most complex dynamic systems from sex to space travel. But in the case of land warfare an explanation is, I think, to be found in the dynamic interaction of leverage and tempo.

Conclusion—manoeuvre multipliers

In the previous chapter I drew a distinction between "fighting multipliers" which acted on physical fighting power and applied to positional warfare and to the actions of the holding force, and "manoeuvre multipliers" which concerned a mobile force under manoeuvre theory. The manoeuvre of this mobile force constitutes a complex dynamic system, and the principal factors which affect the system's development and its ability to exert influence on other systems interact in a cyclic rather than a linear fashion. Just as a local cyclonic air current either spins up into a whirlwind or collapses, the mobile force either gains momentum until it becomes irresistible, or starts to lose momentum and bogs down. I have tried, for the third time and still, I think, without complete success, to represent this graphically in Fig. 29; and I hope this at least gives the vortex-like impression I am trying to convey. To draw this chapter together I will try and "talk" the reader through this schematic.

We first come to two conditions which are essentially extrinsic to the system, in that they largely or wholly depend on circumstances independent of it, but which the success of the mobile force may establish or restore. **Surprise** and **pre-emption** may be achieved or lost at either strategic or operational level. But they are both such powerful multipliers that their sustainment or restoration at operational level will very likely have strategic

COMBAT MULTIPLIERS
(MANOEUVRE THEORY, MOBILE FORCE)

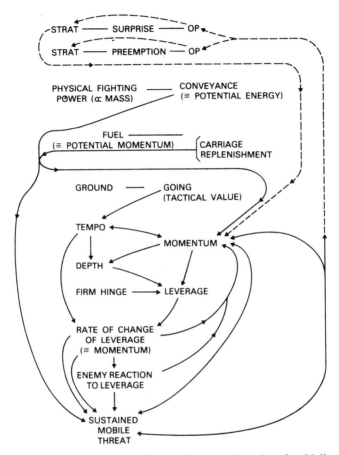

FIG. 29. *Notional flow chart to illustrate the synergetic action of multipliers in manoeuvre theory (see text for explanation).*

repercussions. (By the same token, their sustainment or restoration at tactical level will usually be of operational significance.) The achievement and regaining of operational surprise is evidently a matter of the mobile force's tempo. More of this in Chapter 11. The attainment and restoration of a situation of operational pre-emption relates to the creation and sustainment of the mobile force's threat; this is the precise land counterpart of the "fleet in being" theory (Chapter 8).

This threat is created by two intrinsic characteristics of the mobile force. The use of firepower (from within the mobile force) plays little part in the system, ideally none at all. What matters is the **conveyance of firepower,** providing one essential component of the threat—potential energy. The other key component is potential momentum, the capability of further movement; this the mobile force creates by the **carriage of fuel**. This potential momentum is a wasting asset as the force moves. The need to sustain it is evident in the way the Soviets use heavy-lift helicopters for routine refuelling of their armoured spearheads.

Ground, an extrinsic manoeuvre multiplier, now has to be rated for the going it offers, not its tactical strength. We noted, though, that because of the effect of interior lines and the grain of the ground, the defender may have even more need of good going than the attacker.

We now come full circle to the tentative conclusion I used to prise my way into this study—the threefold influence of **momentum**. First it provides the basic parameter of the system, the **physical manoeuvre value** of the mobile force. We can now describe this value as *mass times tempo* and carry it forward to Chapter 8 in this form. Panning in on the vortex, we can say first that momentum, which varies with tempo for a force of constant mass, represents resistance to change in speed or direction and thus the ability to gain **depth**. This depth represents the length of the lever arm and thus, as long as the hinge between holding force and mobile force holds firm, the **leverage** exercised by the mobile force.

Now leverage is force times length (in our terms *mass times depth*). And momentum, being mass times velocity, can also be represented (as it is in standard dimensional analysis) by "mass times length over time" (MLT^{-1}). But this is also the definition of **rate of change of leverage**, a dynamic quantity. So the rate of change of leverage represents momentum. The development of leverage therefore adds to the momentum of the system, and thus to its tempo, which in turn increases the rate of change of leverage.

While this progressive generation of momentum is evident in historical examples of both blitzkrieg and the deep battle, it is not at first sight easy to explain in physical terms. One looks for an external force acting on the sub-system constituted by the mobile element. Leverage may remain a potential force, in the sense that the mobile force may not attack the enemy's flank and rear. But we know from historical example that it is real. It "turns" him—dislocates him or forces him to pull back (if he can). If the mobile force did attack, the enemy would resist—the physical force would produce a physical reaction. In just the same way the leverage exerted by the mobile force evokes a reaction—a counter-leverage or shouldering action—equal and opposite to it. This I believe is the force from which the mobile force gathers momentum.

Thus one sees how manoeuvre theory depends on the presence and reaction of the third element in the system—the enemy. Like judo, it uses the enemy's strength to defeat him. One also sees why operations based on manoeuvre theory, like the whirlwind, either accelerate to success or quickly collapse. If you lose leverage (by the enemy pulling back) or lose tempo (by being slowed down), the cyclic effect goes into reverse. What is more, the loss of momentum reduces the physical manoeuvre value of the mobile force to its physical fighting power, which may be rather low. Whether "felt", as by the great captains, or analysed, as I have tried to do, this admittedly difficult concept of the threefold significance of momentum lies at the root of an understanding of manoeuvre theory, and thus of the ability to employ it to advantage.

7

The Rotary Wing Revolution

"The ultimate in disposing one's forces is to be without ascertainable shape."
Sun Tzu

"Freedom of movement gives harmony of offensive and defensive power."
Fuller

"The answer (for NATO) lies in matching our increased firepower with a significant increase in mobility, perceiving now the possibilities for tomorrow offered by technology today." Ferdinand von Senger und Etterlin

Introduction—the linear imperative

To a man, the mechanisers of the twenties saw freedom of movement off prepared surfaces as one of the major assets of the "caterpillar track". They envisaged the entire mechanised force, logistic backing and all, rolling freely in tactical formation over the countryside like any fleet sailing in blue water. They were wrong, and for three solid reasons. Even the best of cross-country vehicles moves far more slowly off roads and other prepared surfaces than it does on them. Second, most cross-country vehicles use more deadweight to lift a ton of payload than their roadbound counterparts, and even a vehicle of the same all-up mass uses far more fuel and suffers more wear and tear across country than it does on roads. The result is that a cross-country supply echelon can easily become self-consuming, requiring a greater weight of fuel and stores than it can carry. Even with roadbound supply vehicles, there are many routes in many parts of the world over which only the lightest of forces can be supplied by land. Third, even if the cost of cross-country logistic vehicles could be tolerated, the money and resources could be put to better military effect. Only as the era of mechanised forces as we know them enters late middle age do we see a few examples of priority logistic loads, such as tank ammunition, being given protected cross-country mobility. By and large, the evident restrictions of rail movement, to which Schlieffen, and to some extent, the elder Moltke geared their entire plans from the start of mobilisation to operational success, have been replaced by the linear imperative of controlled movement on roads, the Soviet tank army strung out along the autobahn from Oder to Meuse.

By the same token the pioneers of airborne forces felt they had liberated themselves from the bondage of surface movement. They too were wrong. Throughout the development of flight, and for that matter of space travel, the greatest technical problems and hazards have been associated with leaving and returning to the ground. Figure 30 illustrates how being tied to prepared surfaces imposes a linearity of its own at take-off. In face of modern surveillance sensors, the need to concentrate transport aircraft on the ground for loading is likely to limit airborne operations to brigade level and, because of the risk of losing surprise, severely to restrict their scope. Figure 30 also shows how the flight mode of fixed-wing aircraft prevents paratroops from achieving the *concentration in space and time* on dropping

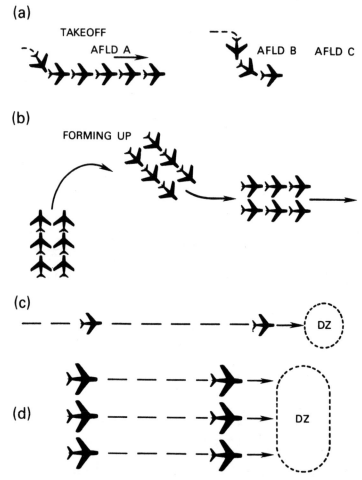

FIG. 30. *Effect of linearity on fixed-wing airborne operations. a. Concentration at airfields, lining up for take-off. b. Forming up. c. Fly-in on single lane—dispersion of paratroops in time. d. Fly-in on multiple lanes—dispersion of paratroops in space.*

which their lack of protected mobility on the ground calls for. This linearity over the dropping zone has proved to be the Achilles heel of paratroops, limiting to tactical level their successful use against organised opposition.

While Fuller spotted this, the only pioneer to do anything about it was Tukhachevskii. *Mechanised* airborne troops played a part in his earliest thinking on deep operation theory. As a result, the Soviet Army was the only one to set about motorising its airborne forces as soon as jeep-type vehicles became available. In the sixties they developed the BMD multipurpose airborne armoured vehicle as a derivative of the BMP1 infantry fighting vehicle. In the seventies they equipped first one-third, then one-half of their airborne battalions with it; and in the eighties they have gone on to field fully mechanised airborne divisions.

From the days of Sun Tzu onwards, the unsung and not widely understood skill of moving troops has been one of the principal hallmarks of successful armies. As already mentioned, it was one of the two keys to German success in the Franco-Prussian War. And in the Second World War even the Anglo-Saxon addicts of attrition found that their ability to fight effectively turned on road movement. To appreciate the full impact of the rotary wing, one must have some understanding of the laws which govern controlled movement.

The layman sees the movement of mechanised troops as analogous to the trips he makes in his car, with a bit added on to allow for the size and number of vehicles. For columns of vehicles with a substantial *pass time* (the time the column takes to pass a point), this kind of thinking gives a completely false picture. As long as running time greatly exceeds pass time—for small bodies of troops moving over long distances, that is—the "motorist's" approach has some validity. And road movement remains a reasonably efficient process, more or less dependent on the physical mobility of the vehicles concerned. In other words, *time to complete* (the earliest time the unit or formation is available at its destination) might be described at "running time plus a bit". But as pass time approaches and then exceeds running time, a totally different picture emerges and the linear imperative really begins to bite. When pass time and running time are equal, the time to complete is twice the running time. Increasing running speed usually leads to disruption of the column by the slower vehicles and a net loss of time. Maintaining normal density, let alone increasing it, is tactically risky within artillery range or in an adverse air situation. All in all, no variation in technique can do more than nibble at the edges of the linear imperative of surface movement.

The helicopter—a double revolution

The Falklands War brought out the role of the helicopter as the workhorse of the modern battlefield, but the scale of the operation as a whole and the very limited lift available after the loss of all but one of the Chinooks on board the *Atlantic Conveyor* made its influence less than revolutionary. And the Soviets seem to have been less enterprising than one would expect in the use of helicopters in Afghanistan. But with existing technology and the kind of helicopter fleet that at least the Soviet Army possesses, operational use of the helicopter can have a far more revolutionary impact on manoeuvre warfare than ever the track did. Let us take as an initial basis for discussion an early version of the Soviet airborne assault brigade (Fig. 31), with sixty attack/assault and twenty-four first-line medium transport helicopters, and a strength probably of some 1900 men. Let us note in passing, before returning to it in the next chapter, that the Soviets regard this brigade as an operational formation and rate its combat worth in the mobile force as equivalent to that of a tank division (with over 10 000 men and about 500 major tactical vehicles).

This brigade obtains its momentum from very high tempo and very small mass, thus solving the movement problem before it starts. An armoured group of eighty-four tactical vehicles moving at "forced march" speed and normal Soviet density has a pass time of only ¼ hour or so. But this helicopter brigade can do the one thing that almost every theorist and analytical historian agrees about—*it can move dispersed and fight concentrated*. What is more, it can lie up dispersed and well back, in comparative

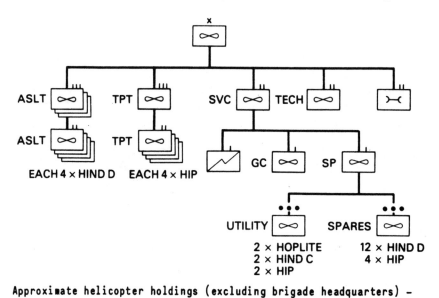

Approximate helicopter holdings (excluding brigade headquarters) –

Mi-24 HIND D 60, Mi-8 HIP 20, Mi-24 HIND C 2, MI-2 HOPLITE 2, **total 84**

Fig. 31. *This organigram represents either an early version of the Soviet airborne assault brigade, or the adaptation of its precursor, the independent assault helicopter regiment.*

safety. In the extreme one can envisage it waiting in dispersed company hides along a lateral, taking off simultaneously, flying nap-of-the-earth in open line, and converging radially on its objective. It would then have zero pass time.

With, say, a 200 kilometre fly-in, its time to complete, deploy and engage would be just under 1 hour. A tank division with the same run-in on one route would take rather over 10 hours to complete, with running time and pass time just about equal. It would then need at least another hour to deploy and bring its artillery into action. But let us forget this and say that the rotary-wing formation's tempo is *ten* times that of the armour. Now the ratios of mass in terms of men and of tactical vehicles, and of running speed (cruising speed) are all around *five* to one. So the helicopter force's having zero pass time *doubles its operational tempo* and thus, in Soviet eyes at least, its combat worth.

This example illustrates well enough the first "revolution of the rotor". Up till now helitroops, like all except Soviet paratroops, have to come down to the mobility of the boot once dismounted. One does not know (or at least I do not know) exactly how the Soviets handle the airborne assault brigade tactically—whether the assault helicopters set down their sections on or before first contact, or whether they operate like infantry fighting vehicles. Certainly the United States Army treats its attack helicopters, which are armed but carry no dismountable troops and are therefore analogous to tanks, essentially as combat *support* weapon systems. But General von Senger und Etterlin, with his "main battle air vehicle" concept, has well and truly set the rotor on its second revolutionary turn. *For a main battle air vehicle uses ground tactically without relying on it for mobility.*

The main battle air vehicle concept

The idea of a tactical vehicle with the operational mobility of a helicopter—a "flying tank"—was a twinkle in at least one German combat developer's eye way back in the late sixties, probably as an offshoot of their abortive experiments of that decade with ultrahigh-mobility tracked vehicles. The idea was well ahead of its time. More important, it was based on the misconception that further development of the rotary wing would yield a cheap, easy-to-fly machine for use at low levels and within ground effect. This notion ignored the characteristics required for nap-of-the-earth flying and, in particular, the phenomenon of recirculation (Fig. 32). This comes into play when the machine is hovering within ground-effect height over rough, mobile surfaces like long grass, or near a vertical surface such as a wall or the edge of a wood. It cancels out the lift obtained from ground effect, and may call for an increase in hover lift as the machine approaches the ground.

As Senger acknowledges, a main battle air vehicle would have to be a full-

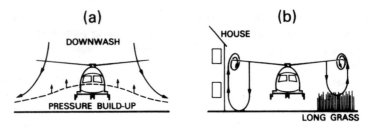

FIG. 32. *When a helicopter is hovering within ground effect (a), but over rough or mobile surfaces (eg long grass), or near a vertical surface,* recirculation *(b) negates ground effect and may even call for more power than free air hover.*

performance helicopter. Such a machine is entirely feasible with eighties technology—in fact a number of current types have the requisite payload and performance—but two current American projects make it much more attractive (Figs. 33 and 34). These are the use of centrifugal contra-rotating rotors to reduce rotor diameter and eliminate the tail rotor; and replacement of the conventional flying controls (collective, cyclic and yaw) with a single miniaturised stick. At the same time helicopters with a maximum take-off mass of around 10 tonnes are beginning to show weight analyses comparable with those of light armoured vehicles (of 15 tonnes or so), making selective armouring to a useful level possible. Three question marks remain. One is the machine's capability on very dark nights and in mist, when a conventional helicopter would be reduced to the mode known as "hover-taxi"; this seems likely to be solved by the nineties.

The other two question marks stand for the problems which, along with cost, will determine whether the military evolution of the rotor in fact follows a similar pattern to that of the track (Table 2). These are endurance and vulnerability. Many throw up their hands in horror at the implications of supplying a helicopter force with the fuel it needs. In fact, over the spectrum of likely running and flying conditions, the fuel consumption of the kind of helicopter we are talking about is not too different from that of,

TABLE 2   *Evolving military role of the rotary wing*

Motorised wheel and track by	Role	Rotor by
1910	service support	1960
1920	combat support	1970
(combat (tank) 1916)		
1940	small high-mobility manoeuvre force (*Panzertruppe*)	1980
1960	mobility base of main manoeuvre force	2000?
2000?	combat/service support and low-intensity ops only	

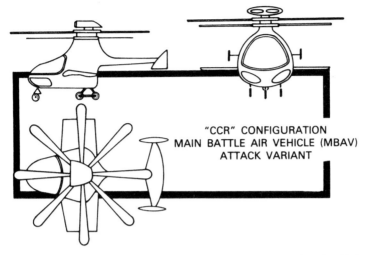

FIG. 33. *Schematic to show concentric contrarotating rotors (advancing blade concept, no tail rotor (NATOR)).*

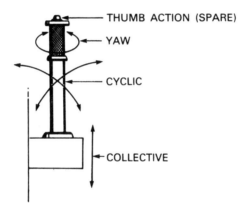

FIG. 34. *Schematic of miniaturised single-stick control.*

the M1 Abrams tank—admittedly a particularly thirsty monster. And the weight of fuel the two can carry (at 20 per cent and 5 per cent of all-up mass respectively) differs by only 1 to 1.5. The difference is that when the tank is stationary it uses rather little fuel, but while the helicopter is hovering it is running at maximum fuel consumption.

As Fig. 35 shows, the problem would be greatly eased if one could keep helicopters circling the battlefield in a kind of collected canter, at "endurance speed" that is; unfortunately they would then become ducks at a shooting gallery. If a helicopter handled like an armoured vehicle could spend some 80 per cent of its time on the ground (Fig. 35, "flight idle"), it

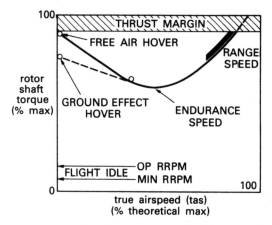

FIG. 35. *Simplified schematic to indicate relative fuel consumption of a helicopter in various flight modes and at "flight idle".*

would have a "battlefield-day endurance" about the same as that of the Centurion Mark 3 tank—roughly 8 hours as opposed to the 24 hours of most modern armoured vehicles. Centurion's limited fuel capacity did pose a problem, but by no means the insuperable one the British user's screams made out. And Centurion could not whip back to safety, refuel and return to its position in 5 or 10 minutes like a helicopter can. Some calculations I have done suggest that, with a crew of three and a "deputy commander" held as a slip crewman at the refuelling point, main battle air vehicles could sustain a genuine round-the-clock capability.

This need to be on the ground when tactically stationary and not in direct contact with the enemy raises the question of agility, to which vulnerability is closely linked. The tacit assumption here, incidentally, is that the helicopter could perform all its surveillance and firepower tasks except firing its tubed armament and launching (as opposed to guiding) its rockets and guided missiles from a "rotor down" position, by means, that is, of a "mast-head sight" (see Fig. 33). (Several systems of this kind are already in service and will undoubtedly evolve along the same lines as the "vision and sighting" systems of armoured vehicles.) Both for armoured vehicles and for helicopters flown nap-of-the-earth, vulnerability turns on movement exposure time and firing exposure time.

Movement exposure time is the time for which all or part of the machine is exposed when crossing gaps between cover. A helicopter and a conventional .tank are about the same height, and the helicopter's need to keep clear of the ground is more than offset by its superior speed and its ability to move instantly in any direction relative to its axis. Again the target area presented by a helicopter and a tank is comparable. The main difference in vulnerability is that the rotor, being at the top, will be exposed more often and for longer than the tank's running gear. All in all, one can say that helicopter and tank will tend to have the same order of movement exposure time and vulnerability on the move.

Firing exposure time is even more critical, because the discharge of a weapon has a very conspicuous signature. Before going into timings, one must underline a major drawback of the helicopter. The tank, with its gun near, in future perhaps *at* the top, need only expose its upper part to fire (Fig. 36, hull down). Because the armament has to be mounted low enough for the projectile itself and the muzzle effects to clear the rotor in its fully forward position, the helicopter, as already pointed out, must come "hull up" to fire, exposing a frontal target with an area over twice that of a conventional tank hull down, and one hundred times that of possible future tanks in a fire position. A tank like M1 Abrams or Leopard 2 coming up from turret down (Fig. 36), firing and dropping back, exposes all or part of its turret for an average of 10 to 12 seconds, 3 or 4 seconds of this after firing.

FIG. 36. *A tank in turret-down (TD) and hull down (HD) positions,* not *to scale. These are normally referred to a target in the same horizontal plane as the observing/firing tank.*

A helicopter like the Sea King, of about the take-off mass we are considering, takes about 10 seconds to "pop up" from "wheels clear" (just off the ground) to free air hover, and 2 to 3 seconds to drop back again. (These figures and the ones which follow were very kindly taken for me during training by the helicopter flight of a nearby Royal Air Force station.) Thus firing exposure times for an agile tank and a main battle air vehicle at the hover are comparable at 12 to 15 seconds. Since decision time, human reaction time, and control mechanism and system response times feature large in this, neither is likely to improve much.

Reverting to the question of endurance, the figures based on Sea King suggest that main battle air vehicles would have to be operated with three levels of alert. One, equivalent to the stand-by state in an armoured vehicle, would be on the ground, engines off. Coming from this to the hover would be a matter of unit minutes. The next higher would be "flight idle", on the ground with the rotor running at operating speed with zero collective pitch; this consumes about one-fifth of fuel required for free air hover (Fig. 35).

(With future more rigid rotors it may be possible to run them at some minimum speed, thus cutting fuel consumption by a further 5 to 10 per cent.) Coming from this state to controlled "wheels clear" hover takes about 30 seconds.

I have analysed this whole question fully elsewhere, and these technical-tactical details are somewhat out of place in this book. But I hope I have said enough to demonstrate that, by the nineties, the main battle air vehicle will be not just a feasible concept but a very attractive one, and that a rotary-wing force equipped with these machines would not be too different in tactical terms from a light armoured force. One cannot yet say whether the primary tactical requirement could best be met by a single type of "assault helicopter" carrying a limited amount of armament and a section or fire team (half section) of men—a successor to the Soviet Mi-24 Hind series—or whether a combination of "attack" version (the tank analogue, AH64 Apache for instance) and an "assault" machine (the infantry fighting vehicle analogue) would be preferable. But it is significant that with the introduction of Mi–28 Havoc, an "attack" machine, the Soviets are going the American way.

There is no problem over direct fire armament. The full spectrum of weaponry required is already in service and in a state of rapid evolution. And interchangeability of armament is an established design feature of both armament packs and helicopters. Indirect fire support is another thing again. There are two basic problems here. One is that a helicopter in flight cannot discharge a tubed weapon with a significant recoil force because the only way it can react to this force is to gain momentum in the opposite direction—to shoot backwards. And with high-angle fire, often an essential for close support in broken terrain if the helicopter is not to expose itself fatally, interference with the rotor becomes impossible to avoid. Available technology offers a simple solution to this, one which may well have appeared in the flesh by the time this book is published.

Since cannon and direct-fire rocket pods can meet much of the low-angle requirement, and since the tactical tempo of a rotary-wing force calls for shock effect, the most attractive types of weapon are the multi-barrelled rocket launcher and the mortar. Either could be mounted in an underslung pod which could be set down in a fire position. Either the detachment could dismount with the weapon and use net radio; or the weapon could be remotely controlled by the helicopter standing off, linked to it by cable or by a secure and interference-proof local system such as a laser telephone. Reserve ammunition would be carried within the helicopter and loaded or transferred to the weapon pod in flight. In fact the reloading problem and the need for a mortar baseplates to be settled by firing make a multi-barrelled rocket launcher of about 120 millimetre calibre look the best bet. This could be provided with a proportion of "smart" (terminally guided) anti-tank rockets and perhaps with some cluster rockets, both being fired selectively or in a mixed salvo. A rough check based on the Soviet BM-21 (40 × 122 mm rockets) suggests that it could be carried with one reload on an unarmoured "fire support" version of the main battle air vehicle.

The heavy-lift option

This idea of setting down a weapon pod provides a link to an alternative concept which at first sight seems to offer the best of both worlds. This is to have a co-designed light armoured family and a heavy-lift helicopter, and to provide a light armoured division with an organic heavy lift for, say, two armoured battalion groups. This would be somewhat analogous to the Soviet tactical helicopter lift of dismounted men when their mechanised divisions get an organic transport helicopter unit—except of course that one is now talking of lifting the armoured vehicles. There will undoubtedly be a substantial requirement for heavy-lift helicopters to support operational rotary-wing formations; after all, the Soviet Army already uses them for immediate logistic support of its tanks. But on closer examination this option has three major drawbacks.

Militarily it is by no means the equivalent of a rotary-wing force. Once set down, the armoured vehicles have only their inherent mobility; the first stage of the rotary-wing revolution is partly wasted, and the second wholly so. Partly for this reason and partly because of their training and tradition, these troops would operate much as they always have; they would not have the scope and tempo of helitroops. Then there is the logistic problem of keeping large numbers of heavy-lift helicopters, and the armoured force, supplied with fuel. Roughly speaking, each heavy-lift helicopter/light armoured vehicle combination would need about four times as much fuel as a main battle air vehicle, or about the same as a platoon of three main battle tanks. To put it another way, a complete fill for the combination would empty a tactical bulk refueller.

Cost

This brings us to the crunch point of cost, which appears to put the "heavy-lift" solution right out of court except as an interim expedient on a small scale. On published figures, an AH64 Apache costs about three times as much as the M1 tank and four and a half times as much as the M2 infantry fighting vehicle. Suppose, conservatively, that the required heavy-lift helicopter would cost twice as much as Apache and, more realistically, that a light mobile propelled gun would cost the same as the M2. Using the United States 1986 force structure as a guideline, two battalion groups would consist of about 120 major tactical vehicles, and a light armoured division would contain ten battalion groups. Thus two battalions' worth of heavy-lift helicopters would cost twice as much as the division's entire holding of major tactical vehicles.

Logistics apart, one would then be trebling the cost of a light armoured division's teeth to gain operational mobility for one-fifth of its combat strength.

If one was to replace the entire division's major tactical vehicles on a one for one basis with main battle air vehicles, which might cost about the same as Apache, the capital cost of the division would increase an intolerable fivefold, and its maintenance cost would also rise substantially. If, however, one bases the comparison on combat worth and takes a five to one ratio as opposed to the Soviets' six or seven to one and the ten to one suggested earlier in this chapter, one arrives at an operational formation of 120 first-line main battle air vehicles for the same capital cost as a light armoured division; the maintenance costs too would seem to be about equal. Thus, if the combat-worth comparison suggested by manoeuvre theory holds, a rotary-wing formation of about the size of the United States (1986) Air Cavalry Attack Brigade or the Soviet Airborne Assault Brigade is at worst a sound investment and at best an excellent one. Soviet practice, American intention and the Senger proposal all suggest that a brigade of give or take one hundred first line machines and two thousand men constitutes the basic rotary-wing operational formation.

Capabilities of helicopter brigades

Let us suppose this force of 120 first-line helicopters to be made up of sixty attack machines (tank equivalent), forty assault machines (infantry fighting vehicle equivalent), and twenty of the fire-support variant carrying multi-barrelled rocket launchers. I suggest this is a balanced force because the attack helicopters, with appropriate armament loads, can carry out part of the role of direct support artillery. Let us also suppose that this brigade would be supported by long-range tube artillery (or naval guns), rocket artillery and fixed-wing air.

This brigade's combination of combat worth and strategic mobility is something few have envisaged, let alone experienced. It probably represents about one hundred C 141B Starlifter loads—say one tenth of the lift of the standard United States airborne division or their proposed "hi-tech" light division. If called upon to do so, it could put about half as many men in foxholes as the 1984 version of the "hi-tech" division and still retain much of its mobile fighting power. Then again, the brigade could be carried in one or at most two large aircraft carriers or, much more interestingly, in three or four of the carrier-sized submarines of which (if a report published in 1983 is correct, page 48) two may have gone down Soviet slipways by the time this book appears. The brigade could be launched off these ships against targets deep inland, avoiding coastal defences. And, given local air superiority, it could operate over long distances without land lines. The transport aircraft and medium and heavy transport helicopters used to maintain the brigade could very quickly lift in light infantry on manpack scales if and when the need arose.

By the same token the operational capability of this helitroop brigade is beyond dispute if it is employed with strategic or operational surprise against soft targets such as political centres, or airfields and bridges far in the enemy's rear. One should note in passing that, if used to seize an airhead, it would allow airborne forces to be flown in on air-landing as opposed to parachute scales; this offers a substantial saving in airlift, especially for mechanised airborne forces of the Soviet type. Its fighting power and shock effect against second-line or logistic troops, headquarters and the like are likewise beyond dispute. Retaining as it does the mobility of the rotor, it could wreak widespread havoc in the enemy's rear.

One of the brigade's key roles is evidently the establishment of a blocking position on the enemy's line of retreat. Here it is fully capable of conducting a hammer-and-anvil action—another reason for it to have a preponderance of attack helicopters (tank equivalents).

The question marks hang over the rotary-wing brigade's ability to hold ground, and to carry out sustained actions against the enemy's main manoeuvre force. Here one must bear in mind that the intensity of indirect fire is already making the holding of ground with infantry at high density a thing of the past. Both high-density defenders and those who concentrate unduly to attack them will be pulverised. So one is already thinking of controlling ground by establishing "anvils of fire", shaped by troops as opposed to filled by them, on key ground, and by practising fire and movement elsewhere. In the blocking role the brigade could expect to come within range of ground force artillery by the time the enemy reacted seriously to its presence. In this event it would be just as capable as any other type of force of conducting a fire-based hammer-and-anvil battle. More generally, one would expect its ability to control ground by surveillance, fire and manoeuvre to be similar to that of a light armoured division. An important point here is that the helicopter's ability to "pop up" greatly increases useful intervisibility distances. Roughly speaking, it provides "area-to-area" intervisibility over "crest-to-crest" distances (Fig. 10, page 68). It is not too hard to get an idea of how a rotary-wing force might control ground by extrapolating from German defensive techniques employing low-level fire and movement by mechanised forces.

Much as I like to work from the bottom up, I find it very difficult to envisage just how helicopters operating tactically in the same role as armoured vehicles would behave. And this is undoubtedly one of the credibility gaps which the advocates of operational rotary-wing forces have to bridge. Evidently they would be no more capable of pushing home an attack against a main manoeuvre force with tactical air defence deployed than light armour would against that force's tanks. On the other hand, given even lightly featured terrain, both light armour and rotary-wing forces are at much less disadvantage against an enemy force with heavy armour coming at them. Light armour can use close country, and to some extent soft going which is awkward for or impassable to heavy armour. And, as we saw, a helicopter force can use ground tactically without depending on it for mobility. Provided that they are content to contain it, nibble at its edges with in-and-out dashes, and employ indirect fire against its centre, both a light armoured force and a helicopter force should be able to attain a favourable ratio of attrition rates against a heavy mechanised force. But they would need freedom to manoeuvre, by giving ground if needs be.

For at all levels these light forces must employ the judo of manoeuvre theory rather than the trading of punches which underlies attrition theory. Since all such forces derive much of their combat worth from momentum rather than from physical fighting power, they must not be employed in situations where they cannot manoeuvre to develop momentum. On the other hand, their grassroots tactical agility probably offsets their lack of physical fighting power (weight per man) to a greater extent than is commonly supposed. We are entering an era of warfare in which it is very much better not to get hit!

Conclusion

Few, I think, would disagree with Fuller when he writes of "military thought, which in recent history has never been less than a generation behind the civilian thought of its day". Being far more revolutionary than the track, the rotor will not easily win the acceptance it evidently deserves. It is surprising that even the world's two most powerful armies will have a substantial operational helicopter force deployed by the mid eighties. We have seen how the rotor drives a coach and four through conventional military wisdom by putting paid to the linear imperative of movement, and by allowing troops to use ground tactically without depending on it for mobility.

But the real significance of the rotor lies a good stratum deeper even than this. With a tempo only one order of magnitude greater than human and animal muscle—infantry on their feet backed by draught horses—could achieve, the *Panzertruppe* still had considerable mass. Its divisions had roughly as many men as infantry divisions, and with organic weight per man four to five times that of the infantry, the *Panzertruppe* still had considerable physical fighting power (Chapter 5). By contrast, helitroops derive most of their combat worth from momentum. Should a helicopter force be deprived of both operational and tactical mobility, of both actual and potential momentum, as it might be by running out of fuel, its combat worth would drop from that of a tank division to that of an infantry battalion. In his concept Senger prepositions fuel and ammunition, flying it in with his skeleton reconnaissance and C^3 advance parties. But it could still get lost or destroyed. Whether helitroops can become an acceptable substitute for a mechanised manoeuvre force, rather than a complement to it, is a question that has to be asked. In the next chapter I shall attempt to indicate how one might set about answering it.

On the other hand, the evolution of rotary-wing forces is but one of at least five trends which at once run parallel and are to a large extent mutually independent. The first and most tangible is the way the combination of surveillance and firepower is putting paid to concepts based on high troop densities. Second, at the other extreme, is the evolution of first and second world cultures away from bellicism (to borrow once again from Michael Howard). Already, given time, world opinion mobilises itself against *any* use of armed force; and this is one factor in Soviet thinking on the "unusability" of organised forces which forms the subject of Chapter 18. Third, there is the efficacy, now being proven anew almost every week, of revolutionary warfare techniques in the shape of "state-sponsored terrorism". In tune with these is another broad influence of technology which I shall examine in Chapter 10—the way technological advance is shifting the

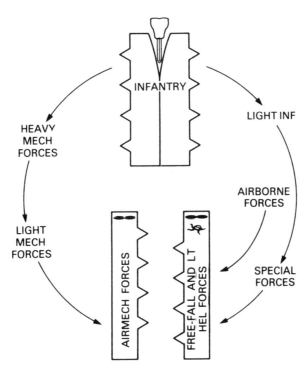

FIG. 37. *Illustration of the notion of technology "turning armies inside out".*

element of chance from the conduct of operations to the achievement and maintenance of surprise.

The fifth trend can be seen as the fruit of these; but it has also gained a life of its own, from communications-induced acceleration of the geopolitical tempo, from the inability of conscript forces to handle modern equipment, and not least from the economic burden of equipping and maintaining mass armed forces. The mass armies of the nineteenth and twentieth centuries, with their clutter of baroque equipment, are beginning to give way to small, light specialised forces. This does not mean that mass armies will soon be disbanded and their heavy metal scrapped; I shall argue in Part 5 that they will join or supplant nuclear arsenals as the unusable deterrent. But the backbone of most armies is still line infantry. Technology is cleaving this backbone of mass down the middle, drawing the two halves apart, and bringing them together back-to-back to form a new spine centred on momentum, a notion I have tried to depict in Fig. 37. On the one hand, heavy mechanised forces are giving way to light ones, and these in turn to airmechanised forces, *alias* helitroops. On the other, the emphasis is swinging from "standard" infantry via light infantry to the combination of special forces, airborne troops and helitroops now represented by the Soviet Airborne Forces. The interface between this ultra-light cavalry and ultra-light infantry is the rotor. The rotary-wing revolution may in the end literally turn armies inside out.

8

Combat Worth

"Thus what is of supreme importance in war is to attack the enemy's strategy, next best is to disrupt his alliances; the next best is to attack his army. The worst policy is to attack cities."   SUN TZU

"Whole campaigns can be conducted at a high level of activity without actual fighting playing any significant part in them."   CLAUSEWITZ

"Moreover, the decision may be produced by the paralysing initial effect of strokes delivered by a comparatively small mechanised element."   LIDDELL HART

"If a solution cannot be reached without battle, this imposes on you the strategic aim to force battle at the time, and under the conditions, most favourable tactically to yourself."   MAHAN

Introduction—the limits of manoeuvre theory

Back in the fifties, when battlefield nuclear weapons were first being discussed, many regarded their distinguishing feature not as the extent to which they could change a situation but as the *suddenness* of that change. This line of thought highlighted a principle which, often tacitly, underlies most theories of war. War is a process of change, and the tempo must not be so fast as to vitiate the sequence of change and response to change. Although first-rate armies are now capable of integrating battlefield nuclear weapons into this pattern—or at least believe themselves to be so—the shock effect of these weapons puts their use very close to the borderline between warfare and meaningless destruction, a border which nuclear and chemical weapons of mass destruction lie beyond. From this pattern of change and response follows a second principle, likewise often tacitly assumed. It is that the opposing forces must be similar enough to interact. This is the grain of truth at the heart of the notion of "like fights like"—a hypothesis in which, as I have said already and shall say again, I for one can find no sense.

Here one must restate three fundamental points. At root manoeuvre theory has nothing to do with vast numbers of men and machines charging about the countryside. Manoeuvre theory is about amplifying the force which a small mass is capable of exerting; it is synonymous with the indirect approach. On the other hand this mass, however small, must be capable of conveying enough physical fighting power to offer a threat that is, or at least is seen by the opposition to be, commensurate with the aim. (I shall examine the question of bluff in Chapter 11). Third, the manoeuvre theory system as a whole must contain an element of mass which remains available to respond to changes in the situation. In familiar terms, there must be a *reserve*, and this reserve should be recreated as it is expended. At the other end of the scale, we have seen in the preceding chapters how the possibility of applying manoeuvre multipliers varies inversely with mass—the outstanding example of this being the effect on tempo of the physical laws governing troop movement. Thus mass limits the effect of the whole synergetic system of manoeuvre multipliers depicted in Fig. 29 (page 113).

Sufficient and minimum mass

Not even the most diehard of addicts of attrition will I think question that tempo enhances combat worth. But in approaching the concept "combat worth", one needs to see whether or not increasing mass or physical fighting power, even at no sacrifice in tempo, would also enhance combat worth.

This must be so within a very limited range. Though they might not put it this way, most people would probably agree that the ideal allocation of troops to tasks lay near the top of the well-sloped section of the diminishing returns curve (Fig. 38)—say at a 75 to 80 per cent probability of complete success (between 4 and 5 to 1 on). This would generally carry with it the near

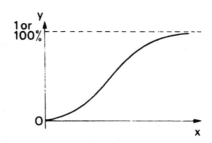

FIG. 38. *Law of diminishing returns, general case.*

certainty of a partial success good enough to set up a favourable pattern of "change and response". Where complete success is of particular importance, it would make sense to improve the chance by going onto the flattening part of the curve if this could be achieved without loss of tempo, or of concentration in time and space. For instance, a Soviet operational manoeuvre group aiming to seize a Rhine crossing might well be reinforced by allocation of a tactical helicopter lift of infantry to the leading tank regiment. But beyond this, increase in mass contributes nothing in theory, and brings a nest of problems in practice.

One thus arrives at a concept of a "sufficient mass" which it is normally pointless to exceed at all, and always pointless to exceed by more than a modest margin of insurance. This stands out clearly both from the Soviet equivalences based on momentum, and from the pattern of development of their mobile force from the forties to the present. In that instance, the right mass and physical fighting power for the job is something over 10 000 men with an organic weight per man of about 4 tonnes (Chapter 5), and give or take 500 major tactical vehicles. The vast tank army of the battlefield nuclear heyday was fine for rolling over a nuclear carpet but unmanageable if real manoeuvre should be called for.

At the other extreme, a responsive system requires a mobile force with enough mass to ensure **flexibility**. This sets a *lower limit to mass*. Thus the need to maintain tempo and concentration in time on the one hand, and the need for flexibility on the other, impose upper and lower limits of mass for a given mission and situation. One is thus led towards the notion of an *optimum mass*, and indeed of an equilibrium between mass, organic weight per man and tempo.

Combat worth

I must now bring into the open the tacit assumption I made in Chapter 5—that for kinetic and chemical energy weapons firepower per tonne of deadweight is roughly constant, so that "organic weight per man" is a sound indicator of firepower. Given this, one can fairly say that the combat worth of the holding force, and the level of threat conveyed by the mobile force—in other words the latter's combat worth if it is forced to fight—will be its *physical fighting power*. This is something which remains unchanged however the force finds itself placed.

If we take *tempo* as standing for the synergetic system of manoeuvre multipliers, we can say that combat worth in manoeuvre, based on momentum, is the product of physical fighting power and tempo—or of mass, organic weight per man and tempo. This definition in fact matches known Soviet thinking on equivalences considerably more closely than just taking the product of mass and tempo. Because tempo is a complex dynamic quantity whose elements interact synergetically, it is something one cannot have enough of. But the dam will not always burst on its own; it may have to be blown to release the floodwaters. For ground forces proper (as opposed to helitroops), tempo will often be limited by going and, in the early stages of an operation, by the tactical situation. By the same token, terrain—or, in the case of long-range intervention, carrying capacity—may limit organic weight per man.

We have seen how the maintenance of tempo and concentration on the one hand, and the need for flexibility on the other set limits to mass. Unfortunately, though, the conventional approach of deriving combat worth from mass and a series of multipliers (which I have used and shall continue to use) does not lead one to a *generally* valid concept of combat worth. By contrast, "mass and multipliers" is an invaluable tool in operational planning, where the requirement is to estimate the combat worth of a given force *in a given situation on given terrain*. Here, the commander has enough fixed values to arrive at a pretty good idea of *relative physical combat worths for the operation envisaged, both of his own force with respect to the enemy, and of the various types of formation available to him with respect to one another.*

This is of course exactly what a commander does by subjective judgement, and I am not suggesting that a string of multiplication sums will help the good general do it any better. In fact the approach outlined above exemplifies both the value and the limitations of an analysis of the physics of war. The analysis provides a set of objective principles or ground rules which may help in forming judgement without unduly restricting the exercise of it, and in building the common outlook among commanders at all levels called for by directive control (Part 4). These ground rules should also prevent the blunders in planning so frequent in military history—they are "guides which warn when it is going to go wrong". By the same token, this discussion of combat worth excellently illustrates the danger of exalting relative concepts to the status of absolutes.

With this reservation in mind, one can look at the problem of strategic planning and force structure. Each strategic aim must be supported by a scenario which postulates situation, terrain and communications, and the existing force structure must be taken as a starting point. This places the strategic planner in a similar position to the operational commander in the field, though with wider margins both of error and of free play. From here the planner proceeds by trial and error. This is in fact very much the way things happen now. But this approach does bring the useful idea of balance—in Montgomery's sense of keeping one's options open. For there is one other great difference between the operational commander and the strategic planner. The latter may be utterly wrong—in using a crystal ball with a range of a decade or two, he may well plan for the wrong intervention in the wrong theatre, and for countering a primary threat derived from the wrong geopolitical situation.

This balance is in fact the safeguard against the commander or the planner being wrong. And the degree of imbalance acceptable diminishes up through the levels as the margin of error grows. The efficient allocation of troops to tasks probably demands high tactical imbalance. The same is partly true of operational imbalance; this is acceptable so long as the basic assumptions over the scope and duration of the operation or campaign hold. If they fall, as they did for Operation Barbarossa when the campaign extended into the Russian winter, disaster may result unless the imbalance can be corrected. Strategic imbalance is surely most dangerous. The assumptions which underlie it are in turn based on political decisions which may be reversed at the drop of a ballot form. To see this, one has only to imagine the state of Britain's defence policy and the British Army if the British Army of the Rhine were to be pulled out of Germany at short notice, say as part of an agreement over a unified neutral Germany. The effect on the United States Army of pulling out 7 (US) Army would be tolerable because 7 (US) Army is part of a much greater whole and its specialised nature thus creates less imbalance.

Interchangeability, neutralisation and annihilation

The Soviet principle of interchangeability of fire and combat troops, of shell and bayonet if you like, seems to go back at least to the nineteenth century, when the French and Tsarist Armies shared a world lead in artillery. Certainly Triandafillov takes it for granted. The concept achieved unquestionable validity in the battlefield nuclear heyday of the sixties; even in the 1980 edition of Babadzhanyan one finds hangovers from earlier editions in which a battlefield nuclear strike and the manoeuvre of a (large) tank army are at once equated and shown to be complementary. But only recent and predicted advances in the application and terminal ballistics of indirect fire have begun to move the West away from its traditional view that the shell neutralises the enemy and the bayonet or machine carbine defeats him. At the same time the current Soviet ammunition norms show scales for "destruction" and "neutralisation" ("suppression"), implying, I think, that only the former can be equated with the effect of troops. So there is a large grey zone here, darkened further by the addict of attrition's insistence on what he would call "cut-and-dried precision of thought" and others might term "thinking in blinkers".

Before feeling our way through this fog, let us establish one respect in which, as we saw in Chapter 6, fire and troops are *not* interchangeable. Once delivered, fire poses no further threat, except perhaps within the limited though important scope of delayed-effect munitions. The results of fire may be devastating at the physical or psychological level, or at both. But they can be seen and measured or estimated; in effect they present the commander of the force fired on with a new discrete situation. The only way to impose a firepower *threat* ("potential energy" as I have called it) on a target is to place projectors where they can bring fire to bear on it. At one extreme this threat is, as we saw, a key component of the combat worth of the mobile force. At the other it lies with long-range aircraft and missiles. This span is one of the foundations of that other Soviet tenet, simultaneity, which we shall be exploring in the next chapter. For the moment let us be absolutely clear that, in the indirect approach which is the essence of manoeuvre theory, the application of fire is in no way comparable to the manoeuvre of a mobile force.

First, though, one must accept Clausewitz's view that, in the last resort, the power of a military force lies in its physical capability to fight and its moral readiness to do so—a view which Mahan, as so often, expresses more lucidly and puts in perspective. This means we must examine interchangeability in terms of fighting. Nobody, I think, has any doubt about the effect of a successful infantry attack. The objective is cleared of enemy, and enemy who do not get away become casualties or prisoners. The defending force is "destroyed" in the common usage of that word. Next let us take the traditional Western view of the role of firepower in this same attack. The artillery provides covering fire, progressively neutralising enemy positions as the infantry comes within view of them; direct fire support weapons, including tanks, "shoot the infantry in" after troop safety forces the artillery to lift. Both indirect and more particularly direct fire may, probably will, destroy a number of targets; but this is a bonus, incidental to neutralisation. The tremendous emphasis placed on co-ordination of the fire plan and the infantry's advance stems from the belief that this neutralisation only lasts as long as the fire is going down.

Strangely, the Western Allies of the Second World War and, I think, the Germans of that vintage too regarded shelling as purely suppressive and bombing as destructive. Perhaps the best known example of this fallacy was the pattern bombing of the German depth positions facing Second Army in Operation Overlord. Putting both sides' accounts together, one sees that this bombing was successful, had a devastating effect, and did effectively knock the Germans out for some hours. But by the time the advancing troops reached these positions, the defenders had recovered and reorganised well enough to offer resistance which resulted in some particularly bloody and protracted fighting. On the other hand, there are a number of instances from the Eastern Front where encircled German forces were able to break out quickly and cleanly as a result of tactical bombing by the Luftwaffe of a sector of the Red Army ring. With good ground-air co-ordination, the effects of the bombing lasted long enough for the troops to take advantage of them. (These operations, incidentally, reflect both the Luftwaffe's gallantry and their readiness to support ground troops at great risk to themselves.)

This gives us, very appropriately, a historical bracket on the duration of effect of high-intensity fire. In other words, we have introduced a notion of **extended neutralisation**, an effect which lasts for minutes or hours after the fire has lifted. While I had not come across this term until I coined it in an earlier book (*Antitank*), it was evident in both Soviet and Western views about the follow-up of battlefield nuclear strikes. We are now at or very near the point at which conventional artillery and tactical air can achieve something approaching the surprise and intensity of the battlefield nuclear strikes envisaged in the sixties. So let us put down this concept of extended neutralisation as a marker.

We can now come at the problem the other way by examining the meaning of "destruction" or, to use the literal translation of Clausewitz's term also adopted in some contexts by the Russians, "annihilation". In a fully revised and therefore presumably valid passage, Clausewitz leaves us in no doubt what he means by this (see quotation page 11). To the attrition-minded "a condition in which it can no longer take part in the conflict" means that the members of the enemy force must be wounded, captured or killed. But manoeuvre theory uses a time base of hours as opposed to days, weeks, months or indeed years. A force which has been bypassed and turned becomes irrelevant to the further development of the operation; what happens to it subsequently is a tactical matter for the holding force. Thus "annihilation" in the Clausewitzian sense comes to mean "putting out of action for a number of hours"—which is nothing more nor less than extended neutralisation. The operationally necessary duration gives us our other marker, and we are now sailing up a clear channel as opposed to wallowing about in the fog.

So it is surprising that the Soviet norms on ammunition scales do not lay down three levels of fire—"simultaneous neutralisation", "extended neutralisation" and "destruction". In fact I find their use of "destruction" in these tables rather ambiguous because it covers both material targets, which certainly can be "destroyed" in the primary meaning of that word, and areas occupied by troops, which probably cannot. In fact they cover this distinction—and make my point—by defining "destruction" differently for point and area targets:

> for *point targets* (almost always materiel) it means a 90 per cent probability that the target is no longer fit for combat.

> for *area targets* a 90 per cent or better chance that at least 50 per cent of the target elements are no longer fit for combat, and/or elements in at least 50 per cent of the target area are unfit for combat (not necessarily the same thing).

What is more, these norms are just a basic scale; several norms may be put down on one target within the same fire plan. I suspect that in some document I have not seen there is a table relating number of norms and rate of fire to duration of neutralisation.

Be this as it may, it seems sensible to steer clear of the rather misleading terms "destruction" and "annihilation" and think simply in terms of *rendering the enemy force operationally irrelevant*. On the one hand, this may be achieved by any combination of extended neutralisation by fire and fighting by combat troops; for this, following one German precedent, I shall use the term **(physical) disruption**. For rendering irrelevant by turning, by the combination of potential energy and potential momentum that makes up the mobile force threat, I shall employ the term "dislocation".

Dislocation, pre-emption and deterrence

Under attrition theory, the process of change and response which is war can only be set and kept in motion by fighting—by bringing about a change in relative strengths. Manoeuvre theory, while fully acknowledging Clausewitz's insistence on the need for physical and moral preparedness to fight, regards fighting as just one means among many of applying armed force—and a rather inelegant last resort at that. This is succinctly put by Sun Tzu, in a quotation to which I shall shamelessly revert again and again:

> "For to win one hundred victories in one hundred battles is not the acme of skill. To subdue the enemy without fighting is the acme of skill."

From this principle one can derive three modes of application of armed force, in increasing order of merit:

dislocation, implying that hostilities have broken out but that victory is to be achieved mainly by manoeuvre;

pre-emption, implying the use of manoeuvre to prevent (in the full sense of that word) the outbreak of hostilities;

deterrence, implying the inhibition of warlike actions without a move from peacetime dispositions.

We accepted earlier (Chapters 2 and 6) that once hostilities had broken out, attrition and manoeuvre theories ceased to be opposites and became complementary—or rather that manoeuvre theory then embraced attrition theory. In operations or strategic actions aimed at dislocation, three types of fighting are likely to occur. There may be a need for attritional action to clear the way for insertion of the mobile force, that is to gain freedom of action or, if you like, operational superiority; and similarly to gain sea and air superiority, at least within the theatre. Second, there is likely to be tactical combat, skirmishing at least, by the mobile force to gain local freedom of action for its manoeuvres. Third, semi-clandestine and clandestine operations by special forces and agents may call for deliberate violence and/or result in outbursts of fighting due to loss of surprise—as for instance in an attack on a headquarters already at partial or full alert. Mobile forces may also become locked in fierce and critical combat, as they do in the encounter battle, in the situation following delivery of the hammer-blow in a hammer-and-anvil defence, or in counter-thrusts against the main or advanced hinge on which an advancing mobile force is pivoting.

Pre-emption is best exemplified by the "fleet in being" theory expounded, with some reservations, by Mahan, who attributes it to the seventeenth-century British sailor, Admiral Tovington, and also links it to some of Jomini's thinking. Mahan states the theory like this:

"The presence of a strong force, even though inferior, near the scene of operations will produce a momentous effect on the enemy's action."

Mutatis mutandis, the broad lines of Mahan's thinking resemble Tukhachevskii's deep operation theory rather closely. In a nutshell, the fleet corresponds to the mobile force, the base or forward base to the (advanced) hinge, and its fortifications to the holding force.

The key words in Mahan's statement are "inferior" and "near", because these imply leverage. He demonstrates how the movement of this inferior fleet relative to the enemy and his objective, accompanied if needs be by the establishment of a forward base, can be used to increase or reduce tension to match the political or military imminence of the threat. Mahan, of course, presupposes two opposing fleets of roughly the same mobility, low by today's standards and separated only by margins of design and seamanship.

One can envisage a modern land counterpart to this in the strategic prepositioning and operational movement of a force, particularly in possible intervention theatres. But with the tempos of modern missile and fixed-wing forces, and perhaps of airmechanised forces, a more sophisticated way to play this game could well lie in states of readiness and alert. The scope this offers is well exemplified by one of the two major pieces of hypocrisy in NATO's position. NATO thinking rules out the possibility of an attack on it launched with strategic surprise, basing virtually the whole of its conventional land capability on a warning period of up to 10 days. As I have argued elsewhere, keeping a force one-third of the size in pre-deployment positions at a genuine readiness of, say, 1 hour—the equivalent of keeping an inferior fleet at sea and positioned well forward—would magnify many times over both the credibility and the actual capability of the counter-threat, thus raising the level of conventional deterrence.

The distinction between pre-emption and deterrence is by no means clear-cut. As I see it, pre-emption implies a departure from peacetime posture, by strategic movement of forces and/or raising the state of readiness or alert. Whether offensive or defensive, pre-emption is a positive act calculated to produce enough leverage, in other words a sufficient and suitably located mobile threat, to force the enemy into military submission or inhibit him from taking the action he apparently intends.

Deterrence, on the other hand, is the leverage exerted on each other by two potential opponents in their peacetime posture. I shall examine these strategic and political aspects of manoeuvre theory more fully in Part 5. For the moment I just want to highlight one multiplier that applies to pre-emption and in some instances to deterrence. The movement or presence of even a token force in a way that applies leverage to the opposition is often enough to demonstrate commitment or to give credibility to aid under a treaty. Thus conventional wisdom has it that the presence of 7 (US) Army and British Army of the Rhine in the Federal Republic deters the Warsaw Pact both by the combat worth of those forces and by the guarantee of involvement that their presence gives.

Human multipliers

I have used the word "physical" *ad nauseam* to qualify combat worth and other terms I have adopted, so as to keep in the forefront of our minds the overriding importance of the human qualities to which Part 4 is devoted. I use the term "*human* multipliers" because genius and a wide range skills at many levels are of the same order of importance as morale. In fact, as all but the British agree, generalship, training and fitness, all mainly matters of brains and aptitudes, are the best basis of morale.

All these factors bear just as heavily on the worth of a force in deterrence or pre-emption as they do once hostilities have broken out. Like tempo, reputation has a synergetic effect. However his fellow Germans may rate Rommel, one of the most striking examples of this, which I personally experienced, was the grip he gained on the British in North Africa. His image and repute, contrasted with the glaring incompetence of the British formation commanders of the Auchinleck era, effectively transferred the respect of junior officers and soldiers from their own superiors to their opponent. In my experience at least, regimental spirit prevented any wavering of loyalty; but this might well have followed in the end, had not Montgomery appreciated the problem and gone to extreme lengths to overcome it. On a lighter note, although the Germans were "the enemy" when I was an infant, I well recall my first remembered nanny saying— "Stop that at once, or Boney'll get you." (Napoleon, she meant, not Fuller!)

Conclusion

Physical fighting power, tempo and momentum are physically valid concepts and, as I believe I have demonstrated, also make military sense as absolute values within manoeuvre theory. So nothing could be simpler, one might think, than to put physical fighting power and tempo together to arrive at "combat worth", a quantity dimensionally the equivalent of momentum. The concept of *relative* combat worth, both between opposing sides and between types of formation on the same side, is clearly an excellent tool when used within the framework of an operational plan or a strategic scenario. The dimensions of combat worth, tonne-kilometres per day, stand for a parameter valid for and familiar to logisticians, but with little apparent meaning for the operational or tactical commander. It is in fact an expression of the "movement of masses" in the most literal sense of that phrase. Similarly, when one tries to approach an absolute definition of combat worth from common sense, one hits a rock.

I think one can fairly say that this rock is terrain, and in particular the duality of its tactical and operational significance. The quality of *going* it offers frequently limits physical mobility—thus tempo and combat worth in manoeuvre—while its *tactical strength* enhances the combat worth of every kind of opposition to manoeuvre. Since terrain also has a large hand both in imposing the need for flexibility and in limiting concentration in time and space, it is a major factor, if not the governing one, in determining the sufficient and minimum masses for a given operation or strategic action.

For just these reasons, the main positive conclusion that leaps out of this chapter is fuel to the fires of the rotary-wing revolution. Because they can exploit the tactical strength of terrain without depending on it for mobility, and because they can disperse, move and concentrate free of the restrictions of linearity, helicopters, as opposed to ultra-high-mobility surface vehicles, are the true means of conducting "naval warfare on land".

An operational helicopter force substantial enough also to act as an independent strategic force is the land equivalent of a blue-water fleet. It not only increases the tempo of manoeuvre by an order of magnitude but, as a "fleet in being", makes manoeuvre theory fully applicable to deterrence and pre-emption. I shall consider the strategic mobility of such a force in the next chapter. As to its size, various analogies from land and sea suggest that two brigades of the kind envisaged in the preceding chapter (about one hundred first line machines each) would represent a minimum, and three such brigades a sufficiency for most operations or strategic actions. I do not for one moment suggest that entire armies should take to the rotary wing; on the other hand, I reckon that the discussion in this chapter also reinforces the final conclusion of the preceding one—that the rotary wing will tend to turn armies inside out and progressively free them from their "baroque" collections of heavy equipment.

Last but not least, seen in relation to high-tempo operations, the concept of extended neutralisation at once elucidates the Soviet concept of interchangeability and resolves the apparent conflict of Soviet and Western views on this subject. Discussion of this has also served to re-emphasise the complementarity of, and interaction between manoeuvre theory and attrition theory—in particular the imperative need for a force to be, and to be seen to be, physically capable of fighting and morally prepared to fight, if it is to exert an effective threat.

9

The Club Sandwich Battle

"164. With all military resources acting in concert, the offensive battle must be founded on the basically simultaneous neutralisation of all depths of the enemy's defence.   PU-36 (Soviet Field Service Regulations 1936)

Introduction—simultaneity

My search of the past for a parallel with the club sandwich battle of the future led me back, courtesy of Liddell Hart and Arrian (Flavius Arrianus), to Alexander the Great's decisive victory at Arbela (or Gaugamela) in 331 B.C. I refrain from quoting this, as the three paragraphs describing the opposing forces' dispositions are about as gripping as the genealogical passages of Kings. The only other analogy that occurred to me was the description of orgies in Steven Marcus's delightful book *The Other Victorians*, memorable because of the resemblance between the mechanics of these performances and the complex steam-engine valve gears invented by Stephenson and others.

So I decided to approach the discussion through the Soviet principle of simultaneity. Soviet authorities from Tukhachevskii onwards accept this principle as fundamental, while Western masters of manoeuvre still tend to pooh-pooh it. I believe this is in part due to the radically different way in which Soviet and Western commanders approach operational planning (pages 107/108). The Russians think inwards from the extremities and thus on the time scale of the operation as a whole. I am fairly certain that Western generals, including Germans of Wehrmacht vintage, envisage the operation as *se déroulant* and apply time scales appropriate to each phase. In Soviet eyes, simultaneity, like interchangeability (page 137), is something between a practical aim and an ideal—a useful way of looking at the problem. Both came to fruition in the heyday of the battlefield nuclear weapon. Since then, advances in mobility and in conventional firepower have made both valid for conventional warfare too.

Because of Western incredulity, I explored this question in some depth in *Red Armour*, and have analysed it further since. Since discussion of simultaneity of action calls for simultaneity of expression, I have drawn my thoughts together in Figs. 39 and 40. The first of these charts compares the

145

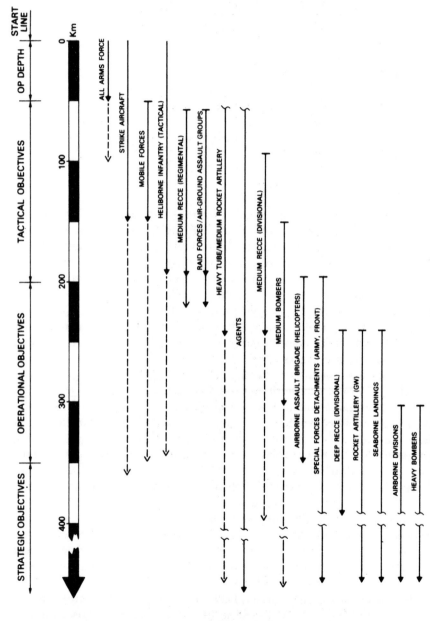

FIG. 39. *Chart to show Soviet use of "forces and resources" to achieve simultaneity.*

SPEED ORDER OF (KPH)	MEANS		NATURE OF DIFFERENCE	TEMPO RATIOS
(10⁴) (HIGH THOUSANDS) 10³ (LOW THOUSANDS)	PROJECTILES FIXED WING	⌐ FAST JETS └ TRANS ACFT	PHYS MOB	4-5:1
10² (HUNDREDS)	ROTOR	⌐ OP FORCE └ TAC GP	PHYS MOB	2-3:1
10¹ (TENS)	TRACK	⌐ FAST TRACKS └ HEAVY TRACKS	PHYS MOB	2:1
10⁰ (UNIT)	BOOT HOLDING FORCE		HANDLING	2-3:1
			PHYS MOB OPPOSING FORCE	2:1

FIG. 40. *Speeds of means of conveyance/projection, and desirable tempo ratios between them.*

"forces and resources" available to the modern Soviet front and theatre commander with typical depths for offensive operations and for strategic actions. The full line shows the preferred depth zone (or range zone) for employment of each, the broken line their physical capability of quasi-simultaneous action beyond this. From this chart one sees at a glance that the whole concept of deployment and employment of the various elements turns on simultaneity; and that simultaneity in turn depends on acceptance of interchangeability. Given this, the various means of bringing pressure to bear make up a well-balanced and continuous spectrum over the full operational—and indeed strategic—depth. On the other hand, simultaneity, again like interchangeability, needs to be taken with a pinch of salt.

It is patently nonsensical to imagine this vast complex of elements all impinging on their initial objectives or targets precisely at H hour. Some of the most important, like the main mobile force, the tactical heliborne force, or the raid forces, depend on the initial success of other components. Others require preliminary action to achieve a suitable air or electronic warfare situation. To convince the down-to-earth Anglo-Saxon that simultaneity is a genuine and workable principle, one must try to explore what the Russian mind makes of the term. Just as in the case of interchangeability, relativity comes into play.

If one is eating out, one expects the meat and vegetables to be served "at the same time". Here a delay of only a minute or two is enough for the meat to start getting cold, the sauce to begin congealing, and the diner to look round for the waiter. If one is conducting some kind of three-sided negotiation by letter, one might fairly say "I heard from X and Y at the same time" meaning on the same day or even on successive days. If one goes into hospital for an operation and arranges to have some other minor condition treated "at the same time", this just means "while I am in hospital"— perhaps a matter of weeks. The common factor here is not chronometric time but the time needed to complete a *change-and-response cycle*, response time, or the "decision loop" as the Americans call it. The Russians evidently regard two actions as "exerting simultaneous pressure" if one follows the other within the enemy's response time at the level affected. I suggest this may be a useful understanding of simultaneity both in the military context and generally.

Relative tempos

Even so, the ability to achieve simultaneity of pressure over a depth of several hundred kilometres evidently depends on the relative tempos of the various components of the manoeuvre theory model. Grouping the elements of Fig. 39 by their means of locomotion or projection, one arrives at Fig. 40. While the order of magnitude into which (fixed-wing) transport aircraft fall depends on the unit of speed chosen, the gradation by orders is otherwise clear-cut, bearing out the notion of a club sandwich. In Chapter 6 (pages 101–109) we discussed the relative velocities of the components of a manoeuvre theory system in general terms and went on to substitute tempo for velocity. We now need to look in more detail at the nature of these differences in tempo and at the tempo ratios between successive elements of the system.

The physical mobility of its equipment sets an upper limit on the tempo a force can achieve. The transport aircraft which carry airborne troops cannot deviate greatly from the tempo represented by their cruising speed. Hélitroops can vary their tempo downwards. But if they fly from their departure area to their objective below "range speed" (about 90 per cent of maximum speed for modern machines) they reduce the chance of surprise, expose themselves avoidably and waste fuel. More important perhaps, their combat worth is so dependent on tempo—in other words on surprise and shock—that it is substantially degraded by slowing down.

With ground troops, by contrast, there is no difficulty in operating below the tempo set by physical mobility unless they move so slowly as to lose much of their indirect protection. The light armoured force mounted in fast tracks with good trafficability is a borderline case. When faced by an enemy with main battle tanks, a force of this kind derives much of its ability to survive from indirect protection as opposed to armour, and not a little of its combat worth from tempo. So it can only be handled in slow time when some extrinsic multiplier such as thick cover or tactically strong ground favours it.

In most advanced armies, however, the holding and mobile elements of the main mechanised force now have the same major tactical vehicles. By the same token, their structures are becoming ever more similar. Over the past 10 years, the tank–infantry ratios in the principal types of Soviet division have converged. When tank battalion strengths as well as numbers of battalions are taken into account, the mechanised division is now almost balanced; and the tank division has a ratio of ten battalions to six as against the previous ten to three. By the nineties, as already mentioned, these two types of division may well have been merged into a single "shock division". The United States "ROAD" armoured and mechanised divisions of the sixties will be reorganising as Types A and B Heavy Divisions as this book appears, with Type A just six to four tank-heavy and Type B balanced. The Federal German Army still has armoured and mechanised divisions with a tank-infantry ratio of about two to one and one to two respectively. But trends in doctrine, force structure and equipment suggest that this could well change in a few years' time. The "armoured" division is now the British Army's only type of mechanised formation; it is balanced, albeit at a level which does more for politicking and peacetime promotion than for combat worth.

There are in fact very strong arguments, some of which we saw in Chapter 6, for the holding force and the initial (heavy track) mobile force having the same physical mobility, and indeed being found from the same type of formation. To develop the leverage which is the key to the turning operation, the holding force must close up to the enemy and maintain contact with him. Ideally it should draw him forward; in the early stages at least it must hold him forward. But sooner or later he is going to pull back. He will either fight a delayed action or attempt a clean break followed by a rapid withdrawal. The holding force must have the physical mobility to maintain contact with him, even in the pursuit situation. The tempo of his withdrawal should be slowed down as a result of envelopment by the mobile force or the insertion of a blocking force; but it may not be. To allow for friction, the holding force should be able to operate at *twice* the tempo of the opposition. And to ensure maintaining contact even in the opening stages of a rout, most of this advantage should be provided by physical mobility rather than handling. This establishes for the holding force both a minimum physical mobility, and a handling tempo in the holding force role—the level above ground, so to speak, of the bottom rung in the mobility ladder.

We saw in Chapter 6 that, much as common sense would suggest, healthy development of the lever arm requires the mobile force to work at a tempo *between two and three times* that of the holding force. If it is less than twice, the mobile force will not be able to get clear fast enough to establish a turning situation, or to maintain that situation if the holding force and the enemy main force come onto the move. If the ratio is much over three, the lever arm may break simply through overstretch, and the hinge between holding force and mobile force becomes dangerously vulnerable to counter-attack.

Achieving this ratio by handling alone poses a very severe training problem. There are certain evident differences in tactics and procedures, many of them well exemplified by Soviet practice. In tank divisions the tanks practise fire and movement by companies, a whole company moving together. (In British jargon, the company is the "tactical unit".) In the mechanised division, the tank companies are larger, and the tactical unit is the platoon. Introducing this lowest level of fire and movement theoretically halves tempo. In the tank division, the mechanised infantry fights mounted unless or until the tactical situation forces it to dismount. In the mechanised division, it normally dismounts for the final stages of an attack, and in defence. In tank formations and battle groups, only the initial orders are given orally and supported by the "operation document"; after that control is exercised by radio. In mechanised battalion groups, certain operations are covered by standing operating procedures (SOPs), but for the rest traditional infantry battle drills (reconnaissance groups, orders groups and so on) are generally followed. I have accumulated a good deal of evidence to suggest that this may temporarily lower tempo by as much as a factor of ten. So on paper there is evidently scope for achieving a twofold or threefold increase in tempo by different handling.

On the other hand, the two types of handling are the outward and visible signs of two different modes of thought. The tank man halts between moves; the infantryman moves between positions. I know of only two examples of the necessary duality of approach and technique having been achieved. One was Manteuffel's Panzergrenadier Division Gross-deutschland; the other was the British motor battalion—a concept in the true Sir John Moore tradition, realised by the regiments now amalgamated as the Royal Green Jackets, and destroyed because its excellence was more than the egalitarianism of postwar Britain could stomach. Having spent much of my service with troops in the infantry support role, I am brutally familiar with this problem in the British Army. It was just as striking in the Bundeswehr, even in the early days when tank and mechanised infantry commanding officers (and some company commanders) were Wehrmacht-trained; now it is even more marked. It has long been a running sore in the United States Army; and a visit I recently made suggests that this is far from healed. In the Soviet Army, inter-arm rivalry burst into the open with the controversy which followed the introduction of BMP1, and has stayed exposed throughout the 15 years or so over which the all-arms battle concept has been developed and pro-mulgated. Since this problem stems from the fact that standing armies are social rather than rational structures, it is unlikely to go away.

Rotor tempo is between five and ten times that of a mobile force based on heavy tracks. This suggests an uncomfortably wide gap between these two rungs—an indication borne out by evident Soviet caution over the operational employment of helitroops. The arguments are precisely the same as those on the ratio between holding force and initial mobile force, and the effect is (or at first was) to restrict the scope of the airborne assault brigade to the tactical-operational borderline. The need is for an extra rung, with a tempo ratio to the initial mobile force of about *two to one*. This is one of the main arguments for a light mechanised force mounted on fast tracks, the other being the need for it in theatres to which heavy tracks cannot be brought or in which they cannot operate. In principal theatres, a force of this kind fits very neatly into the club sandwich battle; it would be passed through after the initial mobile force had established a turning situation, just at the stage when both theory and historical examples suggest that tempo starts to accelerate.

For intervention in secondary theatres, where this light mechanised force would form the initial mobile force, very possibly the holding force as well, environmental and logistic friction are likely to slow tempo down. In any event, the combat worth of a light mechanised force has almost the ideal balance of mass and tempo for extreme flexibility. The technical advance needed to give a force of this kind teeth has already happened. It is the "light mobile protected gun" (to use the American term)—in effect an amphibious light tank with something very like the firepower of a main battle tank, and mobility matching that of the infantry fighting vehicle in all respects. Extraordinarily, at the time of writing, a vehicle of this kind (a successor to PT76) has not yet made a public appearance in the Soviet Army.

I shall revert to this light mechanised force shortly, in the highly controversial context of airborne forces. Before that, I want to develop the picture of the club sandwich battle up to the layer in which helicopters are used operationally.

The club sandwich

One must I think serve the military club sandwich with two large caveats on the side. The use of simple mechanical analogies gives a wholly false impression of firmness on the one hand and rigidity on the other; any operation of war is subject to uncertainties, and its course is often confused. More important, while comprehensiveness makes the club sandwich "with all the works" an invaluable model, complexity makes it a most improbable reality, a Pantagruelian chimera. One might look on it not so much as the sandwich itself, rather as the menu from which the military gourmet can pick fillings to suit the occasion. Once again the ambience will have to be Russian because it is the only one currently on offer; and just as inevitably, the North German Plain (Fig. 13, page 75) will have to serve as a table.

Let us envisage then, a Soviet front opening an offensive operation with a holding force of two all-arms armies less two mechanised divisions. Let us suppose—for I am reasonably sure this will happen soon—that the mechanised division has a "light regiment", in which the main battle tanks are replaced by a mix of light mobile propelled guns and tank destroyers (missile), both having the same mobility as the infantry fighting vehicle, by this time BMP3. These two divisions (both mechanised rather than tank because of the terrain), plus the front's airborne assault brigade and a standard slice of front and army artillery, an army bridging park and an airfield engineer battalion, form the front-level operational manoeuvre group under a corps-level OMG headquarters established as part of the front's order of battle (Fig. 41a). The tank army is held as a third echelon, but the front commander has put an earmark on its airborne assault brigade; and theatre (or probably "principal theatre" has allotted him an additional airborne assault brigade based in Kiev Military District and available on the Elbe by D + 1.

Thanks to excellent operational intelligence, the all-arms army on the right was able to launch a successful slashing attack down an inter-allied corps boundary, and to insert its tank division as an "army-level" OMG by noon on D Day. Although this division is referred to as an OMG and has

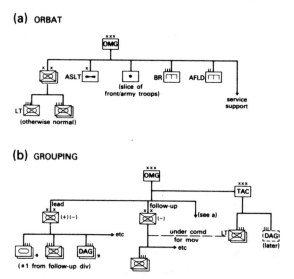

FIG. 41. *a. Possible order of battle of a Soviet "front-level" OMG for operations on the North German Plain. b. Possible initial grouping of this OMG (see text).*

Bremen airport as an operational objective, its priority task is a tactical one—to detach conventional raid forces or air–ground assault groups (page 47) to deal with NATO C^3 centres and artillery capable of delivering nuclear weapons and scatterable minelets. Despite this group's swinging northwards off the main thrust line, the shock effect of its insertion opened a corridor across the Lüneburg Heath and clear of the Hamburg-Hanover autobahn. The front-level OMG was moved up, and launched across that autobahn at 03.00 on D + 1. And there our story begins.

Because of the terrain and his mission, the OMG commander has ordered two regroupings (Fig. 41b). He has detached the light regiments from his two divisions, grouping them under the "forward" (tactical) element of his own headquarters and placing them under command for movement of the follow-up division. And he has switched this division's tank regiment and divisional artillery group to the leading division, leaving it in effect with just six battalion-level task forces and minimum combat support. This weakened division has two tasks. One is to launch raids against three specified targets, in fact all to the south of its axis. The remaining mechanised regiment is to open up, secure and improve the OMG axis and, as soon as possible, a secondary route to the north of it. The OMG commander has strengthened the leading division because, having broken clear across the Weser downstream of the Weser–Aller confluence, it is to detach a mechanised regimental group down the left bank of the river, to join up with the tank division directed onto Bremen airport.

Having cleared the Weser, the leading division, now tank-heavy, has been directed onto Lingen–Elbergen, where the River Ems and the Dortmund–Ems Canal run side by side. The depleted follow-up division will be pretty well spent by the time it closes up to the Weser, at least until it can recover its regiment's worth of raid forces. In terms of our model (Fig. 42) the securing of two routes up to and across the Weser (a minor obstacle in Soviet eyes) will lock the original hinge A, and create an advanced hinge at B, on which the leading division can pivot. Until it can remobilise itself and be replaced by elements of the holding force, the follow-up division's task is to pass the rest of the leading division and the light mechanised group, together with its combat support and essential service support, forward across the Weser.

Once the leading division has successfully bypassed opposition astride the Osnabrück–Bremen autobahn and its leading elements are across the Elbergen–Lingen obstacle (C), the OMG commander, having checked with front, launches his airborne assault brigade onto the bridge at Wesel, with the Rhine crossing at Rees as an alternative objective. (At this point the front commander, who has already briefed his reserve airborne assault brigade for a back-up operation on Rees, brings that brigade to immediate notice.) The OMG commander then flies up to his forward headquarters, moving with the light mechanised group.

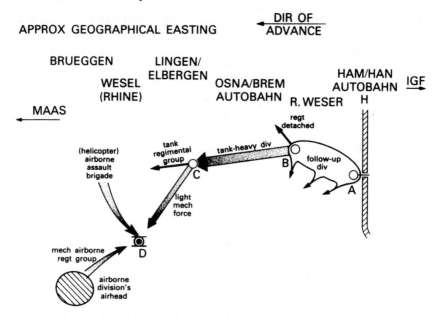

FIG. 42. *The club sandwich model (for geographical layout, cf Fig. 13).*

The leading division's orders are to secure a crossing of the double water obstacle, pass one tank regimental group across, directed onto Apeldoorn and the Dutch motorway running west, then clear and secure the route for the passage of the light group under the OMG commander himself, taking the forward divisional artillery group under command as it passes through. On our model, securing a crossing at Lingen has the effect of locking the hinge at B and creating another advance hinge at C, on which both the light mechanised group (which now has priority) and the forward elements of the original leading division can pivot.

The light mechanised group now races southwards to the Wesel–Rees area to link up with the airborne assault brigade and provide it with artillery support. (Soviet planning calls for this junction to be achieved within 6 hours of the *desant*.) Since the bridge (D) is a fixed geographical location of operational significance, its seizure has the effect of locking the hinge at C and making D an advanced hinge even before the link-up is achieved.

So far in this scenario, one is on reasonably firm ground—figuratively, I mean. The final layer of the club sandwich has become highly questionable; but I will add it and then examine it critically. Once principal theatre headquarters (one level up from front and responsible for the entire strategic offensive against the NATO centre) saw that the northern front-level OMG was rolling nicely, it launched the *ad hoc* airborne corps of three airborne divisions, which the supreme command had allotted, into the

Rhine–Meuse triangle—the heart of European NATO. One division was directed onto Bonn from the northwest, and one eastwards to link up with airborne assault brigades on the Rhine crossings at Düsseldorf and Cologne. The initial operational mission of the northernmost airborne division, with his airhead at the erstwhile NATO airbase at Brüggen, was to launch a BMD-mounted regimental group to link up with whichever of the northerly crossings (probably Wesel or Rees) was seized and established. This division's firm base (E) provides a hinge for the airborne assault brigade seizing the crossing; likewise for the light mechanised group and other troops advancing towards it across the Rhine, and then southwestwards onto the initial strategic objectives.

The future of airborne forces

As well as giving body to the concept of a ladder of tempo ratios, this admittedly idealised model throws up two questions of the highest importance. The first is the employment in opposed or risk landings of large airborne forces carried in transport aircraft. We saw in Chapter 7 how the effect of linearity on the tactical drop denied paratroops on their feet enough concentration in time and space to organise themselves fast enough to ward off the enemy's immediate reaction. Crete apart, paratroops have only made a successful contribution to high-intensity, high-tempo operations when they have been used in a tactical role at very limited depth. This was even truer of the Red Army's few drops into unsecured territory than it was of the drops in support of the Normandy landings and the Rhine crossing.

The Soviets, with Tukhachevskii's concept of *mechanised* airborne forces firmly in mind, overcame this limitation by going first to motorisation, then to partial and later complete mechanisation with the BMD. But this represents a manifold increase both in total lift and in the proportion of specialised aircraft required. And the specialised freight lift is further increased in substantial degree if armoured vehicles and other heavy equipment have to be parachuted in rather than landed. A view which I arrived at by rough calculation and which a number of Western experts in airborne operations seem to have reached by feel is that a Soviet BMD-mounted regimental group (with its immediate combat and service support, that is) is the largest formation that could be dropped by parachute into unsecured territory.

Quite apart from problems of the control of air space, the large number of aircraft needed and the linearity implicit in assembling, loading and despatching them raise two further question marks of Damoclean significance, the hair by which both these swords hang being the maintenance of operational, or even tactical surprise.

Let us take the less severe of the two problems, the fly-in, first. Suppose the force flies on a lo-lo-lo profile direct from the east across Germany to, say, the Rhine–Meuse triangle. Its head will have to fly for 35 to 40 minutes over NATO territory, which is likely to contain observers and ground sensors even if overrun; and the tail will be exposed to risk for significantly longer. An indirect route with full payloads would involve air refuelling, a technique which still seems to present problems at very low levels. And just one aircraft coming up for even a second into radar cover, or acquisition of the force by shipborne radar, would give the game away and expose the force to the full weight of surface-to-air and air-to-air attack without benefit of escort.

The second and still more critical problem is detection of the force on the ground by airborne and satellite-borne sensors. In current practice, aircraft and troops are assembled at a small number of airfields, perhaps one airfield to a brigade requiring a life of two hundred or more machines. Refuelling and checking the aircraft, preparing and loading heavy equipment, and batching the troops into loads ("chalk numbers") is no small matter. Conventionally assembly begins at least 24 hours before the operation is launched, and this is preceded by a considerable period of abnormal air movements and ground activity. One has to agree that, with modern surveillance, surprise is bound to be lost—the more so if all this is going on at several airfields at once, to mount a divisional or larger operation. One is thus forced to look at new tactical concepts and mounting techniques for fixed-wing airborne operations into unsecured territory.

The whole idea of dropping onto or very near the objective, assembling, and seizing the objective before the enemy could make any substantial response stemmed from the fact that, once down, paratroops had the mobility of the boot. Incapable of manoeuvre and short of heavy equipment, they were at the mercy of even the lightest mechanised security force until they had completed their mission and dug in or evaded. By contrast, the last thing mechanised airborne troops want to do is to drop onto or near their objective, forfeiting tactical surprise and exposing themselves to battle when at their weakest. Ideally they should go in at a point an hour or more from two or three possible objectives, before the development of friendly ground force or rotary-wing action discloses which is the most probable one.

If it is going to organise itself tactically and execute a controlled move or a manoeuvre, a mechanised airborne force will do far better to fly into an airhead than to be dropped. What is more, loading men (and more particularly heavy equipment) at landing scales as opposed to parachute scales achieves an important economy in lift because parachutes, containers and platforms are not needed—and this economy lies mainly in the requirement for general and specialised freight aircraft. Let us suppose that, for a divisional operation, one brigade at manpack scales were to be parachute-loaded to drop on and seize the airhead. That brigade's heavy equipment and the rest of the division would be loaded, non-tactically if needs be, for landing as opposed to dropping, and flown in.

This radical change could be reflected to equally good effect in the mounting of the operation. The men of the assault brigade could be loaded at a number of dispersal airfields and strips, thus avoiding protracted concentrations or disturbance of normal patterns of movements and activity. The rest of the mounting could probably be masked within the whole pattern of military and civil air movements, especially in a country such as the Soviet Union whose everyday life depends heavily on air travel. Heavy equipment could be preloaded well in advance and at great depth— beyond the Urals, say—and staged forward to dispersal fields over a period. Troops could in fact be concentrated under cover at airports and embarked in civil aircraft already positioned for scheduled civil flights.

Despite the existence of first-rate opinion to the contrary, I feel reasonably sure that sizeable fixed-wing airborne operations against un-secured territory will remain feasible if an airhead is established as a forward base for the mechanised airborne force, and if semi-clandestine techniques, supported by positive deception, are employed in mounting the operation. I am convinced this is so in a situation of strategic surprise. What is less certain is the scale on which this type of operation would be feasible. This is the kind of problem where "staff check" accuracy is not of much help; but the scope of Soviet airborne operations against the NATO centre would provide an entirely programmable computer exercise, and probably an extremely worthwhile one. Quite apart from feasibility, though, a well-equipped and well-balanced airborne mechanised brigade group might well prove to have a higher combat worth than a more scantily equipped and more unwieldy division. Having established in the previous chapter that combat worth is relative, one needs to take account not just of the number of combat troops likely to be available in the enemy's rear areas, but of their limited physical fighting power and quality.

The weak point in this concept is evidently the seizure of an airhead by dropping a force of men on their feet, relying on fixed-wing aircraft for fire support, particularly when the fly-in will have given at least 30 minutes' warning of a parachute attack. This could far better be done by a rotary-wing assault brigade, particularly if this force was trained and equipped to operate on the "main battle air vehicle" principle (page 121).

There seems every indication that, as increased physical fighting power and higher tempo enhance the combat worth of mobile forces, the key level at which types of formation are differentiated will fall from division to brigade. One might therefore envisage an airborne division, or more probably an *ad hoc* divisional-level task force, made up of four brigade groups—a rotary-wing assault brigade, a light (non-motorised) parachute brigade with a significant free-fall capability, and two airborne mechanised brigades, each type of brigade group having appropriate combat and service support organic to it. Since the dismounted brigade could take over the airhead as a forward base, freeing the helicopter force for a further offensive operation, this force could well have the same operational capability as the *ad hoc* Soviet corps of two to four partly mechanised airborne divisions which features in most seventies and eighties scenarios.

The helicopter-led strategic action

This brings me to a far more radical and interesting line of thought still; and to uphold credibility I should like to make the reader privy to the way I embarked on it. I followed very much the sequence I used earlier in this chapter to construct the club sandwich model on the NATO centre table. As I remarked earlier, the resulting heap struck me as very hard to prepare and almost certain to fall over sideways when being eaten.

At this point the Rhine became my Rubicon. If you could gain control of the key crossings north of the Rhine Gorge, I thought, insert a substantial mechanised airborne force into the heartland of the Rhine–Meuse triangle, and perhaps back this up with a seaborne landing in the Scheldt Estuary, what went on east of the Rhine would really not have too much strategic significance. Even without strategic surprise, the main NATO land forces would be caught the wrong side of the Rhine, facing or even moving the wrong way. Of course the Soviets' mechanised might in its baroque masses would poise itself threateningly and roll across the Inner German Frontier. But taking an "indirect direct approach" to the strategic objectives would change the whole emphasis of the offensive. (Where would one be without Irish?) In terms of manoeuvre theory, the entire Warsaw Pact land force would become the holding force (Sun Tzu's "ordinary force"), its operational manoeuvre groups becoming *tactical* manoeuvre groups, while the rotary and fixed wing airborne forces, together perhaps with their seaborne back-up, would constitute the decisive mobile force ("the extraordinary force"). I felt at the time, and am still inclined to think, that, given the strategic surprise which would be fairly easy to obtain if they led, these fixed and rotary wing forces could be inserted without too much difficulty.

The impact of submarine carriers

Then a piece of information published in 1983 made this line of thought more interesting still. The Soviet Union was reported to be building the first of a series of four or five submarine catamarans the size of the largest United States aircraft carriers. True, later information about a vast (surface) aircraft carrier being built in two halves on the Black Sea cast some doubt on the 1983 report. Be this as it may, though, large nuclear-powered submarine carriers, equipped with both "silent" and high-speed submerged drives, are undoubtedly feasible. Their signatures could well be masked by an escort of hunter-killer and/or missile submarines navigating above and around them. These large craft could undoubtedly carry both rotary-wing forces and amphibious light mechanised forces in substantial strength; and they would need to spend only a matter of minutes on the surface to fly or float these forces off. Let me stress that this small, specialised force operating semi-clandestinely on the borderline of the strategic and operational levels is as different as chalk from cheese from the *tactical* ship-to-shore movement off surface carriers practised by British, Soviet and United States marines.

My layman's interpretation of the naval side of the Falklands War—like that of a good many others outside the Royal Navy—was that surface naval units of any size would not remain viable for much longer; and that, since nuclear propulsion could fit the submarine for every naval role, navies would eventually go underwater. Among other indications, the recent successful launch of a cruise (as opposed to a ballistic) missile from a submerged submarine encourages this view. I could not begin to estimate how many helicopters or light armoured vehicles a submarine carrier might handle. But rule of thumb extrapolation from various known points suggested that a battalion group's worth of either type of force would be a realistic cockshy, perhaps a conservative one.

The mind boggles at the material and human resources the creation of a submarine-borne operational mobile force of this kind would call for. But this has to be viewed in the perspective of the strategic power it would confer and the cost of the "baroque" naval, land and air forces it could replace. The potential of nuclear-powered submarines is well known. I thought I had adequately exposed the potential of the helicopter in Chapter 7, but new facets of it keep on coming to light. The scope offered by combining these two widely different but essentially complementary military systems looks almost boundless.

Conclusion

Three things emerge clearly from the discussions in this chapter. The tempo ratio between two successive components of a manoeuvre system is critical; this makes it difficult to dispense with one or more layers of the club sandwich without destroying its integrity. On the other hand, the "full works" club sandwich, however valuable as a model, is patently not a practical proposition. Even if the resources needed to create an army of this shape were available, dispersing them over so many types of organisation and equipment could scarcely represent the best use of them. And even if such an army could be formed, its employment would be unmanageably complex.

However, one cannot relate these tempo ratios simply to physical mobility. In certain cases flexibility requires some if not all of the difference in tempo to be obtained by different handling techniques. This in turn means that some types of formation will be operating well below their maximum tempo for some, or indeed for most of the time. To maintain their combat worth under these conditions, the contribution made to it by physical fighting power must be high. On the other hand, the potential of very high tempo is too great to be ignored.

This suggests that the tendency will be towards polarisation, exemplified by the probable Soviet move towards a shock division on the one hand, and helicopter and mechanised airborne brigades on the other. In place of the unmanageable club sandwich one will have two courses—a main course based on physical fighting power and thus on mass; and a dessert, better perhaps a savoury, deriving most of its effect from surprise and momentum. The heavy force and the light force will each be capable within itself of applying manoeuvre theory at operational level, of forming a holding force and a mobile force. And the two will interact in this manner at strategic level. The determinant equipments of the one will be the main battle tank and the (heavy) infantry fighting vehicle, with the helicopter filling a range of supporting roles; of the other the helicopter and, probably, the light armoured vehicle, amphibious and airportable. In the heavy combat environment the infantryman on his feet will be hard put to it to survive; within the light force he will have both the traditional task of holding ground (the forward base), and a spectrum of light infantry roles ranging from mountain warfare to special force operations.

This is a tidy picture with a cosy image of progressive conservatism, of socially acceptable evolution. What is more, it fits conventional wisdom about a primary though improbable threat and a viper's nest of more probable secondary threats calling for worldwide intervention. So, once the advanced armies have seen the club sandwiches they are currently preparing topple over or collapse sideways even on manoeuvres, it may well come about.

But even the rather naive scenario we looked at above served to bring out the irrelevance of the heavy forces to the strategic decision once they are turned or otherwise dislocated. Once the helicopter and the light armoured vehicle can be given high and semi-clandestine strategic mobility—something that is technologically feasible and is likely to happen sooner rather than later—they can be employed anywhere in the world with strategic surprise, just as the government-sponsored terrorist can be today. One does not yet have a clear enough picture of warfare within or based on inner space to assess how that would interact strategically with a force of this kind. But what the combination of submarine and helicopter would certainly do is to restore the situation which prevailed up to the eighteenth century, one in which the main problems were to guess the enemy's intention and whereabouts. In Part 5 I shall argue that a submarine-borne force of helicopters and light armour represents not the light but the *massive* end of the probable spectrum of future warlike activities. Heavy forces, preferably without a nuclear arsenal but possibly in conjunction with it, will for some time provide an unusable deterrent, matching the understanding of military strength held by politicians and their electorates, and providing by its inertia a much-needed stabilising force.

PART 3

Luck Management

"The art lies in turning to your advantage any chance that you can possibly foresee; it cannot cover the whims of destiny."   JOMINI

"Audacity is nearly always right, gambling nearly always wrong." LIDDELL HART

10

Technology and Chance

"More and more will the actual men become parts of the machine. . . ." FULLER

"For we live in an age when, if war comes, it will be to the advantage of all to restrict unintended effects." LAURENCE MARTIN

Introduction

It must be years since I heard the phrase "the wonders of science" used other than ironically. Computer-literate primary schoolchildren hardly lift their blasé heads to see a spacecraft sweep across the sky. Yet I can recall how, in the years between the wars, even the most sophisticated of teenagers would pester parents or pedagogues to be taken to see the latest engineering marvel. There were two reasons for this. First, as Koestler put it much later, we saw *Deus* not so much *ex machina* as *in machina*. Victorian materialism still ruled; the Kingdom of God was in this world; sooner rather than later, science would give us a world free of war and want. Now, the tumultuous growth of technology in free-market and mixed economies, in particular of course the nuclear weapon, has shattered this confidence. In Europe—though not yet perhaps in the United States—informed opinion is becoming increasingly sceptical of technology, even actively hostile to it. The broadest effect of technological advance on society is destruction of belief in its own net beneficence. This trend is bound in the long run to influence the application of technology to war.

In the first half of this century even the smaller leaps forward generally still came as bolts from the blue. As the story of penicillin shows, scientists had little idea, even in their own fields, of when and where the next breakthrough would come or whither it would lead. Now, as a rule, the nature and direction of the next breakthrough is widely and accurately forecast; as in the case of controlled nuclear fusion, only the timing is in doubt. Advance has become mainly evolutionary. As a recent BBC television series on discovery by creative imagination showed, however, there is still scope for revolutionary new thinking. Unpredictable step advances will continue to occur; but they are more likely in the biological sciences than in the physical ones. One might fairly say that a second broad

165

effect of technological advance, not least due to computer science, is to enhance its own predictability—to reduce both the appearance and the reality of chance.

Certainly this is true within established disciplines. By contrast vast ignorance—and a good deal of indifference—remains where the effects even of past advances on other fields and on the natural environment are concerned. Over and over again, in agriculture, in medicine, even in such mundane fields as water purification, yesterday's triumph is today's disaster. As I write, a purportedly definitive American study on the "nuclear winter" hypothesis is still in progress. But as far as I can discover, this possibility was not even mooted until over 35 years after Hiroshima. This almost universal failure to examine, let alone to predict broad interactions of advances is at least in some measure due to scientists and engineers "knowing more and more about less and less".

Since the peacetime military establishment of most advanced countries enjoys an unrivalled and largely deserved reputation for blinkered thinking, there is a very sharp moral here for those concerned with future warfare. On the one hand, they need to consider how the rotary wing and further development of the nuclear submarine will interact with each other and with current concepts of mechanised warfare. On the other, they should be questioning, as the Soviets have long been doing and I shall do in Part 5, the practicability of war between large organised forces in the geopolitical and technological setting of the twenty-first century.

Target response

There is one particular aspect of this interaction between fields which is all too little appreciated outside a small circle of defence scientists and humanists specialising in defence studies. Certainly I have encountered very few military men who have an inkling of it. This is the concept of target response, one which applies at every level from the hand gun, or even cold steel, to the fusion warhead. I always find the German term for lethality, *Wirkung im Ziel* (lit. "effect in the target"), helps one to keep it in mind. A bullet may strike a man and pass almost harmlessly through his flesh. Again it may penetrate a vital organ and cause instant death by so doing—a direct or primary effect. But very often the resistance of hard tissue, notably bone, will cause the bullet to tumble, to spread (as happens with a dum-dum) or even to fragment. This is the first stage in a complex series of interactions between projectile and organism, in which the organism's reaction produces indirect or secondary effects far in excess of the primary effect. To take a rather naive example, a bullet striking the rib cage may itself be deflected outwards while causing a fractured piece of rib to penetrate the heart or lung.

The attack of armoured vehicles or ships, where almost the only way to produce a complete or "K" kill with a single hit is to set fire to the ammunition carried by the target, likewise exemplifies the principle well. But to see the full impact one needs to go almost to the other end of the scale, the nuclear weapon of low kiloton yield which might be used on the battlefield or, as a warning shot, against a small centre of population. When I was on the directing staff of the Army Staff College, the initial teaching material on battlefield nuclear weapons was being prepared. One used to examine the effect of a "tactical" weapon on a small town like Camberley and its surroundings, then on troops in the field, "warned and protected" and suitably dispersed. The contrast was so extreme as to make one query the data—until one realised that a great deal of the devastation of the urban target came from secondary effects *within the target*, notably falling and flying masonry, flying glass over an enormous areas, and textile-seated fires over a larger one still. My very limited knowledge of possible directed energy weapons leads me to think that, with them, secondary effects initiated within the target would play a larger part still.

Be this as it may, an understanding of the interaction between attack and target is of enormous importance; but I want to move from nuclear to chemical-energy weapons and to pass from this matter to a broader one still. The increasing destructiveness of high-explosive attack is due partly to increased intensity and improved accuracy of delivery, partly—as explosives technology catches a new breeze after a long spell in the doldrums— to the increased power of a given weight of shell or bombs. These advances in firepower are themselves so great that, with the added benefit of specialised munitions, many effects which 20 years ago would have called for a nuclear weapon can now be achieved with high explosive.

But the value of this growth in destructive power is compounded by increased vulnerability of the target an advanced nation offers. The complexity and dependence on technology of modern societies has both broadened the effect of cutting essential services, notably electricity supply, and grouped key facilities in national computer-based centres. It is doubtful, for instance, whether Britain could keep going today under the weight of bombs and missiles the Germans delivered in the Second World War; and most unlikely that the Federal Republic, or even the German Democratic Republic, could sustain the American and British "strategic" bombing their respective territories suffered in the forties. I am not thinking here of the collapse of political or popular will, but of loss of the level of cohesion and efficiency required to support the war effort and maintain a viable base for the field forces. I shall return to the implications of this question in Part 5, in the contexts of the acceptability of war aims and the usability of large organised forces.

The dominance of firepower

In terms of strategic air attack, though, improvements in high-explosive firepower and changes in target response probably add up to no more than a difference in degree. In warlike actions between organised armed forces, of every type and at every level, we see ourselves as approaching a point at which the dominance of firepower will produce a difference in kind. Given the time lags discussed in Chapter 1, we are in fact already past that point, certainly in terms of planning to make changes, and very possibly in actuality. In the Falklands War an opposition that was certainly second-rate and in some critical respects could fairly be termed *ad hoc* achieved a near-decisive attrition rate against the Royal Navy and its supporting vessels. Since then, the Gulf War has confirmed the ease with which indifferently manned and sometimes obsolescent aircraft can pick off ships at will and at virtually no risk to themselves. Dispassionately viewed, these facts surely put the whole future of major surface naval units in question. Despite the Argentine successes and the Israeli Air Force's ability to overcome the Syrian air defence, the cold facts of weapon system performance suggest that, in a conflict between two first-rate powers with sensible equipment, few aircraft would survive outside earth cover. As I write, a recent American success suggests that ballistic missiles and inner space vehicles too can be dealt with by advanced forms of established technologies. And whenever and however it may materialise, there are the whole fields of directed energy weapons and electromagnetic guns still to be explored and exploited. In sum, one can expect navies to be forced underwater, and air forces to be confined to the nap of the earth.

I stressed earlier that many fire tasks which in the sixties would have required a nuclear weapon can now be tackled conventionally. There is another side to this capability, one which directly affects the role of chance in war. In statistical terms, to achieve a high probability of a given target effect, overkill must be applied. This concept, brutally familiar from the nuclear field, simply means that, on a proportion of occasions, a superfluous amount of damage will be inflicted on the target—in other words ammunition will be wasted. For many targets, Soviet ammunition norms are based on a 90 per cent probability of achieving the required target effect. This calls for a considerable degree of overkill, demonstrating that overkill is attainable with conventional artillery fire. Ninety per cent takes us well up onto the flattening part of the diminishing returns curve (Fig. 38, page 134), so that virtual certainty (99 per cent probability) will be expensive. But it *can* now be done, and this is important because it puts the principle of interchangeability beyond dispute; conventional fire can now offer the same certainty of destruction as a nuclear strike or occupation by combat troops.

While accidents of ground will always provide some kind of cover, the effect of modern firepower on land force tactics is equally revolutionary. Just as we saw in Part 2 how the rotary wing may well turn force structures inside out, firepower is already turning tactical concepts inside out, by replacing the anvil of troops with an anvil of fire (Fig. 5, page 51). The use of combat troops at high density to hold ground or to seize it is already likely to prove highly costly, and may soon become wholly unprofitable. The interesting question is what effect the dominance of firepower will have at operational level.

One school of thought, to which many defence academics on both sides of the Atlantic subscribe, is that it will reduce mobility and bring about a return to positional warfare. The opposite view is that it will put a premium on elusiveness, increasing mobility and reducing mass. On analysis, both these opinions appear rather simplistic, mainly because they ignore the interchangeability of troops and fire (Chapter 8)—in other words the equivalence or complementarity of the movement of troops and the massing of fire. They also underrate the part played by manned and unmanned surveillance, and by communication. Another factor, little understood by soldiers and widely ignored, is the weight of fire a modern fast jet in its strike configuration, flying a lo-lo-lo profile, can put down very rapidly wherever required. With modern artillery and air support, a pair of eyes backed up by an unjammable radio and perhaps a thermal imager becomes the equivalent of at least a (company) combat team, perhaps a battle group.

Again, I shall return to this theme in Part 5. Briefly and in the most general terms possible, I suggest that the long-term effect of dominant firepower will be threefold. It will *disperse mass* in the form of a "net" of small detachments with the dual role of calling down fire and of local quasi-guerrilla action. Because of its low density, the elements of this net will be everywhere and will thus need only the mobility of the boot. It will *transfer mass*, structurally from the combat arms to the artillery, and in deployment from the direct fire zone (as we now understand it) to the formation and protection of mobile fire bases capable of movement at heavy-track tempo (Chapter 9). Thus the third effect will be to *polarise mobility*, for the manoeuvre force still required is likely to be based on the rotor. This line of thought is borne out by recent trends in Soviet thinking on the offensive. The concept of an operational manoeuvre group (OMG) which hives off raid forces against C^3 and indirect fire resources is giving way to more fluid and discontinuous manoeuvre by task forces ("air–ground assault groups" found by "shock divisions") directed onto fire bases—again of course with an operational helicopter force superimposed. As we shall see in Chapter 12, Soviet "professional" reconnaissance and special forces already provide the offensive equivalent of the "net".

Information technology and electronic warfare

As the last sentence suggests and the reader has probably been muttering to himself for the past 5 minutes, all this is really about not firepower but information. For it is really the acquisition, processing and dissemination of information that lies at the root of the speed and accuracy with which fire can now be applied. The accelerating pace of the electronic revolution, and of its invasion of the whole audiovisual field, is already so rapid as to beggar prediction. After experiencing the microchip explosion, I confess myself quite unable to envisage what might happen next; and I frankly doubt whether the rising generation, computer-literate though it may be, has much idea either. From the military point of view, it may be easier to consider what information technology can*not* do, and how far it may be hampered by electronic warfare.

.The laser represents a kind of interface between information technology, where its applications are manifold, and the field of directed energy weapons. As far as I can see there is, however, a clear-cut distinction between the various types of laser used in information technology, and power lasers. On the one hand, progress is widening this gap, by reducing the transfer of power involved in information technology and increasing the power obtainable in weapons and in industrial applications such as cutting metal. On the other, the currently fashionable technique of laser blinding and such tasks as range-taking, boosting low light levels for target identification, or target marking could conceivably be carried out by the same instrument; this suggests that the gap is bridgeable. By and large, though, it seems fair to say that information technology will not become the primary element in systems involving the transfer of power or the displacement of mass. By contrast, it will play an increasingly dominant role in the control of such systems, and spin-off from it may impinge on their primary characteristic.

Usefully if not logically, the term "electronic warfare" has come to mean *interference with* the acquisition and transmission of data by electronic means. As I understand it, perhaps wrongly, it excludes active deception, which I shall cover in the next chapter. Wherever one looks—radar, fusing or jamming for instance—one sees a game of "countermeasures to the *n*th" being played in an infinite variety of expensive forms. This toing and froing makes prediction even harder than it is with advances in electronics. For whatever the trend may be, measure or countermeasure may be on top at any given moment. And in a critical field such as aircraft or missile detection, an edge one way or the other could well be the basis of a decision to go to war. But this high-frequency cycle of positive measure and countermeasure is only one of three. At the other extreme the 50-year cycle postulated in Chapter 1 suggests long-term trends—for instance that navies will at some point be forced to go underwater. In between these is a low-frequency swing which, I suppose, could be said to smooth the short-term perturbations and give direction to the long-term trend. This is the swing that affects development planning, so it might have a frequency of 10 to 15 years. It determines, for instance, whether a particular role will be filled by a manned aircraft or a missile, or whether a new threat calls for a radical change in the design of surface ships or armoured vehicles while the changeover to submarines and helicopters is in progress.

One can perhaps say three things about this third pendulum. Countermeasures apart, the sustained effect of an innovation is almost always less than first appearances suggest. As the general level of sophistication of equipment rises—as the volume of its total technical content increases, if you like—the effect of an advance of given magnitude tends to be less pronounced; this is yet another example of diminishing returns. And except when a countermeasure represents a really big leap forward, the positive measures—the odd powers of n in the countermeasures to the nth game, so to speak—usually stay one jump ahead. So far, for most of the time, the aircraft has been able to get through the air defence, albeit at attrition rates which could not long be sustained; the fuse has continued to defeat the means of frustrating it; and radio communication has kept one jump—or should one say "hop"—ahead of jamming. An analysis on these lines would be a life's work, so one is dependent on subjective feel. And on this basis I would add the impression that advances which extend or impair man's senses, and now his brain, have a more marked and more lasting effect than those which represent extensions of, or constraints on his muscle.

One particular aspect of the impact of electronics on warfare is the **control of air space**, especially air space over an area of land operations. As evidenced by General Bernard Rogers (SACEUR) in a number of public utterances, and by Air Marshal Sir Patrick Hine, Commander 2 ATAF, in a recent address to the Royal United Services Institute, this is currently seen as a problem in search of a solution. It may thus prove an obstacle to enhancement of the scope and tempo of manoeuvre in general, and to the realisation of the rotary wing revolution in particular. The view I have formed, founded on study of Soviet air support and air defence practice and on discussions with various aviators, is that future developments will reshape the problem and make it amenable to radical solutions—given yet another somersault of the military mind.

While the general concept of air superiority must remain valid, that of local or "tactical" air superiority seems to belong to the 50-year cycle now running down. Soon, if not now, any aircraft which climbs out of the nap of the earth into hostile radar vision within range of hostile surface-to-air or air-to-air missiles will be destroyed. For instance, the Royal Air Force considers that even the risk involved in the loop manoeuvre of toss bombing is justified only if the weapon being delivered is a nuclear one. By the same token, as I have stressed elsewhere, a modern strike aircraft delivers such a weight of conventional fire as to put important and sizeable missions within the scope of a single aircraft or at most a pair. The only massed formations will be rotary-wing ones. In sum, outside the nap of the earth, both sides have total control of whatever air space they can reach. The air battle will, I suggest, become an airfield battle—the disruption of runways and the destruction of machines on the ground.

This concentration of activity by widely differing types of aircraft within the nap of the earth appears to present an acute air traffic control problem. Fortunately, tactical nap-of-the-earth (NOE) flying by helicopters mostly takes place at a lower level than NOE flying by fast jets. The clash in fact comes between *contour* flying by helicopters and NOE by fast jets. Since approach flights in a contour flight mode by rotary-wing formations will be planned at higher tactical or operational level, clashes with fast jets should be avoidable by normal means—as long as communications are not dislocated by electronic warfare!

By far the most intractable aspect of this whole problem is undoubtedly the interface between aircraft and air defence, and it is here that radical solutions may help. There seems to be a general feeling that no pilot in his senses, whether he is flying a fast jet or a helicopter (and whichever side he is on), will knowingly enter the airspace controlled by the Soviet *tactical* air defence system, except to make a run-in to a target or objective. The same is not at present true of the air space over NATO troops; but unless it becomes so NATO can forget about manoeuvre by anything larger than a (company) combat team! The reason for these rather extreme statements is the response time available to tactical air defence systems. With everybody flying NOE, no system can do other than engage on contact or not at all. Radar or visual contact between surveillance or launch site and target may be too brief even for an identification-friend-or-foe (IFF) challenge. The only technological solution would appear to be an on-missile IFF system linked to an autodestruct device. However—again provided that communications work—a flip-flop "guns tight/guns free" control system would appear to provide an answer. For the brief period a friendly helicopter force is moving in, the risk of enemy aircraft going unscathed must be accepted. Friendly strike aircraft will generally tend to use an indirect approach to deep targets, both because their bases may be to a flank, and so as to minimise exposure to the enemy's tactical air defence. But air defence could be briefly inhibited for them too.

Despite all these vast grey zones, one may well find that the greatest impact of electronics on warfare will come from a field wholly devoid of direct physical effect—the media. Television is surely already so firmly established as to hold pride of place, though in war, as in all times when routines are disturbed, radio will to some extent come into its own again. By the end of this decade, certainly by the turn of the century, many if not most office and domestic television receivers are likely to have facilities for direct reception of satellites; likewise radio will be in a position to make use of satellites for broadcasting as well as relay, whether or not this is normal peacetime practice. In one way and another, censorship, the principal means of wartime control of information up till now, will be impracticable. Even threats of penalties for watching enemy transmissions will not cut much ice; one thing all forecasters agree about is that, however strongly reinforced, the forces of law and order will have their hands full dealing with major physical disturbances and a surge in violent crime. Even when it becomes possible to take out satellites selectively by pinpoint attack, it is a nice question whether the contestants will destroy each other's surveillance satellites and, I would have thought, a sound bet that their dependence on communications satellites will result in tacit agreement to leave these intact.

As General Sir John Hackett points out in *The Third World War*, the historical aim of censorship has been to keep information from the enemy; but in face of modern surveillance by satellite and other means, the aim becomes the sustainment of public morale on one's own side. This is something on which one has to take a view. The scientific element in my education having left me with a firm belief in openness of information, I regard propaganda and disinformation as the offspring of secrecy and lack of information. Presumably listeners and viewers will continue to trust the sources of news they have learnt to trust; and this will redound to the benefit of free societies practising open information policies, such as the United States and the Federal Republic. As long as this trust is not disturbed by censorship, one cannot see many people getting anything but a good laugh out of some Arab or Russian heavy churning out tales of disaster and prophecies of doom like the voice-over in an advertisement for a lavatory cleaner.

Nevertheless, responsible newscasting will bring scenes of extreme horror into the sitting-room or shelter and—no less important—will disclose alarming information gaps. Under these circumstances, it is surely impossible to predict which way the popular will of the belligerents will jump. One can only speculate on how far television coverage was directly responsible for the collapse of American popular support for the Vietnam War; and how far the more thoughtful elements in the European peace movement are influenced by the almost daily diet of armed violence in the third world and of riotous behaviour in the first. What does seem certain is that television coverage of armed conflict turns world opinion as a whole fairly rapidly against the war covered, and more slowly against the use of armed force to settle disputes.

Then there is the sounding-board effect of television, and of radio amplification of televisual reporting, which has become so familiar from coverage of violent incidents in contexts ranging from "peace protests" through industrial disputes and urban guerrilla activity to other people's wars—Lebanon or the Gulf, for instance. What we do not know—and I at least find hard to envisage—is how one would react to this sounding-board effect in a major war which threatened the existence of oneself and one's family. One must, I think, accept that, although biased or irresponsible reporting greatly enhances it, this resonance is an inherent characteristic of the medium. Even the most informed and intelligent of viewers, who normally discount this effect, may have difficulty in doing so when the actuality, as well as the image, is on their own doorstep and confirms their worst forebodings.

Unfortunately I lack the skills and the data base to analyse this whole problem; all I can do is to throw out some questions in the hope that the appropriate experts may pick them up and try to answer them. My instinct is, though, that management of a body politic accustomed to being saturated with information poses a problem in the political conduct of war just as difficult and just as important as the exercise of command on the military side. The only thing one can say with any certainty is that this problem puts a high premium on strategic surprise and swift decision.

Man and the environment

Historically weather and climate, both directly and through their effects on sea conditions and terrain, have provided the greatest single component of the fortunes of war. Less obvious but, up to the beginning of this century, often more important still was the effect of disease. I have not checked the statement that more armies have been crippled by disease than were ever destroyed in battle, but even in the Second World War, disease remained the dominant cause of casualties in several theatres. All these elemental and environmental effects break down into those derived wholly or mainly from climate, which are generally predictable; and those brought about by meteorological conditions or micro-organisms, which by and large are not. We now generally suppose that "man has conquered the elements"; but it would be well to see how far this is in fact the case.

Until the Second World War made mass air transport a reality, extreme climates tended to exclude from the zones subject to them large-scale activity by organised forces of comparable quality. They did so by direct effects—heat and humidity on the one hand, cold and wind chill on the other—and indirectly by their action on terrain and, in arctic regions, on the sea. There were naval operations, where the micro-environment of the ship, despite all its hardships, tended on balance to mitigate the effects of climate. There were expeditions on the scale we should now describe as special force operations. And there were colonial wars and endless internal security operations against opponents who were disparate but by no means always the worse for being so. But armies as we understand them were mostly the prerogative of imperialist powers and other advanced nations. If they wanted to fight, they generally chose to do it in temperate or sub-tropical seas, or comfortable stretches of countryside preferably in a third party's territory. Great successes were achieved by seamanship and by the engineering and logistic skills needed to overcome difficult terrain. But, as we should now say, the "climatic range" of organised forces was limited.

Nowadays, given the requisite training, clothing, equipment and logistic support, large bodies of troops could, theoretically at least, operate in any climate and season. This statement needs considerable qualification. As both Napoleon and Hitler learnt the hard way in Russia, the requirements under all four heads mentioned may be more than a little out of the ordinary. Extremes of heat and cold require significant amounts of power to make them tolerable; this need and the conditions themselves reduce the performance of machines, particularly of helicopters. For evident reasons, the terrain in extreme climatic zones tends to be undeveloped and more difficult than the average, and this limits both the types and numbers of machines that can be deployed. And some combinations of climate and terrain still offer impossible conditions and may well continue to do so. But there is now a possibility of gaining decisive success by facing and overcoming the hazards of extreme climate just as the great captains of the past did by using extreme terrain. *The saying that the hazards of terrain are always preferable to those of combat now holds good for climate too.*

There has been some advance in my lifetime in the forecasting of general meteorological trends, and in the accuracy of short-term forecasts for areas of open sea and the centres of land masses. But today's predictions for the land/sea interface—coastal waters and land areas with a maritime climate— seem no more reliable than those I recall from hill-walking holidays in childhood. They do not provide a useful basis for planning, while long-range forecasts of every kind have become a standing joke. The failure of meteorology to progress sticks up like a sore thumb among so many scientific success stories and is all the more remarkable when it has had so much help from other fields in data acquisition and processing. Since, as far as I know, the meteorological services are too prudent to publish their track record, one is forced back on subjective judgement. To justify my comments, though, one need do no more than note the inconsistencies of simultaneous BBC radio, BBC television and regional Independent Television forecasts over a few days. Throw into the hat with these the coastal waters forecasts, the shipping forecasts for coastal areas and the forecasts for farmers, and what you pull out may be any kind of weather at all. As a yachtsman I have also used both Coastguard and Royal Air Force forecasts, and these are little better. The only reliable predictions I have come upon are the very short-term ones from (very) local radio stations (who probably do it by looking out of the window), and those in western Ireland, where they just have a tape saying "rain". Eisenhower's decision to launch Overlord was a high-risk one; I believe the risk would be almost as high 40 years on.

By contrast many military activities which 40 years ago turned very heavily on the weather are now largely independent of it. With the exception of local sea conditions for beach landings—probably an obsolescent technique in any event—the two remaining problem areas are visibility and the effect of precipitation on going. There have been recent indications of Soviet doubts about the all-weather capability of fixed-wing aircraft (as opposed to helicopters), but my guess is that these concern visibility, particularly in the context of supporting ground troops. And my impression is that, although they are currently the worst sufferers from it, aircraft will overcome the visibility hazard sooner and better than surface vehicles and shipping—at least at military safety levels. The problem is to replace instrument flying, which has definable limitations of accuracy and does not aid surveillance or target acquisition, with "synthetic visual" flying. This calls for the production by optronic means of an image of the same quality under good conditions as an optical image, and of usable quality under *all* conditions of light and visibility. The technical solution, employing multiple sensors and an image processor, is very nearly there in a number of aircraft and vehicle systems. Since the techniques have applications ranging from entertainment through medicine and defence to aerospace, one can confidently predict a solution by the mid-nineties.

Given radar, navigational aids, the slow speed at which shipping normally moves, and its ability to go slower still, visibility should not be a problem even in crowded waters. Yet it remains a severe one. Few who observe merchant shipping with an informed and interested eye as one does when sailing in the Channel, or read even newspaper accounts of the frequent accidents will be in much doubt that the problem is a human one—lack of training, parrot-like rather than formative training techniques, and sometimes lack of diligence. Hard to explain though it may be, the risk of collision remains a limiting factor in naval operations calling for very high densities of shipping, such as close convoys and landings.

On land, mist and fog will, as now, tend to slow down tempo, because it is not economic to apply the enormously expensive optronic systems mentioned above to driving. Nor is it particularly easy to do so, since driving requires true stereoscopic (binocular) vision. Tactically, a more serious effect still is the impairment of sensory performance. Fog blankets sound as well as obstructing vision. And for the moment at least, even the most sophisticated of mechanised forces relies heavily on the human eye for surveillance and target detection. I know, because I have both done it and had it done to me on exercise, how easy it is to slip through a defence in the early morning mists of autumn. Delay in detection, confused information and difficulty of tactical manoeuvre compound one another to make a coherent response impossible.

The most severe impingement of weather on going is probably not so much precipitation as the onset of a thaw—exemplified by the Russian spring thaw. These conditions make whole areas of normally good going, including all prepared surfaces except for a few metalled roads, virtually impassable for a matter of weeks. The autumn freeze-up and the spring thaw are broadly predictable, but their exact onset and duration are not. Nor, as the Germans found to their cost in the Ukraine, are sudden shifts of temperature across the freezing point. In climates such as that of the

Russian heartland, spring and autumn probably still amount to close seasons—albeit of weeks rather than months—for major land operations. Both in regions which normally experience a frozen winter and elsewhere, heavy snowfalls onto bare ground or packed snow can seriously hamper mobility for a matter of hours or days. These temporary effects are not predictable on an operational time scale. Nor is the timing of seasonal events such as the closing and opening of passes. Rain imposes Clausewitzian friction on all forms of movement. The combination of rain and movement produces mud, which has a general degrading effect on men and machines and may seriously damage some types of equipment. More important from the operational viewpoint, rain can rather quickly render impassable areas of marginal going in general, and the approaches to and exits from water-obstacle crossings in particular.

One can perhaps sum all this up by saying that technological advance has enormously reduced the dependence of warfare on weather, and that its effects are now in a state of transition. Where surface vehicles and men on their feet are concerned, the element of chance introduced by weather is not likely to change much, although the effect of poor visibility will diminish as genuinely all-weather surveillance and sighting systems become more common. The residual influence of weather on surface shipping is something of a mystery of the sea; since it is inexplicable, there is no reason to suppose that it will change much. Fixed and rotary wing aircraft, hitherto the most weather-dependent of all means of transport, look like shedding these shackles in the near future. The upshot of this discussion, as of so many elsewhere in this book, is that the helicopter and the submarine will have a widening edge.

The recent history of infectious disease surely provides one of the sharpest lessons in the vanity of material progress. Classical killers like malaria are stamped out over whole regions, only to reappear a decade later in more virulent form, with resistant strains of carriers and micro-organisms alike. Tourism at jet tempo combines with the understandable carelessness of the ill-informed to import into advanced societies conditions like "legionnaire's disease" and "Lhasa fever". The population has no resistance to these, and there is no specific remedy or proven palliative for them. Less spectacular but possibly more important, specific conditions like hepatitis have appeared at quasi-epidemic level alongside the spectrum of virus diseases known to the layman as "influenza". And this spectrum has been broadened by a seemingly endless flow of rather nonspecific, little understood viral conditions, all of them debilitating and occasionally fatal, and some of them taking weeks or months to clear up. While the virus group of organisms is being contained or forced back on established fronts, it is proving itself a master of manoeuvre, infiltrating with marked success in many ways and at many points.

So far advanced societies have only experienced the current pattern of infectious disease under normal conditions, which are ideal for combatting it. With known types of micro-organism evolving strains resistant to antibiotics or vaccines as the case may be, and with a steady stream of new types or strains of virus against which no vaccine exists, epidemics could floor an army in the field or the complements of large naval units to an operationally significant degree over an operationally significant period. In the fifties and sixties one might have said that disease had ceased to play a part in the fortunes of war, but this would no longer seem to be the case.

What is more, the current pattern and trends have combined with the reality of genetic engineering to create a grey zone between naturally occurring disease and biological warfare. A power which devastated its opponent with bubonic plague or botulinus toxin would merely be digging a moral and probably a physical grave for itself. But there would now be little difficulty in tailoring some nonspecific virus or other so as to increase its virulence and reduce its incubation period. (Incubation periods have already been experimentally cut by as much as 80 per cent.) An army or a population could probably be infected with a modified virus of this kind without its origin being suspected.

Blunders

The only rational justifications for fighting wars as opposed to gaming them are the hopes that chance may operate in one's favour or that the opposition may make what the tennis player calls "forced and unforced errors". We have seen that on balance technological advance reduces the role of chance in the conduct of war. Much harder to say is whether high technology increases or reduces the likelihood of blunders and the gravity of their consequences. While every soldier is adept at preparing for the last war, logisticians seem to carry this skill to the point of repeating the very same unforced errors that have marked the opening phases of past wars. For instance, in certain operations in which I took part, our vehicles had Browning machine guns. But the entire back-up of belted small-arms ammunition was Vickers Mk VIIIZ, incompatible with both our weapons and the infantry's. Replenishment had to be flown out (I think from the United Kingdom), parachuted onto a captured airfield, and moved through a long stretch of unsecured territory. One would like to think that computers made this kind of thing less likely; but one knows very well from day-to-day experience that computers are only as good as the data fed to them. One of the reasons for the United States' failure to rescue the Teheran hostages appears to have been that the helicopters used were naval machines not fitted with the air-intake filters required for desert conditions.

Hard cases make bad law, but for two reasons technological advance appears to increase the chance of unforced error. High technology makes a force dependent on equipment of which commanders and key staff officers, being relatively aged non-specialists, have vast ignorance. This makes them unable to check what their specialists are doing or to apply the mixture of stick and carrot indispensable to effective leadership. Second, basic reliability theory applies; the more complex the system, the greater the probability of failure. The technological solution to this is to build in redundancy—to double and treble up components and complete sub-systems, a technique made familiar to most by the technical problems of manned space flight. But in military terms this means fielding surplus mass over and above the sufficient mass (Chapter 5); and the penalties of this are just as great in mounting an operation as they are in designing an aircraft. As I emphasised in Chapter 9, this, as well as known limitations in Soviet capability, is why I believe the club sandwich battle to be as disastrous a doctrine as it is invaluable a model. It is so large and complex that it is bound to collapse sideways when served or eaten.

On the other hand, I at least can see no reason why technological advance should directly increase the likelihood of forced errors. To the extent that high technology is consonant with momentum, and thus with resistance to change of speed and direction, it may well aggravate their consequences; and common sense and history bear this out. Far more important, though, is the scope high technology gives to the commander with the initiative for varying the tempo of his action, in particular for stepping it up. The pressure he thus places on his opponent is without doubt highly likely to produce forced errors; it may well lead to an inability to make any relevant response.

Conclusion—technology and surprise

For the cumulative thrust of the above discussions is clear enough. The influence of technological advance is not so much to reduce the role of chance in war as to *shift* it from the conduct of war to the moves leading up to hostilities or to a particular operation—*to increase the scope for surprise.* Certainly the tempos made possible by fast tracks and the rotary wing greatly widen the scope for operational and tactical surprise. On the other hand, a distinguished school of thought holds that one particular advance, satellite surveillance, rules out strategic surprise. This question bears on the whole shape of future warfare.

Assume for the moment that two potential belligerents are unable or unwilling to take out each other's surveillance satellites, or at least are not prepared to forfeit strategic surprise by so doing. Suppose too that no means of jamming the satellites' sensors or communications has yet been found—as it certainly will be in the end. Missile sites and military bases receive special attention, so any changes in them will not go unnoticed unless they take place deep enough under the ground not to affect the installation's thermal image. Likewise, any abnormalities of movement or positioning of road, rail, sea and air transport will be spotted. One possibility, to be discussed in the next chapter, is the use of a cover plan to explain the evidence of preparations.

The alternative is to plan, prepare and conduct the war within the restrictions imposed by surveillance. Here one comes back to the actual and possible trends discussed at the end of the last chapter. Helitroops and/or amphibious light mechanised troops held on board submarine carriers, with a proportion of the force constantly on patrol (as missile submarines are now), can be expected to provide a potential for strategic surprise for a considerable time, perhaps—on the 50-year cycle—up to the middle of the next century. I demonstrated in the last chapter how, say, a parachute brigade could be clandestinely concentrated and launched, and how mechanised airborne formations could be loaded at dispersal fields in great depth and "worked" forward without undue perturbation of the normal air movement pattern.

But the fundamental point surely lies in the mental attitude of military men and politicians. The nations in arms of the First and Second World Wars, and the baroque masses now concentrated astride the Inner German Frontier, will soon come to look as antiquated as the trappings of the Field of the Cloth of Gold seemed 50 years ago. Ultimatums and declarations of war already strike one as about as relevant to the modern scene as "Gentlemen of France, fire first." If a nation faced with a *casus belli* is not strong enough to deter the opposition from its peacetime posture or mobile enough to preempt hostile action, the only realistic course open to it is to commit compact but powerful forces, clandestinely assembled and deployed, in an attempt to secure an immediate decision.

To the sceptics let me highlight the close parallel between what I am predicting for the turn of the century in the military sphere, and what is now happening on the economic and industrial side. As was entirely predictable 10 years ago (and was in fact forecast by Shirley Williams in a speech made about 1976), pre-eminence in manufacturing has passed to the third world. We have to learn to live mainly by our heads instead of our hands, backed up by sophisticated instruments whose operation requires rare aptitudes and high levels of skill. By the same token, war between mass armies weighed down with baroque equipment they cannot use properly has become an established third world sport. The advanced world, too vulnerable to survive a war of attrition or mass destruction, must learn to conduct its affairs by the rapier—by the threat or use of small specialised forces exploiting high tempo and strategic surprise.

11

Surprise and Stratagems

"Now war is based on deception. Move when it is advantageous and create changes in the situation by concentration and dispersal of forces." Sun Tzu

"The art is to arrange movements of columns to embrace the widest possible strategic front without exposing them, and to keep them out of the enemy's sight to mask the objective." Jomini

Introduction

Perhaps the one military matter over which there is no dissent is the value of surprise. Yet the addicts of attrition and the masters of manoeuvre show by their actions that they rate surprise very differently. Plans based on attrition theory are deliberate and predictable; frequently, in the name of respectability, they are announced in advance. So they rarely achieve strategic surprise; the opposition is left with little to guess about except the timing. The attrition-minded mostly regard tactical surprise as a bonus. They base their plans on providing enough muscle to win without surprise. In fact one sometimes wonders whether, despite their lip service to it, they do not prefer to *lose* surprise. For surprise suggests uncertainty; in their eyes, emerging bloody but unbowed from a jolly good scrap is preferable to facing themselves and their subordinates with situations which make demands on military skill. They may be right! In fairness, though, one should stress two things. Actions which depend on surprise, such as raids (in the Western sense), are essentially based on manoeuvre theory. Second, however fashionable it may be to damn Eisenhower for caution, he achieved operational surprise in Overlord, thanks to an excellent deception plan, a high-risk decision in face of the weather, and a gut misappreciation by the Germans. In fact the way Overlord developed suggests that without this operational surprise—if the Germans had moved their armour southwest straight away, that is—the invasion might well have been bottled up or driven back into the sea.

In this respect Overlord respected one of the principles of manoeuvre theory. For while masters of manoeuvre do not, if they can help it, allow their operations to depend wholly on surprise, they base their primary plan and the forces required for it on achieving surprise, then make a contingency

181

plan with a more modest aim to cover loss of it. There are of course both historical and theoretical exceptions in which tactical or even operational surprise is unobtainable, or when an opening is going to have to be fought for wherever and whenever it is sought. This is why the Soviets still keep the "heavy break-in" battle in their manuals, and maintain troops equipped and trained to fight it. But these cases are the exceptions which prove the principle of using surprise as a manoeuvre multiplier.

One needs to distinguish between the levels of surprise (strategic, operational and tactical), particularly since the key level of surprise may not be the same as the level of the action. A small usable area of operations, as in North Africa, or a combination of terrain and situation, as in many instances on the Eastern Front, may mean that an operation must be launched with only tactical surprise. And Overlord is an example of a strategic action which gained greatly from, or even turned on the achievement of operational surprise.

Fuller, in what is to my mind his most valuable single contribution to military thinking, distinguishes between "moral surprise" and "material surprise". **Moral surprise** means that the enemy does not know you are coming; in Fuller's view, only moral surprise can achieve an immediate decision. **Material surprise** means that the enemy knows you are coming but cannot do anything to stop you. As I suggested in my conclusions about the dynamics of manoeuvre theory (Fig. 29 and text, pages 112/113), the concept of material surprise, though the less dramatic of the two, is fundamental to manoeuvre theory. For it *makes surprise restorable*, analogous, if you like, to chastity as opposed to virginity. You may or may not achieve moral surprise, but by outdoing the enemy in tempo, by getting and keeping your tempo high enough to put yourself inside his decision loop ("the Boyd Cycle"), you can both ensure material surprise and restore it if lost. What is more, the concept of material surprise suggests that both the value of surprise and the conditions for its achievement should be quantifiable, at least in part.

Quantifying surprise

Let us return to the exotic top two layers of the club sandwich battle of Chapter 9 (pages 154/155) and suppose that the attacker plans to use a helicopter force to seize one of three or four key river crossings or airfields about 50 kilometres from one another—he may go for one of each, but no matter. Let us assume, in line with the discussions of the two preceding chapters, that he assembles an adequate mechanised force under pretext of manoeuvres, and succeeds in concealing the preliminary dispositions for his heliborne and airborne operations. Then he will lose strategic surprise as his first helicopter forces cross the frontier (or if seaborne the coast), and will lose operational surprise once their heading

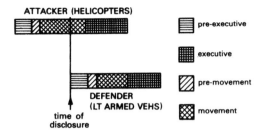

ATTACKER (HELICOPTERS)

pre-executive

executive

DEFENDER
(LT ARMED VEHS)

pre-movement

movement

time of
disclosure

FIG. 43. *Schematic to illustrate how material surprise can be quantified (see text). The defender (very favourably to him) is credited with the same planning and preparation time as the attacker. The attacker moves 200 km in helicopters, the defender 50 km in light armoured vehicles.*

offers an informed guess about the area of their objectives. Let us take this moment as the "time of disclosure" and suppose (favourably to the defender) that the attacking helicopter force is then 200 kilometres from its objective (Fig. 43).

We can now break down the timing of both sides' activities into four quite general elements. Two of these are dependent on movement and two independent of it, but it may be best to take them in chronological order. The first, which I have called **pre-execution time**, is the time taken for the commander and staff to arrive at an outline plan. The attacker will be given his mission and will have received a warning order. The defender must bring his force from whatever state it is in to immediate notice, and make his intelligence appreciation before he can start planning; on the other hand he will presumably have a set of contingency plans. So let us reinforce the argument by leaning towards the defender, and credit both sides with the same pre-execution time.

The second element is **pre-movement time**. This is the period from the commander's decision to the beginning of controlled movement. With a pre-warned helicopter force this tends to zero. For the defender's surface movement, computers pre-loaded with contingency plans should produce an almost instant plan, but orders have to be issued and serials moved to their start points. Again let us unfairly favour the defender by crediting both sides with equal pre-movement time. The third element is **movement time** from the start position to the objective. The fourth element, **execution time**, is independent of controlled movement but includes deployment. In effect it is the time taken for the attacker to seize the objective; or for the defender, if he gets there first, to secure it against attack. In crediting the defender's immediate response with high tempo, one assumes that it would be not powerful enough to dislodge the attacker once he has established himself there. We can now see clearly that the attacker's basic advantage stems from the first two elements in his action, and perhaps part of the third, taking place before disclosure, while the defender can only start to react after disclosure.

This simple model, I suggest, demonstrates four things. Given reasonable knowledge of the defender's state and dispositions, the attacker can shape his plan so as to ensure material surprise, even if he loses moral surprise at the earliest reasonably predictable moment. Second, it provides an example of how physical mobility and the portmanteau concept of tempo (Chapter 6) interact. Because some elements are dependent on movement and others are not, the physical mobility of a force has an absolute value, as well as its relative value with respect to the enemy and other types of friendly forces (Chapter 6). Third, movement speeds apart, we have credited both sides with roughly equal mounting tempo (covering the first three elements) and equal execution tempo (covering the fourth). The attacker's mounting tempo does not bear directly here, because for him the first two elements take place before disclosure. But it is evident how a faster execution tempo will improve his chances of complete success. Fourth, by now crediting the attacker with higher mounting and execution tempos than the defender and removing the line representing "time of disclosure", we can see how, in terms of these four elements, the attacker can not only maintain or if needs be restore material surprise *but can plan to do so.*

Moral surprise—synthetic momentum

Moral surprise is superior to material surprise on both psychological and physical levels. The first of these is almost certainly the decisive one, and this is a matter of subjective judgement on the one side and subjective reaction on the other—the "clash of wills" which I shall look at in Chapter 12. But it appears both feasible and worthwhile to evaluate the physical aspect of moral surprise in terms of mass and tempo. This will depend basically on the defender's state of readiness, and thus on whether the attacker has achieved moral, or at least material, strategic surprise. Given moral strategic surprise, one would expect the defender's mass to be somewhere between 60 and 80 per cent of its nominal value, with organic weight per man (representing equipment readiness) more or less up to scale for the available manpower. One can also form a quantitative idea of the value of moral surprise by looking at the attacker. In discussing Fig. 43 we have so far focused mainly on the part to the right of the "disclosure" line as a means of understanding material surprise.

If we now look to the left of that line, we see (as the defender does not) preparation and movement by the attacker. This suggests that one might see moral surprise as *synthetic momentum.* Thus a force carrying out a surprise mission will have a basic physical combat worth derived from its mass and its actual momentum. Suppose we then re-evaluate this force's tempo on the basis that its whole activity from initial decision to final attack (the entire "attacker" bar left *and* right of the "disclosure" line on the schematic) takes place in the existing time to the right of the "disclosure" line. We now have a synthetic tempo and thus a synthetic value for momentum. By comparing this result with the degradation of the enemy's combat worth through unpreparedness, one should be able to arrive at a fairly safe estimate of the minimum mass one can afford to employ. Theoretically this notion of synthetic momentum provides a kind of upper limit of the value of moral surprise in terms of manoeuvre theory.

Readiness

Theoretically at least, the peacetime manning level would be brought up to over 80 per cent in 48 hours or so; but the time needed for further improvement could be way outside the time scale we are considering. There will be conspicuous peaks just before and during manoeuvres, and corresponding sags after them. Each nation's army shows a consistent and thus predictable pattern in this respect, even if the situation is not permanently monitored and reported by agents—as is almost certainly the case with NATO forces in the Federal Republic. Subject to this limitation on available manpower, infantry can be brought to short or immediate notice fairly quickly, say in a couple of hours or so *plus* the time it takes to marry them up with the trucks or helicopters which are to lift them.

For mechanised combat units, especially tank units, and armoured artillery a major distinction has to be drawn. One can assume that any reasonably trained force will keep its vehicles full of fuel. If it also keeps them battle-stowed, it should be able to turn out (again at available strength) rather faster than an infantry unit. If not, the problem lies in "bombing up" the tanks and guns. From considerable experience, I would say that to bomb up a tank from scratch actually takes the best part of 3 hours and employs all available crew manpower for that period. Allowing for loading ammunition from a dump onto trucks and unpacking it, I reckon a tank battalion would do very well to get itself genuinely ready to move in 7 hours; 10 hours for the head to reach the start point would be a more realistic figure. One may thus be looking at a degradation of mounting tempo by anything from a factor of three upwards. On the other hand, once prepared, troops of all types can be held at 1 hour's notice for considerable periods, both in barracks and in the field.

Strategic surprise

For a demonstration of the immense value of strategic surprise one need go back no further than the Argentinian invasion of the Falklands. How they achieved this, particularly after having telegraphed the punch by their actions on South Georgia, is a matter for historians. But by presenting

Britain and the world with a *fait accompli*, they came within an ace of achieving their political aim, first diplomatically, then—as far as air and sea were concerned—militarily. They used conventional techniques; but higher-grade armed forces could probably have done the job more swiftly and cleanly with special forces alone.

If the United States version of Cuban infiltration of Grenada is accurate, this was a case of a foreign-led coup with a back-up force clandestinely introduced. In this instance, the scale of the whole affair was small enough for the labour force engaged in airfield construction to provide military support, and had the United States not gone in hard with at least operational surprise, a very nasty little war might have resulted. As it was, the United States had to commit three or four times the force initially deployed. Operating on light scales at the end of short sea and air lines over which she had unchallenged control, she was able to reinforce quickly. Sound facts about the early stages of the Soviet takeover of Afghanistan are hard to come by; but it does seem that many of their problems stemmed from the time it took them to move in and deploy their mechanised forces. The relatively slow tempo of this deployment left too long a gap between seizure of control of the political centre and extension of it to key routes and provincial centres. This gave the resistance time to harden its attitudes and to organise.

The lesson is that if sufficient back-up cannot be inserted in advance it must get there as soon as the prepositioned special forces and agents take their first overt action. This is simply an application of the principle of simultaneity. Mechanised forces just cannot achieve this, and even deployment from an airhead taken over or captured at the same time as the coup may be too slow. This is where the helicopter, in future submarine-borne if needs be, bridges the tempo gap.

One might envisage a first-echelon task force of two helicopter brigades and a parachute brigade, the latter clandestinely assembled and launched as outlined in Chapter 9. One helicopter brigade would operate in direct support of the clandestine forces. The other's primary mission would be to seize an airhead. The parachute brigade would be a reserve for the seizure of the airhead; but if all went well it would land in, relieve the helicopter brigade there, and organise the fly-in and deployment of a mechanised airborne force assembled semi-clandestinely from great depth (Chapter 9).

My reason for citing this example is that, with modern mobility, strategic surprise could be achieved with purely military risk—the risk of premature loss of moral surprise. Actions taken before the clandestine forces came into the open and the helicopters took off might well be spotted; but they could scarcely be construed as an act of war. There would be no need for a political cover story; in fact nothing could be worse for the attacker than a political murmur of any kind. By contrast, when large forces have to be assembled under some pretext—as in the hackneyed case of Warsaw Pact manoeuvres—there is a risk of losing moral surprise well before hostilities are opened, and of this triggering an irreversible move into a build-up culminating in war. Thus the risk, and the judgement of it, are elevated from strategic to political level. This inevitably results in a very nice conflict between the soldier's estimate of what he needs and the politician's of what he can get away with. Hitler's seizure of the Rhineland is a classic example of this conflict. In the case of the Warsaw Pact, most estimates suggest that the Soviets are physically capable of mobilising twenty-three of their own divisions in the GDR at short notice. But the largest force so far ever assembled in Warsaw Pact manoeuvres in the German Democratic Republic probably amounts to some 300 000 men—rather under two all-arms and two tank armies. It may or may not be a coincidence that this roughly matches the simultaneous capacity of the east–west routes they might use. What matters is that, since a force of this size has been assembled and manoeuvred several times over the years, the political risk is low. Concentration of a larger force would cause instant raising of NATO's eyebrows.

Special forces and surprise

Having looked at the employment of clandestine forces—special forces and agents, that is—as a strategic spearhead, we should next examine their influence on operational surprise. In the next chapter we shall look at the other side of this coin—the need for operational intelligence; the drama of offensive action by special forces tends to mask their primary operational role of information gathering. The known pattern of Soviet deep reconnaissance and special force deployment, to say nothing of the massive infiltration of the Federal Republic by agents, makes it virtually certain that every NATO headquarters, signals centre and heavy artillery unit—in other words every potential special force or raid target—will be under constant surveillance from the time it leaves its peacetime location or arrives in the theatre on mobilisation. Combat and logistic units would be on a lower priority, perhaps watched by locally recruited agents instructed to report only deviations from their normal pattern. I may be wrong, but from the 11 years or so I have served in Germany since the War, I have gained the impression that major combat units are under constant surveillance in peacetime, and that the watch on movements of individual officers may reach far wider than is generally supposed.

Whatever the details, there is a surveillance and reporting system which, when combined with signals intelligence (SIGINT) and other means, applies the same kind of clamp at operational level that surveillance satellites do at strategic. This massive operational intelligence set-up can be expected to provide a steady flow of first-rate information, on the one hand to operational and higher tactical commanders, and on the other to all concerned with offensive special force operations.

Given that an enemy resource selected as a target is under surveillance, there are five or more ways of dealing with it. In every army, I think, members of the special forces are trained in controlling artillery fire and talking-in air attacks. They could likewise talk-in a helicopter force, whether it was simply delivering fire or was to put in an assault. In the case of a surface raid, the observer makes a rendezvous with the raid force commander before tactical surprise is lost, giving him and his orders group a complete up-to-the-minute rundown on the target, and personally guiding a sub-unit or fighting patrol with a particularly important or difficult mission. (In fact the special force detachment will be at least two and up to five strong.) Finally, if the target is amenable to sabotage as opposed to destruction by concentrated fire or tactical seizure, either the watchers or a back-up special force detachment can do the job for themselves.

However the job is done, the chance of tactical surprise is very high; and from the nature of the targets, their destruction is likely to be of operational significance. One is thus led to ask whether, in the purely military context as opposed to the political one considered earlier, a detachment or group small enough to be clandestinely inserted can achieve moral operational surprise and thus an immediate operational or even strategic decision. My instinct— which I cannot quite see how to support—is that this will only be so in minor theatres where a vulnerable resource—such as a fuel pipeline, a water supply or a rugged mountain pass—is unique, and where the force dependent on it is widely dispersed.

Organised forces engaged in active operations tend to have a certain cohesion and inertia (here in the good sense, as in flywheel), which shields them against incidents which do not physically inhibit their activities. There is a good deal of historical evidence that even the capture or killing of a respected higher commander along with his headquarters does not much affect the immediate course of events. The loss of talent will tell, and a succession of such setbacks chips away at morale; but there is no cataclysm. Perhaps we can draw here on two related concepts developed in Part 2— sufficient mass and sustained threat. Paralysis by shock seems of itself to require the impact of a certain minimum mass. What is more, to exert leverage, a mobile force must retain potential energy (the ability to apply firepower) and potential momentum (the ability to continue moving). In these terms, a special force detachment is more like the human equivalent of firepower. The effect of its action may be devastating, but once it has forfeited both moral surprise and mobility beyond that of the boot, it ceases to pose a credible threat.

The reader may like to join me in speculating where the psychological borderline lies. The issue turns, I think, on this notion of a sustained or regenerated threat. A (company) combat team of assault helicopters might well achieve tactical surprise, and has enough physical fighting power to sustain its threat after it has struck, given that it can refuel and rearm. In fact of course it would use its "potential momentum" to pull out or make a sizeable switch to a second target. A special force detachment which succeeded in evading might in fact continue to pose a real local threat, but this would be on rather a low level; and even at that level the threat would not be credible enough to have a psychological effect. On the other hand, exactly the same action carried out by a team of guerrillas known to have the support of the population would have the same psychological effect as the insertion of a mobile force. This is because a group of guerrillas would be expected to have hide-outs which would allow it to conceal itself, rest, feed and re-arm in safety. In other words, like the mobile force, it would be seen as able to sustain or regenerate its threat and to regain surprise. Nevertheless an individual force of this minute size, however successful, is unlikely to achieve a decisive operational or strategic success by taking on *military* targets.

Security, deception and bluff

In lay circles at least, security of information during the Second World War is widely considered to have been good. Where orthodox military activities were concerned, a mixture of strong leadership, patriotism, rigorous censorship and fear generally worked well. The Dieppe raid can scarcely be counted a security failure, because Churchill still pressed on after intelligence told him that the plan had been blown. I have never seen convincing evidence on whether or not the concentration of Waffen-SS armour in the general area of Arnhem was coincidental or the result of a leak. Be this as it may, both disasters drive home the lesson that few things are worse than ignoring intelligence and pretending you have still moral surprise when you know you have lost it.

At a higher level, the Enigma saga and the fact that Kim Philby was head of "Section D" (the parent substance of Special Operations Executive, SOE), then an instructor with SOE, and later posted to the Secret Intelligence Service proper (MI6) suffice to expose "security" for the farce it generally is. Like passive defence, the most that passive protection of information can do is to buy time; once either is penetrated, it is useless. Long years of working within the framework of the security system have convinced me that, provided it is not pushed to the point of denting morale, it is reasonably effective in keeping unimportant information from unimportant people; but that it provides a cloak within which professional spies, especially spies of conscience, can easily spirit away to their masters the few pieces of information that matter.

In any event, surely not even the hard-nosed persons in curved blinkers who now run many Western countries can still believe in "security" as a means of protecting information except in the narrowest of circles for the shortest of periods. This has become one of the weaknesses the democracies suffer from *vis-à-vis* the authoritarian regimes of the second and third worlds. Almost without exception, Western societies are losing cohesion and stability. They are as deeply divided among themselves as they are penetrated by their potential opponents. Over the past few years, at least one highly responsible person in every leading NATO country has felt morally impelled, at the cost of career and mostly of freedom, to leak classified information. It is not my purpose here to lambast the security system, simply to emphasise what a poor instrument it has become for the achievement of moral surprise—quite apart from the threat to secrecy posed by the spectrum of strategic and operational surveillance.

In Fig. 44 I have attempted to suggest, by means of a notional curve, the way the chance of maintaining moral surprise for a military action decays as

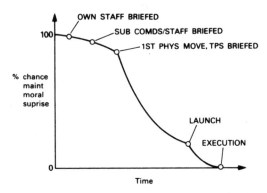

FIG. 44. *Notional curve to suggest the diminishing chance of maintaining moral surprise as preparations for an operation progress.*

the inevitable preparations for it progress. It is worth following these stages through to bring out the point that the maintenance of moral surprise may conflict with the achievement of material surprise. Sacrifice of the one to improve the prospects of the other is certainly a valid area for command decision—all the more so when the leadership aspect is taken into account. In fact, as we shall see in Part 4, the security problem provides yet another argument for directive control. But under any system of troop control there will always be strong and valid arguments which conflict with the conservation of security—the extent of training on new equipment and in special procedures and tactics; the employment of an insurance margin of mass, and/or concentration further forward; and above all the psychological preparation of troops.

With this in mind, back to the curve. Once the commander briefs his key staff, some information is bound to go onto paper or into some form of computer memory. The success of the "bugging" and "hacking" techniques practised by schoolchildren in gaining access to high-grade and purportedly secure data processing systems, likewise the scope for professional computer fraud, suggest that a sophisticated enemy could gain access to supposedly secure systems even without a leak. And in view of the time that elapses from the design of major systems to the end of their service life, a leak somewhere down the line from design office and software studio to field maintenance team seems next to inevitable.

The chance of maintaining secrecy diminishes progressively as subordinate commanders and staffs are briefed and take their own planning action; this is simply a function of the number of individuals, data processing systems and locations involved, the effect being aggravated if information is passed over communications links. The collapse really sets in when the first physical moves are made and troops are briefed, even to cover-story level. The whole thing is thrown open to surveillance; and security of information is now degraded not only by the number of those in the know but by their lower level of reliability. We discussed the problems of final assembly and launch in Chapter 9 and at the beginning of this chapter.

In those discussions, and when examining the changing significance of cover in Chapter 4, one concluded that concealment in face of a first-rate enemy was only to be had from large areas of really dense cover, such as forests, or from going far enough underground to mask the full range of thermal effects—a less than ideal way of setting about a mobile operation. German emphasis on the value of the information they obtained on the Eastern Front from radio intercept suggests that Soviet security left a good deal to be desired. But the Red Army did practise *operativnaya maskirovka* ("operational concealment") extensively, and had great success with it. The Grechko/Vatutin switch of 3 Guards Tank Army and a massive supporting force between the Bukrin and Lyutezh bridgeheads on 25 and 26 October 1943 provides a classic example. The maintenance of moral surprise for a switch of this kind or for forward movement on a similar scale is inconceivable in face of modern surveillance and of the way special forces are now employed to gather information. However, the Soviets were equally keen on active deception—and they have since become increasingly so.

Before considering particular forms of active deception, I want to air an alternative method of protecting information on operational and strategic plans which exploits the potential of computers and guards against their foibles. It is the equivalent of "lunar landscaping" a whole area to conceal defensive works or vestiges of movement, and calls for the production of **multiple contingency plans**. It applies best to initial plans for pre-emption or the opening of hostilities. But on Napoleon's principle of the tree that has many branches bearing fruit, it could well have twofold merit for the development of operations too. The name I have given this technique leaves little need for explanation. You increase your contingency planning effort to draw up a number of alternative plans for each contingency, to take them right down to tactical and logistic detail, and of course to keep them up to date. As I shall bring out in Chapter 16, much of the detailed work could in fact be done by computer, so that the call on high-grade human resources might not greatly increase. These plans, developed as appropriate down through the levels, would be disseminated and held on, say, floppy disks. They would be classified as a concession to the conventional intelligence mind; but the assumption would be that the opposition would acquire them. Thus—and this is the point—the variations on any one theme would have to be numerous enough to face the enemy with an enigma and inhibit him from making a purposeful response in advance. The selected plan could then be implemented at the last minute by a single codeword, which *could* be made the subject of several stages of protection with reasonable hope of success.

Once operations are under way, though, the time and effort needed to maintain this kind of system will diminish, and specific means of **active deception** will be called for. As surveillance techniques advance, the cost and effort of physical deception will come to approach those of the real thing. The days of empty camouflage nets, wooden guns and rubber tanks are, one feels, past. The only way to be sure of success—yet another form of "lunar landscaping"—will be to deploy real formations in a deception role. Up to the assembly area, whatever form that may take, this course calls for very careful consideration of total resources, concentration and reserves. If, as would almost certainly be the case, only one deception force could be fielded, the increased risk of giving the game away early may outweigh the gain from impaling the enemy on the horns of a dilemma. And once a deception force comes into contact, one is really out of the sphere of deception and into that of feints and diversionary actions, which are another thing again.

Here Operation Overlord points the way for the future. As mentioned earlier, Eisenhower's deception plan was extremely successful and perhaps critical to the success of the operation. And a major factor in this—perhaps the key one—was the radio simulation of a phoney formation in Kent and East Sussex. The creation of a phoney force by electronic simulation implies a dangerously high level of signals traffic in the real ones; and computers are not going to make positive electronic deception any easier. Such things as operator and station idiosyncrasies are ideal subjects for computer analysis, storage and retrieval with a minimum of human intervention. On the other hand, a whole array of techniques for eliminating or masking such characteristics are now available. One is into the game of "countermeasures to the *n*th", one ill suited to public airing and in any event best left to the experts. But, all in all, electronics are likely to provide the principal means of active deception.

One interesting offshoot of this line of thought is the use of phoney orders. In the past, with direct voice transmissions, this has, as far as I know, only worked for short periods at low levels, and then only at moments of extreme pressure. I experienced it once myself, and what happened then bears out what I have heard and read of similar experiences both on land and in the air. Whether the imitation of normal working on the net is good or bad, deception is seldom achieved and never lasts long. The most usual effects, often just as serious, are confusion, and hesitancy in using the radio. Now, with computers available to analyse voiceprints and voice synthesis an established technique, things may be rather different. In military applications, and for very good technical reasons, both VHF/FM net radio and radio relay use a limited bandwidth and low-grade amplification. A phoney order could thus be generated in a familiar-sounding voice with relatively low-grade equipment from a simple model and an oral or typed-in instruction. I may be quite wrong, but this appears to be yet another hazard implicit in today's almost total reliance on net radio at tactical levels.

This brief speculation leads one into the field of bluff. The way the terms "deception" and 'bluff' are often used in military contexts leads one to suspect that people take them to be synonymous, or at least to overlap in meaning. True, "bluff" is a form of deception; conversely "deception" comprehends "bluff". But I suggest that a clear distinction can and must be drawn. "Deception" in the military sense in which I have always understood it and have just been using it implies measures *superimposed on a genuine capability* to enhance the chance of success. "Bluff" is the simulation of non-existent capability or the exaggeration of a very limited one. (The word "bluff", incidentally, comes via the great American poker game from the Dutch *"bluffen"*, meaning "to boast".) An essential attribute of a "bluff" is that it will fail completely if called, while the uncovering of deceptive measures will only downgrade the chance of success or restrict its scope.

A bluff must be credible at the physical level; but in war as in poker, the factors which determine whether it amounts to praiseworthy audacity or sheer gambling are mainly psychological. First, the bluffer himself must feel confident he will get away with it; he needs to be on a winning streak. Second, he must be regarded as a winner by both his own side and the opposition. This is one of the dangers, discussed earlier, in a commander becoming a legendary figure to his opponents. Turning once more to personal experience, and once more to Rommel in North Africa, I recall watching a show of force by over one hundred German tanks moving along the Trigh Capuzzo east of ed Duda. (This was probably 15 Panzer Division pulling back from the unsuccessful raid into Egypt, which would put the date as 29 November 1941.) The British still had a useful force of fit tanks concentrated a few kilometres to the south but decided against giving battle. It later emerged that only a dozen or so of the German tanks could both motor and fire; of the rest, those which could fire and many that could not were being towed by those which could motor. Even at that stage and immediately after a failure, Rommel's reputation was such that this amounted to a successful bluff, although it may well have been an unintended one—simply the extrication of a battered force. The moral once again is the need for operational intelligence. More of this in the next chapter, and of the clash of wills in Part 4.

Apart from active deception and bluff, most of the activities traditionally regarded as stratagems have become, or are on the way to becoming, part and parcel of the normality of war. The Trojan horse has become the Spetsnaz "NATO platoon". Those who continue to insist on regarding special force operations and government-sponsored terrorism as unsporting do themselves a threefold injury. They deprive themselves of a powerful weapon; they lay their countries open to direct strategic pre-emption or defeat by these techniques; and they expose their organised forces to intensification by semi-clandestine actions of the leverage exerted by the opponent's mobile force.

Conclusion

For some types of operation, raids in the Western sense, for instance, the usable mass is so small that success or failure turns on the achievement of moral surprise. When restrictions on usable mass are less rigorous, the decision on how far to depend on moral surprise becomes an extremely complex one, in effect a matter of generalship. Increasing mass reduces the chance of achieving moral surprise. By contrast, it may be *worth* increasing mass to gain the calculable asset of material surprise at the cost of the speculative one of moral surprise. Even where decisive initial success must depend on moral surprise, the need to ensure partial success, to attain some fallback aim, or to prevent a failure becoming a disaster may dictate a minimum mass and physical fighting power.

Then come the counter-arguments for reducing mass. One can increase the chance of moral surprise by active deception short of the use of combat troops. One can disperse mass on the lines of the "fleet in being" theory by the out-of-contact movement of combat troops; or one can commit these troops in a diversionary operation. A diversionary movement or operation in advance of the main one can serve to enhance both moral surprise, by taking the enemy's eye off the ball, and/or material surprise by drawing off his reserves. A simultaneous diversion will contribute to material surprise by inhibiting the commitment of enemy reserves. Superimposed on all this more or less quantifiable area, and aimed at the achievement of moral surprise, is the reduction of mass by bluff—something completely dependent on psychological factors and in this instance on subjective judgement.

The other side of the coin is readiness, the Achilles heel of industrial democracies. Mahan puts it like this:

"To prepare for war in time of peace is impracticable to commercial representative nations, because the people in general will not give sufficient heed to military necessities, or to international problems, to feel the pressure which induces readiness."

Readiness is extremely expensive. As I have shown elsewhere, only about one-third of the total standing force available can be kept at high readiness over long periods; thus the cost is self-evident. I believe that by treating unreadiness as a degradation of tempo in the combat worth equation, one can likewise demonstrate the cost of *un*readiness. As we saw in Chapter 8, these estimates can only be relative. But I should not be surprised to find that permanent high readiness generally showed an enhancement of combat worth over the normal peacetime state by a factor greater than three. This would make readiness cost-effective in real terms.

This chapter has explored the borderline between theory and art, as subsequent ones will do. For this reason it well exemplifies both the value and the limitations of military theory, and its resemblance in these respects to "scientific management". By analysing what is amenable to analysis, theory improves understanding of the whole and helps form judgement. Then, by at once narrowing and delineating the grey zones, it allows that trained judgement to focus on them.

12

Intelligence, Risk and Luck

"Now the reason the enlightened prince and the wise general conquer the enemy whenever they move and their achievements surpass those of ordinary men is foreknowledge."   Sun Tzu

"Thus a victorious army wins its victories before seeking battle; an army destined to defeat fights in the hope of winning."   Idem

"Gentlemen, when the enemy is committed to a mistake, we must not interrupt him too soon."   Napoleon (trans. Mahan)

Introduction

With a liking for figures and some experience of low-level research war games, I was long convinced that probability theory ought to be a battle-winning aid in allotting troops to tasks. The Soviet use of "win tables" (as quoted for instance by David Isby) confirms this view—and incidentally throws light on the concepts of minimum and sufficient mass (Chapter 5). This approach is certainly valid for attrition theory, since the chance of winning a particular engagement tells you whether and how far that engagement is likely to contribute to the progressive change in the ratio of relative strengths. Under manoeuvre theory it is the wrong question to ask. The guiding principle lies in the old saw—"If you have to ask how much it costs, you can't afford it." If you have to work out the chance of winning, you should not seek or accept battle; if the enemy forces you to accept battle, you have no option whatever the odds.

One therefore needs to distinguish rather carefully between chance of success, risk and luck. Whether or not it provides a useful basis for decisions, the chance of success is calculable by the kind of techniques discussed in Part 2 and the preceding chapter—Sun Tzu's "calculations". **Risk** then represents the possibility that this predicted chance of success will be degraded by lack of information. **Luck** stands for the possibility of the chance of success being either enhanced (good luck) or degraded (bad luck) by some event that is unpredictable and completely outside either side's control. This does not mean that the notion of "luck management" is an idle one. "Luck only stays with the good general." Like so many clichés,

197

this one, shaped by the elder Moltke, is entirely valid. "Luck management" calls for awareness and flexibility—the one a facet of the art of generalship, the other a product of directive control.

Odds and decisions

The processes by which odds are calculated and the command decision for or against a plan is reached are different in kind. One is basically mathematical, perhaps fudged a bit; the other is subjective. And there are two good reasons why this should be so. One is the "high life" principle set out above; the other is the dominance of the psychological factors. But it would be illuminating, perhaps directly helpful, to establish some kind of relationship between the two. One is really looking for the cut-off points between gambling, audacity and soundness, and trying to express these in terms of probabilities, or easier perhaps of odds. The reader may like to pause at this point and ponder on where he would set these demarcations.

To my perhaps over-cautious mind, evens (50 per cent) or worse definitely constitutes a gamble. In statistical terms one is inclined to push this borderline up to 6 to 4 on (60 per cent) or even 2 to 1 on (67 per cent). If praiseworthy audacity starts at 6 to 4 on, one might see it as extending to the limits of the "probability zone" familiar to gunners—9 to 4 on or 82 per cent. Now this is interesting, because this is the point at which the curve of the law of diminishing returns begins to flatten out (Fig. 37, page 134). (Statisticians will spot that I am committing a mathematical tautology here, but I think it a helpful one in common-sense terms.) In discussing the allocation of troops to tasks, I suggested that an increase beyond this point was an insurance, with the implication that it could well be an over-insurance. This is another way of saying that one is on the borderline between audacity and soundness, soundness here having a mildly derogatory import.

In this chapter one is considering not just the allocation of troops to tasks, but the commander's overall assessment of the chance of success, taking account of psychological factors. At this point the reader might like to draw a mental comparison between his views and my suggestions. The betting man will probably see them as erring wildly on the side of caution. I for my part must admit to having been heavily influenced by Sun Tzu's view, in conjunction with the scope manoeuvre theory offers in seeking or avoiding battle. But I do not think the actual figures matter too much. The important thing surely is for the commander under training to see that, in the military context as in gambling, terms like "a gamble", "rashness", "audacity" and "soundness" are related to an objective baseline, and to appreciate in what parish the chance of his enterprise succeeding might lie.

Information and risk

I am convinced that to the addict of attrition "tactical risk" (meaning tactical and operational risk) is a matter of shape (Fig. 45). Give him a broad, continuous front, with failure constantly being reinforced to keep the line straight and tidy, and he thinks himself safe. Show him the basic situation of manoeuvre theory, with a holding force, a hinge, and a mobile force advancing into the enemy's depth, and he will instantly dub the mobile force's situation a high-risk one. True, this L-shaped posture obeys Tukhachevskii's principle of maximum contact area; and increasing contact area does have an implication of increasing risk. But the reason the addict of attrition—in my view quite erroneously—sees the "L" shape as a high-risk one is because it does not match the shape of his information.

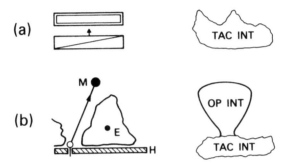

F IG. 45. *Schematic to illustrate the idea of matching the shape of the military posture and that of the intelligence picture, in attritional warfare (a) and manoeuvre warfare (b).*

Like all management decisions, command decisions are based partly on established fact and sound information, partly on information of questionable reliability, and partly on "reasonable" assumptions. These last two categories coincide, because one of the assumptions, tacit or otherwise, is either that the dubious information as a whole has a particular level of reliability, or that certain specific elements in it are correct. A decision-maker bases his plan on "reasonable" assumptions because, if he uses worst-case assumptions, he will get nowhere. So we can look on these "reasonable" assumptions as having a particular degree of favourableness. If they all hold, the plan will have the chance of success the commander thinks it has. If one or more of them turns out less favourably for him, the predicted chance of success will be reduced. It is this reduction which I understand as "risk"— or at least which I shall describe by the word "risk" in this chapter.

Let us slough off the complexities of armies and manoeuvre theory and examine risk in the simpler and more familiar setting of driving a car, and in particular of overtaking. Let us analyse the assumptions that must or may be made by the overtaking driver—analogous to the attacker in war.

The vehicle being overtaken will hold course and speed, or adjust these only in response to conditions, unless its driver indicates otherwise. This has to be taken for granted, but in fact the assumption is a frequent cause of accidents. So here we have an identifiable, but not quantifiable, minimum risk. The fallibility of this assumption is markedly increased if one or more reasonable options are open to the vehicle being overtaken. This is one of the reasons why one should not overtake at a crossroads (the other being emerging traffic). But here we see the information base coming into play. If the branching minor carriageway is an entrance, the probability of the overtaken vehicle using it is greatly reduced. If it is a farm entrance, one would not overtake a cargo truck, a fuel tanker, a tractor or the kind of large, flashy car the Germans so aptly call a *Metzgerwagen* ("butcher's wagon"). But one might well shape up to overtake a whisky tanker, a furniture van or a family car, warning of one's intention with horn or lights. I leave it to the reader to embroider this pattern of sub-assumptions from his own experience. This first assumption concerns the *predictability* of the overtaken driver's behaviour. In fact this behaviour will often include the kind of thwarting response, more or less well concealed, that an enemy might make in war.

The other assumptions the overtaking driver makes concern road space and thus depend on *intervisibility*. If you are on a long straight and can pull out to look at the road in front of the overtaken vehicle before committing yourself, the road-space risk tends to zero. You have 100 per cent sound information. If you are forced to assume that there is no other vehicle or obstruction in front of the vehicle you plan to overtake, two risk elements arise. The vehicle immediately in front of you may itself pull out to overtake; or you may be forced to stay in the oncoming traffic's path beyond the point you have calculated as being clear. You have replaced a key piece of hard information with a favourable assumption—that the road in front of the overtaken vehicle is clear. In particular instances you may feel this to be an acceptable risk, because you can respond by acceleration or braking. You have partially counteracted the risk by *flexibility*, by keeping something in reserve.

Suppose we now make the road undulating. You can see stretches of road a good way ahead and deduce from these being clear that no vehicle moving at reasonable speed can be in the dead ground. Your information is quite extensive, and firm as far as it goes. But it is incomplete, and you have filled it out with the favourable assumption implied by the qualification "moving at reasonable speed". If there is a static obstruction on either lane in the dead ground, still more if there is a stationary vehicle which moves off towards you, you may be in trouble. Once again you have introduced an element of risk to achieve your aim despite a gap in your information. One then comes to overtaking on or approaching a blind bend. Here the key piece of information is lacking; you do not know the road to be clear of oncoming traffic, but as the overtaking driver you (unconsciously) assume it to be so because frustration or aggression blocks your judgement. This action is a gamble, and a losing one because the circumstances which impel you to expose yourself to this risk (heavy traffic, that is) make it likely that there will be oncoming traffic. One sees here the dynamics of a deteriorating situation.

I have flogged this analogy long enough. I hope the reader will find it as useful as I do. If one analyses the whole area of driving in this way, one finds it permeated by a pattern of favourable assumptions—some conscious, some tacit; some truly reasonable, some wild. By the same token, the approach known as "defensive driving" qualifies the standard pattern of "reasonable" assumptions by worst-case assumptions—making it somewhat comparable to Montgomery's principle of balance (keeping your options open). In driving as in war, the art lies in applying the blend of favourable and worst-case assumptions most likely to get you to your objective in good time and good shape.

But to clinch my point about information and risk, and to highlight the fallacy of attrition-orientated thinking about risk, let me press the overtaking analogy just one stage further. You are driving along an open road under good conditions with traffic of mixed types, well spaced out, moving freely in both directions. You wish to overtake the vehicle in front of you. You can see both sides of the road uninterruptedly for a considerable distance; but there is oncoming traffic. You observe this until you have read the pattern, then decide to use a gap in it to overtake. You shape up, change down, signal and at your chosen moment go. Now this is an audacious move because its success relies on your judgement and your skill of execution. But your information is complete and sure; you have made a minimum of assumptions, so there is a minimum of risk. The chance of failure stems from what Jomini would call "the whims of destiny"—here the calamitous failure of your own or someone else's vehicle.

With all this in mind, let us revert to war, and in particular to the commander of an advancing mobile force. Let us stretch even modern technology a bit, and suppose that he has, on a display and in his head, precise, detailed, up-to-the-minute information on terrain, friendly forces (including of course his own) and enemy. He is in the position of the last driver we considered. His situation poses a measure of danger, because he is exposed to the "whims of destiny", and because the skill and judgement of himself and his subordinates may prove inadequate. (For once the phrase so beloved of those who write competition rules fits!) But his situation is a low-risk one. Because his information is perfect, his predicted chance of success is virtually unaffected by assumptions.

Since its outcome differs markedly from common understanding, I have approached this argument with the utmost scepticism. But the only possible conclusion seems to be that the degree of operational tactical risk is mainly dependent *not* on posture, but on the quantity and quality of information available to the commander, and in particular on the match between the shape of his information and the shape of his posture. The Soviets can fairly regard the deep battle as a low-risk operation because they devote substantial resources to the gathering, processing and dissemination of information over the whole depth of the operation.

Operational intelligence

It may not be too much to say that the primary factor in making manoeuvre theory work for you is establishment of a discrete concept of "operational intelligence" and provision of the means to realise it. Even the German concept of "operational reconnaissance" (*operative Aufklärung*) comes nowhere near filling the need, being little different from the Anglo-American concept of "medium" reconnaissance. On the other hand, the British cavalry regiments which long specialised in reconnaissance, such as 11 Hussars and 12 Lancers, achieved such a standard of excellence in these skills that, whenever the situation was at all fluid, they were in effect providing operational intelligence—mostly to commanders and staffs who had not the least idea what to do with it! But to get an inkling of what it is all about, one needs to look again at Fig. 39 (page 149), depicting the way the Soviets implement their principle of simultaneity. From about 15 kilometres ahead of the vanguard, right out to the final operational objectives and beyond into strategic depths, there is an overlapping network of intelligence-gathering resources. The zone of regimental medium reconnaissance merges into its divisional counterpart, and thence into divisional deep reconnaissance, which in turn overlaps with army, front and theatre Spetsnaz detachments. And spread through this entire depth is a veritable host of agents—20 000 of them in West German territory, it is said.

The organisers of battlefield intelligence must turn their entire concept through 90 degrees (Fig. 45, page 199), just as Tukhachevskii did his in switching from the broad front to the deep battle. The notion of a transverse line, however many "antennae" and salients may protrude from it, just will not do. The image needs to be one of a net cast deep.

The effect of this concept of "operational intelligence" on the handling of information is no less radical. One can no longer tidy everything off into frontages and depths and allot these to levels of headquarters. The lowest useful level for collation becomes the controlling operational headquarters, front or army group. By contrast those who need the information quickly are commanders at Soviet regimental level, and in Western armies at battlegroup (battalion combat team) level.

So the network of information gathering has to be matched by a network of information processing and selective transmission. The only conceivable way to tackle this vast problem is by computer, with signals personnel handling inputs from and outputs to the information-gathering agencies, and with intelligence staffs practising a rather rigorous kind of management by exception both in calling for information and in briefing their chiefs of staff and commanders. This as much as their love of centralised control may account for the way the Soviets have poured vast amounts of particularly precious resources into advanced C^3I technology, with systems linking the controlling operational level to the lowest decision-making tactical level (in their case regiment).

The forward and rearward transmission links in this kind of system are evidently vulnerable both to intercept, and to interference by electronic warfare techniques. But to my mind the greater problem by far is how to make them at once manageable and fast enough not to impose a limitation on tempo. I am anything but expert in the capacities and internal techniques of these systems, whatever their origin. But looking at the man/machine interface, in particular at the need to achieve simple and elegant presentation to commanders and to keep headquarters small, the establishment of two or more categories of priority seems indispensable. And here I have in mind priorities not of types of information (which would be normal) but priorities of levels and geographical areas.

NATO has five levels of command from the highest operational headquarters (army group) to the lowest decision-making tactical headquarters (battlegroup, i.e. battalion). In practice, though, this is reduced to four because the national corps fight their own kind of battle, and the army group commander has little or no operational reserve. The Soviet Army has four levels—front, army (or OMG), division (or specialised brigade) and regiment. But a study both of the Soviet concept of operations and of Manstein's defence of the Ukraine suggests that, in the mobile phase at least, not more than two headquarters, one operational and one tactical, are immediately critical to the course of the operation at any one time.

I am not suggesting (or at least not at this stage) that the non-critical headquarters should be bypassed in the chain of command in the way that the elder Moltke bypassed his "army corps" in 1866/7. But if the operational intelligence system is responsive enough, the needs of the critical ones could be given priority in the information handling process, particularly in selection and (human) interpretation. The "inactive" levels would be kept sufficiently up-to-date to be able to accept priority status when the pattern of the operation brought them to the fore. Equally and more obviously, the same principle could be applied to (lateral) sectors and depth zones.

Essential as it may be, operational intelligence in no way obviates the need for tactical intelligence. The two are really quite different in nature. Operational intelligence, like radio or television news, is mainly broadbrush and short-term. Any information that cannot be interpreted and passed on quickly will probably be overtaken by events. Tactical intelligence corresponds to the press. At the higher level (the national dailies) it is concerned with depth reporting, objective analysis, and both interpretative and speculative comment. At low levels, like the local weeklies, tactical intelligence concerns itself with every detail, seeking to build up a fuller local picture of the enemy than he may have himself. This analogy of the broadcasting media and the press is an extremely useful one. It suggests the need for two separate but interlocking systems, certainly employing rather different kinds of people, and probably using different technologies.

Operational intelligence is too important to be left to the quality of officer assigned to intelligence staffs in most Western armies, certainly in the British Army (as a result of which my views may be biased). One can perhaps usefully put together in one's mind the former excellence of British cavalry reconnaissance mentioned above; the reconnaissance capabilities of the helicopter; the superb quality of most armies' special forces; and the fact that, in the Soviet Army, the "second staff officer" (head of intelligence branch) in a headquarters exercises direct command over the "professional" (specialist) reconnaissance elements.

I believe there is a need for a separate staff function, which one might call "reconnaissance", to deal with operational intelligence. This branch would be orientated towards cavalry, army aviation and special forces—whose way of going about things has much in common—and would be manned by staff officers at least equal in quality to the key operations staff (G3) officers—in other words, people with potential for higher command. The head of this branch would have direct access to the commander, and would control the reconnaissance force and any special force detachments assigned to information gathering. This branch would make use of data processing and specialists, but would be based on human talent of top general staff standard.

Given this equivalent of the broadcasting media, the intelligence staff function could continue much as now, handling tactical and general intelligence on a largely computerised basis. This branch would be separate from the reconnaissance branch so as to keep the latter free of bureaucratic detail, but would report either to the head of reconnaissance branch or to the chief of staff (senior staff officer) and not have direct access to the commander. To avoid increasing the number of officers in lower head-quarters, this intelligence function could be carried out by NCOs at brigade and battalion levels, the existing intelligence officer becoming the reconnaissance officer—an appointment which used to exist in the British tank battalion (and which I myself once held). I shall come back to this topic in Chapter 16, in the context of staff organisation.

Luck

As this last discussion suggests, the complexity of modern warfare forces one to qualify Moltke's dictum. Nowadays luck only stays with the good general *who has a good system of command and control.* For even after we have separated out predictable chance of success and risk, it would be quite wrong to suppose that in talking of "luck" one implies nothing more than Jomini's "whims of destiny". "General's luck" surely comprehends three distinct though related elements—the creation of opportunity, the spotting of opportunity, and the exploitation of opportunity. Only in the second of these does pure chance, the unpredictable whim of destiny, play a part.

At its least positive, the creation of luck depends on being aware of predictable contingencies—possible events outside one's control with a better than even chance of occurring. The first step in this process of creative thinking is *to include and retain within the span of one's awareness information which may not seem directly relevant to one's aim.* The next step is to shape one's plan so as to take advantage of the contingency if it arises, without courting disaster if it does not. Suppose for instance one is planning an autumn offensive with a dog-leg thrust-line which runs along a littoral backed by high mountains which are snow-covered in winter; and that high passes offer a choice of short cuts (Fig. 46). For both tactical and

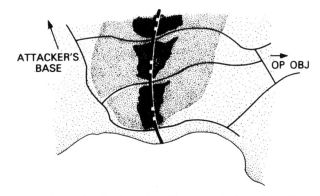

FIG. 46. *Sketch map of notional terrain to illustrate main thrust line on littoral, with possible use of passes if still open.*

meteorological reasons, it would be patent folly to base one's plan on the passes, even with a contingency plan using the littoral. On the other hand, the littoral constitutes a long natural defile, so you are likely to be blocked and forced to fight a break-in battle. You therefore deploy in this sense, but hold a suitable part of your high-tempo resources well back. Then, if the passes are still open when you have drawn the enemy main force forward along the littoral to the neck of the defile, you can seize the exits of the passes with paratroops or helitroops and whip your reserve through them.

The most positive way of creating luck is undoubtedly forcing the opposition into blunders. The setting up of forced errors may sometimes involve a lure or even a trap; but generally, in war as in tennis, it is a matter of tempo. Here one comes back to Fuller's classification of surprise (page 182). If you achieve moral surprise, the enemy may fail to produce any effective response, and you will obtain an immediate material or psychological decision. If you gain and maintain material surprise, especially if you can progressively widen the edge of your tempo over the enemy's response—get further and further inside his decision loop—you will sooner or later force him into a blunder. What is more, you will probably be able to predict the nature of this blunder in time to poise yourself to exploit it—whether by delivering a death blow or, Napoleonically, by giving him rope to hang himself.

Predicting the nature of the blunder leads into the second of the categories I postulated—spotting luck. This is another reason why operational intelligence, and excellence in reporting it to the commander are of such immeasurable importance. For if one side of that coin is the minimisation of risk, the other is the spotting of opportunity. Once again one is looking at a fairly wide spectrum of possibilities. The "lucky" general may set the whole thing in train by asking the right questions of his reconnaissance staff. Or he may see an opening from the information they feed to him. Or again, since picking staff is a key aspect of generalship, they may suggest one to him.

Then there is the question of probability and imminence. The opportunity may be some way off in space and time, at the end of a whole chain of interdependent contingencies. Or it may exist and demand "action this minute". It may concern the enemy directly, or it may be some extraneous circumstance which has moved from the area of pure chance into that of predictability. In fact what matters here is the ability to spot the possible significance of something that seems at once trivial and wholly irrelevant. This is really an aspect of the creative thinking that lies at the root of all innovation and may manifest itself in literary or artistic talent, entrepreneurial flair, management (and thus command) ability, or the pioneering spark in the driest and hardest of scientific fields.

But neither the creation or the appreciation of opportunity is of much use without the ability to exploit it. So one comes back yet again to that overworked word *flexibility*, or better perhaps responsiveness. Even if a brilliant commander spots an opening before it has become as much as a twinkle in his opponent's eye, he will not be much further forward unless he can respond swiftly and appropriately. If his subordinates and their staffs, and his troops, are trained only to act on detailed orders and to obey complex SOPs to the letter regardless of circumstance, he cannot hope to get them to do something extraordinary at the drop of a hat. He must transmit his *idea* instantly and certainly to the mind of the subordinate commander who is to implement it, then leave the latter to interpret and develop it. This, as we shall see, is the essence of directive control.

Conclusion

In these three chapters I have attempted to cast some light on an aspect of war which many, even while acknowledging its reality and importance, prefer to leave as a convenient mystery—one which can be trimmed a little to suit their ends. While I would be the last to deny the reality of the whims of destiny and the art of generalship, I think I have demonstrated that down-to-earth argument and analysis can strip away most of the veils which surround these concepts. It then becomes easier both to identify and to nurture a talent for the art of generalship, which is in fact nothing more nor less than a particular form of creative thinking.

Of the conclusions I have drawn from this whole area, I would rate three as being of key significance. One is the supreme and ever-growing importance of surprise, and in particular of what the discreet charms of material surprise have to offer, even when the glamour of moral surprise is absent. Then there is the role of information both in preventing impairment of the predicted chance of success, and in positively enhancing it; here there is a need for the shape and character of information to match those of the operational posture. Finally, one returns yet again to the stuff of which manoeuvre theory is made—the tempo and responsiveness to be had from directive control.

PART 4

The Round Boulder

"Thus the potential of troops skilfully commanded in battle may be compared to that of round boulders which roll down from mountain heights." SUN TZU

"On the field of battle the happiest inspiration (*coup d'oeil*) is often only a recollection." NAPOLEON (trans. MAHAN)

"Battle experience overcomes friction, from troopers and riflemen up to the divisional commander." CLAUSEWITZ

"*Concentration* sums up in itself all the other factors, the entire alphabet of military efficiency in war." JOMINI

"A plan, like a tree, must have branches—if it is to bear fruit. A plan with a single aim is apt to prove a barren pole." LIDDELL HART (after NAPOLEON)

13

"The Clash of Wills"

"The experienced general can be in no doubt that war is a great drama, in which a thousand moral or physical causes may exert more or less force, and which cannot be reduced to mathematical calculations." JOMINI

Introduction—political and popular will

In probing the mysteries of chance I felt—and I hope the reader will agree—that I was just about keeping a big toe on the bottom. Now one must face up to Clausewitz's uncharacteristic assertion, quoted earlier (page 13), that the great captains always have acted by "feel", and that this is the way things will always be done. Once again, one can do no more than try to narrow the grey zone by bracketing it on it like any pre-electronic gunner— and with about as much chance of actually hitting the target!

In the sea and the air, fluid media where man depends wholly on machines, decisions are influenced to a greater or lesser extent by subjective judgements; but once battle is joined the issue is determined in a rather clear-cut physical way. The contest is conducted by large, discrete units which, to all intents and purposes, can only be in one of rather few discrete states. Degrees of damage may occur, but a ship is basically fit, crippled or sunk, and an aircraft fit, able to limp to a safe landing, or crashed. Outside minor tactics, the only choice which lies open to the captain of a damaged craft of either kind is whether to break off the engagement or to try and hang on. Like modern land warfare, the actuality of war at sea and in the air lies somewhere between Lanchester's Linear and Square Laws (pages 79/80); but the issue is decided by a relatively small number of separate engagements. Sometimes, as in the case of the German surface warships in the Second World War, the destruction of a single unit changes the whole operational or strategic situation.

From this reference point, let us turn to individual man by considering, on the one hand, the breaking of popular will (as in the Haldane/ Fuller/Liddell Hart doctrine of chemical warfare), and on the other the mechanism by which a classical "high port in the moonlight" infantry attack succeeds or fails. Certainly events in Britain and Germany between the thirties and the fifties suggest an extremely low correlation between both political and popular will on the one hand and physical reality on the other—a hypothesis largely confirmed by historical evidence before and since that period. A strong leader who manages to acquire a legendary image is evidently a much more powerful factor.

In the past, politicians of the type apt to gain power in a bellicist society could count on high office shielding them and their families against both the dangers and the hardships of war. In face of terrorism, these people seem to draw personal courage from a source they might describe as "my sense of service, your ambition, his lust for power". But whatever their leaders' motives, first and second world governments of the nineteenth and twentieth centuries generally seem ready to make war regardless of the odds and to prosecute it regardless of the outcome, apparently seeing the destruction of their nation as preferable to loss of office. A few generals welcome war, to put their theories to the test, because they believe it glorious, or—like the unfortunate Clausewitz—as a way to promotion and a higher income. But even in supposedly militaristic societies, only a very small proportion of top military men are of this mind. Every key figure in the Reichswehr was opposed to Ludendorff's views about war for war's sake; and it seems fairly clear that Beck's resignation from the appointment of Chief of General Staff in 1938 was based on moral objections to Hitler's plans as well as on professional reservations about the Wehrmacht's readiness. In fact Goering's boastful and swaggering aggressiveness sticks up like a sore thumb and was, it seems, deeply resented at all levels in the Luftwaffe.

In advanced countries where the political and military hierarchies are separate, military opinion generally seems to lie—as indeed it should— many leagues closer to realism than the attitude of government or people. One is faced with a nice paradox here. True, as the saw attributed to Talleyrand has it, "war is much too serious a thing to be left to military men". Yet this is not, as commonly supposed, because military men's judgement on issues of peace and war is unsound; but rather because, as I shall be arguing shortly and most military writers and historians agree, the military men who rise to the top in peace are very often incapable of conducting a war.

But if political and popular will bear little relation to the facts of the case, they bear even less relationship to each other, unless the political leader is strong to the point of Draconianism. Where popular opinion is free to express itself, it seems to pass through three quite sharply differentiated phases. The first of these, as evinced by the welcome given to Chamberlain on his return from Munich in 1938, and by the "nuclear despair" which has weighed down much of Western Europe's bodies politic since the deployment of Tomahawk and Pershing 2 began, is rejection of war at almost any politico-economic price. War being (as Marxism–Leninism with undoubted truth affirms) a means of maintaining and strengthening the status quo in domestic politics, bellicism is the prerogative of the ruling class or, nowadays, of the party in power and its agencies.

By contrast even the token use of armed force against the nation instantly hardens public opinion behind the government. One enters a phase where the will to resist *increases with* the damage inflicted. The reaction of both the British and the German populations to "terror bombing", a fair term I think for the pattern bombing of centres of culture and population, shows that acts seen as aimed at breaking the popular will rather than gaining military advantage simply reinforce determination to resist, carrying it far beyond the limits of the rational. One sees here a certain connection with the conditions generally said to be necessary for political revolution; as conditions deteriorate, opposition to the existing leadership fades.

Beyond a certain point, popular feeling enters a third phase of resignation and passive acceptance. Once the opposing force is and is seen to be overwhelming, the will to resist collapses. One sees this in the feeble resistance offered by German Jewry to the holocaust, and in the way this grew feebler still as it became clearer what was happening. One sees it in the collapse of Japan under nuclear attack; and Britain, being likewise a geographically small country, would surely have capitulated under equivalent attack by Germany. One sees all three phases in the reaction of a mind to pain and fear.

The key point in all this is perhaps the very sharp swing of public opinion behind the government the moment a military affront takes place—a phenomenon understood and exploited by Britain's Thatcher government in its handling of the Falklands situation. In the absence of a patently overwhelming threat to which the opponent has no counter, the implementation of a political aim by bringing armed force to bear directly on the popular will calls for strategic moral surprise. If this is lost and the defending government has time to rally its people behind it, the attacker is unlikely to achieve a quick decision. This puts a high premium on pre-emption. If the attacker can position himself to impose an immediate and severe threat without being spotted, he can deliver an ultimatum before the defender's political will has hardened or his public opinion can be mobilised. The other motif which will carry right through this part of the book is the tenuous nature of the relationship between government policy and public opinion, and between both of these and reality.

The infantry attack

One of my favourite operational research stories bears this out. Shortly after the war a team carried out a field study on a rather basic tactical exercise, in which they measured four elements—one could scarcely call them quantities. These were—the actual situation at the point of contact, the information passed back on it, the orders issued by the headquarters in response to this, and the action taken by the forward troops as a result. The team found the correlation to be remarkably low—much, I think, as any open-minded and experienced soldier would expect. Several years later, when the establishment concerned acquired its first reasonably powerful computer, the former team leader decided to program and run this simple exercise in order to gain experience with the machine. When the whole thing had been set up and run on the original lines, some wit had the notion of randomising it—marrying up, say Situation A with the report on Situation D, the orders issued as a result of Report C, and the troops' action following Orders B. According to the computer, history or at least folklore relates, this made very little difference to the interactions between the forward troops and the enemy.

More seriously, I have never seen any objective explanation of the mechanism by which an infantry attack fails; nor has my questioning ever evoked any offer of one. True, in the First World War and some colonial wars attacks were pressed home blindly until not a man was left standing, or until just a few survivors leapt into the defender's trenches to be instantly set upon. But anybody who supported or observed infantry attacks in the Second World War knows that this is the exception. (In my very limited experience I had the privilege of supporting Australians, the Guards, Highlanders and Indian Army infantry—all universally regarded as among the finest fighting troops in the world.) The decisive stage was usually between the last bound (or intermediate objective) and the final objective, when the attacking infantry had already taken some casualties and suffered some disruption. One minute there was fire and movement; the next there was just fire, and the leading companies were reported "pinned down". Sometimes intensification of covering fire and/or an assumption of the lead by the tanks would get the attack going again; sometimes the reserve company would pass through and get a footing on the objective, clearing the way for the original leaders to close up. Sometimes the attack would fail, and they would pull back to the intermediate objective.

My question is, though, just what made these extremely brave and well-trained men go to ground when they did—often in an exposed position where they soon drew artillery fire. From reading too, I am convinced that this is a common phenomenon; it was in fact to prevent just such a loss of momentum that Lieutenant-Colonel "H" Jones VC so heroically rushed an Argentinian machine gun post at Goose Green, at the cost of his own life and those of most members of his tactical headquarters.

The success of this splendid example of professional judgement and extreme physical courage acting in concert, and the outcome of similar actions further back in history, suggest that, even at this low and extremely physical level, the outcome turns on what we normally call a "clash of wills". The problem is that we all talk blithely about "psychological victory" and the "clash of wills" without understanding what we mean. I only hope this rather tentative discussion will spark some specialist into studying the problem in depth. For I suspect that, if we really understood the mechanism by which an infantry attack is slowed down and pinned down, we should be a good deal further towards explaining the psychological interaction of opposing commanders at operational level in manoeuvre warfare.

Once again let us go for a long bracket on this. On the one hand there are the cases, mentioned above, in which the defeat of the attack is entirely physical. On the other, a battalion commander who sees one of his forward companies getting a mauling may halt it on an intermediate objective and pass a reserve company through. We might try and explain what makes a commanding officer trade off tempo for mass in this way. Perhaps his thoughts run something like this:

> "B Company on the right is having a fairly easy passage, but what I see and hear on the radio suggests that A Company has taken quite a few casualties already, including some section commanders. Certainly their fire and movement's getting a bit sticky. The final bound is a nasty one for both. If A Company gets pinned down, they'll both be stuck in open ground. They'll get shot to pieces and have God's own job pulling back. So I must tell A Company to go to ground and pass C Company through. This'll mean holding B Company back, but they have reasonable cover right up to the intermediate objective and on it."

Snap decision as this may be, it is evidently a conscious act of professional judgement, a calculated response to an observed situation which represents a change from that predicted in the initial plan. The battalion commander has extrapolated forward in time from A Company's attrition rate during the first phase of the attack, and concluded that they will not be strong enough to reach the objective. At this level he expresses this judgement in a positive command decision—to pass a reserve company through.

Now let us consider what might happen if the CO let A Company press on. Troops of the quality I have indicated are unlikely to grind to a halt even if a leading platoon loses, say, its whole headquarters and a section commander. What probably happens is that the company commander unconsciously extrapolates forward, just as his CO did, and (as he would probably put it) "senses" that he does not have the strength to get a foothold on the objective. If his forward platoons are exposed, he cannot very well order them to halt. Probably he will not order them forward from the final company bound, and report back that he is pinned down. The other possibility is that a leading platoon suffers such casualties that it is no longer able to function as a platoon—a situation familiar two or three levels higher up.

The point is that *we do not know how this phenomenon we call "being pinned down" arises or exactly what it represents.* We are one level below war diaries or logs; and since those who have experienced this will see it as a failure, they will long since have distorted their recall by rationalisation. So it may not be easy to find out.

Loyalties

There are a fair number of recorded instances, on both sides in both World Wars for example, and in Vietnam, of waverers being shot in the back by the company sergeant-major or whoever. But fear of this in no way serves to explain the coherent behaviour of good troops advancing under heavy fire. The key to it is evidently group loyalty, combined, as General Sir John Hackett puts it, with "a readiness to offer your life to the enemy". Most authorities agree that there are two main levels of loyalty, which Anthony Sampson has aptly dubbed the "pack" and the "tribe". Certainly all agree on the importance of "regimental spirit". But my experience, shared I know by many others, has been that this dominant cult object "the Regiment" is really a focus of loyalty for the officers' and sergeants' messes. It is beyond the scope of the junior ranks' gut reaction.

Looking at commerce and industry, Anthony Sampson reckons a "pack" may number up to ten or a dozen, and a "tribe" up to several hundred—roughly the size of a British "one-unit" regiment. In the British Army at least, the upper focus of the junior ranks' loyalty is almost certainly the company of about a hundred men. The lower focus is less clear-cut. Rather oddly perhaps, it does not seem to be the platoon, or even the section (of ten give or take) in manpower-heavy organisations. What matters appears to be the smallest functional group—the tank crew, the gun detachment, the fire team. Lower still, there is a tendency towards what one might call non-sexual pair bonding, sometimes encouraged by the "buddy system" under which two named men look after each other; but this is essentially defensive and protective. The key object of loyalty in achieving coherent behaviour under fire is almost certainly the company.

Moral and physical courage

There are many well-known techniques for cultivating this loyalty. But at the risk of sounding cynical I would suggest that the strength and reliability of it in achieving cohesion stems from the fact that most men have more physical courage than moral courage. Once they feel themselves to be full members of a close-knit group which forms the object of their loyalty, facing almost certain death probably becomes easier for them than deviating from the behaviour pattern they know the group expects. At the lower levels of an organisation, moral courage acts disruptively rather than creatively. This is probably why most armed forces—and most employers if they think they can get away with it—seek to dehumanise people as part of their basic training. My reason for the digression about loyalties and for making this last point is that, at some link along the chain of command, moral courage becomes creative, and physical courage ceases to be of primary importance. My feel is that this changeover occurs at the level which crosses the boundaries of regimental spirit—division in the Soviet Army and brigade in most others.

Physical courage naturally remains a major element in the exercise of leadership and in a higher commander's image; the principle that no one should ask another to do something that he cannot and would not do himself is a fundamental one. But the *command decisions* the operational commander makes rarely touch his physical courage. Even the most ardent proponents of forward command spend only a small proportion of their time sensing the battlefield or leading from the front. At operational level the commander needs the moral courage to keep his judgement unclouded when forced to accept short-term setbacks for the sake of long-term aims, or to follow a course which he knows will cause heavy casualties among men who trust and respect him. Above all, he needs moral courage to make big decisions fast and to stick to them.

Pegs and holes

Unfortunately excellence of *military* judgement and the courage of their convictions are qualities which seldom bring men to the top in peacetime. As stressed in Chapter 1, armies are not rational organisations but social ones. In the three armies I know reasonably well, a long period of peace has allowed military considerations as such to give way to two underlying aims. In decisions affecting the army as a whole, the governing factor is conservation of the social structure; in internecine strife, between arms for instance, it is the control of manpower. Occasionally, as it always will, real talent breaks through; but by and large the key to success is conformism. This is a harsh judgement, but one borne out by two indisputable facts. In inter-service rivalry, the single-service chiefs switch their aim from conservation of structure to control of manpower. And the heavier the political pressure for greater warlike efficiency and cost-effectiveness, the further the emphasis within the services shifts away from military effectiveness and towards social conservation.

Having lived with 15 years of financial squeeze on the British Army and observed another dozen or so, I find it hard to blame those at the top for this attitude. They are reduced to hanging onto a cliff by their toenails, not daring to move for fear of losing the little they have. One sees the same attitude in businessmen in a constantly contracting economy. Their approach is at once more honest, because they do not suffer a conflict of aims, and more conspicuous, because one can compare them directly with their counterparts in expanding economies.

In both cases loss of confidence is inevitable. This is only one reason why, almost without exception since mass armies and professional officers came in, nations going to war have had to spend the first phase of the conflict replacing most of their peacetime commanders. This happened to a considerable extent even in the Wehrmacht. The problem is how this rather quaint custom can be upheld in face of the tempo and scope for surprise offered by modern technology.

A second factor is undoubtedly age. If officers are to be given a full-length career in peacetime, the age zone for successive levels of promotion is at least 5 years too high for exercise of the corresponding level of command in the field. I say "at least" because the days when career officers were the exception, and many wartime examples since then, show that young men have great success in high command. In Chapter 15, for an entirely different reason, I shall suggest limiting the duration of commissions. In any event, with second and third careers becoming the norm for able people, it should be possible to knock as much as 10 years off the normal retirement age for officers, now 55 in some armies and 60 in others. This would still leave open the possibility of extended service for those reaching the highest ranks in appointments where they were essentially professional advisers to government; there the requirement is for breadth of experience and maturity of judgement.

But the whole thing goes much deeper than this. Clausewitz writes that "outstanding commanders never come from the class of knowledgeable or even scholarly officers". Mellenthin, paraphrasing Bernhardi (a German general and author of the First World War era), puts it like this—"Purely 'routine' soldiers—that is to say, the strictly practical—will and must fail as soon as they are challenged by the great and difficult problems of modern warfare." Neither Napoleon nor Nelson would have survived positive vetting. Marlborough too, with a wife indiscreet enough to reveal that (on returning from a campaign) "his Lordship pleasured himself of me twice before removing his boots", might have found himself barred from the corridors of power. When one really looks at them, one sees that the senior officer in peace and the general in war are mostly two quite different animals. The only genuine link between them is a body of professional knowledge and skill, itself none too wide in scope and none too firm in validity. One must draw a sharp distinction here between *technical* knowledge (in the broad and proper sense of that word) and decision-making ability. At tactical levels technical knowledge (of Bernhardi's "routine" soldiers), like physical courage, predominates. At higher levels, staff officers and specialists require excellent technical knowledge and great skill in applying it. Technical knowledge straddles a command decision with two phases of activity—briefing and implementation; but its sole direct influence on the decision is to keep this within the bounds of feasibility.

Looking at industry and commerce, one is forced to question whether operational command in the field should necessarily be given to career officers. In those civilian areas there is a fairly clear-cut divide between top line management (the equivalent of strategic and operational command) and the rest. A few succeed in battling their way up through the organisation and arrive at this divide with enough momentum to carry them across it. But many top executive appointments, especially those seen as hot seats, are filled by a small group of people who move from industry to industry, or between industry and commerce. (Sir Michael Edwardes provides a recent British example of this, Ian McGregor a more recent but less happy one!) These are perhaps the men to whom high command in war should go.

The Soviets do appear to have a system of this kind. Naturally enough its exact nature is protected; and no less naturally its significance is probably not exactly what Western eyes might read into it. But discussion of this topic with John Erickson suggests to me that it might be a three-pronged system something like this, with the special powers of the General Staff as the bar carrying the tines. Strategic and operational commanders for war are nominated in peacetime. Only rarely are they the peacetime commanders. They may be prepositioned within the formation, either in the headquarters itself (say as first deputy commander) or as commanders or chiefs of staff one or two levels down. Alternatively, they may be placed in key positions within the Ministry of Defence and its agencies, or in the defence industry, the criterion for these posts being the need for frequent real-life decisions in peacetime. The third prong is the relatively junior General Staff officer (colonel or even lieutenant-colonel) who is sent into field headquarters down to division armed with detailed orders, which the nominal commander is bound to accept, and with special powers, such as authority to move and commit reserves. David Longley, the Aberdeen historian who advised me on the sociopolitical aspects of *Red Armour*, may have hit the nail on the head in suggesting a power link between the General Staff and the KGB.

For Western armies the insertion either of civilian top managers or of predesignated officers would be an extreme notion indeed. Even if it led to better strategic and operational decisions, the introduction of civilians would further weaken the professional quality of the peacetime officer corps by removing the ultimate carrot. As a social organisation, the peacetime army would withhold loyalty from an intruder of this kind; many examples from the Second World War suggest extreme resistance even to a regular soldier posted in as a "company doctor".

On the other hand, there are three related reasons why many officers who have developed in peacetime are unsound as commanders in war. One, of which much more in the next chapter, is that they have learnt not to delegate because, in the intense competition for promotion, a single error by a subordinate could wreck their career.

The second concerns character. The same careerist pressures, stemming mainly from the social aspect of an army's nature and nowadays reinforced by the demands of the security system, impose on an officer the strictest conformity to a code which sets him apart both from his men and from society as a whole. If he or his wife puts so much as the tip of a little toe out of place—curtains. (The United States Army even has (or at least used to have) a booklet on etiquette and conduct issued to a wife on her husband's promotion to general rank.) All this may encourage strictness but is scarcely calculated to foster the other four attributes Sun Tzu calls for in a general—wisdom, sincerity, humanity and courage.

Then one might say that the underlying aim of a career officer's training, like that of a pilot or a ship's master, is to fit him to take a critical decision in the unlikely event of his being called upon to do so. The emergency decisions the captain of an aircraft or ship may have to make are essentially physical ones dependent on technical expertise. Strategic and operational command decisions are different in kind because they call for judgements on the behaviour of other human beings—both enemy and subordinates. Every day the peacetime commander has to make trivial administrative decisions within the artificial convention of peacetime soldiering. Even the decisions he makes on exercise are aimed at winning his superior's favour rather than military advantage; he has everything to lose and nothing to gain by audacity. The pressures towards soundness, and the disproportionate effect on his future of the trivial decisions he takes in peacetime, impose undue stress on a career officer and atrophy his judgement when he is faced with a decision that really matters.

By contrast, the top executive is making practical decisions every day and thriving on them. He gets some wrong, but his track record and the very fact of his selection bolster his confidence. If he wants a change, or if a board sacks him, he just picks up a job invitation from the top of the pile. He creates his own style of management; and the better he is at decision-making, the more freedom he has to follow the life style of his choice. He is in much the same position as a commander in war.

Putting all this together, one sees a glimmering of a possible solution. By the time he comes to be selected for promotion to lieutenant-colonel, a career officer is fully formed, and enough ought to be known about him to single him out as a higher commander in wartime. The few officers so selected should be seconded to top executive appointments through the good offices of the appropriate national association (such as the Institute of Directors or the Confederation of British Industry). Apart from a few days of military study each year, they would then pursue a career in commerce and industry, the only restriction on this being availability for instant recall. Those who failed to make the grade would be slotted back appropriately into the peacetime army structure. In the event of war or a decision on intervention, these men could be in the key command appointments within hours. As an alternative or, better still, a complement to a system of this kind, successful reserve army officers (in Britain the few who rise to command their regiments and qualify on the Territorial Officers' staff course), together with a few directly recruited up-and-coming top managers, could be placed in a special reserve pool. Members of this pool would carry out a small amount of study and training each year to keep them in touch, and would be earmarked for a proportion of field command appointments, as well as for key logistic posts.

I simply do not know whether any system of this kind be workable within the framework of a modern industrial democracy. But if it were, it would provide round pegs for the round holes of war, while still giving the square pegs the chance to fill even the biggest and best square holes of peace. Should war break out or a major intervention be decided on, younger officers would still have an opportunity to make a name for themselves on active service and move to the top that way.

Unity of command

The more one looks into the German side of the Second World War, the more one reluctantly comes to realise that Hitler made some notable contributions to the success of blitzkrieg. For it was he, in the name of the *Führerprinzip*, who abolished the sharing of responsibility between commander and chief of staff, placing the burden of decision squarely on the commander's shoulders. He also attempted to do away with "staff channels", here meaning the right of officers in General Staff appointments to communicate direct to their counterparts one level up on "matters of command and personnel". A similar system prevailed in the Red Army from the time during the Second World War at which Stalin abolished the *troika* (commander, chief of staff, "commissar"), and appears to be perpetuated in the Soviet Army of today.

We shall see in subsequent chapters the constructive role staff channels can play in the conduct of an operation, but it should be possible to allow for this without giving senior staff officers the chance to go behind their commander's back on less urgent matters. The arguments that Mellenthin, for instance, puts forward for the Continental chief-of-staff system have force; and it may well suit the armies which follow it. Interestingly I have observed that sharing of decision-making responsibility, as by joint chief executives or "directors" (in the German sense) seems to work well on the Continent. But this is almost always disastrous in Britain and is, I think, little liked in the United States. There seems to me to be a clear-cut demarcation line, at philosophical and practical levels alike, between extreme delegation and the sharing of responsibility.

Not surprisingly perhaps, the emphasis that armies place on "officer mystique" seems to vary inversely with the past competence and integrity of their officer corps. While the Queen's Commission held by British officers is to my mind something of enormous significance and value, the position of the officer as the local embodiment of the sovereign is surely something that went out with physically rallying round colours, or perhaps with the growth of armies beyond the size and shape which a single great captain could directly control. Both when serving and since, I have always seen officer mystique and the privileges which surround it as a device to uphold discipline in face of an individual officer's blatant incompetence, misjudgement or misconduct. Officer mystique at once draws a veil round the reality and draws a quasi-canonical distinction between the office and the holder of it.

I must admit that my argument fails to explain the way the Russians, Tsarist and Soviet alike, have managed to combine intense officer mystique with a strong general staff. But the Germans, with a General Staff at once able, coherent and dedicated, seem to have set little store by mystique. For them, privilege has to be earned by the proper exercise of responsibility. This is quite a different thing; in fact it is a principle which appears essential in any hierarchic organisation, quite simply to provide the decision-makers with the time and facilities they need. Where privilege has been abolished, as for a short time in the Red Army, or more recently and for a longer one in the Chinese Army, it has come back again. In irregular and revolutionary forces it grows up, often in rather quaint forms, as leaders earn respect.

Praiseworthy and valuable as they are in other ways, regimental spirit and patriotism combine with officer mystique to enshrine the commander as a unique figurehead. This leads not only to absolute respect for unity of command, but beyond that to the "strong commander", symbolised for me at least by de Gaulle. Adept as he was at arousing loyalty from a distance, not one officer from the armoured division he commanded in 1940 joined him in the Free French forces. At least he lived up better than most to his own ideal—the "man of character" he depicted in *Le Fil de l'Epée*—"His dynamic puts his stamp on events, he turns them to his advantage, makes them his own. . . . See how straight and proud he stands and looks you in the eye. He can accept orders . . . but he burns to impose his will, to crack the whip of his resolve." De Gaulle surrounded himself with a void which symbolised his detachment and superiority, not allowing even his Chief of Staff through the barrier. He ruled by fear, remaining silent when courtesy at least called for speech, and speaking mainly to damn or deflate. Like many successful commanders and top managers, he controlled his information inputs rigorously, yet usually made correct decisions in good time, leaving his more fully briefed staff gaping.

This image of the strong commander is fundamental to Soviet officers' attitudes towards their subordinates. It also found a good deal of favour in the British and United States Armies of the Second World War. But for reasons which will emerge in the chapters that follow, the view of strong commanders taken by senior Wehrmacht officers I have talked to is ambivalent to say the least. There is in fact a nice distinction to be drawn here. The "strong" commander is apt to "impose his will on the situation" to the extent of ignoring it. He fights the battle according to the picture of it he wants to see. This works rather well as long as things are going more or less according to plan, his incisiveness accelerating the tempo. But it compounds setbacks when the things begin to go awry. I recall a phrase I heard Mellenthin use—"missions in blinkers". In the defence of the Ukraine at least, a remarkably high proportion of specific German failures were due to "strong" commanders imposing their will two or three levels down—notably by insisting that armoured divisions attacked as soon as their head cleared the dispersal point of a move.

While a "strong" commander may get his way, his attitude hangs a question mark over his ability even when things are going well for him. The truly able commander, by contrast, enjoys relationships with his staff and subordinates which are based on respect rather than fear. He may, as Manstein did, exploit this respect by being not just professionally exacting but personally impossible. Yet the resulting tensions, like those in a quarrelsome or violent marriage, may strengthen and deepen the relationship, satisfy all concerned, and bear much fruit.

Styles of command

Certainly any system of command-staff relationships and troop control must be flexible enough to accept a gamut of command styles. Perhaps I can illustrate this with a quartet of caricatures I used in an earlier book:

> Major-General A must be able to slap his men between the shoulder blades or exhort them on the video, then lead them into battle head-and-shoulders out of his hatch, helmetless and with pistol or carbine waving—what time his deputy and staff get on with the mundane business of fighting the battle.

> Major-General B must be able to sit tight-lipped in his command vehicle, with map, felt-tip, calculator and computer terminal, orchestrating every sub-unit move with the intensity and uniqueness of a van Karajan—what time his subordinates down through the ranks know that he is giving them the best chance of winning and the least chance of dying.

> As the crunch-point approaches, General X turns away from the map and display unit, tells his orderly to pour him a vodka and tonic, and takes a stroll through the rose garden of his chateau of the moment, sipping and sniffing away. Suddenly he turns on his heel and calls— "Launch the reserve—Plan 2." This may be the first time for several days that he has allowed military activity to interfere with his life style. Yet everybody under his command knows that his decision will be a

winner; and as, he expects, they will have done everything that needed to be done.

Lieutenant-General Y's chopper is vaulting the hedges and ducking under the powerlines, swerving now and then to avoid a burst from a ZSU23/4 as it flies down the line of contact until he issues the order to go by firing a signal pistol, maybe flourishing it at a lurking Havoc.

Each one of these figures of fun may be a battle-winning commander and may become a war-winning one—as long as he is free to do his thing and the system can shape itself round this. As Mellenthin remarks, no one man can conceivably deal with all the things that have to be done in the conduct of a modern operation. So it does not matter too much what the commander does, as long as it leads him to make correct and timely decisions. Jomini's discussion of the selection of a commander-in-chief brings this out well. The commander, he says, must be experienced and tough, a strong character with well-developed personal qualities, moral courage and a grasp of principles. The chief of staff must complement the commander. So his most important qualities are likely to be intellectual ability, openness and loyalty. Yet this counterpoint of personality and brain has its dangers. History has seen far too many figureheads, royal and otherwise, who have thrived for a while on decisions made for them but been found wanting when the crunch came. Just as dependence on officer mystique varies inversely with professional quality, the importance of "leadership qualities" varies inversely with decision-making ability. As the Wehrmacht demonstrated and we shall see in the next chapter, the key to successful command is neither love nor fear but *respect*.

Conclusion—appearance and reality

Having established a long bracket and explored various aspects of higher command, we may now be in a better position to determine what this expression "the clash of wills" really means. At all levels the basis for decision is *not* the physical situation as last reported or observed, but the *commander's mental picture of the situation as it will shortly develop*. At low levels with the two sides locked in conflict, neither commander has much freedom of action. If we except, as we have, the rare occasions when an engagement is pushed to its physical limits, he goes on as planned as long as he feels he can. If this does not allow him to accomplish his mission, he in effect abandons it. The attacking company commander either takes his objective, or stops short and reports himself "pinned down". The defending company commander either wards off the attack, or has to pull out. It is enough for either to observe the situation. Neither knows who his opponent is; nor does he need to.

There are two essential differences in kind between these company commanders whose actions are governed by attrition theory and their superiors at operational level conducting manoeuvre warfare. The operational commanders have a wide choice of genuinely differing options. Second, they know each other's identities; they should know each other's characteristics from intelligence profiles; they may know each other personally. So their actual aim becomes *the creation of a picture of defeat in each others' minds.* The physical situation they seek to achieve must be such as to generate this picture; but it is *not* fundamental to the outcome. This places the operational level of manoeuvre warfare—still more the strategic level, of course—at not one remove from attritional warfare but two. The outcome turns neither on the seizing and holding of ground nor on the dislocation or disruption of forces and resources, *but on the pictures in the opposing commanders' minds.*

One can I think demonstrate this by a spot of *reductio ad absurdum.* Suppose that General Ivan has an electronic capability which allows him to suppress completely the genuine information flowing into General Tom's headquarters and replace it by controlled disinformation, without General Tom becoming aware of this. Then General Tom's operational decisions and the orders issued as a result would be based on his interpretation of a wholly fictional situation. He would be a puppet on a string, dancing to General Ivan's tune.

Coming back to the margins of reality, let us now suppose that General Tom has thoroughly bad information on the opposition and that General Yuri (who replaced Ivan on the outbreak of hostilities) knows this. General Yuri will shape the development of the operation so as to reinforce this false impression and build it up to form a picture of defeat. The better General Tom's initial information, the more General Yuri's plan must depend on solid military achievement as opposed to deception, bluff and disinformation.

Thus in reality, where both sides' initial and subsequent information is reasonably sound, there is an extremely subtle interaction in the commander's mind between the picture he wants to paint in his opponent's mind and the physical actions he must execute to paint it. These actions must evidently include physical achievements like putting a mobile force into a turning position, destroying crucial delivery means or communications centres, and perhaps using a helicopter force to seize a key crossing or an airhead in depth. But the real purpose of these achievements is to provide a background of credibility, on which a layer of deception, bluff and disinformation is superimposed to make the finished picture.

I have accepted the "clash of wills" as a convenient label, partly because it is widely understood as representing the psychological conflict between opposing commanders, partly because the word "minds" in this context has a misleading connotation of "hearts and minds" (influencing the popular will). But I believe the image conjured up by "the clash of wills" is a false one. This is *not* a psychological analogue of two fat Bavarians elbow-wrestling across their brimming *Steine*, or of two "men of character" sitting in their caravans glowering at photographs of each other and "willing" each other to succumb. What we are talking about at root is *the creation and manipulation of information*, something calling for creative thinking and great subtlety of presentation. The actual forces of which a commander disposes are the materials and tools he uses in realising his creation.

Willpower is the principal supporting actor in this drama, and plays a double role. It sets the threshold at which a commander will see his mental picture of the situation as representing defeat and succumb to his opponent. By the same token, the best way for an operational commander to avoid being manipulated is evidently to sense the situation for himself—in other words to practise forward command. Willpower also determines the ability of the two commanders to implant their picture and their plan in the minds of their respective subordinates. For, as we shall see, one of the two fundamentals of directive control, and thus of responsiveness, is the implantation of an idea into the heads of subordinates whose minds are tuned to receive it accurately.

14

Directive Control

"War is an act of human intercourse—a social act."   CLAUSEWITZ

"All orders will have to be as brief as possible. They should be based on a profound appreciation of possibilities and probabilities which . . . will generally lead to a series of alternatives."   FULLER

"The command of troops is an art, a free creative activity based on character, ability and power of intellect."   HDV 100/1, Truppenführung, 1962

Introduction—the meaning of *Auftragstaktik*

Some modern commentators have used the above quotation to claim that Clausewitz was a greater thinker than Sun Tzu because he recommends the maintenance of all forms of communication with the enemy, while Sun Tzu (in the "Close the passes" passage) favours the severance of all links save the clash of arms. My gut reaction to Clausewitz's remark is one of explosive revulsion; calling war an act of communication is like calling rape an act of love. But I believe this reaction is as wide of the mark as the interpretation I opened with. One saw in the previous chapter how a commander's ultimate aim should be to implant a picture of defeat in his opponent's mind by creating and manipulating information. This, I now believe, is what Clausewitz was driving at. We have also seen at various points the need for the communication of ideas and interpretations of information upwards and downwards through the levels of command. It is this aspect of communication which lies at the root of *Auftragstaktik*.

In his article "Der Auftrag", Ose takes us back to the Prussian *Exerzierreglement* of 1806:

> "*Long winded orders on dispositions must not be given before a battle.* (The commander-in-chief) looks at as much of the ground as he can, if time allows gives his divisional commanders the general idea in a few words, and shows them the general layout of the ground on which the army is to form up. The manner of deployment is left to them; fastest is best. The commander-in-chief cannot be everywhere. He must always keep the picture as a whole in his mind's eye and shape it, mainly by sound handling of the reserves."

In something of a desperate effort to get the meaning of *Auftragstaktik* across to its English-speaking Allies, the Bundeswehr worked up an English-language presentation, in which the script writers understandably but disastrously rendered *Auftrag* as mission, and *Auftragstaktik* as "mission-type control". Audience and subsequent readers naturally linked this to their term "mission" and thus to Paragraph 2 of the standard NATO operation order. As I recently heard Senger, strongly backed by his colleagues, point out, the essence of *Auftragstaktik* is concerned with Paragraphs 3a and sometimes 3b of the NATO form of order—general outline and allocation of troops to tasks. The 1933 edition of *Truppenführung* ("Command and control"), drafted mainly by Beck, differs little in this respect from its 1921 counterpart, presumably inspired by Seeckt.

A glance at either suggests that, in this context, the American/NATO term "mission" is closer to the German *Entschluss* (normally "resolution"), while *Auftrag* would best be represented by the more mundane term "task". Thus one might render the Beck version, which is slightly the clearer of the two, something like this:

> "36. Command is based on task *(Auftrag)* and situation. The task lays down the aim to be achieved, which the commander charged with achieving it must keep in the forefront of his mind.

> "37. Task and situation give rise to the mission *(Entschluss)*. . . . The mission must be a clearly-defined aim to be pursued with all one's powers. . . . The commander must leave his subordinates freedom of action, to the extent that doing so does not imperil his intention *(Absicht)*."

The 1962 (Bundeswehr) version, quoted as an epigraph, goes further, stressing the need to "take immediate action in accordance with the superior commander's thinking" in the absence of a set task. This serves to highlight the contrast between *Auftragstaktik* and its opposite *Befehlstaktik*, rendered by the Bundeswehr as "detailed-order tactics" but maybe more happily as "control by detailed order".

Back in the tactical nuclear heyday of the sixties, the British Army realised that detailed orders would not work on the nuclear battlefield because the situation after delivering or receiving a strike was too unpredictable. At this time British thinking was dominated by the "Western school", mainly made up of cavalry officers of high intellect to whom the possibility of a subordinate moving a muscle other than by numbers was not wholly unthinkable. The "operation order" was replaced under certain circumstances by an "operational directive" very much on the lines of *Auftragstaktik*. "Operational" was used here in the former Anglo-American sense; it must be discarded because the principles of

Auftragstaktik run through all levels. But "directive" (in contrast to "order") precisely reflects the spirit of *Auftragstaktik*. So I propose to render the term as "**directive control**". (This discussion, incidentally, provides a textbook example of the dangers of translation, especially between German on the one hand and English and the Romance languages on the other; one has to dissect out the underlying thought and express it in a radically different way.)

Parameters of command

But before pursuing this dissection of directive control, I should like to take a broader look at the parameters of command. Figure 47 uses triplanar Cartesian coordinates (a third dimension, z, superimposed on the familiar x and y of graphs) to represent the three main variables in the exercise of command. If all three axes are drawn of equal length, this model represents a sphere—a hollow globe, if you like—any point within which represents some particular command technique. Unfortunately one cannot blob in

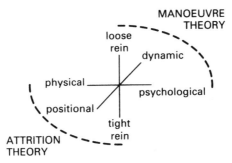

FIG. 47. *The parameters of command.*

points on a spatial model within the plane of the printed page. But if the reader does this mentally, I think he will see the Anglo-French command of the First World War as way out to the lower left, with the Eisenhower/ Bradley broad front approach somewhere between this and the centre. Blitzkrieg, as an example of directive control, will be top right, with the Soviet system purporting to be up there with it but in fact dragged down to the bottom right by lack of trust and excessive complexity. More broadly, the lower left hemisphere represents attrition theory, and the upper right one manoeuvre theory.

In any given theatre at any given time, the physical aspect of war, which we discussed so fully in Part 2 and Chapter 11, the technological state of the art, and the prevailing politico-economic constraints (notably the politico-economic value of territory) squeeze this theoretical sphere into a cigar-shaped form along the "loose rein–tight rein" axis. In other words, the degree of control is the main choice an army has. But the model also brings out how the system of control must match the theory employed. Manoeuvre theory, with its emphasis on tempo and dynamic effects and thus on responsiveness, is not really compatible with control by detailed orders. To repeat a metaphor I used before, time-lapse photography of movements executed by numbers will never generate dynamic forces. Conversely, there is a fundamental contradiction between the Bundeswehr's doctrine of directive control and its concept of positional defence; a subordinate cannot exercise initiative to much effect if he is pinned to an eight-figure grid reference. One can see this conflict in the arguments raging in the Federal Republic over tactics and force structure for the nineties—also in the way that, by a psychological quirk, the current version of their command manual lays even more emphasis on the subordinate's freedom of action.

Germans past and present, the Soviets since 1942, and the United States Army's "Reformists" evidently all see movement from bottom left to top right of this model as representing some kind of growth of military potential, a concept one stage broader again than combat worth. The Soviets are stuck with a contradiction that could prove a veritable Achilles heel; the Germans, ironically, are held down in the same quarter by the converse of the same contradiction. This makes it all the more important for the United States Army, and the British if—as now looks possible—it goes that way, to reach upwards and outwards with the strong right arm of manoeuvre theory.

The basis of directive control

The real basis of directive control, meriting a chapter to itself, is an unbroken chain of trust and mutual respect running from the controlling operational commander to the tank or section commander. But in trying to come to grips with the concept, I found it helpful to consider its physical aspects first, so that I had a clearer idea of what this moral basis had to provide. Americans and Britons can perhaps best see the principle of directive control as the vertical counterpart of team spirit. A sports team, an ocean racing or rowing crew, or a climbing rope is small and collocated, so that only one level of command is necessary. There is the skipper or leader, and there are the members. (This remains true even when a coach is in charge, because the command function is then divided—he exercises control, and the captain exercises leadership.)

Here the aim is known to all. The method is worked out in advance by a technique of discussion, in which all participate, decision making by the skipper, and briefing. If a situation calling for a change in technique or tactics arises during a game or race, the skipper simply gives a brief command or a prearranged codeword, and the team responds. The game is mostly conducted by *the members themselves reading the instantaneous local situation and reacting to it in accordance with their understanding of the aim and plan.* It may happen, though, that a response of this kind made in good faith will adversely affect the overall situation. Some of these secondary effects are inherent in the rules of a game, the established practices of a sport, or the design of a yacht. These permanent limitations can be dealt with by a set of drills and instructions developed and rehearsed in training. Other secondary effects derive from the occasion—opposition tactics, weather conditions, or the characteristics of a rock face. The skipper and his advisers must find out about these special limitations in advance, brief the team members on them, and lay down any resulting variations in their standard drills or limitations on their actions.

In a single sporting event taken in isolation, the aim is simple and invariable—to win. To complete this analogy between sport and war, we therefore need to envisage the winning of a league or series, or the completion of a climbing expedition, thus creating a higher intention to which the winning of a single event or the surmounting of a single face must be subordinated. One of the principles which now comes into play is economy of force; but the ramification I want to explore is modification of the aim of individual events. The skipper of a yacht may quite properly decide to sail for a comfortable second place by keeping the third and fourth boats covered rather than put on a press of sail and risk being dismasted in a wild chase after a boat way ahead of him. If conditions worsen during a climb, the leader would be doubly correct in switching to an easier route; he would be conserving his forces and making sure he was poised for the next stage. In neither case would the man in charge on the spot be expected to consult the owner of the yacht or the sponsor of the expedition—any more than a foredeck hand faced with a jammed winch would consult the watchkeeper before making the sheet onto another. The higher intention is sacrosanct. The immediate aim may have to be modified or abandoned to uphold it. And the man to take this decision is the man on the spot.

In the directive control of troops, *a commander must regard his superior's intention as sacrosanct,* and make its attainment the underlying purpose of everything he does. He will be given a **task** of his own, and be told the **resources** he has to carry it out and any **constraints** on how he does so. Within this framework his plan will be a matter for discussion upwards, sideways and downwards if time allows; but it will not be made for him. The crunch point here is *the status of the task set to the subordinate commander.* The Bundeswehr's current command manual puts it like this:

"*No* 1005. The superior commander determines the definition of the object (*Zielsetzung*) of the operation, makes resources available and coordinates with other sectors.

"His intention and the task (*Auftrag*) set by him are the overriding factors (*massgebend*) in determining the thinking and action of the

subordinate commander, who is responsible for carrying out the task
set him; he is to be left as much freedom of execution as possible."

I think the reader will now see why I have given the American/NATO term
"mission" a wide berth. *Massgebend* is I suppose the second strongest of the
group of German words for "authoritative, definitive, decisive"; it stops a
long way short of implying absolute obligation. And the first determinant
for the subordinate is the superior commander's intention, *not* the task set
him. From the written evidence, discussion with senior German officers,
and historical examples I am in no doubt that, under the German version of
directive control, *the subordinate commander is free to modify the task set him
without referring back, if he is satisfied that further pursuit of that aim would
not represent the best use of his resources in furtherance of his superior's
intention.*

Perhaps the best support for this interpretation is a negative evidence.
The Wehrmacht had its share of "strong" commanders who sought to bend
the situation to their will rather than to respond to it. They frustrated
directive control by laying down "missions in blinkers" (to use
Mellenthin's phrase again), and by standing pat on these even when the
executing commander formally protested. As recounted in the previous
chapter, this practice accounted for many of the specific German failures in
the defence of the Ukraine. The criticism of fellow participants and German
historians is unequivocally directed not at the failure of the subordinate but
at the obstinacy of the superior.

I apologise for having made heavy weather of this rather simple point. But
on the one hand it is fundamental to the successful implementation of
manoeuvre theory, especially at today's and tomorrow's tempos. On the
other, it contradicts not only the Anglo-Saxon understanding of military
discipline, but the attitude and usages of American, British *and German*
society in all other fields except sport. Almost needless to say, it is in total
conflict with the Russian way of doing things—a traditional attitude heavily
reinforced by Marxism–Leninism.

Two up and two down

"An order is a good basis for discussion" has long been my favourite
military saying. Nevertheless, when I saw such emphasis laid on telephone
discussions, especially between chiefs of staff, in written accounts of the
Wehrmacht's doings in the East, I took this to be just the kind of
amplification of situation reports that one sees going on between levels in the
British and United States Armies. Not until I had the chance of listening to
and questioning those actually concerned did I realise that "discussion"
meant a great deal more than this. Personal and telephone discussions, often
extending two levels up and two down from the focal headquarters, played

two key parts in the German system, as I believe they or their modern counterparts must in any system of directive control.

The first concomitant of freedom of action is immediate and full reporting; these discussions served to keep key staff officers fully in a common picture, thus allowing them to brief their commanders at any moment. The second concomitant of this freedom is unity of thought; these discussions between men who were at once like-minded and fiercely proud of their independence of mind served both to harmonise thinking through the levels and to refine it. The implantation of images in the opposing commander's mind which we saw in the previous chapter is one side of the coin of "war as an act of human intercourse"; the communication of ideas between commanders at various levels is the other. I make no apology for reiterating that the root of directive control lies in the sharing of ideas and interpretations by minds well-attuned to one another. Perhaps this notion, at once so akin to the performance of music and so foreign to the Anglo-Saxon military mind, also lies at the root of the semantic problems I have wrestled with above.

Yet the freedom on which directive control rests brings with it the need for fundamental constraints quite distinct from the specific constraints called for by co-ordination. Thinking two up may be something new to the stolid addict of attrition whose outlook is even more heavily blinkered than his mission, but the need to think two down is something every company commander in every army is taught. In many German orders one in fact finds *tasking two levels down*, from army group to corps or from army to division. To the extent that the principles of directive control were observed in these instances, this will only have been done after the plan had been discussed through the levels concerned, and any overriding of the views of executing commanders explained. But from studying the plans in question one gains the impression that tasking two down, while going well beyond the scope of normal co-ordinating constraints, was in fact necessary to give the operation coherence. This really comes back to the point I made when discussing operational intelligence in Chapter 12—that at any given stage of an operation (in this case the planning stage) only two levels of headquarters, one operational and one tactical, have a key part to play. The *planning and controlling* operational headquarters, say army, sets the tasks for the highest tactical formation (division). The role of corps, the *executing* operational headquarters, is to help the divisions carry out these tasks, and to direct them in the sense of the army commander's intention as the operation develops. One can trace a similar pattern within the tactical levels.

Once again one comes back to a moral psychological aspect of the system. Dedication to the superior commander's intention combined with independence of mind is the precise opposite of the attitude that often seemed to prevail among the Western Allies in the Second World War—profound mistrust of a superior combined with enforced blind obedience to his every word. On the British side, it is probably fair to say that this attitude stemmed from an excess of regimental spirit—too much of a good thing— and from a nostalgic extension of "regimental" spirit to brigades and divisions, as in the case of the Desert Rats (7 Armoured Division). The speed with which Guards Armoured Division worked itself up to a peak of excellence was, I suggest, due not so much to superior quality of officers and men, high though this was, as to a unity of purpose stemming from unity of spirit and tradition. More of this in a moment.

Forward command

If proof is needed of these comments on the Western Allies, it is to be found in the rejection of the practice of forward command by the British Army, and I think by the United States Army, and in its frequent and successful use by the Wehrmacht. As I see it, part of the tacit agreement which permits effective working despite mistrust and resentment between levels is non-interference. The superior commander issues his orders. They are completely binding on his subordinate as far as they go—and they may go a very long way. The *quid pro quo* which allows the subordinate to salve his pride and maintain the respect of *his* subordinates is that he is not interfered with as long as he is willing and able to stay within the bounds of these orders. The only hypothesis which can explain Anglo-Saxon objections to forward command is that the trust implied by this very limited delegation is really no more than a mask for lack of trust.

For forward command is nothing more nor less than a continuation of the practice followed by commanders-in-chief before the days of mass armies. A distinguishing mark of the great captain was to place himself at a focal point from which he could at once direct the battle from personal observation and exercise leadership—either simply by his presence or, if needs be, by a personal act of bravery. If we look at two outstanding German examples from the Second World War—Rommel on the Meuse (in 1940) and Manteuffel at Targul Frumos—we see the higher tactical commander actually assuming command of the key sub-unit and leading it in the critical phase of the action. At the times in question Rommel was commanding 7 Panzer Division, and Manteuffel Panzergrenadier Division Grossdeutschland. Thus, although the latter was handled more like a panzer corps, both men were at the time commanding at the highest *tactical* level. I know of no instance of an operational commander actually taking over a battalion or company, though this may well have happened.

As Hasso von Manteuffel put it:

> "The place of all commanders of armour up to the divisional commander is *on* the battlefield, and within this wherever they have the best view of the terrain and good communication with the hard

core of the tanks. I was always located where I could see and hear what was going on "in front", that is, near the enemy, and around myself—namely at the focal point. Nothing and nobody can replace a personal impression."

Nonetheless, Rommel in North Africa frequently directed the battle from a light command vehicle or his light aircraft, and used to take his beloved *Mammut* (a captured British armoured command vehicle) into the direct fire zone. On at least two occasions in the fighting of spring 1941 around Tobruk, he diverted and moved with a battery or troop of 88-mm dual-purpose guns, without however actually assuming command of it. From an operational level, he writes in much the same vein as Manteuffel:

"It is of the utmost importance to the commander to have a good knowledge of the battlefield and of his own and the enemy's positions on the ground. It is often not a question of which of the opposing commanders is the higher qualified mentally, or which has the greater experience, but which of them has the better *grasp of the battlefield* (my italics). This is particularly the case when a situation develops the outcome of which cannot be estimated. Then the commander must go up to see for himself; reports received second-hand rarely give the information he needs for his decisions."

The desire to see for oneself, to "sense" the situation, seems to be a deep-seated need of human beings when exercising control. The yachtsman stays up in the cockpit and faces the weather although he has an enclosed helm position; he in fact gains a significant amount of information from hearing and feel too. The tank commander opens his hatch and sticks his head out, knowing that he is likely to get shot, although the expensive optics in his cupola give him all the vision he *theoretically* needs. By the same token, I doubt whether higher tactical and operational commanders will ever find holographic maps or video and computer displays a substitute for being on the spot.

Like the Wehrmacht, the Soviet Army seems to draw a distinction between the way tactical and operational commanders exercise control. It would be stupid to pretend that Russian officers are lacking in courage. There are many wartime examples of Red Army divisional commanders leading from the front; and one gathers that the commander of a mechanised division would assume personal command of his divisional tank battalion (of almost sixty tanks) and lead it into action, if the situation became critical enough for him to commit it. By contrast the Soviet Army seems to be digging itself a pit by its massive investment in C^3 technology at operational levels and reaching down to regiment. Reading between the lines of certain passages written in the heyday of the battlefield nuclear weapon, one gathers that nuclear strikes provided operational commanders with a watertight excuse to interfere in the tactical battle, and that the swing away from these weapons has left that practice very much alive and kicking. As I understand it, an army or even a front commander has the facilities to sit in his main headquarters and exercise direct detailed control certainly of a battalion and probably of a company. If the problems to which forward command proper gives rise in Western armies are anything to go by, this "forward command from the rear" is likely to be disastrous for morale. (As well, it strikes me, as offering an excellent line for a limerick!)

But before leaving this topic, I want to clear some ground for the next chapter by probing British opposition to forward command a little deeper. Surely no one can dispute that it makes sense for the most talented and experienced man concerned to weigh up a criticial situation on the spot and decide how to deal with it, all the more when it is one he himself has contrived. As we saw in the previous chapter, lack of confidence in one's superiors may be justified in the early stages of a war, when key posts are still filled by their peacetime occupants. But I suspect that the root cause is regimental spirit run riot, and that St Michael himself would not be trusted unless he was wearing—or at least had once worn—the right cap badge. Personal loyalty to a higher commander does not seem to be enough. There always remains a gut feeling that he may be got at by all those gunners and sappers around him—or whatever. Being a British social institution, the British Army doubtless mirrors the extraordinary, I think unique, trait of British society—that it only functions to any great effect under the adversary system. In fairness though, one reads of this internecine strife in other armed forces of other periods.

Apart from a few special cases in which the regimental spirit has been extended one or two levels up, among them the Guards Armoured Division, the only examples I know of in which unreserved loyalty and real cohesion has been achieved beyond regiments or the equivalent have turned on solidly founded and openly acknowledged elitism. The three major instances which spring to mind are Guderian's *Panzertruppe*, the Soviet Airborne Forces and the Israeli Armoured Corps. In the course of the long drawn-out post-mortems which followed the Yom Kippur War, a heated and at least partly public debate took place over whether the Armoured Corps should retain its elite status. Israeli society purports to be extremely anti-elitist; and the status and repute of the Armoured Corps was unquestionably leading to weaknesses and less than superb morale in other parts of their army. Nevertheless, a conscious decision (not a tautology in this case, I think) was taken to conserve the Armoured Corps' elite status.

Even an unashamed elitist like myself can see the rub in this. Our world is not Alice's. If some elements in an army are elite, others almost as important are going to be less than elite, putting us back on square one as far as mutual trust and cohesion are concerned. So one is forced to look for an acceptable face of elitism that will not produce this imbalance and divergence. The examples above suggest that this might lie in the sharing of a mumbo-jumbo; and there is much else to reinforce this view. In the British Army, the Brigade of Guards and the Parachute Regiment are multi-unit families united in the one case by their status as Household Troops, in the other by parachuting. Before their parent regiments were formally amalgamated, the Green Jackets were given common identity by the tradition of Sir John Moore in discipline and training, and by their role as motor battalions during and after the Second World War. By contrast, because it shares its mumbo-jumbo with the cavalry regiments, the Royal Tank Regiment has never enjoyed solid cohesion but steered a middle course between unifiers and separatists. Extending the argument, one finds a genuine bond between, say, parachutists, commandos or special forces of different armies, whether or not they are allied—and the same is even truer of sailors and airmen.

The conclusion which I draw from this is that the sharing of a mumbo-jumbo offers a means of extending regimental spirit beyond a single unit without diluting it, and that this should be a prime consideration in designing a force to operate under directive control.

Standing operating procedures (SOPs)

I recently heard a leading British proponent of manoeuvre theory mutter, half to himself and half to the assembled company—"But how are we going to do these complicated things without detailed orders?" He in fact knew the answer better than most, but he was still aghast at the idea of launching a complex army or corps operation on the back of an envelope. The answer lies in SOPs. But it has to be a carefully balanced answer. The scope and nature of SOPs are critical, the attitude of commanders and staffs towards them no less so—and the same goes for much C^3 technology! In a word, SOPs must be slaves restricted to servile tasks. They must not have free men's tasks entrusted to them. Above all they must never become masters.

Cautious as I am about underestimating the Soviets, it strikes me that they have not so much fallen into this trap as steered themselves carefully and inexorably into it. They know very well that their operational concept calls for the responsiveness offered by directive control. But the Russian love of autocracy and bureaucracy, the extraordinary paranoia bred by Marxism–Leninism out of the Russian temperament, still more the appalling relations through their ranks and the essential passivity of their run-of-the-mill officers, have led them to try and combine the flexibility and tempo of directive control with the certainties of detailed orders. The fuss they make about "operational quality" at higher levels and "initiative" at lower tells its own story. To resolve this contradiction they have built up a canon of extremely detailed SOPs, norms and models (computer and "steam") so massive that few can grasp its details even in the calm of an academy, fewer could be said to know their way about it, and no one man could conceivably have everything he needs at his fingertips. We have already seen in Chapter 9 how the complexity of the club sandwich battle becomes self-defeating. Imagination boggles at the thought of trying to conduct it by "forward command from the rear" employing "directive control by detailed order". (Once again, a couple of pieces of Irish make the point better than pages of English!)

SOPs designed to support directive control must themselves respect the principle of directive control. The criterion is how far their subject calls for the exercise of judgement. An SOP is really the verbal analogue of a data processing system. Routine and technical matters can be covered in entirety by SOPs, just as the calculations and optimisations concerned can be left entirely to computers. Artillery provides a good example of a "mixed" function (Fig. 48). The handling of the guns is a tactical matter calling for

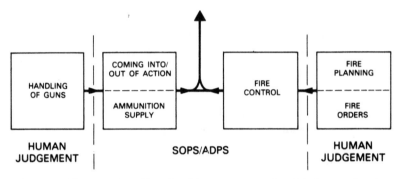

FIG. 48. *Elements of artillery handling as an example of judgemental and routine/standard functions.*

judgement; once an artillery officer's judgement has been formed by instilling into him certain broad principles and guidelines, he needs data but no written instructions. Bringing guns into and out of action and supplying them with ammunition is a matter of routine except in emergencies; SOPs provide the basis of training and serve as an aide-memoire in the field. Once a fire task is ordered, its execution is best left to a data processing system, which can also handle routine inputs such as meteor without human intervention. But fire planning and *ad hoc* calls for fire are tactical matters calling for trained human judgement. I very much wonder whether the sheafs of documentation the Soviets use have any advantage whatever over NATO artillery voice procedure employed by talented, well-trained officers or NCOs and skilled operators. Radio procedures themselves excellently demonstrate the proper interface between SOP and free play. Their purpose is to enable communication, not to restrict it.

I am convinced that the British and former German practice of excluding SOPs and school solutions from tactics is correct, still more that any attempt to lay down standard solutions to problems of operational command would be folly. By contrast, the drills for execution of the basic minor tactical movements of an infantry or tank platoon must be standardised and rammed home until they become instinctive. Deployment and battle drills provide an interesting middle ground. Sometimes the standard pattern fills the bill, but quite often it has to be changed or telescoped. The best approach to this is probably a combination of SOPs and "management by exception". Unless the commander orders otherwise, the standard procedure is followed. Most of the time he will only need to specify departures from it, but occasionally he will have to get the thing done in a completely different way, using the SOP simply as a reference base. This seems to me greatly preferable to having a whole set of SOPs, say for normal, hasty and crash deployment, none of which are quite going to fill any particular bill.

There is a much stronger reason for this approach, though. SOPs, like the Regulations for Avoiding Collisions at Sea, have got to be few enough and simple enough for trained men who are constantly exercising or rehearsing their calling not just to memorise them but to follow them "instinctively". You should only have to go to the book for occasional cases; and then you should know that the rule you want is there, and just where to find it. Thus SOPs must be few and simple. Their content and expression must be refined by trial. They must be changed only when absolutely necessary. And the procedures must be designed for ease of training even at some cost in efficiency.

In sum SOPs must provide a framework of discipline within which the trained mind can safely roam free. Their purpose is not to restrict human judgement, but to free it for the tasks only it can perform; not to exclude it from the primary control loop, but to sustain it there.

Conclusion—the mechanics of directive control

The be-all and end-all of directive control is mutual trust and respect, leaving the subordinate free to act as he thinks fit in furtherance of his superior's intention, and assuring him of support even if he makes an error of judgement. Thus the mechanics of directive control are extremely simple—as they must be if they are to further this principle rather than frustrate it. Headquarters must be small, simple and supple, designed round a minimal nucleus of commander and key staff officers. Certainly the Germans felt that it was better to stretch key officers to breaking point than to work a system of reliefs. These officers need good but simple comfort, as the small-boat sailor might expect; vast "gin palaces" like American and British headquarters are wholly inconsistent with the principle and practice of directive control.

The need for frequent, untrammelled discussion between levels is paramount; it should extend over any five levels (two levels up and two down). By the same token, misunderstandings may be more serious than they are under control by detailed order, because they may go undetected for much longer. Thus, electronic warfare or no, reliable, secure, high-capacity voice communications are essential. Each link should be capable of extension upwards or downwards by relay. Data links between signals/ computer centres serving each headquarters are likewise essential. And the local links between these centres and the headquarters themselves must provide teleprint and facsimile facilities. Then there is the golden rule ignored, as far as I know, only by the British Army and until recently by the United States Army. All electronic and electrical communications systems, however reliable and counter-measure-proof they may appear, must be backed by a system in which a written message is carried by an officer or soldier. The best vehicle for this at higher levels is evidently the light helicopter. Lower down the motorcycle mostly seems unbeatable, but there are combinations of climate, terrain and security situation which call for two men in a jeep.

Emphasising the need for freedom of action to be set in a firm framework, the Germans of Wehrmacht vintage set great store by written executive or confirmatory orders. These were extremely short and simple. An army order for a major operation might fit on one quarto page and would never extend beyond three or four. The purpose of these orders was to get everyone off to a clean start on common ground. They were not cluttered with intelligence, executive and logistic detail which could be dealt with on staff channels. They set out simply and clearly the controlling commander's **intention**, his subordinates' **tasks**, the **resources** available to them, and the **constraints** they must observe.

15

The Supple Chain

"All in all it seems, as the above suggests, that an unusual spirit, of independence of those above and acceptance of responsibility, has grown up throughout the Prussian officer corps as it has in no other army. . . . Prussian officers will not stand for being hemmed in by rules and stereotypes as happens in Russia, Austria or Britain. . . . We follow the more natural course of giving scope to every individual's talent, of using a looser rein. We back up every success as a matter of course—even when it runs counter to the intentions of a commander-in-chief . . . . The subordinate commander exploits every advantage by taking initiatives off his own bat, without his superior's knowledge or approval." PRINCE FREDERICK OF PRUSSIA (in an 1860 essay)

Introduction

Some Germans claim that directive control as practised before and during the elder Moltke's time and reincarnated in the elite Reichswehr was the product of a unique combination of human qualities and social circumstance. They may well be right. I sought far and wide, ranging back to the Classics and focusing on the Bible and on Tennyson at his heavier, for a quotable quote that favoured trusting one's subordinates, let alone respecting them—a fruitless quest whose further pursuit I offer to the reader as a small competition with no prizes. So let us be absolutely clear what we are talking about—*a chain of trust and mutual respect running unbroken between theatre or army commander and tank or section commander.*

I must admit, though, that this metaphor of a chain fails in one respect. A chain is as strong as its weakest link. In any command or management hierarchy there will be weak links, sometimes undisclosed but more often widely recognised as such. The chain of directive control must be strong enough as a whole to generate a kind of magnetic force which bridges these weak links. One might perhaps regard this limited function as the proper role of officer mystique, were that concept not so mightily abused in officer corps where privilege goes hand in hand with incompetence and irresponsibility. For directive control will only work if that despised being, the "average" officer, combines in himself in far from average degree creative flair, dedication, intellectual as well as moral integrity, and professional competence.

In this chapter I want to examine whether this chain can be established in an army based on an open industrial democracy and, if so, how.

241

The "Junker" society

Since some British lexicographers evidently regard "junker" as a term of abuse, let me say that I am using it, shorn for the moment of moralistic connotations, as shorthand for "an aristocratic Prussian country squire" (its secondary meaning in German). While the military tradition goes back at least to the days of Frederick the Great, one is thinking primarily of the period from the rise of Bismarck to the end of the First World War, culminating in the formative years of the Wehrmacht's great captains. Unfortunately but unsurprisingly, Germany has not to my knowledge fathered a G. M. Trevelyan, an Arthur Bryant or an Alan Taylor; historical accounts lie well outside my turgidity tolerance zone. The novelists, short-story writers and diarists I have read seem to take the squirearchy for granted and concentrate on rural eccentrics and urban sophisticates. Even Thomas Mann's *Buddenbrooks*, in many respects a key work of social documentary fiction, only helps by providing a parallel to *its* family's equivalents in British society. In fact it was *Mach's Gut, du*, a little book of *belles lettres* by Ebba von Senger und Etterlin, reminiscing about her early childhood in the twenties, that gave me a link to my own experience of the English squirearchy.

One might then envisage the Prussian officer's background as an intensely paternalistic, quasi-feudal society, marked above all by stability. Even in the twenties, it remained virtually untouched by the Industrial Revolution. The squire, who was apt to come and go for purposes unknown at least to the children, was a veritable patriarch to his family and his domain, though his lady exercised a good deal of influence from the hearth. The aristocracy was Christian mostly by convention rather than personal faith, with Catholics and Protestants alike heavily slanted towards puritanism. Yet as with their counterparts in Britain, the driving force of most male aristocrats seemed to lie outside Christian belief, in a sense of duty and service to some unspecified ideal. Perhaps one could better call this a mythos, for in the German case it had strong overtones of the Nordic mythology which found expression in Wagner. For the ladies music was a key formative influence, and the ability to sing and play an important social asset; but with this exception the Junkers' attitude to the arts was marked by respect rather than passion.

As a rule—latterly at least—there was not much money about. Then again, there did not seem to be any great need for it, except to conserve the family home, generally in name at least a castle, and to modernise it to the extent decency permitted. All the essentials of life came from the estate. When a stay in the city or at Court was called for, the "old boy net" of this numerically small caste came to the rescue. For there seems to have been a far sharper demarcation between rural and urban aristocracy than was the case in Britain, with the Court providing the link between the two. Although of the highest social standing, the Junkers strike me as having far more in common with the English yeomen than with the English, French or Russian aristocracy. Sexual *mores* apart, one finds a closer parallel still in the Scottish landed gentry.

In this thumbnail sketch there are two traits we need to seize on. One is this rather mystical dedication. The other, related to it but only implied above, is the closeness and excellence of relations between squire and "subjects". There was an absolute demarcation between social and other relations, with vertical *social* intermingling restricted to certain traditional forms and occasions. This allowed all kinds of relationships even remotely involving a functional link to flourish. Being mutually dependent, the community was bound by trust. Anybody who betrayed this trust, as by getting a girl in the family way or by petty theft, was either brought sharply into line or driven out. By the same token the squire's managerial skills and acceptance of responsibility, the professional skills of doctor and school-master (not yet socially acceptable), and the craftsmanship of manual workers all earned respect because they were indispensable. (In fact one sees here a parallel with the military hierarchy of officer, senior NCO, junior rank.) Unlike in England, the squire's children often seem to have started their education at the village school, although they would later have a governess or tutor before going to a private school in the city.

Since it is hard to imagine anything more different from a modern urban society, we need to look one level deeper still for a principle which has general application. I suggest it may be *the acknowledgement and unreserved acceptance of mutual dependence.*

Problem interfaces through the ranks

Before exploring how these junkers became officers, let us come at the issue from the other end with a look at the problem interfaces through the ranks of a modern army. This is something that needs to be faced with complete frankness and seldom is. In soldiering as in other callings, the prime motivating force of those who succeed is indisputably ambition. My impression is that love of power comes later, with the enjoyment of it. (Hard to avoid a string of hackneyed quotations here!) In peacetime the spur is mostly a comfortable standard of living and upward social mobility, often for the sake of wife and children rather than self. In war it is surely fame. Ambition of this kind is a healthy, acceptable and even admirable quality when its influence is openly or evenly tacitly acknowledged. Only when individuals, especially those in high positions, delude themselves into believing that they themselves and others are altruistically motivated do the rubs start to fester.

In these terms, a problem may arise between any two ranks across which a critical selection barrier operates, the more so when the same team contains, in the lower rank, a mix of aspirants and failures. Where this occurs depends on the pattern of officer training. In the British and Federal German Armies, the only hurdle that gives rise to this rub among officers within a battalion is eligibility and selection for staff training. From the next promotion (or not) onwards, sheep and goats tend to follow divergent paths. Thus there is a potential problem interface between a battalion commander and some of his company commanders.

In the Soviet and United States systems (a Soviet battalion being in this respect the equivalent of a Western company, and so on), there are two stages of higher training—arms academy and General Staff Academy, Command and Staff College and Army War College. The first of these hurdles affects selection to command of a Soviet regiment or an American battalion, the second of a Soviet division or an American brigade. Thus less than ideal cohesion may arise at two levels. Admittedly this is of little importance in the Soviet Army which, at least from division downwards (between General Staff officers and the rest, that is) operates on an imposed discipline upheld by open abuse and fear. But it seems a reasonable principle that *a commander's direct subordinate commanders should all be fully eligible for command at his level*—though they may not attain it.

To an outsider, problems might seem most likely to arise at the officer/NCO interface. In the Soviet Army this became so serious that, in 1972, they introduced a new type of warrant officer (*praporschchik/michman*) as "the officer's right-hand man", a link between officer and NCO! A less than healthy feeling of "us and them" was, in my experience, always present in the United States Army and seems to have been aggravated by Vietnam. I suspect it may still be serious from the very intensity of the conscious efforts now being made to build bridges and mend fences. One has to bear in mind here that, improbable as it may seem, United States society is built up of complex stratifications in a number of different planes; it may thus present a more intractable problem in this respect than European societies which are just plain "class-ridden'. One might expect to see this problem at its worst in a deeply divided Britain with an officer corps still heavily dependent on privilege and mystique. There are perhaps four reasons why the opposite is the case. By far the most important of these is the trickle of commissioning from the ranks, of which more in a moment. Then there is the professional and institutional strength of the British Army's sergeants messes (which include warrant officers), coupled with the tacit acknowledgement that regimental officers rely heavily on their senior ranks to provide the professional expertise they themselves often lack. Third comes the strength of regimental spirit; and fourth the high regard in which the character and qualifications of these senior ranks are widely held outside the armed forces.

All the interfaces so far discussed represent minor weaknesses in a strong chain, and the problems they pose look manageable. The link which is so patently weak that one might think it a "break-safe" is the *subaltern in his salad days.* This weakness pervades every advanced army I know or have studied except the German, and is most pronounced of all in some small European armies such as the Dutch. All these armies (including the Soviet Army) take the bulk, or at least the potential cream, of their career officers from school or university and put them straight into officer academies of an extraordinary similarity. The resulting weakness, of which most experienced officers must be aware but are prevented by the code of their mystique from acknowledging, is demonstrably due to the system of officer selection and training. I say demonstrably, because it is shown up by an examination of the German system; likewise of the Israeli system, which increasingly seems to have taken the German approach too far.

German structure and training

Most armies have far too many officers. Table 3, comparing a German wartime tank battalion and a British unit of about the same strength in tanks and personnel, brings this home in a flash. If one takes account of specialists included in the German establishment but classed as attached in the British case, the German battalion has half the number of officers. The principle that this example so vividly illustrates is that the German Army has always regarded its career officers strictly as *top management or professional-level specialists.* Middle management, including command of rather over 50 per cent of platoons, is found from the somewhat complex structure of senior non-commissioned ranks. Outside field-force units, administrative posts and the like are filled by reserve officers, by commissioning from the ranks, and (now) by officers with short-service commissions. A trickle of conversions from the last two categories serves to keep the career officer cadre topped up against wastage.

In other armies the officer structure spreads as a matter of policy into middle management, seemingly to the tune of 40 or 50 per cent. This has four adverse effects. It produces sufficient concentrations of young officers in field force units for them to form a social clique in which professional competence is strictly démodée, and whose behaviour brings officers into disrepute with soldiers, and the army as a whole with the outside world. It creates a functional overlap at middle-management level between officers and NCOs, causing confusion over their respective status. It dilutes the quality of officer. And it creates a pyramid with a base so wide as to distort the career structure and give rise to frustration at the critical levels of selection.

The second feature of the German system, less marked perhaps in the Bundeswehr than in its predecessors, is the early yet rigorous selection of officers for the General Staff. Two further differences derive from this. Officers are groomed for stardom from the moment of selection rather than on passing out well from the Staff College—typically perhaps 7 or 8 years

TABLE 3. *Comparisons of Officer Strengths*

a	Panzerbattalion 1944		Officers	b	Armoured regiment (typical post war) (HE)		Officers
	Battalion Headquarters				**Regimental Headquarters**		
	CO	Major			CO	Lieutenant Colonel	
	Adjutant	Lieutenant	3		2 I/C	Major	5
	Asst Adjutant	2/Lieutenant			Adjutant	Captain	
					IO	Lieutenant	
					RHQ Troop Leader	2/Lieutenant	
	Headquarter Company				**Headquarters Squadron**		
	OC (Echelon Commander)	Lieutenant or Captain			OC	Major	
	Signals Officer	Lieutenant	3		2 I/C	Captain	
	Tank Troop Leader	Lieutenant			Regimental Signals Officer	Captain/Lieutenant	
					MTO	Captain/Lieutenant	
	Support Company				Quartermaster	?	
	OC (Doubles as Bn 2IC)	Captain			Technical Quartermaster	?	10
	Technical Officer (Mech)	Captain			Medical Officer	Captain	
	Technical Officer (Armaments)	Lieutenant	3		EME	Captain	
	Administrative Officer	Lieutenant			Asst EME	2/Lieutenant	
	Paymaster	?			Paymaster	?	
	Tank Companies (3 or 4)	each:			**Armoured Squadrons** (3)	each:	
	OC	Captain	2.5		OC	Major	7 × 3
	Troop Leaders (1 or 2)	2/Lieutenants	9		2 I/C	Captain	(21)
					Battle Captain	Captain	
		Average per Coy			Troop Leaders (4)	Lieutenants or	
		Average per Bn				2/Lieutenants	
	TOTAL (Average) 20 Officers				**TOTAL 36 Officers**		

earlier. (Interestingly the British Army moved in both these directions in the early seventies with the introduction of a junior staff course.) Third, as a combination of directive control and allowance for casualties requires, these officers are trained *three levels up*, so that they can assume command one level up and hold their own in discussions two levels up from there. As an extension of this, potential General Staff officers are given the feel of operational command early on. For instance, among the exercises in which Hindenburg "commanded" as a captain was one where he played army commander in a campaign in East Prussia and Poland which he was later to fight in that role.

Great as the emphasis which battle-tried senior German officers place on this early imparting of "operational feel" may be, they do not regard it as the touchstone of the Wehrmacht's success in practising directive control. The strength of the chain of trust and mutual respect they attribute squarely to the fact that, traditionally as now, *all German career officers serve a spell in the ranks*. This is not just something that is good for the other chap's soul. Three officers, at least one of whom served this apprenticeship on the Eastern Front, and all of whom later served with distinction in the Bundeswehr, have told me straight out that they regarded this experience as essential to their formation as officers. In no other way, they argued, could they have gained a real understanding of the men they were to command or—more important still—acquired *the genuine respect for those below them in rank* that directive control calls for. One of these same men in fact paid the penalty of outspokenness in a successful battle with a Social Democratic Federal Government to uphold this very principle—a fact which I found doubly interesting since, as I recall, it was a British *Labour* Government which blocked one fairly modest effort to broaden the base of British officer recruitment.

Admittedly some of the German boys did (in the past at least) attend a "cadet school", and most of them were (and are) earmarked as potential officers from the start. But this is not the kind of lip-service the British Army from time to time pays in the form of a "potential officers' troop" or whatever at a training regiment. The German boy first joins his regiment as a normal private soldier. If all goes well, he gets his first stripe after 6 months, and then works his way up to a rank which one might describe in British terms as "officer-cadet-lance-sergeant". He then spends a year at the Officers School (formerly the Infantry School) learning infantry tactics and the social niceties. Then follows *a whole year* (not 6 weeks of socialising as in the British Army) at his arm school, and—after this 2-year absence—a further probationary year back with his regiment as an ensign. Only then is his commission as a lieutenant confirmed. The next rank up is *Oberleutnant* (first lieutenant) in which he may find himself in a highly responsible appointment like battalion adjutant.

In modern times this system has one serious drawback, aggravated in fact by the way German universities work. If a boy leaves school at 19 with his *Abitur*, he will be 24 by the time he is finally commissioned. He is then expected to spend 3 or 4 years with troops. Again uniquely (to the best of my knowledge), his basic officer training includes no substantial academic element; and by the time he is free to leave his regiment, an officer who is a university candidate faces three problems. He is at an awkward age for university; he has lost the knack of study; and he cannot afford the 4 or 5 years most German university courses require. He therefore goes for 3 years to one of a number of Bundeswehr colleges. As many of those colleges' academic staff seem to feel—and as anybody who has been associated with analogous institutions will know—they can in no way compare with a proper university as far as development of intellect and character are concerned.

In fairness one must say two things. British professional opinion was, and as far as I know still is, just as solidly and seriously opposed to passing potential officers through the ranks as German opinion is for it. Within the first and second worlds, the Germans are (as far as I know) in a minority of one on this issue, with the French sitting on the fence. The majority view rests, I think, on two planks. One is the continuing need for officer mystique to uphold discipline and the status of the Queen's Commission (or its equivalent) in face of the impression created by bad officers. This is held to require a difference in kind between officer and soldier which, being entirely unnatural, can only be created by social artefacts. Then again, the officer who has been through the ranks is claimed to be unpopular with soldiers just because he knows the wrinkles junior ranks use to make life more tolerable. This was probably a valid point in the British Army of the thirties and the early war years. Whether it remains so after the social revolution of the postwar period and (in Britain at least) the broadening of the base of officer recruitment is another thing again. My only reason for supposing that this thinking still has some force is the way some wise and experienced senior ranks see one of their roles as a buffer between the soldier as he really is, and the image of him the officer needs if he is to strike the right balance between organisation and individual. I can only comment that, to my eyes at least, this approach compares poorly with the German one as a basis for trust.

Second and by contrast, identification of officer with soldier can evidently go too far. In the conscription-based Israeli Defence Forces there is, theoretically at least, no preliminary earmarking of officers. Everybody starts on the same footing. Men (and in a few cases women) must earn selection as NCOs, complete an NCOs' course, and prove themselves as tank, detachment or section commanders with their regiments before being considered for officer training—a 6-month course heavily oriented towards character development and leadership. The Israeli officer is commissioned after 2 years; he then serves 2 more years full time (a total of 4 years as opposed to the basic 3) before being considered for a long-service commission.

Like the Germans, the Israeli forces have a small officer corps—only 6 per cent of total strength. Their regimental system is much stronger even than the British one, particularly where officers are concerned. They have (or had until recently) a manpower pool of unrivalled quality to choose from. And through most of the country's existence they have been able to give most of their soldiers experience of active service, at least in low-intensity operations. Yet I like many others see a steady deterioration of command skills from the peak of excellence demonstrated in the Six Days War, even among their elite Armoured Corps. That War seemed to have produced a crop of up-and-coming young commanders. But once the hand of Moshe Dayan—well up in my personal list of the great captains of history—came off the military helm, the Army's operational performance became more and more pedestrian. The conduct of the First Lebanon Invasion revealed a military ham-handedness rivalled only by its political ineptitude. And in the Second Lebanon Invasion—as the UN Security Council vote of August 1984 showed—some of the Six Days War's bright young men managed by their actions to dent the sympathy for Israel of every Western nation bar the United States.

Thus we have a spectrum of selection and training systems ranging from the American, British and Soviet at one end, through the French (with any wrong ideas learned during token service in the ranks quickly rubbed off at St Cyr) and the German, to the Israeli. This leads one to ask two questions. The first is what distinguishes, or *ought* to distinguish, the officer from the senior rank. I suggest it may be the same quality that is acknowledged to separate top management from middle management—*creative imagination*. In the officer, though not necessarily in the civilian manager, this has to be combined in one individual with the professional competence and leadership qualities called for by directive control. Since the Jewish people is more generously endowed with creative imagination than any other, it may be that the Israeli system has gone too far in the direction of egalitarianism. Either those who designed it deliberately opted for soundness rather than brilliance; or selection is faulty; or the struggle for a commission puts out the flame. Thus an army wishing to practise manoeuvre theory by directive control should not be looking for an "officer and gentleman", an "officer and manager", or a "commissioned super-soldier", but for something in between.

Socio-economic background

Many Germans question whether their present army's officer corps will show the same command talent as members of the Wehrmacht's General Staff, and indeed whether the prerequisites for the exercise of directive control exist in the open industrial democracies of today. Certainly the key features of the Junker's background were stability and cohesion. Just as certainly, the Second World War destroyed the social fabric of Britain and Germany, among other Western countries. Since then, the "third industrial revolution" and the transfer of classical manufacturing industry to the third world has launched Western Europe into what may prove to be a Gibbonian decline, making it a demi-continent of societies which are politically and culturally unstable and divided amongst themselves. And, although cushioned by size and wealth, the United States is in much the same boat.

People from different generations and walks of life no longer have even a semblance of common purpose. In a climate of financial uncertainty overshadowed by the nuclear despair which increasingly dominates the European mind since the deployment of Tomahawk and Pershing 2, most men are very understandably out for the short-term benefit of themselves and their families. The deep-seated split of opinion over possession and deployment of nuclear weapons, compounded in Britain by the electoral system and everywhere except perhaps in France by ever poorer quality of government, is tearing societies further and further apart. Before long it may even eat into the cohesion of armed forces. In fact this is yet another case of a phenomenon taking a decade to cross the Atlantic. Superimposed on the long-term economic trends, Western Europe is experiencing the same kind of doubts and disruption which split the American body politic and armed forces over the Vietnam issue, and from which the United States has recently begun to recover.

I have painted a deliberately gloomy picture—though one not too far, I think, from present and future actuality—in order to bring out the problems facing the armed forces of a disunited society. Things have not changed much; Sun Tzu writes of "the ruler's moral influence" as the first prerequisite for military success. Without unity of purpose through the ranks and among their families, it is hard indeed to build and maintain the level of morale needed for effective control by detailed orders, let alone to achieve the bond of trust implicit in directive control.

One is thus forced to embark on an extremely dangerous path—that of creating a military sub-culture. I shall consider in Chapter 19 the threat to the freedom of the individual imposed by a universal cellular militia. Those countries which have a system of this genre (Denmark, Sweden, Switzerland and Israel) are all at root united societies. By contrast I have lost count of the number of United Nations members ruled by their military or by governments placed and kept in power by the armed forces. We now know that practically anything *can* 'happen here", whether here in Britain, the Federal Republic, France, the Netherlands or the United States. So let us for the moemtn focus on the political threat implicit in the existence of long-service standing forces.

One saw the first danger in Britain in the sixties, with the ending of conscription and the butchery of the reserve forces. Even where strong local links exist, the standing forces, notably the Regular Army, have become divorced from society as a whole. This is perhaps no more than an accentuation of a trend which has been evident in England since the days of Cromwell, and was one of our earlier and more enduring exports to the United States. Over the past 25 years, however, the tip of an exceptionally ugly and menacing iceberg has manifested itself more than once in Britain, France, Germany and the United States. Prudence dictates gobbledygook here. So let us content ourselves with "extra-parliamentary activity of a paramilitary nature", and let who runs read.

But a military sub-culture, like a militarist culture, is apt to bring in its wake a third danger, at once more subtle and more serious. A sub-culture must be built on a unifying aim, and for a military sub-culture the only realistic aim is the effective waging of war. In the worst case (as manifested in Germany after the fall of Bismarck, in the Schlieffen–younger Moltke–Ludendorff succession), this aim degenerates into the glorification of war as an end in itself. Others come to terms with their *raison d'être* by achieving a *metastable* mental state immortalised in United States Strategic Air Command's motto—"Peace is our profession". Being founded on hypocrisy, albeit at subconscious level, this attitude provides a less than ideal basis for a bond of trust between officers and their soldiers, many of whom for some strange reason seem unable to perform the required mental gymnastics.

This said, let us suppose that, despite alarming sways and lurches from time to time, some way of straddling this razor edge has been found—as by and large it probably has been in Britain's case. Or, more realistically in one sense but less so in another, that a united and stable democratic society requires standing forces to defend itself or to pursue what one might call more outward-looking political aims. Within this framework we can return to the more manageable problem of creating sound relationships through the ranks.

Conclusion—a possible system

To draw the above discussions together, I should like to postulate the bare bones of a system which might meet the requirements of directive control. I shall do so in British terms; these will be familiar to many readers and, though I have studied other systems in depth, I lack a comparable "feel" for them. Rather than set up a grand design which somebody might be rash enough to take as a blueprint, I shall employ manoeuvre theory, attacking the soft edges of the problem in the hope that the hard core will then crumble before me.

The first trick is evidently to follow the example of many of history's most successful armies and restrict the *size of the active officer corps to 5 or 6 per cent of total strength*—as opposed to 15 per cent and upwards! This single act provides a double boost to morale. It clearly identifies the officer with top management and narrows the base of his career pyramid; no less important, it opens the full span of middle management to senior ranks. It should also improve the quality of that notoriously inadequate being, the average officer.

The next move here, again killing at least two birds with one stone, is to limit *all* commissions and engagements to 20 years, with a maximum of 16 or so spent as an officer. This ties with current Royal Air Force practice, and with the British Army's first option point for pension. Commissioned service would be extended by selection for 10 or 15 years, give or take, as now in the RAF; with a further automatic extension for those promoted to three star rank (as currently in most services). Many have questioned the British "careers to 55" approach ever since its inception. By the time any change of this kind could be implemented, a two- or three-career working life will have become an accepted pattern, even the norm perhaps, throughout the Western World. A combination of selection beyond 20 years with generous terminal payment and pension, and with preferential entry to attractive second careers should offer economy, sharper incentive to do well, and improved quality.

The next requirement is a *baton in every knapsack*—or more precisely (as best exemplified by the Tsarist Army and the British Army of today) lieutenant-colonel's badges in every knapsack, with a baton wherever you like to envisage it but destined for the next generation. To my mind, this controlled upward social mobility is the British Army's most admirable single trait. But it is not achieved by equality of opportunity in the first year or two of service (such as the Israeli system offers). Men of limited education, perhaps from limited or difficult backgrounds, need time and opportunity within the service to develop themselves.

In fact the British Army system would surely be hard to better. A minute proportion of men are *selected for commissioning in their late twenties*, often after being tested as staff-sergeant platoon commanders. They have an outside chance of qualifying for general staff training; one or two surmount this hurdle too and join the mainstream of career officers. A rather larger number of soldiers gain commissions in their late thirties from the senior ranks (warrant officer in the British case). These splendid professionals fill administrative appointments within field-force units, instructional and administrative posts in schools, and quartermaster appointments proper. One of the more respectable reasons often put forward for restricting commissioning from these sources is dilution of the quality of sergeants messes. My impression from experience of the British Army is that these two streams together could provide about 3 per cent of total strength, or *about one-half of a small officer corps*, without dilution of quality before or after commissioning.

At this point we need a spot of figuring to reset our sights. Take the British and United States Armies at their existing strengths as a reference base. The two changes suggested above would reduce the size of the young officer intake *to* (not *by*) almost one-sixth of what it is now—say to one-fifth (20 per cent). A substantial proportion of this residue would be graduate specialists of various kinds, mainly engineers and doctors, whose status rests on their professional qualification. If the British Army followed the excellent practice of many other services and instituted a "secretarial" corps, the same route would be open to graduates of several other disciplines too. (These specialists might be post-graduate direct entries or "university cadets" (roughly United States ROTC), in each case much as now, or army apprentices who matriculated.) Similarly, there is no argument save tradition against splitting the sappers into "combat engineers" and the rest, a pattern long since found in some armies. *We are then left with the young entry to the teeth arms*—armour, artillery, aviation, combat engineers and infantry (including airborne). *This would amount to only some 10 per cent of the present annual intake.* I stress this point to pre-empt the likely financial counterstroke!

Lengths of engagement and other conditions of enlisted service are too dependent on socio-economic conditions at the place and time in question to merit discussion in general terms. Both the Federal German and United States Armies, likewise I understand the French, have had great problems recently over the quality of senior NCO and the number of men extending beyond the crucial 12-year point to fill senior general-duty and specialist appointments. (A far more serious problem still in the Soviet Army, but that is another story!) In considering the recruitment and selection of mainstream officers, one should thus also seek to ensure an ample and healthy flow of talent up through the enlisted ranks.

The suggestion I am about to offer as one possible solution to both these problems rests on the principle of the British "junior leaders" system—now, like most other things British and military, castrated by tightening of the purse-strings. Boys would have to join junior leaders units at 16, and leave them (as now) on enlisting for man's service (or opting out) at 18. They would follow a curriculum based on "Hahnist" principles (see also Chapter 20), combining secondary education (including matriculation) with adventure training, sport, and military basics. Boys would gain promotion on a trainee rank structure, not only up to junior regimental sergeant-major (as now) but to "junior commander" (of "officer" status).

These units would become the sole route of entry for career officers commissioned young into the teeth arms, and the main one for potential senior ranks. Candidates for early commissioning would not be earmarked in advance, though they might well show early. They would have both to gain their academic qualifications and to win their spurs as junior leaders in face of extremely hot competition—all the more so since only about one-quarter of the officer corps, or under 2 per cent of total strength, would gain commissions in this way. Those not selected for early commissioning could, as now, join their units as private soldiers, but with their experience and "junior" attainments to fit them for early promotion.

I am fairly certain that the price of not putting officers fully through the ranks (as the Germans and the Israelis do) is the elimination of any form of "officer school" as such. Soldiers and civilians alike are blind to any merits these places may have, seeing them as temples of officer mystique, and their courses as mere initiation rites. So those selected for commissioning would be given probationary status as ensigns or whatever, comparable to that of midshipmen in navies. They would spend one year at their *arms or corps school*, under the immediate supervision of an officer of their own regiment in regimentally-based arms. This course would cover general professional subjects, special-to-arm curricula, the requisite minimum of social polish, and advanced training in a chosen arduous sport. Success would depend on both qualifications and recommendations, those who failed *on any aspect* being offered reversion to the ranks or discharge. The successful ones would spend a further probationary year with their regiments as ensigns before acceptance for a 3-year provisional commission as second-lieutenants.

This system would have young men joining their regiments as ensigns at 19 and receiving provisional commissions at 20. They would have surmounted a series of hurdles which were in fact tough and, more important still, were seen to be tough by their fellow junior leaders, now the bulk of their NCOs. After a total of 4 years with troops, they would still be young enough (at 23) to take a degree before embarking on preparation for staff training. This suggestion surely gives officers and their men enough in common to forge a bond of trust and mutual respect. It does not overcome the problem of having inexperienced officers in junior commands. But with a smaller number of young officers in a unit, and good middle management back-up, this seems marginally preferable to sending young men off to spend their salad days at university. In the event of war, the lieutenants (first lieutenants) reading for degrees would be available to fill these posts.

This route would be the predominant one for entry to the *general staff* and qualification for command above company level; in fact, on the figures I have used, everyone following it successfully should receive staff training. I would see three supplementary sources. One, already mentioned, is the selection for staff training of men commissioned in their late twenties from staff-sergeant rank; as a matter of policy, the numbers from the other two together should not exceed the number from this source. The second would cater for good honours graduates of outstanding personal qualities with at least 5 years' service on short-service commissions in a teeth arm. Third, as in most armies now, some specialists would attend staff training on a quota basis to fit them for senior appointments in their own corps. Again as now, a very few might be nominated for general staff appointments in field formations after outstanding performance on staff training, and thus admitted to the general staff.

In this illustrative scheme I have sought to combine what I see as the best elements of the conventional, German and Israeli systems so as to provide a coherent body of officers and long-service soldiers, while also catering for specialists. This system would seem equally apt for the long-service core of a professional army, or the professional nucleus of a conscript army or militia. The nub of the idea is to place potential officers and young soldiers in fair competition, but in a synthetic, forcing-house environment rather than in field-force units. The scheme bridges the interface between officer and senior rank in the way called for by directive control, at the cost of creating—or rather acknowledging—one between teeth-arm officers and specialists. This teeth/tail interface arises from the need to offset the cost of putting suitable teeth-arm officers through university when they are on a fairly high salary. In the ideal, it could largely be bridged by applying the "extended junior leaders" principle to army apprentice schools and, as now, by graduating the bulk of the engineers in house. Be this as it may, I hope I have at least demonstrated that success in forging the chain of trust calls for a middle-of-the-road system involving both officers and NCOs, rather than any extreme solution. And I believe tomorrow's officer material would welcome a challenge of this kind.

16

Of Popinjays and Pards

"Thus, one able to gain the victory by modifying his tactics in accordance with the enemy situation may be said to be divine." Sun Tzu

"Great achievements, little show; more reality than appearance." Schlieffen

Introduction—the battle for the primary loop

Over the past 40 years, the Soviet Army has improved the tempo of mounting an operation by a factor of almost four, maintaining symmetry of time with its improved tempo of execution (Chapters 3 and 6). Since high mounting tempo is at first sight the basis of responsiveness, one might expect Soviet mobile forces to be formidable indeed. In fact there is good reason to suppose that the Soviets have compounded their inbuilt inflexibility by misusing C^3 technology to exercise "forward command from the rear". Swiftness they may have, but it may often be what Sun Tzu calls "blundering swiftness". As long as he retains the initiative, the attacker can get away with this by exploiting momentum—a kind of steam-roller effect. The defender by contrast must combine speed with precision in his response. Conditioned as it may be by extraneous factors, the way the Soviet Army seems to have gone in exploiting technology is just one example of the misuse of computer technology. As any computer or management consultant will tell you, gross mistakes in the application of automatic control and data processing are to be found in every field of science, technology and management.

Many of these expensive nonsenses are due to hard selling and the pressures of fashion on the one hand, and to a monumental lack of understanding on the other. But I believe there is more to it than this. Even informed users are ambivalent about the part the human organism should continue to play in the primary control loop. This is a genuine problem of immense importance in the military sphere, at every level from anti-tank guided weapons to operational command decisions. Good decision-makers welcome the way scientific management techniques in general, and computer technology in particular, both provide better data and narrow down the grey zone within which human judgement has to be exercised. So

257

far, so good. But beyond this the road turns into a primrose path leading to "the elimination of human fallibility" from the system by making the primary control loop fully automatic. I suspect too that technologists' own distaste for responsibility is reflected in their preference for handing over to the machine.

On the other hand, the type of man who makes a good manager or commander thrives on responsibility; decisions would be meat and drink to him were it not that the tougher and harsher they are the more he relishes them. Narrowing down the grey zone reduces his job satisfaction, makes him feel fenced in. Above all, he wants to be right in there pitching. I suggest this second attitude is the right one, at least where military command is concerned, and for two very good reasons. Until computers can be given a synaptic and associative network analogous to that of the brains of man and the higher animals, they can only be as good as their inputs. Even the most sophisticated software is not creative; it just distances man from machine by shifting the interface towards man. The system may be able to spot some kinds of errors in data; but it cannot remedy the limitations and misconceptions that go into its programming. By transferring functions from man to machine, one is not eliminating fallibility but transferring it from end-user to operators, and to the designers of hardware and software. More important by far, however strong an impression of original thought it may give, a computer is in fact incapable of creative synthesis. It does what it has been told to very well, and performs the tricks it has been taught very nicely. *But no way can it "pull something out of the bag" when faced with the unexpected.*

This is why I at least am convinced that, just as we still put an expensive human brain, sometimes two, in a strike aircraft, every kind of commander at every level must be kept fairly and squarely in the primary control loop. By the same token, he still needs the support of human brainpower. My purpose in this chapter is to apply these principles to an analysis of staff functions and suggest lines along which staffs might be reorganised. But first I want to air two general points fundamental to the exercise of directive control.

Commander and senior staff officer

We had some discussion on the principle of unity of command back in Chapter 13, but it is now time to come to grips with the nitty-gritty of it. One might reasonably suppose the term to mean that the responsibility for decisions and their consequences rests on one man. In the event, though, the unison of preaching contrasts with the discords of practice. One can perhaps single out four key points on the spectrum of such variations:

British practice. Only exceptionally, and then only at the very highest levels, does one find a deputy commander or chief of staff. To cater for emergencies, a subordinate or specialist headquarters is designated as alternative headquarters. The staff is run by the head of the operations (G3) branch, who is *primus inter pares* with the senior administrative staff officer. Plans normally originate with the commander and are devilled by the staff, then brought back to the commander for decision, and finally implemented by the staff.

The United States system. Headquarters down to brigade level have a deputy commander, who is assigned specific sub-tasks (like the conduct of a river crossing) and generally remains at the headquarters while the commander "roves". Then there is an "executive officer", analogous to the first officer in a ship, who does not form part of a staff branch but co-ordinates staff activities. The principal branch heads have access to the commander.

The German system from 1938 onwards. There is no deputy except perhaps at strategic level. The chief of staff would take over temporarily if the commander was killed; and briefing two up and two down (pages 232/233) safeguards against loss of continuity if a headquarters is destroyed. Above division, the chief of staff is divorced from a staff branch. He does not share command responsibility, but has the right to express disagreement in writing. Plans may originate with either commander or staff. In fact, this basis produced a wide spread of results, some commanders holding themselves aloof and giving oracular decisions, others working with their chiefs of staff as a two-man team.

The former German and current Soviet system. The Soviet Army now provides for a deputy at operational levels, probably as a hangover from the battlefield nuclear heyday. Headquarters from corps (Soviet "army") level upwards have a chief of staff who shares responsibility (and kudos) with the commander. (In fact, as we saw earlier, real control may be vested in the chief of staff.)

The first infringement of unity of command lies in the presence of a **deputy commander**. At first glance this seems an essential precaution if there is a significant risk of the commander becoming a casualty. But a harder look suggests otherwise. Unless the commander is incapacitated in the middle of the battle, there is time to get someone else in. On the decision-making side, the last thing a deputy commander taking over in mid-stream can do is change horses; this would simply destroy cohesion and impair morale. The senior staff officer should be perfectly capable of co-ordinating subordinate commanders in implementing the original plan—just as he is capable of running the formation in peacetime or rest periods when the commander is away. As for leadership, the occasions when a deputy could have instant impact would be rare indeed. However well-intentioned, his cutting a dash before taking over would be bound to impair the formation's loyalty to its commander. In a field headquarters, then, the deputy and all his works probably amount to a palpable chunk of superfluous fat.

By contrast the **chief of staff** issue is genuinely controversial; in fact it raises three distinct problems. The first again concerns size. Despite differences in practice and nomenclature, the British, Federal German and Soviet armies seem to share a consensus that a co-ordinator is a waste of food at division and below but justified from corps (army) upwards. The second question is this one of shared responsibility. Shared responsibility must mean shared control, or more precisely retention of a measure of control within the general staff even if the commander is not a member of it. The reasons for this concept seem to be historical, in that the commander might be a princeling or other non-professional figurehead; and in the Second World War political. Hitler changed the system to frustrate the General Staff, whom he saw with some justice as over-cautious. Stalin, under pressure of imminent defeat, took the political horse out of the *troika* but kept a share of control with the General Staff—a reasonable move, perhaps, after he had purged all the talented commanders but preserved a few brilliant staff officers! One can see no good military reason for preserving this custom.

The third and more interesting problem area is the way commander and senior staff officer work together. This will largely depend, as it undoubtedly should, on their respective personalities and the commander's style (in the Western, not the Russian sense, pages 223–225). But one can probe beyond this to the commander's function. Like a queen bee, he is at once creator and inspirer of effort (though he is unlikely to exercise leadership by hormonal secretion). Anything he has to do to implement his creative thinking detracts from both these functions. By the same token, he must be mollycoddled whenever the exercise of one or both of his proper functions does not dictate otherwise—as it does in the exercise of forward command. On the other side of this coin, the senior staff officer's role is to pamper the commander's mind, just as the role of his steward and orderly is to pamper his body.

I use these extreme terms at some cost to good taste both to dispel fashionable images of the commander as some kind of social worker who runs a Boy Scout troop in his spare time, and because they highlight the functional relationship between commander and staff.

Jumping ahead for a moment, I would almost say that commander is to staff as staff is to computer. This does not mean, though, that staff officers should be subservient. As Jomini puts it, they should have been picked for competence and brainpower just as the commander is picked for flair and character. One of the staff's roles in executing the commander's will is to interact vigorously with him in shaping that will. This is teamwork at its highest. Most authorities agree that a commander should have both an active say and a veto in the selection of his senior staff officer; I would add that the senior staff officer too should be allowed to "place himself on the transfer list" without prejudice to his future.

Headquarters size and structure

This need for commander and key staff to work as a team compounds with the physical arguments for keeping headquarters small. Germans of Wehrmacht vintage see this as essential to the proper exercise of directive control. In their view, an operational level headquarters should have only ten or a dozen officers, and a minimum of supporting personnel—this meaning a minimum, not the kind of circus that traipses around in the wake of American and British formation commanders. To make the rest of my argument credible, I should stress that both the Germans and the Soviets are evidently against working staffs in shifts. The loss of continuity is unacceptable; and if the key man is off duty when a crisis occurs, it takes too long to rouse and brief him. They apparently consider it preferable to overstretch staff officers for the period during which a given headquarters is playing the operational or tactical lead (pages 203, 233).

On this basis, a dozen officers including the commander and combat support advisers might suffice (Table 4). This command post would be capable of hiving off a tactical headquarters or forward command post of commander and two staff officers for limited periods.

I shall explain the innovations in this suggestion in a moment. But the need to keep headquarters small strikes me as so important from every point of view that one ought to take it as a starting point. Few would dispute that the British and United States Armies have gone wrong in this respect and have led their German allies some way down this primrose path. The false thinking may lie in starting with the notion of a "main" headquarters, from which a "tactical" and "rear" headquarters are split off. This makes the focus of control more of a bladder than a ganglion. Better surely to begin, as the Germans did and the Soviets always have done, with the idea of a compact but sub-divisible command post, then to think in terms of giving it the support it needs (Fig. 49). The communications terminal at the command post will itself need to provide a secure voice link with its forward offshoot. If this is to consist of just one helicopter or two light vehicles, it cannot and probably need not handle data or facsimile. But it must have the means to join lower-level command nets after clearance through signals channels.

The command post must be supported via secure voice, data and facsimile links by a communications and computing centre. This would also be a convenient location for detailed intelligence work, so let us call it

TABLE 4. *Operational level command post*

commander
senior staff officer (co-ordinator)
two operations staff
two "reconnaissance" staff (page 204)
one adviser each—
    artillery
    engineer
    air (fixed and rotary wing)
one "interface" officer each for—
    intelligence
    communications
    logistics

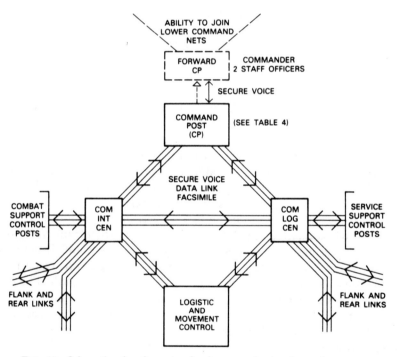

FIG. 49. *Schematic of a formation headquarters developed round a compact command post.*

COMINTCEN. Combat support headquarters would likewise be organised on a command post basis, and would link into this centre. Naturally it would also have outward links of all types.

If one is going to rely on computers for some staff functions, and on high-grade communications for the achievement of high tempo, both types of facilities, *and data storage*, must be duplicated at separate locations to minimise tactical risk. Logically, then, one might parallel the

COMINTCEN with a COMLOGCEN, which would provide, as well as the requisite duplication, a focus for logistic work and communications support for service support control posts. As a further precaution, the COMINTCEN would have a small logistics team, and the COMLOGCEN a small intelligence team. A logistic control point, analogous to the command post and also serving as a movement control centre, completes the picture.

It may seem folly not to duplicate the most important element of all, the command post. If the command post is split and only one element of it survives, that element is best placed to assume control. If the whole lot goes, then the superior or a designated subordinate command post takes over. This exploits the principle that, out of four or five levels of command, only two will be fully active at any one time (pages 203, 233). Since the active command post is the one most likely to be destroyed, replacing it with a second eleven is unacceptable. Far better to move in another first eleven which does not have too much on its hands at the moment—the more so as this approach ties in with the "two up and two down" briefing essential to directive control.

I have neither the expertise nor the data to examine the cost-effectiveness of standardisation, but it does strike me that, in a headquarters structured in this way, technical and administrative personnel, and materiel, would not vary too much with level. It might well pay to establish standard "bricks" which could serve any level of headquarters between, say, army group and division or brigade.

Mounting tempo and staff functions

I started by structuring the command post because, on the basis of first-rate vicarious experience, I am convinced that, in this instance, "small" is not just beautiful but in the fullest sense vital. Clearly, though, any rethinking and restructuring must exploit modern C^3 technology. Since one gets a much cleaner model from an offensive operation (simply because the attacker by definition has the initiative), I shall once more use the study of a Soviet tank army or front-level OMG offensive that I developed in *Red Armour* and, in more detail, for my contribution to the March 1984 Symposium at the United States Army War College. The nub of the matter is that the Soviet Army appears to have reduced the mounting time for an operation of this kind, in step with the execution time, by a factor of three to four between 1945 and, say, 1980. What follows are my deductions from this acceleration, backed by a few factual pointers.

Figure 50 sets out the rough timings. The gestation period of the controlling operational headquarters (army/OMG) appears to be unchanged at 11 to 12 hours from receipt of orders, extended by a similar period (or repeated as the case may be) if there is a major change of plan. By contrast

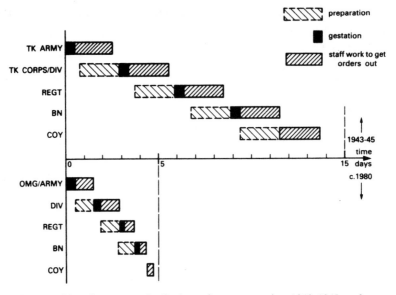

Fig. 50. *Mounting tempos of a Soviet tank army operation, 1943–1945, and an OMG operation (say 1980).*

the time taken to get the "operation document" out has been halved. The feature of Soviet wartime practice which seems strange to Western eyes—and which I therefore checked with some care—is that the (then) period of 48 to 60 hours to get orders out was repeated at each level down to battalion, rather than diminishing down the levels as one would expect. This gives a remarkably consistent figure of 15 days from order to launch.

The use of data and facsimile links to pass advance information and detailed orders downwards means that *divisional* (tactical) planning should be completed within 48 hours of the receipt of orders by army/OMG. If we assume that similar techniques are used down to regiment, we find that leading company commanders can receive their very simple orders 4 to 5 days from the word go, which is about the time they should have completed replenishment in the assembly area.

The defender cannot, of course, afford 12 hours' gestation time. For him it is a question of choosing a contingency plan and putting it into effect as it stands or with minor changes. As we saw (pages 191/192), the details of these contingency plans can be prerecorded and distributed on floppy disks (or perhaps in future using the branched video disk technique), leaving only a brief directive on any changes and the code word for implementation to be passed. This system not only helps security but gives the defender a chance to obtain and maintain material surprise—to offset the attacker's advantage of interior lines and get inside his decision loop. Thus the gain in tempo offered by a combination of computerisation and directive control is of even more importance to the defender than to the attacker.

Nonetheless, an offensive operation once again provides a clearer model for analysing this improvement. One can break down the types of staff work involved in mounting an offensive operation into three categories:

work calling mainly for human judgement (H);
work best done by a mix of human and computer resources (HC);
work best done by computer, with very simple special-to-occasion inputs (C).

Table 5 analyses under these heads the successive steps in mounting an offensive operation, which are broadly representative of the principal staff functions of a formation headquarters in the field.

TABLE 5. *Computerisation of staff functions*

Intelligence collation	HC
Operational/tactical planning	H
Choice of plan	H
Concentration—planning/movement orders	C
Allocation of troops to tasks	H
Outline fire planning	HC
Detailed fire planning	C
Engineer planning	HC
Operational movement (out of contact)	C
Preparation of operation directive	HC
Logistic planning	HC
Logistic detailing	C
Preparation of logistic orders	C

How it would work

Readers may quibble over the detail of this breakdown, but I doubt they will dispute its essence. At this point we can marry it up with the headquarters structure suggested above on the basis of compactness.

The command post, with its co-ordinator, operations branch, and "reconnaissance" branch (i.e. priority intelligence, page 204), is responsible for the "H" functions, promulgating its directives through the COMINTCEN. The "reconnaissance" branch receives inputs from the "interface" intelligence officer, and may put specific questions to him, or to the information-gathering resources under its own control. A two-way interaction goes on between the co-ordinator, the operations branch and if needs be the commander on the one hand and the combat support advisers on the other. The latter in turn pass directives via the COMINTCEN to their command posts for detailing and implementation. A similar but less detailed exchange goes on between the logistics "interface" officer and the co-ordinator; this generates outputs, *including controlled movement out of contact*, to the COMLOGCEN.

I have coined the term "interface officer" not just to be trendy but to bring out the fact that these links must be experienced and senior officers, perhaps even branch heads. There are three reasons why junior liaison officers would not do. First, these officers must be able to give the best possible specialist advice. Second, they will have to draw up the directives which go to the "INT" element of the COMINTCEN, and to the COMLOGCEN. Third and most important, they must be too good to be browbeaten by the commander and the operations staff. Unless they can get their point of view across and make it stick, there is every chance of the commander opting for a plan which he cannot execute.

The role of the communications interface officer is rather different; it is a nice point whether or not this should be the commanding officer of the signals/headquarters battalion. The interface officer's immediate function is to see that the command post facilities run properly. However, he will also have a dual advisory role of critical importance. He must ensure that the options considered are within the resources of the C^3 set-up; less obvious but just as important, he must advise on the electronic warfare implications of the options being considered. Then he must issue executive directives to the COMINTCEN and COMLOGCEN. It is a nice point whether the CO should be at the command post (as interface officer), or at the COMINTCEN, because the functioning of the two communications and computing centres is essential to the exercise of operational and higher tactical command. As I already stressed (page 240) there must be back-up systems, but calculating by steam and communicating by wheel are bound to result in severe degradation of tempo.

If computerisation is to work, the signals arm must also accept responsibility for software management. Certainly programming skills, and probably some systems analysis capacity, will be required at COMINTCEN/COMLOGCEN level. A particular problem of the extensive use of APDS in the field is the updating of software at the lower levels; unless a foolproof program for doing this automatically can be devised, an exchange of disks at COMINTCEN/COMLOGCEN level may be the only answer.

Conclusion—two major changes

I slipped in one of the two major changes I have suggested without justifying it. This is the transfer of the planning and control of controlled movement from operations (G3) to logistics (G4)—an idea which I picked up from Jomini's description of the French practice of his time, and which seems to fit computerisation like a glove. The operations staff must of course lay down the moves of combat forces in outline. But much of the heat is taken out of the movement problem by the ability of computers not just to work out movement orders but to optimise the use of road space, to respond instantly to changes in the situation, and to make far more effective use of switch routes and staging areas than any human staff could. This change would of itself relieve the operations staff of one of its worst chores—and one of the most frequent causes of snarl-ups. Movement is the kind of thing the feeblest of computers does much better than the ablest of men.

The second and greater change is not so much an innovation as the fusion of historical fact and existing trends. Armies which have succeeded in manoeuvre warfare have had small headquarters; and advances in electronics, both directly and due to the electronic warfare threat, are having a decisive influence on organisation and procedures in the C^3I sphere. So far electronics have been superimposed on existing structures, resulting in Topsy-like growth and duplication. The time must have come for a rethink.

What I have tried to do is simply to isolate the core of the functions of forming, making and implementing decisions, and the officers needed to perform these functions. I have then added back the essential advisers, who in fact form part of the "decision team". This team needs to receive certain inputs and to make certain outputs. I have provided for these by adding "interface officers" who double as advisers. The only fat I have allowed this command post is that needed for hiving off a forward element.

Most advanced armies now deploy signals centres separately from headquarters proper, and duplicate these centres in separate locations. So all I have done is to transfer the wholly or mainly computerised staff functions to these centres, forming what I have called a COMINTCEN and a COMLOGCEN. Combat and service support control posts, each separately located, tag onto these centres just as the command post does; and there is a small staff-manned point for physical control of movement.

Communications and computer-related facilities are resources on which the exercise of operational and tactical command is now considered to turn—probably to a greater extent than it really does. So for both psychological and technological reasons, formations would initially have to retain an organic headquarters/signals unit, of which the command-post personnel and materiel would form a sub-unit. But I suspect this is only the beginning of the story—and here again I am projecting forward from current trends rather than innovating. I have no idea how many megabytes the data to be held at a COMINTCEN or COMLOGCEN would amount to, or what proportion of this would be special-to-level or special-to-formation. But given the right combination of storage capacity and speed and certainty of data transfer, there would be no need to tie a particular centre to a particular level or to an individual formation. One could then set about generating SOPs to standardise the interfaces between these centres and command and control posts. This is an ideal area for SOPs; since most of them would in fact be incorporated in computer software, there is a good chance of their being properly observed.

This step offers a great leap forward both in flexibility and in economy of resources. For it would then be possible to divorce these centres from formations and establish a centrally controlled lattice over the entire area of operations. Command posts at all levels from the controlling operational headquarters to brigade, together with their related combat support command posts and service support control posts, would simply "plug in" to the nearest pair of centres. Similarly, with a physical transfer of staff officers and specialists amounting to no more than a single medium helicopter lift, a COMLOGCEN could be converted into a COMINTCEN, and *vice versa*. This would allow communications and computing resources on the operational and intelligence side to be boosted near operational centres of effort, with logistics temporarily handled at a greater geographical distance. What is more, this ability to switch channels within a lattice would make life extremely difficult for the opposition's signals intelligence organisation.

But the feasibility or otherwise of a lattice system does not touch the heart of the matter. The successful application of manoeuvre theory turns on speed and precision of response, doubly so when one bears in mind the effects of Clausewitzian friction. Responsiveness calls for directive control. Directive control at once requires and enables the command function proper to be exercised by close-knit teams working in compact command posts. These posts are easy to move and to conceal, and their compactness keeps hangers-on out of the hair of the people who matter. In fact, if the commander practised forward command freely, his command post could enjoy something like the seclusion of a monastic reserve. Surely nothing could be more conducive to the quality of decision-making on which success in manoeuvre warfare turns!

PART 5

Ends and Means

"The legitimate object of war is a more perfect peace."
(Inscription on General Sherman's statue, Washington DC)

17

Acceptable Aims

> "The national objective ... (should be) ... the resumption and progressive continuance of what may be termed the peace-time policy, with the shortest and least costly interruption of the normal life of the country." LIDDELL HART

Introduction—the ultimate sport

I am not clear at just what stage in the Christian era war took on the likeness of a sport. Certainly not in the Gothic Wars of the sixth century conducted by Belisarius and chronicled by Procopius. Belisarius, in fact, seems to have provided history's outstanding example of the minimum use of armed force as a back-up to political and economic pressure, and of the employment of threat and pre-emption as opposed to fighting. Yet by the time of that mockery of holiness and classicism alike, the Holy Roman Empire, the pattern of "kings' wars" (then in fact mostly dukes' wars), which reached its apotheosis in the eighteenth century, was well established. My personal view, from amateurish dippings into the past, is that European civilisation's attitude to war, the bellicism which Michael Howard brings out so well, derives from the Moorish and Mongol influences of the Dark Ages and the period of emergence from them. One can surely trace a link between the rules of war (such as they were) which grew up during Crusades, the mediaeval code of chivalry, and the concepts of both "sporting" and "gentlemanly" behaviour. Certainly the last two have always struck me as owing much more to Islam than to the Christian ethic *per se*, or to the humanism bred by Classicism out of Christianity in the shape of the Renaissance.

Be this as it may, up to the middle of this century war was essentially conducted in the same way as a team game, with an ethos (excellently elucidated by General Sir John Hackett in his *Profession of Arms*), a code of written and unwritten rules, an opening and final whistle, occasionally even a half-time break. Though I do not know an example of the contestants changing ends, they have frequently changed sides. For the period between the abandonment of the charming mediaeval custom of pillage, massacre and rape, and Napoleon's ravagement of the tradition of "kings' wars", this sporting analogy seems both rather precise and morally unexceptionable.

271

Even the mass slaughter of the First World War failed, as I well recall, even to dent the surface of the bellicist attitude of the British upper and middle classes. With one honourable exception, every pedagogue who taught or tutored me for long enough to influence my views was steeped in bellicism—many using the glories of war to justify some very strange views on life in general.

Even the use of air power in the Second World War did not, in my experience, greatly change matters. The holocaust overshadowed all other horrors, leaving little sympathy for Germany's postwar sufferings. And it was a long time before the release of German and Soviet film brought the injury inflicted on the Soviet Union into the realm of the imaginable for Western bodies politic. Only the Western countries which had suffered German occupation (and then with the major exception of France) started to move towards the traditional neutrals in rejecting war as an instrument of policy.

Now, in Western Europe at least, grassroots opinion in the bodies politic has begun to swing. There is a gathering tide not so much of pacifism, in the strict sense of submission to armed force, as of "anti-bellicism", a refusal to accept the use of armed force as an instrument of policy. This has been brought about by two trends, ranging along the two extremes of concepts of war. On the one hand, the nuclear threat, symbolised for many by the Cuban missile crisis of 1962, is seen by all but the most blinkered for the madness it is. At the other, revolutionary warfare in all its forms, and now state-sponsored terrorism too, have blurred the dividing line between peace and war. Above all, almost every violent act, ranging from assassination to surprise invasion, has achieved or at least advanced its political aim. By contrast, governments have failed to do more than hold their own, even on home ground, against subversive movements—the IRA in Ulster, ETA in the Basque country of France and Spain, the Bader-Meinhoff Gang and the Red Army Faction in the Federal Republic, and the Red Brigades in Italy, to name but the ones closest to home. The employment of organised forces (as we now understand them) to wage war is suffering not just from increasing moral rejection but from a credibility crevasse widened almost daily by some freak avalanche. The states one knew as peace and war are progressively merging into a metastable condition threatened alike by shifting and by collapse.

Since it is pretty evident that "a more perfect peace" is a long way off, I want to apply the thoughts set out earlier in this book to the situation facing the first and second worlds. In an effort to postulate some broad principles of reasonable endurance though limited in scope, I shall start with the long-term and then, in the last two chapters, come back to the Warsaw Pact–NATO confrontation and the revolutionary warfare threat.

My broad long-term scenario is this. The first and second worlds are increasingly being forced to intervene militarily, with mixed success, in their respective third world spheres of influence. They are gradually burying the hatchet and lining themselves up, along with a China playing the same kind of role that France does *vis-à-vis* NATO, against a threat from the South. This threat, generated and driven by Islam militant, has grown from the economic threat of the seventies and the state sponsored terrorism of the eighties to one of massive organised forces backed by nuclear weapons. Shi'ite Fundamentalist influence straddles the northern tropics from Malaysia to Morocco; some regimes friendly either to Washington or to Moscow are still holding, but few of these can be seen as stable. Israel, towards which the West has considerably cooled and the Soviet Union is discreetly warming, remains a focus of turbulence, under mounting direct threat despite its military excellence and nuclear capability. I am not indulging in an exercise in "future history", simply inviting the reader to look another 50-year cycle ahead at a picture which at once is reasonably credible and represents a substantial shift from the present one.

War aims

Holy wars apart, most wars in history, including revolutionary wars, have been started to further a fairly well defined politico-economic aim and conducted in accordance with this. Many of these aims, like many of the historical practices of war, would be seen today as totally unacceptable, sometimes as ridiculous. But, partly because warlike resources were still based on human and animal muscle, the effort and sacrifice was by and large attuned both to the importance of the aim and to the degree of success achieved. Both sides evidently kept their eyes open for situations which offered a chance of a negotiated compromise. Reading Jomini, I am far from convinced that Napoleon's concept of "absolute war" meant much more than the relentless employment of all available resources to achieve a defined aim. Nor do I think that Clausewitz's statements about "absolute war", qualified to death as they are, can be blamed for war having, as Liddell Hart puts it, "got out of control". Ironically it was the threefold synergetic effect of the elder Moltke's successes, the misinterpretation of Clausewitz abroad, and the progressive shift (through Schlieffen, the younger Moltke and Ludendorff) to a belief in war for war's sake that pushed war over the top. Sun Tzu's advice about not destroying the enemy nation was forgotten. Positive war aims, whose attainment would represent genuine politico-economic benefit, gave way to negative ones based on hatred. Or if the initial aims were positive, these were overridden as the war developed by insistence on "destroying the enemy". Liddell Hart and others regarded the First World War as exemplifying this transition. But surely it was not in the same league as the Second, where Allied insistence on unconditional surrender set in train the decline of Caucasian civilisation.

Again, as is shown by the readiness with which nations changed sides both during wars and between them, European wars between the thirteenth and the nineteenth centuries were largely fought between like nations or alliances. Culture, ideology (in the shape of Christianity) and the ruling class's working scale of values were common to them. The Russian Revolution put paid to this; and the economic price demanded of Germany for losing the First World War bred yet another radical "ism". So instead of sharing a common foundation, Europe and North America were now divided by three mutually opposed ideologies. Or so it seemed; only much later did the liberal democracies come to realise that the political range was not a straight line drawn from right to left, or even the Eysenck grid, so much as a circular continuum with authoritarianism, be it of the left or of the right, at one pole, and liberalism at the other. In fact failure to recognise this lies at the root of NATO's problems in the eighties. Faced with almost a worldful of unacceptable governments, the United States instinctively favours those of the "right", while the gut reaction of her European allies prefers those on the "left".

The Second World War's legacy of gross economic and social destabilisation and unresolved ideological conflict has led to what one might call "ideological Balkanisation"—a trend equally pronounced inside the great religions and across the spectrum of socialism. At the same time, the overwhelming strategic success of revolutionary warfare in all its divers manifestations, increasingly reinforced by the sounding-board effect of the media, has led the most "sub-Balkan" of factions to resort to violence—often with results disproportionate to their size or to the validity of their cause. Revolutionary warfare has stretched out both its arms to embrace government sponsored terrorism with one, and organised crime with the other.

Marx's view that the root cause of all wars is economic may have had force when he expressed it, but evidently has little today. In fact almost from very early times onwards authoritarian governments, oligarchies and dictatorships alike, have been giving that other Marxist dictum about the primary role of armies being to preserve the internal status quo a rather broader interpretation than its author probably intended. The creation of a situation calling for a military response abroad to alleviate political difficulties at home is an age-old trick of autocrats. The events of the early eighties in Central America, the Caribbean and the South Atlantic indicate that it is increasingly finding favour with democratically elected governments of the right too. The point I want to make is that we have moved out of an era of genuine and limited politico-economic war aims into one of sweeping political aspirations either triggered by ideological conflict (including differences of religion or sect), or masking some quite different internal or external intent.

One consequence of this, to my mind a favourable one, is the way it has acted in concert with the nuclear threat to weaken the confidence of bodies politic in elected governments, and to foster dissidence in authoritarian societies. These influences, combined with the collectivist trend sometimes referred to as "modern socialism", have already swung some advanced societies, notably Canada and the smaller nation states of northwest Europe, perhaps Australasia too, away from their traditional bellicist attitude. Stephen King-Hall's cry of "Better red than dead" still has a considerable following. But the mass centre towards which shifting opinion, informed and populist alike, seems to be gravitating lies somewhere between bellicism—that is, acceptance of declared war between organised forces as a permissible instrument of policy—and pacifism, in the strict sense of declining to offer any resistance whatever may befall.

Being essentially devoid of political overtones, this attitude is likewise distinct from neutralism; one can envisage circumstances in which a country adopting a purely defensive posture might enter into an alliance to the extent of offering facilities. The posture is summed up in the slogan "just defence"; but I think one must do better than this, especially in Britain, where the phrase has been adopted as the name of yet another of these puzzling fringe associations. "Passivism" would do fine if it did not sound much more like pacifism than its meaning implies. "Protectionism" being reserved for the economic field, I shall coin the term "**protectivism**", and define it as "*a policy in which resort to armed force is rejected as an active instrument of policy but accepted as a means of protecting a country's existing territory and territorial waters against armed force*". I shall explore this policy in depth in the next chapter.

Military aims

For the moment I want to examine the problems posed to those concerned with the framing of military aims as a result of "war having got out of control", of politico-economic sense having been largely replaced by ideological passion, and of a nuclear and chemical threat so devastating that it ceases to be a means of achieving a politico-economic aim. The practice of issuing ultimatums after pre-emptive action which poses an overwhelming threat seems likely to survive, since this makes entire strategic sense, doubly so with today's operational tempos. But there seems little moral or practical justification for continuing the farcical sequence of ultimatum—declaration of war. Where they cannot attain their aim by pre-emption, aggressors will employ strategic surprise in one or more forms, ranging from terrorism to a strategic *desant*.

Where one or both sides has a nuclear or offensive chemical capability, the nature of the interaction between diplomatic and military means will eventually change under the pressure of political realism. Oddly enough, this trend is best brought out in Soviet writing on the "unusability" of various means of waging war, of which more in the next chapter. As soldiers and administrators within NATO—in contrast to its more strident member governments—already tacitly accept, military victory by conventional means would not be a sound aim if it carried the opposition across the nuclear threshold. The history of the last 30 years has conclusively demonstrated that, given time, world opinion mobilises against a war, especially against participation of the members of the first or second world in armed conflict. This tide of opinion amounts to a rejection of war as a means of settling a dispute, with very little regard for the rights and wrongs of the case. Since the strength of the reaction is redoubled when either of the superpowers is involved, the pressure which would build up in the United Nations over any form of hostilities between the superpowers would be so high that, unless the contestants were hysterically bent on mutual destruction, they would find it hard to ignore. The proper aim of conventional armed forces may therefore be not to defeat the enemy but to *restabilise* the situation at some different level, thus allowing some form of negotiation or mediation to resume. In sum, *diplomacy becomes a continuation of war by other means*. For instance, if we take the scenario of General Sir John Hackett's *The Third World War* to a point short of the Birmingham–Minsk nuclear exchange, we might envisage a truce on a line some hundred or more kilometres west of the present Inner German Frontier, followed by a negotiated peace. This is not a pipe dream but the re-establishment of a pattern maintained from earliest historical times up to the beginning of this century.

To say that we should have to fight the next war with the forces already in position would be a truism were it not a dangerous half-truth. The likelihood of pre-emption and strategic surprise puts a premium on **readiness**. In an earlier book, *Antitank*, I suggested that both the deterrent and combat worth of the standing NATO forces in the Federal Republic would be greatly enhanced if even one-third of them at a time were held at genuinely high readiness. To my mind this argument is of such importance as a general principle that I shall rehearse it here, despite having touched on it in Chapter 11.

The reliability of every kind of equipment I can think of is best ensured by keeping it in a fully serviceable state and exercising it regularly. The cost of replacement of short- and medium-life elements is usually more than offset by the saving in unscheduled maintenance effort. Conventional thinking on readiness requires men to be ready in a few minutes so that they can devote the rest of the time to their machines. Given the realisation that machines thrive on a high state of readiness and men do not, one can devise readiness procedures which do not adversely affect morale.

With the kind of readiness procedures most armies practice it is indeed impossible to hold more than one-third of a force even at moderate readiness over long periods in peacetime. But I have calculated that, with conditions and dispositions such as one finds in the Federal Republic, a sensible approach would allow *half* the force to be held at short enough notice to counter strategic surprise. If, for the sake of simplicity, we take a force of two divisions, each of three brigade groups or task forces, with a division serving 6 months on standby, the pattern might look something like Table 6. The figures in it may look over-detailed for a broad proposal, but they are based on a good deal of experience of nominal and actual readiness states under a wide variety of conditions.

TABLE 6. *Readiness pattern for a force of two divisions*

Division A (standby)
Standby forward covering force (10-day turnround)
one battle group (battalion combat team) at 1 hour's notice
in or just behind deployment area

Standby covering force (1 month turnround)
one brigade group less one battle group, equipment and
maintenance/preparation team in/behind deployment area,
rest of men in barracks, force at 3 hours' notice to 75 per
cent strength, 6 hours to "99 per cent"

Standby main force
In barracks, at 3 hours' notice to 67 per cent strength, 6
hours to 90 per cent

Division B (brigade groups on 2-month turnround)
one brigade group at 9 hours' notice to 75 per cent strength
one brigade group at 24 hours' notice to 67 per cent strength
one brigade group stood down

In sum, a bird in the hand is worth two in the bush! I have dealt with readiness under the head of "aims" because it is of the highest importance and is extremely difficult to achieve in peacetime. So much so, in fact, that it should become a major factor in the basic decisions about force levels and maintenance costs which are fed into the defence budget. To use the distinction I drew in Chapter 14, a sufficient state of readiness will with luck deter a strategic-surprise attack; and, in accordance with the fleet in being theory, the ability to raise this level rapidly could well pre-empt any such venture.

But, as we have seen, both preventive moves and manoeuvre warfare are paper tigers unless they are backed by the mind and the muscle for a fight. So one is forced to rethink conventional military aims in the light of a "reversible reaction" between diplomacy and armed force. The strategic aim here is clear enough—*restabilisation* at some new equilibrium. This will almost by definition call for the defender to pay some price, probably of territory, which he will hope to regain in part or in full by negotiation. The defender's initial operational aim will be *containment* in the accepted sense of that term—the halting of the attacker with a minimum ceding of space for a maximum gain in time.

But one now comes face to face with the age-old military principle of "going over to the offensive", traditionally with a view to gaining a military decision. It is at this point that a change is needed. Operational commanders must learn to think in terms not of victory, which may lead to nuclear or chemical disaster, but of "doing enough" to turn the tide. This calls for extreme finesse of judgement and delicacy of execution. Amongst other things, it requires, as Nelson put it, that "officers should have political courage".

Clearly a passive defence, the holding of a line of containment, is unlikely to discourage a determined enemy from further enterprise or bring him to the negotiating table. Offensive defence at tactical level makes the defender's point more forcibly, but tends to result in an interrupted line of contact, or at best in a saw-toothed one—too fluid and untidy a situation to provide much of a basis for a truce.

Thus the defender must probably resort to some kind of *controlled operational counterstroke*. This must be at once bold enough to imprint an image of a turning tide in the attacking commander's mind, and restricted enough in scope not to push him over the nuclear or chemical threshold. It need not in fact be completely successful in the sense of being driven right home. On the other hand, excellent operational intelligence is needed to minimise the risk of the defender's operational reserve being encircled or destroyed. For the tide would then gather force in favour of the attacker, and the defender might be forced to resort to a nuclear or chemical response. In terms of the eighties and nineties, I suggest that the example General Sir John Hackett uses in *The Third World War* will do very nicely. This is a counter-offensive up the line of the Münster–Osnabrück–Bremen autobahn (Fig. 13, page 75), aimed at cutting off the "Krefeld salient" (roughly the bottom left black arrowhead on the sketch map) and at frustrating the use by the Warsaw Pact of the airfield and port facilities at Bremen.

Clausewitz would undoubtedly have argued that the imposition of constraints like this on operational aims runs contrary to "the grammar of war"; represents a degree of political control which conflicts with the nature of war; or calls for a precision incompatible with the friction of war. Most military men, addicts of attrition and masters of manoeuvre alike, would probably agree with him. Yet I suggest that both the credibility and the capability of a conventional deterrent turns on this requirement. I would accept that this kind of fine tuning was out of the question as long as chance played a major part in the conduct of war. It probably remained impossible as long as speed and precision of response was restricted by physical mobility and the linear laws of movement. But for the future, as I think I have demonstrated in the detailed discussions earlier in this book, the sensible application of technology permits fine tuning of this kind—when combined with excellence of training, the responsiveness of directive control and, above all, decision-making of the highest quality.

If forces which are and are seen to be capable of meeting the demands of restabilisation cannot be developed, we are probably faced with two alternatives. Either the Soviet views on the unusability of organised forces, which I shall discuss in the next chapter, will come to be generally accepted, and revolutionary warfare will become endemic the world over. Or any tilting of the balance of power between East and West, or later perhaps North and South, seems extremely likely to result in an inexorable tide of destabilisation carrying one side or the other across the nuclear threshold.

Operational concepts

Nevertheless, the requirements set above for the aim of the operational counterstroke probably represent about the most severe set of constraints that any dynamic system could tolerate. On the NATO centre, which inevitably dominates one's thinking on major war scenarios, there is a further constraint which could well prove to be the last straw. This is the immense politico-economic value of the Federal Republic's territory. The Bundeswehr has been directed by its government to commit itself to a forward positional defence. This policy is entirely understandable, in fact unarguable. But tying the hands of the largest of NATO's three significant land-force contingents behind their backs augurs ill for containment. I shall discuss this is Chapter 19. For the moment I want to draw a general moral.

Historically, the device of a buffer state has often proved successful in preventing or limiting wars between major powers. Either they have respected it and kept apart. Or, more frequently, they have used it as an area in which their forces could have free play without too much commitment on either side—at the expense of the buffer. At the time of Yalta, nothing could have looked more expendable to Churchill, Roosevelt and Stalin alike than German territory, the German economy, or the German people. Their intention appears to have been to create an occupied buffer state with an agreed line of demarcation. Should physical clashes arise between the ex-allies, the depth either side of the Inner German Frontier should suffice to absorb them. Less than 10 years later, "the same stone which the builders refused: was become the head-stone of the corner". The attainment of a vengeful and improper war aim quickly resulted in an unusually imperfect peace.

Even on attrition theory, it is military madness to suppose that an offensive such as the Warsaw Pact might launch could be brought up solid, creating a static continuous front of First World War character within a few kilometres of the Inner German Frontier. Any line of this kind is going to be turned by *desanty*, or penetrated, or both, dislocating the bulk of the Federal German Army. To quote the German proverb—"What does not bend will break." The Germans understand this better than most; but they cannot accept it psychologically or acknowledge it politically. They also know better than most that a pre-emptive incursion into satellite territory, or even an early counterstroke across the Inner German Frontier, would never be accepted by other European members of NATO and, because of the predictable destabilisation of the satellite regimes, might well push the Soviets over the nuclear threshold. This political inability to *reculer pour mieux sauter*, rather than shortage of troops, is in my view the real reason why the NATO centre has such a low nuclear threshold. More of that too in Chapter 19.

Conclusion

A strategic aim of restabilisation and gaining time must logically make the defender pay some price. And his only currency is space. If organised forces as we know them can in fact be employed to accomplish a strategic aim of restabilisation with operational aims of containment and controlled counterstroke, the military commander must have freedom to manoeuvre in depth. And depth means depth. When Manstein was operating on the Donets and arguing with Hitler about the need for bold manoeuvre "while we still have enough depth in Russian territory", he had almost 1200 kilometres of Soviet territory behind him, and a further 800 or so to the nearest point on German soil proper. The depth from the Inner German Frontier to Cape Finistère is only about 1250 kilometres.

The kind of depths Manstein had in mind for operational manoeuvre might well make strategic sense in terms of intervention on the Asian or African land mass. The problem is, then, how to reduce the depth needed to destroy the momentum of an offensive of the scale and nature threatened by the Warsaw Pact to something that might be politically acceptable within the dimensions of the European theatre. In the next chapter I shall argue that large organised forces should not be the sole or even the principal means of achieving this. Then, having attempted to peer 50 or 60 years into the future, I shall come back to the beginning of the next century and consider how the NATO centre might best be defended if the existing confrontation across the Inner German Frontier still prevails.

I would close, though, by re-emphasising the way in which a combination of a high and speedily enhanced state of readiness and manoeuvre warfare offer a land counterpart to a fleet in being as an instrument of deterrence and pre-emption. Here, employing the thrust of Mahan's thinking, I would see a frontier zone of unmanned fortifications (pages 87–92) as the operational equivalent of a fortified forward naval base. The facts that such a zone is geographically located forward of the manoeuvre force (the fleet), and that the manoeuvre force is not logistically dependent on it, do not, I think, invalidate this argument. A fortified zone fulfils four roles. It acts both as a shield and as a tripwire. It degrades the attacker's initial tempo and thus, in the relative terms that matter, enhances the defender's tempo—perhaps even to the point of giving the defender at least the tactical initiative. Herein, I suggest, lies the clue to a resilient yet highly resistant defence. Finally, as long as operations remain within its sphere of influence, it contributes to the mass of the defender's holding force.

18

The Relevance of Organised Forces

> "The sages who, at [the Geneva Disarmament Conference] in 1932, sought the definition of a purely defensive weapon probably did not suspect that, if they had found it, the discovery would have completely changed the destiny of man by bringing to the world an age in which he would have lived without fear."
>
> FERRERO (trans. LIDDELL HART)

Introduction—the Soviet concept of "unusability"

The Soviets seem to have written more, and more coherently, than anybody else about the "unusability" of organised forces. The fact is as surprising as the reason is ironic. One of the fundamental tenets of Marxism–Leninism is that the *primary* role of armies in capitalist states is not to fight foreign wars but to maintain the internal status quo, and thus the dominance of the ruling class. Under Communism the necessity for this does not arise (*sic*), so the only role of armed forces is an external one. I have adopted the ugly and not entirely appropriate word "unusability" because Lider and his colleagues (and I think others before them) have used it and made it stick. The Russian word *negodnost'* has a rather more interesting connotation around the area of "unsuitable", "inappropriate"; it is in fact the word they use of a person unfit for military service. By the standards of Russian writing on politico-strategic matters and of the translations and comments of most Sovietologists, the meaning of "unusability" is remarkably clear. *Organised forces are considered to be "unusable" if total military success would result in a net politico-economic loss.*

This is both a rational position and a half-way house between bellicism and the span of anti-bellicist attitudes. It is somewhat to the "left" of the true Clausewitzian position in its implication that the political aim must be economically justifiable—a variation on another fundamental Marxist theme. After Berlin, Hungary and Czechoslovakia the idea of there being no need to use organised forces for repression merits at best a horse laugh. But one must in fairness concede that the Soviet Union has not used her own armed forces aggressively outside her acknowledged sphere of influence except in Afghanistan. And there the results have been so disastrous as to

283

make it worth recording that Soviet views on "unusability" were established long before then.

Other underlying trends

Leaving aside for the moment the advance of technology and the decline of bellicism, one sees two powerful trends which diminish the relevance of organised forces—or at least of large organised forces. The first of these is historical. It can be summed up as the almost total lack of success—one is tempted to say the helplessness— of organised forces against the divers techniques of revolutionary warfare. As stressed in the previous chapter, advanced societies are hard put to it even to hold their own on home ground against these manifestations; and when the first or second world intervenes in the third, even with seemingly overwhelming force as in Afghanistan, it gets a very bloody nose indeed. Templar's operations in Malaya (as it then was) still seem to be the only modern instance of successful intervention against an indigenous movement. Some would parallel with this the defeat of the Indonesians in Borneo; this was certainly a supreme example of success by professional special forces against the *techniques* of revolutionary warfare, but my understanding is that the opposition was basically extraneous to the island's population.

Jomini is perhaps the best of the standard authorities on this subject. Elucidating his thesis by numerous historical examples, among them Napoleon's problems in the Tyrol and in Spain, he sums it up like this:

> "It is above all when hostile populations are supported by a sizeable core of disciplined troops that a war of this kind poses immense problems. You have but one army. Your adversaries have an army *and* a complete nation in arms—or at any rate most of one. Everyone, everywhere is armed. Every individual is planning your destruction. Everyone, even the non-combatant, has a stake in damaging your cause. You have to be very careful where you make camp. And outside the confines of this camp, everything becomes hostile, multiplying in a thousand ways the difficulties you encounter at every step."

For me, this is the clearest pointer to the future I have so far unearthed. But there is a key distinction to be made. Malaya apart, the only occasions when movements using the techniques of revolutionary warfare have run into trouble is when they have progressed in to Mao Tse Tung's "Phase three", the formation of organised units with heavy equipment. Where battalions exist, God is just as much for the big ones as he was in Voltaire's day. Expressed in modern terms, Jomini's point concerns a defence based on a standing force plus a militia, presupposing that the defender is on home ground.

The second trend, observable in most of Western Europe and the whole of North America, is the declining trust democratic bodies politic place in their political leaders. A steady decline in quality of the individuals who enter political life—still more of those who succeed in it—is rather like a steering fault in one's own car. Because one is living with it all the time, one has no idea when it started and fails to sense that it is getting worse. I do not propose to explore this theme in depth, but I will sketch a purely personal view of it as an indication of what I mean, for any reader whose hackles are as yet not permanently set in the upper register.

Competition to get into higher education and to get a job after completing it seems to have resulted in some degeneration of the scope and breadth of liberal education at the highest levels. The extinction of the polymath has led to a shortage of people who have rubbed shoulders at least with several major disciplines, if not with "many". Even the men and women most talented in their own fields often seem lacking in the human qualities of wisdom and judgement. And these are the qualities which make for good government. There are three events which lie in the back of my mind as markers for this decline—Adlai Stevenson's divorce, the death of Ian Macleod, and (as I have always interpreted it) the framing of Willi Brandt. Only France, with its acceptance of meritocracy and its coherent system of education from the village school to the quaternary stage, the *grandes écoles*, still seems able to get first-rate people to the top of public life.

These remarks may be the ravings of an elitist in his dotage, but I do not think so. A liberal American mathematician and author I met for the first time not long ago responded to my polite "your current administration" with "the Reagan gang". And in Britain we see the remaining handful of politicians of integrity and wisdom sandwiched between a *poujadiste* government and a quasi-Marxist opposition. Of the larger liberal democracies, only in France, which de Gaulle appears to have endowed with a system that suits her, and the Federal Republic, which seems to have got proportional representation about right with its 5 per cent cut-off point, can lay any pretensions to being well run. The smaller liberal democracies of Western Europe, along with Canada, seem to do much better. But whether this is because they have abandoned bellicism, because "small is beautiful", or simply because "the grass is always greener" I do not know.

I have used a subjective view to put this point about declining quality under the spotlight because it is the only way I can bring it to the reader's attention quickly and simply. But if opinion polls mean anything at all—and the way politicians loathe them tends to confirm that they mean a good deal—one cannot doubt that, in Europe at least, the proportion of voters content to entrust their governments with dangerous toys, or even to permit them ideas about dangerous toys, is continuously and ever more sharply on the decline. Within the 50-year cycle beginning now and reaching to the middle years of the twenty-first century, this trend is bound to have a radical effect on defence policies.

From MAD-ness to lunacy

Returning to the end of the 50-year cycle that straddles the mid-twentieth century, one sees a rapid decline in the credibility of the nuclear deterrent. This has been accelerated in 1983 and 1984 by the left-and-right of theatre weapons and the nuclear winter hypothesis. Interestingly, on the previous two occasions when NATO has deployed medium range ballistic missiles, they have been withdrawn again after a few years; one can only hope the present batch will go the same way. All seem agreed that they fulfil no military purpose—or at least none that could not have been equally well served in less provocative ways. But, as the European peace movements have rightly if indirectly perceived, their existence pre-empts the use of battlefield nuclear weapons and thus destroys the credibility of NATO's reliance on them.

Let me be the first to sympathise with American displeasure at Europe's reaction to Tomahawk and Pershing 2. Helmut Schmidt asked for them. NATO backed him. The United States, at considerable cost to other defence programmes, provided them—by which time even moderate European opinion had turned against them. The crunch point here is surely the profound mistrust European electorates show towards their own political leadership, in this instance projected onto the United States administration.

I have always subscribed to the "metropolitan" theory of nuclear deterrence, first outlined to me many years ago by General Sir John Hackett. (In fairness, though, I should say that he does not agree with the particular argument I am about to put forward.) According to this theory, the real value of possessing nuclear weapons is that they pre-empt nuclear attack on the possessor's metropolitan territory. Up till now, ever since John Foster Dulles steered United States policy away from "massive retaliation" and towards "flexible response", there has been no clearly defined threshold between the discharge of a few unit-kiloton weapons over troops on the NATO centre, and the strategic nuclear exchange which neither superpower can have the least intention of launching. On the previous occasions when medium range missiles were deployed, they plugged a perceptible gap in military capability, and they were not designated "theatre weapons". Now there is a threshold—the confines of Europe. There is no longer anything to restrain the superpowers from wiping out each other's spheres of influence in Europe without much risk of their metropolitan territories being destroyed. Thus one can expect "first use" on the battlefield to escalate instantly to a full-scale European exchange.

There are drawbacks for both sides in this situation. On the one hand, NATO's threat of first use on the battlefield becomes something of a paper tiger. SACEUR is never going to get European governments to agree to release; and if the United States went it alone, her European allies would have good reason to sue instantly for peace—as some would undoubtedly do. In one's more cynical moments, one might suppose that the Soviet Union would welcome a chance to destroy the Federal Republic at the same time as having her turbulent satellites eliminated by courtesy of Uncle Sam. Fortunately, though, under the prevailing weather systems, Mother Russia could expect a swingeing dose of tropospheric fallout slap across her bosom.

Whatever the United States administration may promise about "all for one and one for all", the deployment of theatre weapons makes the European exchange not just a realistic option which any President would almost certainly exercise, but a morally and theoretically *correct* option from the viewpoint of the United States authorities. The first duty of a government and the proper object of a defence policy is to protect its people from harm. Fortunately again, though, Western Europe does have a trump as long as Britain and France possess submarine-based nuclear weapon systems, however small in scale. These forces would not be destroyed in a European exchange, and would be able to deliver a strategic strike against Soviet metropolitan territory. I very much doubt whether the Soviets would get out their binoculars to look at the labels! This is the old theory of the "trigger deterrent" in new and more constructive guise. Taking the metropolitan and trigger "theories" together, I believe that, even should NATO crumble or she leave the alliance, Britain must for the time being retain an independent submarine-based nuclear deterrent.

As I write, the definitive American study on the "nuclear winter" is still under way. But as megatonnages rise, authoritative scientific opinion in East and West alike seems to be hardening in favour of this hypothesis. Quite apart from hard data and quantitative predictions, the hypothesis seems a probable one because it is in tune with the broad current trend of discovery. From agriculture to preventive medicine, those who interfere massively with biological systems and ecosystems patently have very little understanding of the possible or probable consequences of their actions. And as these unforeseen consequences come home to roost, they are almost always adverse. To take two other examples from the nuclear field, there is now some reason to suppose that the radiation doses to which American and British servicemen were deliberately exposed in the early days are producing unforeseen carcinogenic and genetic effects in the long term. And in Britain at least the incidence of child leukaemia in areas exposed to artificial radiation via discharges into the atmosphere or the sea is giving cause for disquiet. If predictions of a "nuclear winter" are confirmed, even at a fairly low probability, MAD-ness surely becomes sheer lunacy, and the credibility of the nuclear deterrent finally goes out of the window.

Non-nuclear deterrence

Whether or not this happens, the nuclear threat may be superseded by the threat or actuality of "Star Wars" fought in space with directed energy weapons or electromagnetic cannon. But the disclosure that current United States work is focused on the use of established technology to intercept ballistic missiles coincides with most of the other evidence to put the idea of a decisive struggle for the domination of inner space into the next 50-year cycle but one. We therefore have to look at a period in which the nuclear deterrent has lost credibility and there is no extraterrestrial substitute. Already, many tasks that would have called for a nuclear weapon 20 years ago can be accomplished with conventional firepower. As we saw in Chapter 10 and elsewhere, and as all authoritative opinion seems to agree, we are entering a period of dominance of firepower. Large organised forces deployed at high density with a panoply of baroque equipment will become unusable in the very literal sense that they will be shot to pieces.

Yet the tempo of historical development and the realities of the present situation make it unthinkable that these large forces will soon be disbanded or much reduced. With nuclear back-up ruled out, NATO will have to achieve a conventional balance of power—something that I shall, in the next chapter, suggest as entirely feasible. Likewise both the first and second worlds will have to retain both a nuclear deterrent and substantial organised forces in face of the third world threat. In terms of this threat the nuclear winter hypothesis will not apply for a long time to come. Some of the more honest military writing, even in militarily advanced countries like Pakistan, confirms the evidence of the Gulf War. Even should some third world nations eventually attain the level of technological skills which allows advanced equipment to be used effectively, there is no sign of their developing the command ability to handle mechanised or airmechanised forces in manoeuvre warfare, or to exploit the dominance of firepower. It will still take an array of bayonets to deter them.

Given a rough balance of power between them, the first and second worlds' large organised forces look set to replace nuclear weapons as the unusable deterrent. They must continue to exist and to be credible, but their use in war would be most unlikely to result in a net politico-economic gain to either aggressor or defender. At most it will be possible to sharpen the peacetime state of deterrence by pre-emptive actions—by applying the "fleet in being" theory in the shape either of troop movements or, more probably, of playing tunes on an overt alert and readiness system.

Usable forms of armed force

Putting all the arguments above and in the previous chapter together, one perceives a trend of which two aspects have already become evident. One is the increasing emphasis being placed by most advanced powers, most of all by the Soviet Union, on the development and expansion of **special forces** in the accepted sense of that term—as represented by SAS, SBS, the United States Rangers and Spetsnaz. Looking 30 or so years ahead to the mid-point of the next 50-year cycle, I would be inclined to see special forces as the focal point of land-force structures (Fig. 51). I do not mean to imply that special forces will be the largest component numerically, but that, like mechanised troops now, and helitroops in the nearer future, they will become the decisive instrument of offensive action at operational and strategic levels.

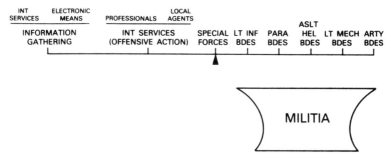

FIG. 51. *Long-term force balance.*

The second aspect can best be described as jumping on the other side of the same bandwagon. It is the twin-warp pattern in which revolutionary warfare is evolving. On the one hand, the progression foreseen by Mao Tse Tung, and so far successfully practised only by him, is being modified. "Phase three" used to be the formation of organised units, some of them with heavy equipment. These battalions, later to be combined into at least brigades, were to fight in the manner of organised forces, either on their own or alongside such forces. The outcome of attempts, as for instance by the PLO, to move into this phase has varied from the rather ineffective to the hilarious. The requisite powers of organisation, command skills and mechanical aptitudes are generally lacking. As a result, these movements are tending to steer clear of the attritional phase three, preferring to extend the scope of Phase two—offensive guerrilla operations employing the principles of manoeuvre theory. The second thread, which links official and revolutionary forces, is government sponsored terrorism. It is, I think, fair to say that *"my* defensive use of gallant special forces in the cause of freedom" is *"your* subversionary activism in violation of international law" and *"his* government sponsored terrorism".

The common factor in all this—the broad trend in fact—is the spread of the realisation that *armed force will only be "usable" by exploiting strategic surprise to establish a pre-emptive situation.* This approach differs somewhat from the form of pre-emption I considered earlier in this book, in that one or more surprise acts of violence may be needed to set up the pre-emptive posture. The terrorist with the nuclear weapon in his suitcase may have to hijack an aircraft to get to his target and then to put it out of action. More realistically, the problem is not to execute the guerrilla or special force operation, but to achieve a situation of change and response—to build on success in a way that offers the flexibility needed to achieve a fruitful negotiated settlement. This is why I believe the submarine helicopter carrier to be such an immensely powerful concept, and the submarine transport of light mechanised forces to approach it in significance. We come back to the way-out scenario I depicted in Chapter 9, where compact, highly mobile paratroops, helitroops and mechanised airborne troops operate *in support of special forces and agents*. Like the somewhat analogous one of making the helicopter a combat weapon system rather than a combat support one, or the changeover from detailed orders to directive control, this concept presents few physical problems. It just calls on the military mind to execute a mental somersault.

Land force structures

Before looking at future force structures in any detail, we need to rid ourselves of a sacred cow—the division. This is in fact no more than another step down an evolutionary path marked out by technological advance. The "division" is an ancient and important tactical concept, but the idea of a division as the key organisational formation (rather as the battalion is the key unit) does not seem to go back much beyond the middle of the nineteenth century. As I have remarked elsewhere in various contexts, the more recent the tradition, the hotter and more irrational the defence of it. It would be surprising if our current concept of a division was worth more than two 50-year cycles; and there are in fact three specific arguments against it.

First, the discussion on airborne forces in Chapter 9 suggested that a brigade was the most that could be put into unsecured territory, and in Chapter 7 we noted wide agreement on a brigade of about one hundred first-line machines as the best size for an operational rotary-wing force. In terms of the NATO centre, an armoured division is probably still the minimum operational force; but in a mixed force operating on the flanks of NATO or in intervention, a light mechanised brigade would certainly have operational impact. Second, as the United States 1986 force structure and many other exercises, including my own studies, suggest, any attempt to produce a balanced self-contained division results in an unwieldy one. This is due mainly to the introduction of a substantial rotary-wing element, and to the shift from 1/3 towards 1/1 in the ratio of artillery to combat arms. This change of ratio is an inevitable concomitant of the dominance of firepower; it ought to be encouraged as strongly as it will undoubtedly be resisted. But it does produce a *prima facie* problem by putting the tactical commander and the supporting artillery commander at the same level. In most armies this problem is easily solved by making the artillery group a "regiment" of *x* battalions, commanded by a colonel, and placing it in a brigade commanded by a one-star general. Third, a division with its main subordinate formations all of a kind, like the proposed United States "light infantry" and "hi-tech light" divisions, is too large to be a manageable component of an intervention force dependent on airlift. I shall therefore base this discussion on the brigade.

Let us take special forces as the focus of the structure. To one side of it, and equivalent to the evolution of special forces in the 50-year cycle now ending, one might expect to see a pronounced growth in the offensive activities of clandestine agencies such as the CIA and the KGB, with permanent members forming a cadre for cells of locally recruited agents. With advanced technology playing a steadily growing part in collecting and processing information, the relative importance of information-gathering and offensive actions in these agencies might in fact become much what it is in special forces today. Similarly the balance of emphasis in special forces would shift in the direction of offensive action.

On the "organised" side of the special forces, one will surely see emphasis on the "semi-special forces", in which numbers are less important than quality of man and equipment—paratroops, helitroops and commandos/light infantry. These "usable" manoeuvre forces would be designed to provide a conventional offensive capability *at tactical level*, and to support special force operations. I would foresee heavy mechanised formations remaining as the backbone of the "unusable" conventional deterrent; and I shall discuss the possible reincarnation of line infantry separately below.

In these terms one might expect to see the five types of brigade depicted in Fig. 51. The first four of these need no further explanation. The parachute, light and light mechanised brigades would have appropriate artillery regiments (see above) organic to them, together with other combat and service support elements. Once technology permitted, the helicopter brigade would be given artillery support in the shape of multi-barrelled rocket launchers (pages 126/127). The artillery brigade is a fairly radical concept (as compared, for instance, with the Soviet formation of that name), though not an entirely new one. As I see it, this brigade would provide a mobile fire base capable of producing concentrations of fire of great weight and intensity, and of several types. It would have an organic local security force, perhaps one light mechanised battalion found by the artillery itself, and a light mechanised battery in each artillery battalion. The point I want to make is the need to recognise the dominance of firepower not just by increasing the ratio of artillery support but by fielding a formation dedicated to mass indirect fire.

Home defence

What I have said above is in effect a projection of current and discernible future trends. To the unbiased eye it represents a technology-led evolution rather than a revolution. The radical note in it is struck by the emphasis on strategic surprise. This amounts to an abandonment of the notion of legalising war by declaring it, and the recognition of a continuous state of ideological and economic conflict which may find violent expression at any time and at any place.

I now want to consider the military implications of a defence policy which means just what it says—one in which a government rids itself of bellicist and imperialist hankerings after past glories, and accepts that the proper goal of a defence policy is the safety of its people and its territory. This "protectivism" implies economic self-sufficiency at an acceptable level, an aim to which France has long successfully held and towards which other West European nations now seem to be working. A protectivist policy is probably not for the superpowers; and as long as the NATO–Warsaw Pact confrontation persists, the switch to it cannot be embarked on precipitately. But protectivism has so far proved wholly successful for Europe's two best-run countries, Sweden and Switzerland. Denmark has gone as far down the same road as it can while remaining within NATO; and, if public opinion means anything at all, Belgium, the Netherlands and Norway would follow suit were it not that their geographical position within NATO attracts activity by the larger members of the Alliance. If the Federal Republic's next general election results in a Social Democrat/Green coalition, the trickle of discussion about a militia could quickly become a torrent, leaving Britain with little option but to pull back within her frontiers.

Everybody shrinks from even discussing policies of this kind for fear of offending the Americans. I am by no means convinced that a move in this direction would "offend the Americans". They are not noted for wearing blinkers; they favour frankness; and they have at least as great a stake as European NATO members in avoiding any sudden change which might lead to destabilisation. Apart from the grafting on of the Bundeswehr and the withdrawal of France from the military organisation, NATO has remained virtually unchanged for almost 40 years. Despite the accelerating tempo of the times, it has—as far as I can trace—outlived any similar grouping of free nation states. Change must come; and the Alliance will only uphold its purpose if that change comes openly and gradually.

In any event, manoeuvre forces of the kind depicted above, their naval and air counterparts, and a minimal nuclear capability are extremely expensive. On the other hand, a purely static defence would be ineffective, open to destruction in detail. It therefore seems economically and militarily reasonable to postulate a level of manoeuvre forces capable only of *tactical* action against a major opponent, but powerful enough to have operational or strategic impact against an enemy numerically weak or grossly inferior in quality. I see this as more than a mere concession to the traditionalists. Convinced as I am that the real future threat comes from the south, not the east, I see both a submarine-borne nuclear capability and a compact manoeuvre force capable of long-range intervention with strategic surprise as essential. And for the foreseeable future this must be on a national basis to prevent potential enemies from dividing and conquering. To illustrate the kind of thing I mean, I would envisage a British Army with a manoeuvre force of 40 000 to 45 000 all ranks. This would be home-based and might be made up on the lines of Table 7. It would be complemented by two composite Royal Marines Brigades, submarine-borne, each composed of a special force company (SBS), an assault helicopter battalion, a light mechanised battalion, and a commando battalion, with appropriate combat and service support. Only the Marine Brigades, the SAS Brigade and the Parachute Brigades would be engaged, designed and equipped for service outside the United Kingdom. One Marine and one Parachute Brigade, and an appropriate slice of the SAS, would be held at high readiness for intervention, or prepositioned to pre-empt a threat.

TABLE 7. *Possible composition of a future British Army manoeuvre force*

one special force "brigade" (SAS)
two parachute brigades
two assault helicopter brigades (perhaps the Guards)
three light infantry brigades
three light mechanised brigades (one Household Cavalry)
four artillery brigades (see text above)

These formations would in fact be self-contained brigade groups, with, where appropriate, an organic artillery regiment of from one to three battalions, and appropriate engineer and service support elements. In shot-estimating a manpower figure of 40 000(+), I have assumed that they would average some 3000 all ranks. Since they would share some training and most administrative facilities with the militia, one might hope to get away with a 60/40 teeth/tail ratio, giving a total manpower requirement of about 70 000.

The line infantry, territorially based in Britain as in many countries, would become a **militia**—or, if you like, a Territorial Army in the true sense. Militia service would be universal for all fit men *and women*, initially perhaps between 25 and 30. There would be no exemptions, but on call-out those in key professions such as medicine would continue to do their job within the militia. I am inclined to think that, by the time a scheme like this could conceivably be introduced, public opinion would favour the inclusion of women in militia combat units; but this is not a key point, since there is plenty of scope for employing them elsewhere.

Based on small and homogeneous populations, the Swedish, Swiss and Danish models may be misleading for countries like Britain. Three tiers would probably be needed—a full-time professional nucleus, a part-time volunteer cadre (comparable to the present Territorial Army), and the majority, committed only to compulsory part-time training. Many will argue that the larger of today's open industrial societies are not suitable vehicles for a militia. They may well be right especially, one has to admit, where Britain is concerned. But I would ask these doubters to consider whether an "open" society whose "free" citizens cannot be trusted to hold arms and ammunition at home represents an entity that *should* be defended in moral terms or that *can* be defended in military ones. Sun Tzu's dictum on "moral authority" strikes home here.

I have taken a 5-year age band to provide a force of rather over three million. Since a proportion of officer and NCO positions should be open to conscripts, this might call for a part-time volunteer cadre of 300 000, and a professional nucleus of 30 000, bringing the standing army as a whole to about 100 000.

This militia would be equipped and trained only for operation on its home ground in a fairly narrow sense. No provision would be made for accommodating or feeding personnel away from home, or for transporting them; nor would there appear to be any need for periods of full-time training. Specialists would be provided within the volunteer cadre, which *would* need some full-time training. The conscripts' training would have two thrusts. One would range from the simple defence of a locality to offensive quasi-guerrilla tactics such as tank hunting and sabotage, with emphasis on information-gathering too; the other would concern civil defence and disaster relief. They would be organised on conventional infantry lines down to fire teams (half sections). In areas occupied by the enemy, these half sections would become "resistance" cells. The command chain would be narrowly localised, so that it could operate clandestinely if needs be. It would be in every way desirable to expand this force by taking a wider age bracket. I have simply taken as a start one which looks socially feasible and produces an amount of manpower which should be economically and organisationally manageable.

The third key element in any future home defence would be **unmanned fortifications** of the kind discussed in Chapter 5, but extended to provide the static elements of air and coastal defences. They would be complemented by the land-force manoeuvre element described above, by a light naval force, and by short-range interceptor/strike aircraft. As the Swedes are continually finding, coasts have to be vigilantly defended against infiltration; but an assault landing across beaches does not seem a particularly promising form of *desant* for the future.

As we have seen, the seaborne helicopter threat is totally unpredictable, and can only be countered by a mixture of immediate local defence and manoeuvre. But it is limited in size. *The prime requirement for unmanned fortifications appears to be to prevent an invader landing transport aircraft.* In the United Kingdom as in many European countries, there is a shortage of unprepared surfaces on which a transport aircraft can land with any hope of taking off again. One of the priority tasks for the militia would be to barricade suitable stretches of main road with vehicles. Aerodromes of every kind are another thing again. As part of the peacetime preparation for home defence, military air bases, civilian airports and sports airfields should be combined and the number reduced to what is economically essential; these should be priority areas for all elements of the defence. All other airfields and strips could then be destroyed. For the United Kingdom at least, defence against an invasion by organised forces would start by being a battle for the airfields.

The dangers of a militia

I should not have put forward this notion of a protectivist defence policy were I not convinced that it catches the tide of political opinion, especially among the young; and that it would not only be acceptable to most democratic bodies politic, but is the only posture that will be politically acceptable in 20 or 30 years time. Trying to look ahead, I am very doubtful how long a submarine-borne nuclear capability would be supported, or whether even a very limited intervention force would remain acceptable through the coming 50-year cycle.

There is, however, one danger of immeasurable gravity that faces a liberal democracy seeking to base its defence on a militia. This is the temptation to use the militia as a "third force" (a *gendarmerie,* that is) to maintain law and order in face of genuinely internal conflicts. This problem is perfectly exemplified by the violence and lawlessness of the miners' strike which Britain is suffering as I write. Evidently the militia must be under some kind of military law when it is called out. Just as evidently, it would be crazy not to be able to call out this force for disaster relief. It may be easy enough to include in the legislation setting up the militia a definition of the circumstances in which it may be called out. But there is nothing to stop a government simply ignoring these restrictions; or taking emergency powers and overriding them; or concocting a scenario in which the internal unrest is linked to an external threat.

The United States governmental system, with a written constitution and a set of checks and balances between Administration and Congress, provides a safeguard. But it is hard indeed to see how a country governed by its parliament in principle and its cabinet in practice can be adequately protected against this abuse. This may be a point at which the head of state must become politically involved by having the right to consult the judiciary before giving assent. One solution is to create a professional "third force", for which I shall argue in Chapter 20; this would also fit in to the total defence picture. In any event it surely goes without saying that, as Kielmansegg stresses in discussing its Federal German counterpart, this militia must be an integral part of the armed forces proper. What is more, the concept must be generated through a major party's manifesto at a general election, and in no way fostered by pressure groups or by any form of extraparliamentary activity; and it must be mainly based on universal service, not volunteers.

Conclusion

In this chapter I have attempted to pull together the various broad threads of argument likely to shape the future pattern of Western Europe's defence policies. I have drawn on discussions earlier in the book to outline the shape armed forces might take under a truly defensive defence policy. I know that I differ from most who think along similar lines in advocating the retention of some minimal submarine-borne nuclear capability. But I think one must accept the impossibility of weathering a nuclear attack with a population the size and density of Britain's or the Federal Republic's. Given this impossibility, unilateral nuclear disarmament may result in our (literal) annihilation to satisfy the passing whim of some tyrant or religious fanatic in the third world.

The retention of an intervention force is likewise debatable. But I have tried to pitch this at the level which might be needed to rescue one's diplomats or one's citizens from the kind of barbaric threat that has become an everyday experience.

For home defence against any threat ranging from invasion by organised forces to externally-inspired subversion, I have satisfied the requirements of manoeuvre theory—a holding "force" (manned and unmanned) and a mobile force—while restraining the mobile land, sea and air forces to a tactical rather than an operational level. They are not strong enough either to embark on an offensive against a major enemy; or to "go over to the offensive" as opposed to warding off and containing the threat. This may strike many readers as defeatist fantasy. But in the next chapter I shall move back in time and demonstrate, from quite different premises, how the future defence of the NATO centre links the present situation to my way-out notions.

19

Defence of the NATO Centre

"Our conventional forces must be sufficiently robust to serve as more than just a 'delayed trip wire' for escalation. The problem which faces NATO is *not* to seek a new strategy; Flexible Response is as valid today as when first elaborated in the 1960's. Rather, we must determine, within a reasonable level of resource commitment, how best we can strengthen our conventional forces so that they can play the crucial role which flexible response demands of them. Our task, in short, is to find the means to maintain an effective deterrence by keeping our strategy of Flexible Response flexible."   GENERAL BERNARD W. ROGERS, SACEUR (1983)

Introduction—NATO's rotten planks

Even under the Soviet regime, the Russian sense of humour remains at once sharp and rumbustious. Among Moscow's 1984-vintage in-jokes is a habit of referring to the EEC as "Lenin's rope" ("Give the capitalist countries enough rope . . ."). Certainly squabbling and bureaucracy within the so aptly nicknamed Common Market has driven me, a convinced European of four decades' standing, to look across the Atlantic and the North Sea rather than the Channel. More seriously, discord among EEC members is probably a graver threat to the cohesion of NATO than divergences between United States foreign policy and European views. The ethnic make-up of the American body politic creates a force of attraction between the United States and many European countries besides Britain. For the moment, then, let us assume that the Atlantic Alliance will hold even if the form of the NATO military organisation changes.

Even so, before one can discuss the NATO centre sensibly in military terms, one must highlight the defects in the Organisation's platform. The most glaring of these is the weakness of the southern flank. With an internally wavering Greece and Turkey at each other's throats, Italy chronically unstable, Spain an unknown quantity, and Portugal's capability at best questionable, the United States Sixth Fleet is the only real obstacle to a strategic turning movement into the South of France, with Libya or Algeria as a forward base. It is thus prudent to think, if not to speak, of an open flank along the Alps, the Massif Central and the Pyrenees.

The second rotten plank is NATO's proclaimed and real reliance on a warning period of up to 10 days, when Soviet capabilities increasingly favour the use of strategic surprise. Exercises like the Reforger series, Crusader 80 and Lion Heart go surprisingly well. But they would need to proceed at the speed of light to have much strategic significance. These forces might contribute to a counterstroke. But whether the Warsaw Pact advance is contained or the nuclear threshold crossed will almost certainly turn on the performance of the standing forces located in the Federal Republic and the Rhine–Meuse triangle. This same antiquated notion of a build-up and a warning period is used to justify the refusal of most NATO governments to meet the cost of keeping a good proportion of the assigned forces at a high enough state of readiness to pre-empt or counter strategic surprise (Chapter 17).

A third grey zone is the military weakness and potential discord which stem from the Federal Republic's attitude. This feeling manifests itself from time to time in the United States Congress, and in her media, generally disguised as resentment against the failure of European NATO as a whole to pull its weight. (A view entirely valid in its own right!) Since 1973, the Federal German government has insisted not just on having its cake and eating it, but on getting its Allies to provide the icing. This must, I think, have been the thought at the back of Field Marshal Sir Edwin Bramall's mind when he talked to the Royal United Services Institute in February 1982. One can write off as an accident of history the way the nation with the world's fourth strongest economy and plenty of high-grade manpower has managed to get others to contribute at least half the men and money needed to defend it. Less forgivable is the mounting political pressure since 1973 to commit the entire Federal German Army's field force to a linear forward defence, which the Germans and everyone else know would be broken. Up to about 1982, one might fairly have added that it was military folly too for NATO to pin down in forward defence the troops best fitted for operational manoeuvre in depth. While no-one would suggest that the Bundeswehr was ever in the same league as the Wehrmacht, it was at that time still led by Wehrmacht-trained officers. By contrast, the United States Army (as it was and is honest enough to own) was suffering from the post-Vietnam backlash in terms of morale and quality of enlisted men. And British Army of the Rhine was once again busy brooding goose eggs. Now, with the Wehrmacht influence gone, the Bundeswehr seems to be heading towards ever deeper dugouts and ever more ponderous equipment. With the United States Army well out of its seventies trough and turning to manoeuvre theory, and with the British swinging back to the intellectual cavalry approach of the early sixties, a static role may well be the right one for the Bundeswehr.

This does not alter the most riling aspect of all—the Federal Government's persistent refusal to agree to a frontier obstacle belt in peacetime. Significantly but incredibly, this constraint extends to the Max Planck Institute's study of a protectivist defence policy. The authorities appear to feel that such a zone would symbolise perpetuation of the division of Germany.

This may be so. If they were prepared to defend themselves with their own men and money, fair enough! but with the military advantage to Britain, for instance, of defending herself in Germany rapidly diminishing, the Germans should surely offer this in return for a continuing Allied presence. The possibilities offered by unmanned fortifications, and the trends discussed below, make a permanent fortified belt along the Inner German Frontier not just a desirable add-on but an essential component of the future defence of the NATO centre.

Land-force levels

To put figures on all this, the standing ground forces assigned to the NATO centre and stationed in the Federal Republic comprise just six first-rate corps, of which three are German, two American and one British. The assigned contributions of other armies, whether stationed in the Federal Republic or behind it, are widely seen as penetrations about to happen. With virtually no first-rate reserves in depth, and literally no operational reserve for the army group commanders, the outcome of the conventional battle is an open enough issue to put the nuclear threshold uncomfortably low—certainly to preclude NATO from making any even remotely honest declaration of "no first use". Much would depend on the air situation, and estimates of this vary so widely that they are not much help.

By contrast there is a fairly solid body of opinion which holds that two more first-rate corps in being would produce a very different picture. In *The Third World War*, which was based on exhaustive analysis, General Sir John Hackett postulates a newly formed and slightly shaky 2 (BR) Corps, and depicts the Warsaw Pact advance as being halted astride the lower Rhine. If each army group commander had a powerful mechanised corps with a rotary-wing element under his hand as operational reserve, the stabilisation called for in Chapter 17 could almost certainly be achieved. The reason for this is that the Warsaw Pact's usable mass is restricted by route saturation (page 80).

Since the United States already finds two corps, these additional forces would evidently have to come from the Federal Republic itself and Britain. NATO shares almost one-half of the gross world product between under one-eighth of the world population; it is thus absurd to argue that the "Alliance" could not afford these forces. Admittedly the Federal Republic has an awkward dip in her demographic pattern, but she could form an additional corps simply by increasing full-time conscript service from 15 months to 22 months instead of the proposed 18. With a declaration of "no first use" as a quid pro quo, this would probably be supported by the SPD left, and very possibly by the Greens. And although this expansion of the

Army would scarcely dent Britain's manpower surplus, I would guess that the balance of cost after trading off or postponing the British Trident project would find wide political acceptance. One might even argue that this raising of the nuclear threshold would show an economic benefit by improving European popular morale. If the Germans were not prepared to accept more British troops on their territory, the appropriate Anglo-American response is best expressed in a recipe often recommended by schoolboys.

Tactical concept

As Frederick the Great more than once discovered to his cost, operational brilliance is no substitute for tactical soundness. Even if the next 20 years or so sees an Anglo-American swing to manoeuvre theory, it is in technology-led tactical development that the real problems of the near and middle future lie. So I think it makes sense to address the tactical level first. Within this, the direction of evolution of the mobile force is fairly clear, with light tracks complementing heavy tracks, and the rotor playing a progressively larger part. Tempo and densities apart, the only foreseeable tactical innovation is the development of the rotary-wing assault. It is in the holding force that the revolution must come. I see it in four stages.

I should like to take as a point of departure the Livsey active defence, although this is now in some respects superseded by airland battle. This consisted in essence (Fig. 52a) of a lattice of "last ditch" strong points; within this lattice a series of tactical hammer and anvil actions, and other types of blocking action or short sharp punch would be conducted. As I see it, the principle was to break down the Soviet regiment–battalion command link by repeatedly getting inside its decision loop. The British "framework battle" was rather similar, although it had only one type of anvil. The first stage of development is to superimpose on the hammer and anvil tactic a third element, which I have called a "**net**" and the Germans call a "sponge", to exploit the hindering terrain, urban and otherwise, which lies on enemy thrust lines (Fig. 52b).

This net consists of light infantry, reinforced by gunner and sapper detachments down to platoon level, and deployed at 5 per cent, *never* more than 10 per cent, of normal infantry density. This makes a platoon responsible for a sector 2 to 3 kilometres wide and up to 7 kilometres deep. Within this, the platoon employs quasi-guerrilla tactics while having call through its gunner on artillery and air support. In typical rural hindering terrain, it might employ two sections to put out four to six tank-hunting patrols, and deploy the headquarters (which has an extra fire team) and the third section in an ambush, into which the bulk of the sapper support would probably go. There is in fact a need for a "network of nets", so that they can pull back through one another on foot, avoiding the main battle.

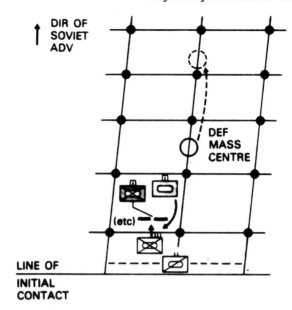

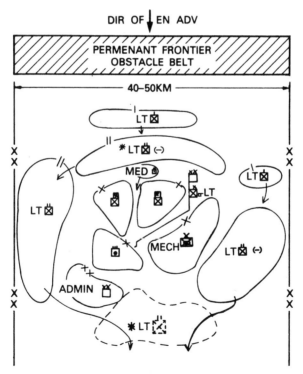

FIG. 52. *a. Schematic indicating principle of "active defence". b. Schematic of hammer, anvil and net.*

The net's task is not attrition, but mobility denial in the broadest sense, based on the blocking of routes. The aim is to pose a sufficient threat to force the enemy to move up massed infantry, dismount it, and clear through the hindering terrain on foot. Quite apart from the repercussions on his movement plan, nobody with experience of clearing through under threat of opposition will be in any doubt of what this would do to the attacker's tempo.

The second stage is along the same lines but calls for a more drastic shift in the balance of the force structure. Franz Uhle-Wetter (at the time of writing Commander 5 Panzer Division) puts it forward in his book *Gefechtsfeld Mitteleuropa* ("Battlefield Central Europe"). It is to confine NATO mechanised forces to the terrain best suited to them, and to cover the rest—about 50 per cent of Federal German territory, he reckons—with light infantry well backed up with artillery, and with fixed- and rotary-wing air. This light infantry would use a mix of conventional and quasi-guerrilla tactics; it would also act as a security force against the whole span of special force and subversive threats.

Acceptance of the "net" or "sponge" concept seems to be steadily spreading, though there is much argument about just how it should be found. And Lieutenant General John R. Galvin, at the time of writing Commanding General 7 (US) Corps and evidently a rising star, has publicly endorsed Uhle-Wetter's view. So these first two stages seem to have reached the point of being non-controversial, however difficult it may prove to implement them with reasonable speed. The third stage is more radical, in that it literally turns defensive tactics inside out. It can best be summed up as *the replacement of the anvil of troops by an anvil of fire.*

The growing dominance of firepower, which I have so heavily stressed in Chapter 10 and elsewhere, has already reached a point at which deployment of both armour and infantry at high densities is extremely dangerous, and movement at conventional densities is apt to be difficult even without an air threat. As Soviet ammunition norms and much other evidence show, it is now possible to achieve extended neutralisation, and destruction of materiel when required, with a realistic expenditure of ammunition. This capability is further enhanced if the fire is observed as opposed to predicted; still more if direct fire is employed to shape and contain the target, to thicken up the indirect fire, and to pick off any key targets with distinctive visual signatures.

This transforms the defensive holding force, or anvil, from a rock on which the enemy must pound to a shell (as in oyster, not gun) into which he must be drawn (Fig. 5, page 51). The positions forming this shell also serve as local pivots for sniping tanks, tank destroyers and helicopters, as well as protecting artillery observers. Evidently this concept calls for some form of tactical defile. If there is no natural obstacle at the end of it, an artificial one may have to be created with minelets delivered by artillery and/or scattered from helicopters and vehicles. And the flanks may require a "net" to stop the defile being turned and to extend the scope for observed fire and anti-tank sniping. The minor tactics of this anvil of fire need a good deal of thought; but the principle is clear enough once one makes the requisite mental somersault.

The fourth stage is radical enough even for my taste; and I see it as of outstanding importance because it links the present to the long-term concept I depicted in the previous chapter. Since it is bred by the anvil of fire out of the net, I shall call it the "**universal net**". Rather than try to illustrate it schematically, I would invite the reader to shake a pepper pot over a map. The entire area of operations is covered by a net, very much of the kind I have described. This could well be found by a militia. The artillery observers would have to be professionals or volunteer reservists; for the rest, local knowledge and the immediate threat to homes would more than offset any limitations of training. And a militia would be ideally placed to go to ground when overrun, at least continuing to gather information. The problem in NATO terms is that a universal net of this kind should—in fact *must*—be found by indigenous troops, militia or otherwise. But this universal net is simply an extension of Uhle-Wetter's thinking; and there is a growing movement, supported by General Kielmannsegg among other men of distinction, for a militia element *within the Bundeswehr* (as opposed to a "third force"). So the concept could be a great deal more realistic and more quickly attainable than it looks at first glance.

The enormous military advantage that a universal net offers the defender is that his holding force is permanently in place. He is freed from the tactical risks of moving it. He can create an instant anvil of fire wherever he wants just by thickening up the net, ideally with a helicopter force, while his mobile force has free play on the surface routes. Conversely, the attacker is faced at every step he takes with a threat he cannot identify in advance because it does not concentrate or move. In Sun Tzu's phraseology it is "shapeless". He may destroy some of it in detail and displace more. But he will have to do this with men on their feet, and he will find this a very slow job indeed.

NATO's present massive mechanised forces are not very well suited to the support of a universal net. There is a need for brigade-sized task forces of the kind depicted in the previous chapter, and in particular for the mobile self-protecting artillery brigades suggested there. One can in fact see a way of linking this universal net concept to the existing shape of the NATO Alliance. The net force must, I think, be indigenous. But if the problems of low-level inter-army co-operation could be overcome, some of these tactical mobile forces could come from Britain and the United States, say to the tune of one corps' worth each, while those two Armies would each provide one corps as operational reserve, and the Germans themselves two corps. I do not want to probe this delicate interface between theory and practice too hard; but I hope I have said enough to suggest that smooth progress from the present to the long-term future is not inconceivable.

Operational concepts

At present the army group commanders on the NATO centre do not have a great deal of say in the conduct of operations. The most they can hope to do is to co-ordinate and support the various national corps battles, each fought in the way the national army concerned prefers. As the Germans would see it there is no operational reserve, and thus no operational level. I have suggested above middle- and long-term remedies for this situation; but in fact the depth in front of the Rhine and the politico-economic value of the Federal Republic's territory leaves little scope for operational manoeuvre of the kind practised by the Wehrmacht on the Eastern Front.

The purpose of a true operational reserve would perhaps be twofold. Being held well back, it could be used to clear up a runaway breakout or to counter a strategic turning movement. And, once containment had been achieved, its existence would ensure that fresh troops were available to deliver the measured counterstroke needed to restabilise the situation (Chapter 17). But for the moment I think one must join the Americans in regarding the corps battle as an operation, calling for an operational concept.

In these terms the Bundeswehr's operational concept is clear enough—the tightest possible forward defence, some 50 kilometres deep, with only tactical reserves and only tactical counter-attacks (in the strict sense of moves to restore the position). The United States **airland battle** concept is likewise, as I see it, limited to a depth of between 30 and 50 kilometres as far as manoeuvre by ground forces is concerned.

For this reason, many authorities, among them General Sir John Hackett, see a profound conflict between airland battle, as developed by General Donn Starry and now widely propounded in the United States itself, and "**strike deep**", the doctrine proclaimed by General Rogers in his capacity as SACEUR. In terms of peacetime provision—and that is what matters—there is certainly a resource conflict between the two concepts. The very expensive surveillance and weapon systems called for by strike deep can only be provided at some cost or other to the materiel needed for the corps battle. But I cannot see a fundamental conflict; and a little exercise in *reductio ad absurdum* confirms this view. It is inconceivable that a defender would devote his whole effort to striking the follow-on forces deep in Warsaw Pact territory while giving the leading echelons a free run. It is just as unthinkable that he would concentrate wholly on dealing with the attacker's leading troops, leaving the follow-on free to pass through these and hit him at full strength and full steam. As I understand it, the operational purpose of interdicting the follow-on forces is to create "windows" between the echelons, into which higher tactical and operational hammer-blows can be launched. This gives priority to firepower which can be delivered either tactically, as ultra-deep defensive fires to ease immediate pressure; or operationally, to weaken, disrupt and if possible halt the follow-up.

The airland battle and strike deep thus seem to coalesce in the defensive concept perhaps best—if inelegantly—described as the "**anvil and triple hammer**" (Fig. 53). No matter for the moment whether the anvil is of troops or of fire. The first hammer is a low-level tracked one, say a tank-heavy battle group within the anvil brigade. Its purpose in life is counter-attack to restore the anvil or, if the anvil is based on a defile, to deal with

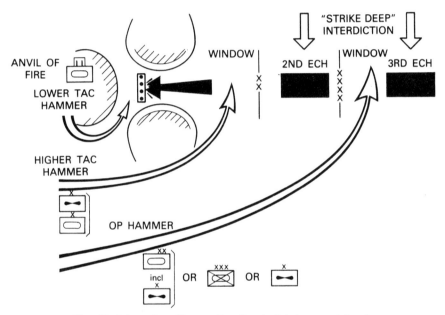

FIG. 53. *Schematic to illustrate "anvil and triple hammer defence".*

anything that emerges from the throat. The higher tactical hammer, which might consist of a tank-heavy brigade with strong helicopter support, or a helicopter force such as the Air Cavalry Attack Brigade (ACAB) of the United States' 1986 organisation, delivers the classic hammer-blow exemplified by Manteuffel at Targul Frumos, either hooking into the depth behind the attacker's leading formation, or passing through the anvil and disrupting the attacker as if with a battering ram. With all the emphasis on manoeuvre and turning, one needs to recall that this frontal hammer-blow, aimed at literally shattering a disorganised and weakened force as if it were a flawed pot, was a tactic the Germans used with great success on the Eastern Front.

It is the third hammer, the operational one, which represents the interface between the two American concepts. This must by definition have a direct effect on the strategic situation. Given the pattern of threat, this means that it will have to impact both on the enemy's follow-up forces and on his resupply system. The counter-offensive against Bremen depicted in General Hackett's *The Third World War* is an excellent example of a relatively modest operation with just such an aim. It is perhaps within the broad scope of this operational hammer-blow that the crunch over resources really comes.

Suppose the operation to be carried out by an United States 86 Heavy Division Type A, or by a panzer division with an attack helicopter regiment under command (the British "armoured" division being too small). This formation will require massive support from long-range artillery and fixed-wing air throughout the operation, as indeed would a larger force—say a corps, or the equivalent of a Soviet front-level OMG. On the other hand, if this stroke is to accomplish its operational aim of dislocation and destruction as opposed to just getting a short-lived toehold on a designated piece of real estate, something has got to be done about the enemy follow-up forces in greater depth still. If one has the resources to interdict these as well as supporting the operational hammer, one is on the way to developing a club sandwich counter-offensive. In particular, with the armoured force as a forward base or hinge, the ACAB could back up interdiction by a further swift hammer-blow.

The short answer is that you can win—whatever "winning" may entail—with inferior resources. But you must have enough resources to implement a realistic plan without being forced to resort to the doublethink that parsimony imposes on NATO's top military men. The more interesting question strikes me as being whether a commander of the kind needed to execute a counter-offensive like this swiftly and fairly painlessly would be psychologically capable of pulling his punch in the way called for in Chapter 16. Success on the ground will produce the same kind of situation as an operational encounter battle, with large mobile forces laid alongside each other, each trying to bite the other's tail. This is an extremely unstable situation in itself, doubly so since the Soviet concept of operations regards it as the ideal point of departure for a bigger and better offensive. The need is for the defender to deal extremely quickly with the forces enveloped. Something like this may well be the idea underlying recent Soviet thinking on double envelopment and encirclement. More practically perhaps from NATO's point of view, it argues strongly for the geographical objective of the operational hammer-blow to be the coast, or the bank of a really substantial water obstacle. This operational ploy featured large in the thinking of those two masters of manoeuvre, Triandafillov and Tukhachevskii; but the Soviets and everyone else seem rather to have lost sight of it since.

Counterstroke and counter-threat

This operational hammer-blow, supported by interdiction in strategic depth, brings one to think of defences which are agressive at the operational or even the strategic level. A counterstroke across the Inner German Frontier is something that, for evident and perfectly good reasons, the Germans have been discussing ever since the Bundeswehr was formed. (They tend to deny this, but I first took part in and listened to such discussions at social events in 1960, and had many such experiences in the early and late sixties.) Much more recently this thinking has been developed along two lines in the United States. One, which I shall call the **counterstroke**, favours the launching of an all-out offensive operation into Warsaw Pact territory as an *immediate response* to any Warsaw Pact intrusion across the IGF. The other, which I shall call **counter-threat**, is based on a similar, but if anything rather deeper, *pre-emptive* move—a northward-turning hook through Czechoslovakia and thence in the general direction of, say, Danzig. This would turn the GDR, so far generally thought to be more "politically reliable" than the other satellites, and the Group of Soviet Forces in Germany (GSFG). Success would evidently depend on bringing the Czech and Polish peoples out in revolt. In these terms the main operation could well be supported by a major subversive operation in the former Baltic States. On latest form, one might reasonably hope that the East Germans would in fact also stage a revolt.

Before looking at the military aspects of these concepts, one might do well to consider the politico-strategic side. The present Federal German Government would be likely to support such a move, but a Social-Democratic successor almost certainly would not. With the possible exception of the present (Thatcher) British government, other European members of NATO could be expected to oppose anything like this to the point of opting out. The Americans may argue that there is no real difference between conducting air operations East of the IGF and crossing it with ground troops; but I am fairly sure that, in everybody else's mind, the psychological difference is one of kind.

The Soviets might well expect to regain military control of the situation before counter-revolutions in the satellites could take much effect. If they failed to do so, it is very hard to see how they could long abstain from a nuclear or mass-chemical response. They might well be able to live with the loss of manpower and economic resources, but surely they could not accept the loss of face in the third world that would result from the collapse of their East European empire. However little the West may like it, the Soviet Union enjoys something more than the unqualified formal support of governments in many third world countries, and of revolutionary movements in others. A number of "non-aligned" nations rely on her for military and/or economic aid; and still more are prepared to give her moral support.

No matter whether the NATO thrust was pre-emptive or an immediate response, few can doubt which way a vote in the United Nations General Assembly, however ineffective, would go. Even in the Security Council, it might take a United States veto to inhibit censure—as, after all, did the vote on Israel in August 1984.

Given the extent to which the Federal Republic is penetrated by Warsaw Pact intelligence, it is inconceivable that the counter-threat could be implemented with moral strategic surprise. Failing this, both concepts are open to four fundamental military objections. First, even if NATO's conventional standing force levels were raised as suggested above, this operation would require a shock group of the two corps postulated as an operational reserve for the middle term; there would be only six first-rate corps left in a defensive posture, and this merely replicates the present situation. Second, the NATO thrust would be on *exterior lines relative to both its flanks*—to GSFG on the one side and the bulk of the Soviet forces in Poland and Kiev Military District on the other. Third, the operation would be a high-risk one even given excellent operational intelligence; for it would rely in greater measure or less on popular uprisings to prevent interference with its flanks. Fourth, GSFG, an immensely powerful force and a self-contained one in the short term, would have two options open; probably it would be strong enough to pursue both. It could drive south-southeast to the Alps astride Munich, and then sweep northwestwards, pivoting on, say, Nuremberg; and/or it could execute the eastward thrust across the North German Plain onto Wesel–Rees, thence swinging south into the Rhine–Meuse triangle, and/or driving onwards for the North Sea/Channel coast. So far from protecting the politico-economically precious territory of the Federal Republic, counterstroke and counter-threat alike would most probably accelerate its occupation.

Conclusion—threat assessment

Having analysed and expounded the Warsaw Pact threat in *Red Armour* and used it as a model in this book, I thought I would for once consider it last rather than first. To start with, it seems to me as unlikely that the Soviet government would seek to "march against NATO" as that NATO would "march on Moscow". On the other hand, what the Soviets would call "the reunification of Germany from the East" must be a tempting political aim for them. Very understandably, the Second World War engraved a genuine fear of Germany deep on the Russian national consciousness, and this fear is compounded by Marxist–Leninist paranoia. With the present levels and states of readiness of NATO's standing forces, the Soviets may reckon that they could gain moral and material strategic surprise, and achieve their strategic aim within 48 hours. They may well count on hesitation among NATO's other European members about getting themselves atomised for

Germany's sake—and they might well prove to be right when the chips were down. The Russians do not have a monopoly of recall, as the trauma of Reagan's visit to the Bitburg war cemetery showed.

On the other hand, I believe there is little understanding in the West of the scope and extent of the part played by the *turning movement* in Russian (and I mean Russian) military thinking. As *we* struggle to come to grips with the idea of the turning *operation, their* thoughts seem more and more to be moving towards *strategic turning movements based on desanty.* The power and tempo of a Warsaw Pact offensive on the NATO centre is limited by route saturation to a level which NATO, strengthened as discussed above, could match. If the Rhine–Meuse triangle were to be covered by NATO with a standing operational reserve, the Soviets would surely think in terms of the South of France, if they could get at it, and Northeast Scotland, which is perhaps more accessible to them. All in all, their capability to do this kind of thing is increasing.

Thus an open-minded and fundamental analysis of the threat to NATO points to the need for defence in depth—not just the depth from the IGF to the Rhine, but the entire depth of Western Europe. This, I suggest, calls first for standing forces in Germany of a strength and readiness sufficient to block a direct assault with very little risk of having to resort to nuclear weapons. Then, taking account of purely military trends, for the progressive conversion of this force to a "universal net" defence behind a fortified frontier zone; this would be based on a German militia, but have some of its mobile elements contributed by the United States and Britain. In tune with this shift, the universal net of a militia-based defence, with mobile support, should be spread over the whole depth and breadth of European NATO.

A long-term policy on these broad lines would serve three political ends. It would progressively ease the Russian fear of German aggression. It would replace the no longer credible nuclear deterrent with both a visible conventional deterrent and a genuinely effective defence against the scope of Soviet strategic turning operations. And it would bring about the truly defensive, protectivist posture that European bodies politic increasingly seem to seek, without the dangers of increased imbalance or sudden destabilisation.

20

Small-force Manoeuvre Theory

"The crux here is making the subjective and the objective correspond well with each other." MAO TSE TUNG (trans. GRIFFITH)

"Some people are intelligent in knowing themselves but stupid in knowing their opponents, and others the other way round; neither kind can solve the problem of learning and applying the laws of war." Ibid.

"Attack may be changed into defense and defense into attack; advance may be turned into retreat and retreat into advance; containing forces may be turned into assault forces, and assault forces into containing forces." Ibid.

"The ability to run away is precisely one of the characteristics of guerrillas. Running away is the chief means of getting out of passivity and regaining the initiative." Ibid.

"Flexible employment of forces is more indispensable in guerrilla warfare than in regular warfare. . . . and the chief ways of employing the forces consist in dispersing, concentrating and shifting them. . . . In general, the shifting of forces should be done secretly and swiftly." Ibid.

Introduction—soldiers and guerrillas

The two most significant forms of modern land warfare, manoeuvre warfare and revolutionary warfare, both derive from Sun Tzu. The one apparently passed to the Russians via Genghis Khan, to be re-expressed by Triandafillov and Tukhachevskii. And it was on Sun Tzu, Lenin and Tukhachevskii that Mao Tse Tung drew for his doctrine of revolutionary warfare. This doctrine was developed and latinised by Che Guevara; but in my view, Mao Tse Tung's statement of it remains of more general application. I hope the multiple epigraph will serve to demonstrate both the common origin of the two theories, and their fundamental similarity.

I had intended to call this final chapter "Manoeuvre theory against revolutionary warfare", but I now see a continuum of the application of armed force linking positional warfare by mass armies and terrorism. Large-force manoeuvre warfare, small-force manoeuvre warfare and guerrilla warfare are adjacent segments of this continuum.

311

There is, however, one distinction between organised forces and guerrillas which one must draw in unequivocal terms—the motivation of the combatants. Revolutionary fighters are by definition politically or religiously motivated—or both. While Che Guevara insists on total dedication to the cause even at the cost of keeping numbers down and thus slowing development of the movement, Mao Tse Tung accepts, with the realism characteristic of him, that developing his Phase two (widespread guerrilla operations), still more the move to Phase three (organised units) is going to dilute the strength of individual motivation. Nevertheless, he insists that the building of coherence and morale must be based on personal dedication, and that this can be achieved by indoctrination. At the same time, there is a good deal of evidence that successful groups develop not just team spirit but a kind of tribal or "regimental" lore which reinforces and may to some extent supplant devotion to the cause.

The motivation of the soldier in an established army is more complex. Here I want to look more closely at the individual, as opposed to the group, than I did in Part 4. I often puzzle over the way the whole shape of my political outlook was determined by the Spanish Civil War, which I followed in the papers with schoolboy interest in a period of deep personal grief, while the only event in the Second World War which had the least political effect on me was Churchill's decision for a positive alliance with the Soviet Union (which I was dead against). Like others of my generation, I am often asked by younger people what made me—or "people"—fight in that war. The general assumption among those who have not experienced war is that people are motivated by patriotism. But I do not think this is so. Now that Christianity and humanism alike have shifted their ground from Renaissance-based and individualism to collectivism, Western soldiers in a conventional "Third World War" might be motivated by some relatively lofty idea of protecting the group. But for my money—and one finds this feeling widely expressed by the First World War poets—one fights to preserve one's family and above all one's way of life. This is perhaps why the bravest people on the battlefield are those with the most to lose.

While I respect the soldierly ethic so lucidly and elegantly set out by General Sir John Hackett in *The Profession of Arms*, this entire approach, which derives I think from the Crusades and the mediaeval code of chivalry, is wholly alien to my thinking. These soldierly codes range from the balanced and tolerant to the fanatical. In their extreme forms, that of the *Samurai* for instance, they demand a dedication at least as great as that of the revolutionary fighter. But in the Caucasian culture at least, they do not touch a significant proportion of the soldiers in mass armies. For them, motivation to fight is compounded of a wholly laudable resolve to defend hearth and home, and an excess of physical courage over moral courage which leads them to conform. This is why it has always struck me as folly to begin military training with a vicious process of dehumanisation.

Why revolutionary forces win

Oddly enough, nature and strength of motivation does not seem to affect bravery in combat nearly as much as it does skill. Mao Tse Tung argues that civilians are quickly and easily turned into guerrillas because the best training for war is war. (Incidentally, he argues much the same way where commanders are concerned.) At the time of writing one does not yet know what will happen in Afghanistan, nor in whose favour a settlement in El Salvador might emerge. But I can think of only two cases in which a movement employing the techniques of revolutionary warfare has not at least held its own. And many have fully achieved their political aim. One case of failure is in Nicaragua, and here the reason is crystal clear. The Sandinista government may not be a model of multi-party liberal democracy; but it broadly if crudely represents the popular will, while the Contras, largely created by and entirely dependent on CIA support, are a phoney movement which is conspicuously failing to "win hearts and minds". The Contras will ultimately be defeated unless the United States intervenes massively with organised forces; and Jomini's teaching combines with the Vietnam experience to suggest that even these would have a rough ride.

The other instance is Templar's success in Malaya (as it then was). Admittedly the revolutionary movement there was limited in numbers and received only patchy support from the population; and admittedly the British had a powerful psychological weapon in *Merdeka*, the promise of independence. But Templar won by getting a force composed mainly of conscript townsmen to master the jungle, and to outplay the guerrillas at their own game. This approach carries a key lesson in itself; but above all, perhaps, it was a triumph of training and positive morale building. Once again, Borneo offers a parallel case, though to my mind not an entirely analogous one. Interestingly, every national serviceman I have met who fought in Malaya recalls the experience with a shudder, but with immense satisfaction, acknowledging it to have been a key formative influence in his life. This contrasts very markedly with the reaction of similar men who fought in Korea, or participated in the numerous unsuccessful campaigns of the decolonialisation era. And the stalemate in Northern Ireland evokes loathing even in career officers and long-service soldiers.

Even when one makes the fullest possible allowance for the advantages conferred by dedication and popular support, one is forced to conclude that the span of military techniques covered by the term "revolutionary" warfare may actually represent a more effective way of waging war than operations by organised forces. Fascinatingly, this brings one full circle both to Soviet views on the unusability of organised forces (Chapter 18); and to Uhle-Wetter's thesis (page 302), one aspect of which is that, even in a contest between two first-rate armies, sophisticated equipment can easily become more of a liability than an asset. This exemplifies Sun Tzu's and Mao's principle of fitting the response to the situation, the subjective to the objective. But since, unlike irregular forces, established armies cannot use war to train for war, one comes back to this question of training.

Philosophies of training

I devoted a whole chapter to the selection and training of officers and NCOs, but have so far said little about the basic training of soldiers. While there is ample room for improvement in every national organisation I know of for training conscripts, this is inevitably something of a mass production process. It may then be more helpful to consider the training of men for a small volunteer force and rely on spin-off from this to modify the sausage-machines. There are two fundamentally different philosophies of training, both of which I have not only witnessed but experienced. I shall call them **"gung-hoism"** and **"Hahnism"** (after Kurt Hahn, the founder of Salem, Gordonstoun, and their offshoots). I think this latter term a fair one because the approach it represents was injected into the Royal Navy by the Duke of Edinburgh, then a serving officer, and happened to catch the tide of the British Army's thinking about the importance of remnants on the nuclear battlefield.

Gung-hoism is very fashionable at the moment. Its aims might be summed up as mental and physical toughness, basic team spirit and instant obedience; in other words, it is based on the close combat at high densities called for by attrition theory, and on conventional wisdom concerning the use of organised forces in counter-insurgency. It proceeds by dehumanising a man, motivating him with an ardent "regimental" spirit, and rebuilding him in a very specific image. The technique is epitomised by the "P Company" course of the British Parachute Brigade, and employed by the French Paras, and in the United States by Airborne Forces, Infantry (and to some extent Armor), and Marines. The Royal Marines' basic commando course and the United States Rangers' training are at least as arduous but place more emphasis on accomplishment and responsibility, less on dehumanisation—a subtle but important difference. These examples of those who base their training on gung-hoism will leave nobody in any doubt that it is outstandingly successful in accomplishing its aims. As I see it, gung-hoism is the bottom-level equivalent of the training philosophy that underlies Sandhurst, St Cyr, West Point, and even more markedly the crack Moscow Higher All-Arms School with a name as long as your arm. Certainly the British Army swung violently back from Hahnism to gung-hoism when members of the postwar output from Sandhurst came to command their regiments. And the prevalence of gung-hoism, is why, in Chapter 15, I suggested that potential officers should go through a "junior leaders" type of training and selection rather than through the ranks as such.

Having recently come to see a good deal of Kurt Hahn's principles in action, I must admit to the profoundest of doubts about them in an educational context. For better of for worse, they have become severely watered down by time, scale, and the elimination of real danger. But at a deeper level I often wonder how Kurt Hahn's ideas would have been received in Britain (for instance) had he not won the supreme accolade of being slung out by the Nazis. Some of those who knew him tell me that he saw a close resemblance between his philosophy and the Benedictine Rule— and a nobler model than this is hard to imagine. Yet to my libertarian mind the very concepts of "preparation for leadership" and "moral leadership" are extremely dangerous unless firmly contained within some greater whole such as a democratic constitution. This said, Hahnism is an ideal basis for training modern armed forces.

The essence of Hahnism is that the individual is in no way dehumanised or forced. He is placed in a carefully though discreetly controlled environment designed to foster the development from within of certain aspects of character. This is backed up by a number of special environments which offer high challenge and entail an element, however remote, of real danger to life. For training soldiers, most of these challenges will be mainly physical; and both general and special environments will be designed to encourage individual initiative in a setting of team spirit. This approach applies intense pressure to the subjects, and a small proportion, 4 or 5 per cent maybe, will crack under it and drop out. All the better. The rest will develop into full, mature personalities, mentally alert, physically tough, resilient, determined to make the most of themselves, and happy to work within an accepted discipline.

Hahnism is in fact the basis of the "junior leaders" training I discussed in Chapter 15. But in fairness, I am less than sanguine about its working in the setting of a basic training unit mainly made up of run-of-the-mill recruits; to achieve the right atmosphere, one would have to have training companies in field force units. Some argue that this kind of self-generating discipline, which is really only one step beyond the "accepted discipline" of the British cavalry tradition, will not work in circumstances which demand tight control and instant obedience, such as the conventional approach to counter-insurgency. This I suggest has been disproved once and for all by the performance of Royal Armoured Corps and Royal Artillery units in Northern Ireland. They have carried out these tricky infantry roles just as effectively as the line infantry and the Parachute Regiment, seemingly with an even lower proportion of breaches of discipline and excesses.

Countering revolutionary warfare

This brings us to a dividing line which badly needs redrawing. By and large, British commanders in Northern Ireland and American ones in the counter-guerrilla phase of the Vietnam War have not followed Templar's example. They have moved from the procedures of "aid to the civil power" to more or less conventional infantry tactics, using armoured vehicles for protected mobility, but still relying on a show of force and retaining severe restrictions on the use of firepower. In dealing with violent revolutionary movements there will often be—as there would be, for example, if troops were brought in to deal with the British miners' strike in progress as I write—an initial phase in which the army's role is essentially pre-emptive. Troops deploy conspicuously at high densities in support of the police as a warning of what may happen next. As a personal view, I have always felt this to be a misuse of troops, just as "anti-riot squads" are a misuse of normal police. Powerful as the counter-arguments are, it may well be better on balance to fill this grey zone with a "third force" on French lines, leaving the police and the army to the roles for which they are constituted and trained. My reasons for this view are twofold. I have always seen it as wrong on the one hand to expose police to mass violence and the concerted use of firearms, and on the other to expect soldiers "to offer their lives to the enemy" without permitting them unrestricted use of firepower.

The existence of a third force allows the army to enter the lists in a proper military role, with the clear-cut aim of eliminating the subversive movement from the nation's territory. The overlap required is not between the *overt* activities of police and army; here there should be not even an interface but a demarcation zone filled by a third force. The overlap should be between special forces and military intelligence on the one hand, and special branch (police) and national intelligence services on the other. One of the many unpleasing characteristics of the intelligence world is its proneness to internecine strife, but let us suppose for a moment that this kind of co-operation could be achieved.

One then has a situation in which revolutionary warfare and military activity to counter it can develop in parallel. Both start at a covert, non-violent level. Phase one is countered by a "hearts and minds" campaign, and by the undercover deployment of special forces, possibly culminating in a surprise strike aimed, say, at capturing the leader or the main arms cache. If, despite this, the revolutionary movement is able to go over to Phase two, widespread and continuing guerilla activity, the army must be free to counter this by adopting the same tactics, again supported by a psychological warfare effort. And, as Templar's men did, it must do both better than its opponents.

The spectrum of revolutionary warfare represents both the most probable form by far of future armed conflict in the first and second worlds, and the most effective means of first and second world intervention in the third. This is the thought underlying my contention that special forces should be at the mass centre of future armies, with "semi-special" forces next in priority to them (Chapter 18). Let us look at this for a moment through Soviet eyes. Their Airborne Forces, soon to be in name the separate service they are in fact, include their special forces, Spetsnaz. The "professional" strength of Spetsnaz proper is considerable, and the KGB and Ministry of Internal Affairs have similar forces of their own. But the Soviets' stated aim is to train every man in the Airborne Forces "to Spetsnaz standards". Let us suppose for a moment that this means what it says, not just teaching them free-fall parachuting, the hallmark of Spetsnaz; let us also suppose, not unreasonably, that the Soviets do the same with their Marine divisions. This would give them the best part of 100 000 men equally capable of undercover operation, quasi-guerrilla tactics *and* high-density raids. True, the effectiveness for a given effort of all these types of activity diminishes as their intensity increases; true also that expansion on this scale would bring in its wake some dilution of quality. But even when the fullest allowance is made for these spoiling factors, both the threat posed by such a force and its potency as an instrument of intervention are mind-boggling.

Speaking for a moment in purely military terms, the Israelis use this three-pronged approach to excellent effect. The 7000 or so troops put into the Lebanon by Britain, France, Italy and the United States confined themselves to "aiding the civil power" and presenting the Shi'ites with prestige targets. One cannot help wondering just what the outcome would have been if they had been deployed into the country in undercover patrols and quasi-guerrilla groups, supported by heliborne strike forces held embarked—all this with the aim of eliminating the irregular foreign elements and of forcing the various indigenous bands to disengage. I am sure this would have been political madness; but it provides a model for assessing the military value of this approach if and when direct intervention against revolutionary movements becomes imperative.

Intervention

Whatever the moral rights and wrongs of it, the superpowers are evidently not going to abstain from intervention when they see their "vital interests" threatened, or when they reckon they can gain an advantage before world opinion can react. Even countries with a protectivist defence policy based on home defence may be forced to intervene to rescue diplomats or nationals. And the day might come when superpower relations warm sufficiently to allow the United Nations to form an intervention force with teeth. A situation calling for intervention may arise from a specific localised threat (the Teheran Embassy hostages); a Phase one subversive movement (Grenada); a conflict between movements operating in Phases two and three (Lebanon); actions by a country's national organised forces (Tanzania vs Idi Amin's Uganda); foreign organised forces supporting a subversive movement (Libya in Chad); or outright invasion (Falklands).

Intervention is most likely to take place at the end of long air and/or sea lines. It may involve land operations across large stretches of undeveloped territory, which may or may not be unsecured or hostile. Revolutionary movements will have the advantage of playing at home, or at least in an area with an ethnically and culturally similar population. Indigenous organised forces are likely to be massive, and may be excellently equipped. With known exceptions, such as Israel or Pakistan, their overall quality will be low. But elite groups may be good tactically, and forces which are generally second-rate may be greatly stiffened by "advisers" at particular times and places. Aircrew are likely to be up to first world standards, even if they are not "advisers" or mercenaries.

Generally speaking, massive intervention by organised forces seems to be at best unduly costly, and at worst disastrous. One wonders whether the Argentines in the Falklands could not have been softened up, if not broken or driven out, by special force operations, culminating perhaps in a heliborne strike; and whether the very successful British operations on the Argentine mainland could not have been greatly extended. The United States got off fairly lightly in Grenada in terms of casualties caused and received. But with the information that must have been available to them on the threat, they could surely have done the job much more neatly and cheaply, and evoked much less umbrage, with a clandestine "Phase one" and a quasi-guerrilla "Phase two". The Soviets must be wishing that, if they had to go into Afghanistan at all, they had done it by using the revolutionary warfare techniques they preach. Contrast these operations with the way the Israelis at Entebbe, the Germans at Mogadishu (and by request elsewhere since then), and the British and French special forces on several occasions, have achieved total success with a surprise strike. All this does seem to argue strongly for the "unusability" of large organised forces—as in a different way does Vietnam.

By contrast, intervention by special force and quasi-guerrilla operations is not going to achieve a quick decision against large organised forces operating on their home ground. Problems of strategic mobility will limit both the physical fighting power (organic weight per man, Chapter 5) and the mass of the organised force that can be inserted. Part of this force must evidently be employed to secure and develop a firm base around the airhead or port. Outside this base, the application of manoeuvre theory will allow these compact, light intervention forces to exploit their quality and gain a decision against superior numbers. If they get bogged down in attrition warfare at the end of long exterior lines, they will at best achieve stalemate and probably lose.

It is easy to say that present and erstwhile great powers ought to learn to use a rapier rather than a bludgeon. But the mental somersault called for is a political rather than a military one. A bellicist culture which regards a declaration of war as making organised mass slaughter morally and socially acceptable is more or less bound to condemn strategic surprise, let alone clandestine operations, as something between unsporting and criminal. If one accepts and projects the evidence of the past 50 years, one can be in little doubt that stealth and surprise are the ways of revolutionary warfare now, and will become the ways of international warfare by the twenty-first century.

Suitably motivated, trained and led, the soldier of the advanced democracies should gain just as much of an edge in clandestine and small-force operations from his personal qualities and the technology at his disposal as he does in organised warfare. Even when playing away, he ought to be able to do the other man's thing and do it better. Just as fortunately, there is no contradiction between the professional back-up needed by a home defence militia and the forces required for interventions based on the principles of manoeuvre theory.

Conclusion—a politico-legal device

There remain, then, these three theories of war—attrition theory, manoeuvre theory and the doctrine of revolutionary war. All these lie on a continuum; and attrition theory becomes complementary to the others once fighting between organised and/or irregular forces breaks out. But just as, within manoeuvre theory, offence and defence are opposite aspects of the same continuum, so, within the continuum of the threat and use of armed force, attrition warfare lies at one pole, while manoeuvre warfare and revolutionary warfare adjoin each other astride the opposite pole (Fig. 54).

FIG. 54. *Attrition-manoeuvre continuum.*

Manoeuvre theory and Mao Tse Tung's doctrine have a common ancestor and have interbred at various stages of their evolution. In fact the Mao doctrine is an evolutionary refinement of manoeuvre theory, accomplished by stripping the latter of its trappings of military convention.

To match this, governments must shed their hidebound attitudes to peace and war. They must find a way of applying armed force to frustrate the violent actions of their foes at the least possible cost in time, resources and above all blood—in other words, with the least possible disturbance of peacetime life and relationships. By the same token, established armed forces need to do more than just master high-intensity manoeuvre warfare between large forces with baroque equipment. They have to go one step further and structure, equip and train themselves to employ the techniques of revolutionary warfare—to beat the opposition at their own game on their own ground.

Given free rein, surprise is a matchless combat multiplier. Revolutionary warfare exploits it to carry the principle of economy of force to lengths unimaginable to the conventional military mind. As I write this, one or two men, some simple electronics, and 10 kilograms or so of commercial explosive have just come within a whisker of killing the entire British cabinet, with the stated political aim of getting British troops out of Ulster. The perpetrators were (they claim) the IRA; *mutatis mutandis*, they might just as well have been a Muslim fundamentalist group—or the KGB. Despite defence budgets of billions, neither the British government nor the administration of any other advanced democratic nation has any effective means of preventing such incidents, or of bringing the culprits swiftly to book. This makes little sense. If terrorism and subversion are allowed to succeed, some group will sooner or later achieve pre-emption by applying a level of blackmail a government cannot withstand.

On the other hand, democratic governments rest on the rule of law, and must so rest. Then again, declarations of war are no way to inhibit or counter an enemy who acts with strategic surprise. More important still, the police procedures of liberal democracies are no way at all to counter an opponent employing the techniques of revolutionary warfare. There is a need for legal devices which would entitle a government to respond instantly in the one case and ruthlessly in the other. We must sooner or later face the fact that the direct and indirect effects of the tumultuous growth of technology are sweeping us from an era of stability and the rule of law into one of anarchy and violence. One aspect of the problem lies in aggression by organised forces and irregular operations by armed forces and other official government agencies (such as the KGB or the CIA). Here the only answer seems to lie in treaties of non-aggression and mutual support, coupled with a defence policy which provides extremely high readiness—just in case. A militia-based defence, backed by small standing forces, fills the bill to a T.

By contrast, there *is* a need to "declare war" on organisations, government-backed and otherwise, and individuals who resort to violence for politico-economic ends. In earlier times of lawlessness, the device of outlawry worked remarkably well and was rightly much feared. An appropriate constitutional device would provide for the outlawing of an organisation and/or named individuals and their associates. This measure would be far more sweeping than the present practice of "declaring an organisation illegal". Individual outlaws and known members of outlawed organisations would have the same legal status as hostile combatants at war with the outlawing state. This state would then be entitled to employ against them both the gamut of revolutionary warfare techniques and, if appropriate, unrestrained action by organised forces. It would also endeavour to persuade friendly nations to outlaw these individuals and groups; enabling clauses, somewhat analogous to extradition treaties, could be incorporated in the network of agreements mentioned above. Irregular operations of every kind constitute the most likely form of future armed conflict; they should be understood and acknowledged for what they are—a way of war!

Even with a "third force", operating on the principle of minimum force, as a buffer, both the decision to outlaw and the balance between immediacy and safeguards would pose nice constitutional problems. Perhaps a cabinet or an executive president could invoke provisional outlawry by simple proclamation, to be upheld or rejected within, say, 3 days by a quorum of all branches of government (including the judiciary). This would be finally confirmed by the normal legislative process. This is a matter for lawyers and politicians. Many will argue that such a move would give free play to the rogue governments which rule over most of the world; but rogue governments use these techniques anyway. For my part, I would simply highlight the irony by which advanced democratic societies may only learn to apply armed force effectively for their own protection once they come to eschew it as an active instrument of policy.

Bibliography

[*Note:* For a fuller list of Soviet material researched, please see the Bibliography to my book *Red Armour*]

Books

ADAN, AVRAHAM ("Bren"). *On the Banks of Suez: an Israeli General's Personal Account of the Yom Kippur War*, London, Arms and Armour Press, 1980.

ARON, RAYMOND. *La rencontre des deux révolutions* (photocopy used, publishing details not traced).

—— *Penser la guerre, Clausewitz*, Paris, Gallimard, 1976 (*also* translation: *Clausewitz, Philosopher of War*, London, Routledge, 1983).

BABADZHANYAN, MARSHAL OF ARMOURED FORCES A. KH. (ed.). *Tanki i tankovye voiska* (Tanks and tank forces) (new edition), Moscow, Voenizdat, 1980.

CARVER, FIELD MARSHAL THE LORD. *The Apostles of Mobility: the theory and practice of armoured warfare*, London, Weidenfeld & Nicholson, 1979.

VON CLAUSEWITZ, CARL. *Vom Kriege* (On War) (16th edn), Bonn, Dümmlers Verlag, 1952 (with a critique by Dr Werner Hahlweg).

CLUTTERBUCK, PROFESSOR RICHARD L. *Living with Terrorism*, London, Faber, 1975.

—— *Britain in Agony: Growth of Political Violence*, London, Faber, 1978.

—— *Guerrillas and Terrorists*, Ohio, University Press, 1981.

—— *The Media and Political Violence*, London, MacMillan, 1983.

COOPER, MATTHEW. *The German Army 1933–45*, London, Macdonald and Jane's, 1978.

VAN CREFELD, MARTIN. *Supplying War*, Cambridge, Syndics of Cambridge University Press, 1977, and New York and Melbourne.

—— *Fighting Power: German and US Army Performance, 1939–1945*, New York, Greenwood Press, 1982, and London, Arms and Armour Press.

DEUTSCHER, ISAAC, *The Prophet Armed*, Oxford, OUP.

DRUZHININ, COLONEL GENERAL V. V. and COLONEL (TECHNICAL) D. S. KONTOROV. *Ideya, algoritim, reshenie* (Concept, algorithm, decision), Moscow, Voenizdat, 1972.

DUFFY, CHRISTOPHER. *Russia's Military Way to the West*, London, Routledge & Kegan Paul, 1981.

ENGELMANN, J. *Manstein: Stratege und Truppenführer*, Friedberg, Podzun-Pallas Verlag, 1982.

ERICKSON, JOHN. *The Soviet High Command*, London, Macmillan, 1962, and New York, St Martin's Press (reprinted Boulder (Col.), Westview Press, 1984).

—— *The Road to Stalingrad*, London, Weidenfeld & Nicholson, 1982.

—— (with Richard Simpkin). *Deep Battle—the genius of Marshal Tukhachevskii*. (Brassey's forthcoming 1986).

ESAME, H. *Patton the Commander*, London, Batsford, 1974.

FULLER, J. F. C. *The Reformation of War*, London, Hutchinson, 1923.

—— *Foundations of the Science of War*, London, Hutchinson, 1926.

—— *On Future Warfare*, London, Sifton Praed, 1928.

—— *Armoured Warfare*, London, Eyre & Spottiswoode, 1943 (reprinted New York, Greenwood, 1983).

DE GAULLE, GENERAL CHARLES. *La Discorde chez l'ennemi*, 1944*.
—— *Le Fil de l'Epée*, Paris, Plon, 1926(?).
—— *Vers l'armée de métier*, 1934*. (*Latest publishing details not available).
GUDERIAN, COLONEL-GENERAL HEINZ. *Panzer Leader* (trans. Fitzgibbon), London, Michael Joseph, 1952, and New York, E. P. Dutton.
—— *Panzer-Marsch!* (ed. B.-G. Oskar Munzel), Munich, Schild-Verlag, 1955 (2nd edn 1957)
HACKETT, GENERAL SIR JOHN. *The Third World War, a future history* (with others), London, Sidgwick & Jackson, 1978, and New York, Macmillan.
—— *The Third World War, the untold story* (with others), London, Sidgwick & Jackson, 1982, and New York, Macmillan.
—— *The Profession of Arms*, London, Sidgwick & Jackson, 1983.
HEMSLEY, JOHN. *Soviet Troop Control*, Oxford, Brassey's, 1982.
HESS, WOLF. *Mein Vater Rudolf Hess*, Munich, Langen Müller, 1984.
HOWARD, MICHAEL. *The Causes of War and Other Essays*, (2nd edn), London, Unwin Paperbacks, 1984.
HUARD, PAUL. *Le Colonel de Gaulle et ses Blindés*, Paris, Plon, 1980.
ISBY, DAVID. *Weapons and Tactics of the Soviet Army*, London, Jane's, 1981.
DE JOMINI, LE BARON ANTOINE. *Precis de l'art de la Guerre* (2 vols.), Paris, Anselin/ G.-Laguionie, 1983.
KEEGAN, JOHN. *World Armies*, London, Macmillan, 1983.
—— (with Joseph C. Darracott). *Nature of War*, London, Cape, 1981.
KITSON, GENERAL SIR FRANCIS. *Low Intensity Operations: Subversion, Insurgency and Peacekeeping*, London, Faber, 1971.
LANCHESTER, F. *Aircraft in Warfare, the Dawn of the Fourth Arm*, London, Constable, 1916.
LENIN, V. I. *Collected Works* (4th edn), Vol. 21 (August 1914–December 1915), London, Lawrence and Wishart, 1964 (Lenin on Clausewitz, 304–305).
LIDDELL HART, SIR BASIL (see also Mao Tse Tung, Sun Tzu). *Paris, or the Future of War*, London, Kegan Paul, Trench, Trubner, 1925 and New York, Dutton (monograph in series "To-day and tomorrow").
—— *The Revolution in Warfare*, London, Faber & Faber, 1946.
—— *The Rommel Papers* (ed. B.H.L.H., trans. Findlay), London, Collins, 1953, and New York, Harcourt Bruce Jovanovitch.
—— *Strategy, the Indirect Approach*, London, Faber & Faber, (3rd edn) 1954.
—— *The Sword and the Pen* (ed. Adrian L. H.), New York, Crowell, 1976.
LIDER, JULIAN. *Military Force—an analysis of Marxist-Leninist concepts* Farnborough (Hants), Gower, 1981.
LOSIK, PROFESSOR MARSHAL OF ARMOURED FORCES (ed.), *Stroitel'stvo i boevoe priminenie sovetskikh tankovykh voisk v Velikoi Otechestvennoi Voiny* (The structure and employment of Soviet tank forces in the Second World War), Moscow, Voenizdat, 1979.
LUCAS, J. and M. COOPER. *Panzergrenadiers*, London, Macdonald and Jane's, 1979.
MAHAN, A. T. *Naval Strategy—compared and contrasted with the principle and practice of military operations on land*, London, Sampson, Low, Marston; 1911 (reprinted New York, Greenwood, 1975).
VON MANSTEIN, FIELD MARSHALL ERICH, *Verlorene Siege* (1957), Bonn, Athenaum Verlag.
——*Aus einem Soldatenleben* (1958), Bonn, Athenaum Verlag.
MAO TSE TUNG and CHE GUEVARA. *Guerrilla Warfare* (trans. Griffith) (foreword by Liddell Hart), London, Cassell, 1962.
MARTIN, PROFESSOR LAURENCE. *The Two-Edged Sword* (the Reith Lectures 1981), London, Weidenfeld & Nicholson, 1982.
VON MELLENTHIN, MAJOR-GENERAL F. W. *German Generals of World War II*, University of Oklahoma Press, 1978.
—— *Panzer Battles*, London, Futura Books, 1979.
MOSTOVENKO, V. D. *Tanki* (Tanks), Moscow, Voenizdat, 1956 (see also under von Senger).
RADZIEVSKII, PROFESSOR ARMY GENERAL A. I. *Dictionary of Basic Military Terms* (trans. DGIS Ottowa), Moscow, Voenizdat, 1966, Washington DC, (under auspices of) USAF, 1977 (in series "Soviet Military Thought").
—— *Tankovyi udar* (Offensive tank operations), Moscow, Voenizdat, 1977.
SAATY, T. L. *Mathematical Methods of OR*, New York, McGraw Hill, 1959.

SARGENT, WILLIAM. *Battle for the Mind*, London, Heinemann, 1957.

SAVKIN, V. Ye. *Basic Principles of Operational Art and Tactics* (*A Soviet View*), Moscow, Voenizdat, 1972 Washington DC, (under auspices of) USAF, 1974 (in series "Soviet Military Thought").

SCOTT, HARRIET, FAST and WILLIAM F. *The Armed Forces of the USSR*, 1979.

—— *The Soviet Art of War—doctrine, strategy and tactics*, 1982. Both Boulder (Col.), Westview Press, and London, Arms and Armour Press.

VON SENGER und ETTERLIN, GENERAL (a.D.) Dr F. M. *Der Gegenschlag:* Neckargemünd, Vohwinkel Verlag, 1959.

—— *Panzergrenadiere*, 1961.

—— *Die Roten Panzer—Geschichte der Sowjetischen Panzertruppen 1920–1960* (ed.), 1963 (see also Mostovenko). Both Munich, J. F. Lehmanns Verlag.

(SOVIET GENERAL STAFF). *"PU–36"* (Soviet Field Service Regulations 1936) Moscow, Voenizdat, 1937 (certainly masterminded and probably drafted by Marshal Tukhachevskii).

STANHOPE, HENRY. *The Soldiers: an Anatomy of the British Army*, London, Hamish Hamilton, 1979.

SUN TZU. *The Art of War* (trans. Griffith, foreword by Liddell Hart), Oxford, OUP (Clarendon), 1963.

"SUVOROV, VIKTOR" (nom de plume of Soviet officer defector). *The Liberators*, 1981.

—— *Inside the Soviet Army*, 1982. Both London, Hamish Hamilton.

TAYLOR, A. J. P. *The Course of German History: a survey of the development of Germany since 1815*, London, Hamish Hamilton, 1945.

TRIANDAFILLOV, V. K. *Kharakter operatsii sovremennykh armii* (The character of the operations of modern armies), Moscow, Voenizdat, (3rd edn) 1936, (4th edn) 1937.

TRYTHALL, A. J. *'Boney' Fuller: The Intellectual General*, London, Cassell, 1977.

TUKHACHEVSKII, MARSHALL of the SOVIET UNION M. N. *Uzbrannye proizvedenye* (selected works), (2 vols.), Moscow, Voenizdat, 1964 (see also Soviet General Staff).

UHLE-WETTER, MAJOR GENERAL FRANZ. *Gefechtsfeld Mitteleuropa* (Battlefield Central Europe) (3rd edn), Koblenz, Bernard & Graefe Verlag, 1981.

(UNITED STATES ARMY ARMOR SCHOOL). *Airland Battle 2000* (a collection of readings from professional journals).

(UNITED STATES ARMY INFANTRY SCHOOL). *Mechanized Infantry: Past, Present, Future*, Reference ATSH-CDT, 23 April 1979.

UNITED STATES ARMY, TRAINING AND DOCTRINE COMMAND) *FM100-2-1: Soviet Army Operations and Tactics*.

—— *FM100-2-2: Soviet Army Specialized Warfare and Rear Area Support*.

—— *FM100-2-3: Soviet Army Troops Organization and Equipment*. All due out 1984/5.

—— *FM 100–5 Operations*, August 1982.

(UNITED STATES ARMY WAR COLLEGE). *German Military Thinking—selected papers on German theory and doctrine* (May 1983).

—— *Soviet Operational Concepts* (June 1980). (ten articles from *Voyennaya mysl'* (Military Thought), the restricted Soviet General Staff periodical). Both Art of War Colloquium publications.

VIGOR, P. H. *Soviet Blitzkrieg Theory*, London, Macmillan, 1983.

Papers and extracts—unpublished/limited publication

KLINK, DR ERNST. *Die Begriffe "Operation" und "operativ" in ihrer militärischen Verwendung in Deutschland*, Freiburg-im-Breisgau, Militärgeschichtliches Forschungsamt, 1958 (copy marked *Ausarbeitung für Führungsvorschrift* i.e. "ideas draft for Command and Control Regulations) (courtesy of United States Army War College).

VON MANTEUFFEL, GENERAL HASSO. *Some thoughts on the employment of the Panzergrenadier Division Grossdeutschland in the defensive and tank battle of Targul Frumos (Rumania), 2–5 May 1944* (typescript, December 1948) (a copy of this paper, with maps, was given to me by General Sir Desmond Fitzpatrick, GCB DSO MBE MC, when I was a student at Staff College in 1951. I presented it to the Staff College Library in 1971, and later obtained a copy from them without the maps—which were in any event almost unintelligible).

(REICHSWEHRMINISTERIUM, TRUPPENAMT). *Reise des Chefs des Truppenamts nach Russland, August/September 1928)* (Visit of the Chief of the Army General Staff to Russia). Reference: Nr.231/28 geh-Kdos. T3V, Berlin, 17.11.1928 (kindly provided from his research papers by Professor John Erickson).

(UNITED STATES ARMY AIR ASSAULT CORPS). *The Air Assault Corps and the Light Division)* (undated).

(UNITED STATES ARMY ARMOR SCHOOL). *Battlefield Management System* (BMS) ("white paper" discussion draft, 9 May 1984).

(UNITED STATES ARMY INFANTRY SCHOOL). *7th Infantry Division (Light Division). 9th Infantry Division (Hi-Tech Light Division)*. Briefing folders.

(UNITED STATES ARMY OFFICE OF MILITARY HISTORY). *Russian Airborne Operations*. Ref MS P-116, 1952 (translation from German).

Articles

[*Note*: For ease of access, articles are listed chronologically by periodicals.]

Armada International

4–5/80	"Airborne Anti-tank Warfare" (Parts 1 & 2), Konrad Alder.
(36–75)	
(74–104)	
2/83	"Helicopterborne Anti-armour Warfare. Illustrated by AH-64", Mark
(7,77)	Lambert.

ARMOR Magazine

May/Jun 80	"Soviet Combined Arms Operations", Professor John Erickson.
(16–21)	
Nov/Dec 80	"Increased Combat Power" (1986 force structure), LTC Ralph G.
(30–34)	Rosenberg.
Jan/Feb 81	"Mission-oriented Command and Control", (Bundeswehr, Fu.H.III.2).
(12–16)	
Jul/Aug 81	"Training for Maneuver Warfare", LTG William R. Richardson.
(31–34)	
Jan/Feb 82	"The Armor Force in the Airland Battle", MAJ Michael S. Lancaster.
(26–32)	
Mar/Apr 82	"Armor Aviation", CPT Thomas H. Trant.
(26–29)	
Sep/Oct 82	"Airland Battle's Power Punch", CPT Marc C. Baur.
(38–41)	
Jan/Feb 83	"Airland Battle Defeat Mechanisms", MAJ Michael S. Lancaster and
(35–37)	Jon Clemens.
May/Jun 83	"The LHX Pursuit Helicopter Squadron", CPT Greg R. Hampton.
(26–29)	

British Army Review

66(Dec 80)	"Bricks without Straw" (review article—de Gaulle), Richard Simpkin.
(10–13)	
72(Dec 82)	"Hammer, Anvil and Net", Richard Simpkin.
(11–21)	
(45–48)	"Lanchester's Square Law", Fergus Daly.
74(Aug 83)	"The French Home Defence System", Maj A. J. Abbott, MBE.
(19–24)	
78(Dec 84)	"Manoeuvre Theory and the Small Army", Richard Simpkin.
(5–13)	

Defence

Sep 81   "Military Helicopters" (composite feature).
(636–650)

Défense nationale

[*Note*: I had great difficulty in gaining access to this periodical, which I finally did thanks to the British Library Lending Division. I have not yet had an opportunity to research pre-1984 issues.]

Jan 84   "La Stratégie, et ses sources", Louis le Hégarat.
(25–41)
(165–168)   "Le concept suédois de défense globale", Michel Darfren.
Mar 84   "La stratégie, théorie d'une pratique", Louis de Hégarat.
(51–67)
(152–157)   "Réforme de l'Ecole spéciale militaire de Saint-Cyr et politique de recrutement et de formation des cadres", Georges Vincent.
May 84   "La stratégie totale de l'URSS", René Cagnat.
(67–80)
Jul 84   "L'Airland Battle et le nouveau débat doctrinal dans l'OTAN" (Part 1),
(89–104)   Robert A. Gessert.
(9–22)   "Défenses alternatives, 1—Défense classique et nucléaire tactique", Maurice Faivre.
Aug/Sep 84   "L'Airland Battle et le nouveau débat doctrinal dans l'OTAN" (Part 2),
(23–42)   Robert A. Gessert.
Oct 84   "Défenses alternatives, 2—D'autres formes de défense", Maurice Faivre.
(27–42)

Europäische Wehrkunde (et al.)

[*Note:* This is the successor to *Wehrwissenschaftliche Rundschau* (WWR), which itself was the post-war reincarnation of *Militärwissenschaftliche Rundschau*. Again I have had problems in gaining regular access to this periodical, and have not yet fully researched back numbers. I have also grouped here a single entry for *Vierteljahreshefte für Zeitgeschichte* (VFZ).]

VFZ/1 (53)   "Reichswehr und Rote Armee", Helm Speidel.
(9–45)
WWR/9 (62)   "Die geheime Luftrüstung der Reichswehr und Ihre Auswirkung auf den
(540–549)   Flugzeugbestand der Luftwaffe zum Beginn des Zweiten Weltkrieges", Karl-Heinz Völker.
EW6/82   "Nessie" und die Miliz—Anmerkungen als Beitrag zur Klärung",
(252–256)   General a.D. J. A. Graf Kielmansegg.
(264–265)   "Der 'Auftrag'—Eine deutsche militärische Tradition", Dieter Ose.
2/84   "Militärische Aussichten in den nächsten dreissig Jahren", G.-L., a.D.
(82–89)   Carl-Gero von Ilsemann.
(90–94)   "Konzeptionelle Vorstellungen für die gepanzerten Kampftruppen der 90er Jahre", OT i.G. Gero Koch.
4/84
(209–214)   "Die 'deutsche Frage' als ein Kernproblem der Friedensordnung in Europa", OT i.G. Gerhard Hubatschek.
(224–230)   "Die Führungsinformationssystem des Heeres (HEROS)", OTL i.G. F-J Schächter.
7/84   "Renaissance der Infanterie", OT i.G. Gero Koch.
(409–413)

Flight International

Feb 79   "Battlefield Helicopters", D. Richardson, G. Warwick, M. Lambert.
(319–327)

Infantry

Mar/Apr 84 (14–16)	"Infantry Division, Light" (editorial feature).
Jul/Aug 84 (10–31)	Five-article feature on heavy-light forces and related topics.
Sep/Oct 84 (14–31)	Five-article feature on leadership and command.

International Defense Review

[*Note:* For articles on Soviet armed forces up to 9/82, see *Red Armour* Bibliography.]

8/78 (1247–52)	"AH-64: the US Army's Advanced Attack Helicopter", J. Philip Geddes.
3/80 (400–406)	"Helicopters for the Central Front—Part 1", Mark Hewish.
6/83	"Soviet Operational Manoeuvre Groups—a closer look", C. J. Dick.
9/83 (1210–16)	"Spetsnaz—the Soviet Union's special forces", "Viktor Suvorov" (nom de plume).
(1241–45)	"Flying the AH-64 Apache", Mark Lambert.
10/83 (1391–95)	"The Warsaw Pact Strategic Offensive—the OMG in context", John G. Hines and Phillip A. Peterson.
11/83 (1551–56)	"The Airland Battle 2000 Controversy—who is being short-sighted?", Ramon Lopez.
12/83 (1715–22)	"Soviet Doctrine, Equipment, Design and Organization—an integrated approach to war", C. J. Dick.
2/84 (123–124)	"The Real Danger to World Security is Nuclear Proliferation", General Sir John Hackett.
4/84 (380)	"Some Thoughts on Operational Manoeuvre Groups", Dr Juan Carlos Murguizir.
(389–392)	"Sun Tzu and Soviet Strategy", Thomas Ries.
(473–478)	"Fire and Manoeuvre—the German armoured corps and combined-arms operations", K. G. Benz.
5/84 (559–566)	"The Soviet Helicopters on the Battlefield", C. H. Donnelly.
(585–588)	"LHX—helicopter program of the century", Ramon Lopez.
9/84 (1183–91)	"Low Intensity Conflict—an operational perspective", M. G. Donald, R. Morelli and Maj Michael M. Ferguson.
(1211)	"The US Army's 9th Infantry Division", Sutton Berry, Jr.

Military Review

Mar 81	"Extending the Battlefield", General Donn A Starry (see also under Books, US ARMY ARMOR SCHOOL, *Airland Battle 2000*)

Military Technology

5/83 (38–60)	"Strike Deep": a new concept for NATO, General Bernard W. Rogers, SACEUR.
	"Requirements and weaponry" (for Strike Deep), Erhard Heckmann.
3/84 (82–92)	"Countering the OMG", Richard Simpkin.
8/84 (62–82)	"Flying Tanks?—a tactical-technical analysis of the 'main battle air vehicle' concept", Richard Simpkin.

RUSI Journal

125/2 (June 80) (32–37)	"Doubts and Difficulties Confronting a Would-be Soviet Attacker", P. H. Vigor.

126/? (81) (45–52)	"The Soviet Biological and Chemical Warfare Threat", Charles J. Dick.
127/2 (June 82) (17–22)	"British Land Forces: the Future", Field Marshal Sir Edwin Bramall, GCB, OBE, MC
127/4 (Dec 82) (3–6)	"NATO: The Next Decade", General Bernard W. Rogers.
128/1 (Mar 83) (39–43)	"Force Strategy, Blitzkrieg Strategy and the Economic Difficulties: Nazi Grand Strategy in the 1930s", Professor Williamson Murray.
(52–60)	"Heirs of Genghis Khan: the Influence of the Tartar-Mongols on the Imperial Russian and Soviet Armies", Christopher Bellamy.
128/2 (Jun 83) (7–10)	"Conventional Defence of Europe", Field Marshal the Lord Carver.
(11–15)	"New Operational Dimensions", General Dr F. M. von Senger und Etterlin.
128/3 (Sep 83) (9–12)	"The Continental Commitment and the Special Relationship in 20th Century British Foreign Policy", Professor Paul Kennedy.
128/4 (Dec 83) (50–56)	"Military Power in Soviet Strategy against NATO", Phillip A. Petersen and John G. Hines.
129/1 (Mar 84) (46–48)	"Europe and the Security of Russia", Dr Edwina Moreton.
129/2 (Jun 84) (20–26)	"The Impact of Surprise and Initiative in War", Corelli Barnett.
(27–32)	"The Light Attack Helicopter in World War III", Col. J. N. W. Moss and Col. J. L. Waddy.
129/3 (Sep 84) (17–22)	"A Positive Approach to Terrorism: the Call for an Elite Counter-Force in Canada", Lt-Col. (Retd) G. Davidson-Smith.
(50–58)	"Antecedents of the Modern Soviet Operational Manoeuvre Group (OMG)", Chris Bellamy.
(59–66)	"Concepts of Land/Air Operations in the Central Region", Parts 1 and 2, General Sir Nigel Bagnall and Air Marshal Sir Patrick Hine.

Soldat und Technik

5/82 (266–268)	"Hughes AH-64—ein Kampfhubschrauber modernster Art", Hans-J. Kreker.
6/82 (316–317)	"Mi-8/HIP- —Meistgebauter sowjetischer Hubschrauber und seine Varianten", OTL Günter Lippert.

Teknika i vooruzhenye

[*Note:* I only gained access to this periodical at the beginning of 1984, and have not yet had a chance to research back numbers.]

1/84 (10–11)	"Podvizhnost' tankov" (Tank mobility), S. Vygodskiy.
2/84 (10–11)	"Mnogotselevoi armciskii vertolet" (The multipurpose army helicopter), Col. (Tech.) Dr V. Volodko.
(12–13)	"Bronyetankovaya tekhnika v osobykh ysloviyakh" (Armoured vehicle technology under special conditions), Lt-Col. (Tech.) M. Igol'nikov, Lt-Col. (Tech.) B. Zaslavskii, and Maj. (Tech.) A. Rykov.

Truppenpraxis

3/82	"Gedanken über die Gepanzerten Kampftruppen der Zukunft", Gero Koch & Bauers.
7/83	"Gedanken über den Einsatz der Panzergrenadiere der Zukunft", Schütze & Remuel.
11/83 (812–814)	"Gedanken zum Gefecht der gepanzerten Kampftruppen", B.-G. Gerd Röhrs.

12/83	"Panzergrenadiere 90" OT i.G. Gero Koch.
(880–886)	
2/84	"Die Entwicklung der sowjetischen Militärstrategie von 1945 bis heute", Maj i. G. Jürgen Hübschen.
3/84	"Die Entwicklung der sowjetischen Streitkräfte in den Jahren
(155–158)	1970–1983", Maj i.G. Jürgen Hübschen.
4/84	"Panzeraufklärungstruppe: Aufklärung oder Kampf als Hauptauf-
(251–256)	gabe?", OT i.G. Gero Koch.
(265–269)	"Der israelische Offizier: Zentrale Figur für den Zusammenhalt der Truppe", Maj Richard Gabriel USAR & Col Reuven Gal IDF (original—"The Israeli Officer: Lynchpin of unit cohesion", *Army Magazine*, Nov 83).
5/84	"Kampf gegen gepanzerte Kräfte in Mitteleuropa", G.-L. Meinhard
(325–332)	Glanz (also as "Defeating Enemy Armour", *NATO's Sixteen Nations* special 1/83).
8/84	"Gewässerzone in der Forward Combat Zone (FCZ)", OTL Gustov
(582–587)	Lünenborg.
(604–607)	"Der Einsatz mittlerer Transportflugzeuge in der vorderen Kampfzone—Möglichkeiten und Grenzen", Maj i.G. H.-W. Ahrens.
9/84	"Anweisung für Führung und Einsatz" (AnwFE 700/108 VS-Nfd), OTL
(674–679)	i.G. Klaus Hammel.

Voenno-istoricheskii zhurnal

1/65	"Razvitie teorii sovetsckogo operativnogo iskusstba v 30-e gody", Part 1
(34–46)	(Development of the theory of Soviet operational art in the 30s), G. Isserson.
3/65	(Part 2 of above.)
(46–61)	
7/65	"Izbrannye proizvedeniya M N Tukhachevskogo" (review article) (The selected works of M N Tukhachevskii), Professor Col-General N. Lomov.
5/75	"Sovetskoe operativnoe iskusstvo v kampanii 1945 goda v Evrope"
(28–35)	(Soviet operational art in the 1945 European campaign), Army General S. Sokolov.
(36–43)	"Taktika sovetskikh voisk v zavershayushchem periode voiny v Evrope" (The tactics of Soviet forces in the closing stages of the war in Europe), Professor Army General A. Radzievskii (while head of Frunze Military Academy).
2/76	"Vvod tankovykh armii v proryv" (The commitment of tank armies to
(19–26)	the break-in), Professor Army General A. Radzievskii.
8/76	"Razvitie teorii strategicheskoi nastupatel' noi operatsii v 1945–1953 gg."
(38–45)	(The development of the theory of strategic offensive operations, 1945–53), Maj-Gen. M. Cherednichenko.
9/77	"Vstrechnye srazheniya tankovykh armii v nastupatel'nykh operat-
(24–33)	siyakh" (Encounter battles of tank armies in offensive operations), Col. B. Frolov.
2/78	"Razvitie taktiki obshchevoiskovykh soedinenii" (The development of
(27–34)	the tactics of all-arms formations), Professor Army General A. Radzievskii.
9/79	"Kharakternye cherti razvitiya i primeneniya tankovykh voisk"
(25–32)	(Characteristic features of the development and employment of tank forces), Maj-Gen. of Tank Forces I. Krupchenko.
9/80	"Sposoby vedeniya vysokomanevrennykh boevykh deistvii bronetanko-
(18–25)	vymi i mekhanizirovannymi voiskami po opytu Belorusskoi i Vislo-Oderskoi operatsii" (Questions of the conduct of the high-tempo manoeuvre battle—based on the actions of armoured and mechanised forces in the Belorussian and Vistula-Oder operations), Professor Marshal of Armoured Forces O. Losik.

6/81
(12–20)
"Sposoby razvitiya yspekha v operativnoi glubine silami tankovykh armii, tanovykh i mekhanizirovannykh korpusov" (Problems of the exploitation of success at operational depth with the forces of tank armies, and tank and mechanised corps), Professor Maj-Gen of Tank Forces I. Krupchenko.

8/82
(13–16)
"Operativnaya maskirovka" (Concealment and deception at operational level), Col-Gen. P. Mel'nikov.

11/82
(42–48)
"Boevoe priminenie bronetankovykh i mekhannizorovannykh voisk" (The combat employment of armoured and mechanised forces), Professor Marshal of Armoured Forces O. Losik.

6/83
(26–33)
"O nekotorykh voprosakh razvitiya strategii i operativnogo iskusstva v kurskoi bitve" (Soviet questions about the development of the strategic and operational art in the Battle of Kursk), Army General A. Luchinskii.

7/83
(19–25)
"Ocobennosti primeneniya bronetankovykh i mekhanizirovannykh voisk v Kurskoi bitve" (Special factors affecting the employment of armoured and mechanised forces in the Battle of Kursk), Professor Maj-Gen. of Tank Forces I. Krupchenko.

10/83
(16–22)
"O nekotorykh tendentsiyakh razvitiya teorii i praktiki nastupatel'nykh operatsii grupp frontov" (Some tendencies in the theory and practice of front-level operational groups), Col-Gen. V. Karpov and Professor Maj-Gen N. Zubkov.

11/83
(11–19)
"O nekotorykh tendentsiyakh v sozdanii i ispol'zovanii udarnykh gruppirovok po opyty frontovykh nastupatel'nykh operatsii Velikoi Otechstvennoi voiny" (Some trends in the structure and employment of offensive groupings as shown by front-level offensive operations in World War II), Colonel B. Petrov.

1/84
(10–21)
(31–37)
"O stile raboty voenachal'nikov" (Style in the exercise of command), Army General P. Lashchenko.
"Nekotorye osobennosti organizatsii i vedenya armeiskikh nastupatel'nykh operatsii v lesistobolotistoi mesnosti" (Some special factors in the organisation and conduct of army offensive operations in overgrown marshy terrain), Col. (Retd) F. Utenkov.

4/84
"Otrazhenie kontrudarov krupnykh gruppirovok protivnika v khode frontovykh nastupatel'nykh operatsii Velikoi Otechestvennoi voiny" (The repulse of counter-offensives by major enemy groupings against (Soviet) front-level offensive operations of World War II), Lt-Gen. A. Evseev.

5/84
(15–23)
"Nekotorye voprosy podgotovki i vedenya posledovatel'nykh po glubine frontovykh nastupatel'nykh operatsii" (Some questions of the mounting and conduct of follow-on phases in depth in front-level offensive operations), Col-Gen. M. Bezkhrebtyi.

6/84
(10–60)
"Sovetskoe voennoe iskusstvo v Belorusskoi operatsii 1944 goda" (Soviet military art in the Belorussian operation of 1944) (group of articles, including Losik on armour).

8/84
(24–31)
"Organizatsiya i sovershenie marshei tankovymi i mekhanizorovannymi soedinenyami v gody Velikoi Otechstvennoi voiny" (The planning and execution of controlled moves of tank and mechanised formations in World War II), Professor Maj-Gen of Tank Forces I. Krupchenko.

9/84
(12–21)
"Opyt organizatsii i vedeniya krupnykh tankovykh srazhenii v gody Velikoi Otechestvennoi voiny" (Lessons from the mounting and conduct of major tank battles in World War II), Professor Marshal of Armed Forces O. Losik.

Voennyi vestnik

[*Note:* Since January 1981, *VV* has been running a regular section on "The Theory and Practice of the All-Arms Battle". Taken together, these sections constitute a kind of informal tactical manual, but it is evidently impossible to list this in full.]

8/75 "O primenenii BMP v boyu" (Battle employment of the BMP), Col. E.
(49–50) Kamenskii.
(55–57) "Na BMP vo vstrechnom boyu" (The BMP in the encounter battle), Col.
E. Brudno.
12/75 "O primenenii BMP v boyu" (BMP in battle—comments on previous
(55/57) articles), Capt. V. Chernikov and Lieut. V. Varenik.
3/76 "BMP v boyu" (The BMP in battle—final article of series), Col–Gen V.
(19–22) Merimskii (at the time deputy director of combat preparedness).
4/76 "Upravlenie voiskami—na uroven' sovremennykh trebovanii"
(47–51) (Command and control—what it means today), Col. Gen. D. Grinkevich
(at the time C of S, Group of Soviet Forces Germany).
8/76 "Operativnost' v upravlenii voiskami" ('Operational quality' in the
(49–53) command of forces), Col-Gen. M. Tyagunov.
9/76 "Manevr—dusha taktiki" (Manoeuvre—the soul of tactics), Col. V.
(35–38) Savel'ev and Lieut-Col. V. Shkepast.
4/77 "Manevr—klyuch k pobede" (Manoeuvre—the key to victory), Col. P.
(68–71) Simchenkov.
12/77 "Prinimaya reshenie na boi . . ." ((Decision-making in battle, in the series
(67–70) 'Sophisticated techniques in real life'), Col. V. Matveev and Lieut-Col.
A. Malishev.
4/79 "Aktual'naya problema sovremennogo boya" (Current problems of
(12–16) modern combat), Col-Gen. V. Yakushin (written while Chief of General
Staff, Land Forces).
7/79 "Komandir i shtab" (The commander and his staff), Col. P. Simchenkov.
(28–33)
2/83 "Batal'on nastupaet s khody" (Hasty battalion attack) (editorial). [*Note*:
(20–27) The importance of this article is that it confirms a mounting tempo of
18–22 hours.]
7/83 "Vo vzaimodeistvii i taktycheskim vozdushnym desantom" (Co-
(34–37) operation with a tactical helicopter force), Lt-Col. V. Peusher.
10/83(?) "Razvedka i tempi prodvizheniya" (Reconnaissance and rates of ad-
(12–15) vance), Majors A. Sagakyantz and N. Kolomychenko.
11/83 "Po moryu—v tyl protivnika" (By sea into the enemy rear), Col. B.
(16–19) Skripnichenko.
(58–59) "Peredovoi otryad forsiret reku" (The vanguard in the opposed crossing),
Col. R. Baikeev.
2/84 "Sovremennyi nactupatel'nyi boi" (The modern offensive battle),
(26–31) Colonels P. Konoplya and A. Malyshev.
6/84 "Upravleniyu—vnimanie osoboe" (Focus on command), V. Khaidorov.
8/84 "Vstrechnyi boi" (The encounter battle), A. Zheltoukhov.
(15–18)

Wehrtechnik

5/82 "Drei Jahre Panzerabwehrhubschrauberregimenter im Heer: Auftrag,
(69–74) Gliederung Erfahrung", István Csoboth.
6/82 "Militärische Hubschrabuer—Technik und Taktik", B.-G. Dr H Tiedgen
(23–24) (part of report on 14th Helicopter Forum, Bückeburg, 1982).
8/83 "Die Panzerabwehr der Kampftruppen: Eine Voraussetzung für die
(18–25) Vorneverteidigung", Edelfried Baginski.
12/83 "Roboter auf dem Gefechtsfeld: Ersetzt der Kampfautomat der
(75) Kampfpanzer" (editorial item).
5/84 "In Erwartung des Panzerabwehrhubschraubers 2", B.-G. Dr H. Tiedgen
(45–47) (interview).
7/84 "Stärkung der konventionellen Verteidigungsfähigkeit", Wolfgang
(14–23) Altenburg.
8/84 "Führungssysteme im bündnisweiten Verbund", G.-L. Eberhard
(52–59) Eimler (airforce C^3 systems).

9/84   "Die Rolle der Luftstreitkräfte in der NATO", G.-L. Eberhard Eimler.
(46–60)

10/84   "Aufklärung im Heer: Lücken werden geschlossen", Wolfgang Flume.
(20–25)

Index